CORE TAX ANNUALS

Capital Gains Tax 2010/11

CORE TAX ANNUALS

Capital Gains Tax 2010/11

Rebecca Cave FCA CTA MBA

and

Iris Wünschmann-Lyall MA (Cantab) TEP

Series General Editor: Mark McLaughlin CTA (Fellow) ATT TEP

Bloomsbury Professional

Bloomsbury Professional Ltd, Maxwelton House, 41–43 Boltro Road, Haywards Heath, West Sussex, RH16 1BJ

A CIP Catalogue record for this book is available from the British Library.

ISBN: 978 1 84766 517 1

Typeset by Phoenix Photosetting, Chatham, Kent
Printed and bound in Great Britain by CPI William Clowes, Beccles, Suffolk

Preface

Capital Gains Tax Annual 2010/11 is the fifth edition of this publication, one of the six 'Core Tax Annuals' series published by Bloomsbury Professional. It aims to provide a clear and a quick guide to the taxation of capital gains for busy tax practitioners and taxpayers alike. We have taken a practical approach to the subject, concentrating on the most commonly found transactions and reliefs. The commentary is cross referenced to the tax legislation, as well as to the HMRC Manuals and the HMRC website where appropriate. We have also incorporated over 130 examples to illustrate how the computational rules work in practice.

This tax year has seen an unprecedented mid-year change in the rates of CGT, effective from 23 June 2010, which has had implications for a number of CGT reliefs and deeming provisions as outlined in Chapter 1. The new HMRC powers and penalties are also discussed in Chapter 1 together with a summary of the revised time limits for submitting claims, elections and raising tax assessments.

The commentary in Chapter 5 on UK residence and domicile as it affects the taxpayer's liability to CGT has been revised to reflect changes introduced by case law and HMRC practice in this area. The election which remittance basis users can make with regard to foreign losses is explained in full in this chapter. The discussion of incorporation relief in Chapter 15 has also been expanded to include more worked examples.

The second Finance Act for 2010 introduced a new mechanism for calculating entrepreneurs' relief and a revised election concerning qualifying corporate bonds, both of which are explained in Chapter 11. A third Finance Act for 2010 is expected to be passed in November 2010, and this edition takes into account announcements concerning draft legislation and regulations that were released before 31 July 2010.

To cater for readers who are looking at gains that originated before 6 April 2008, we have retained commentary on taper relief in Chapter 17, and have included commentary on a recent significant case on this relief.

All of the examples in this edition have been updated and several new examples have been added. We hope you enjoy using this book and would welcome any suggestions for improvements or changes.

Preface

The first edition of the book was written by Andrew Goodall, together with Toby Harris, Iris Wünschmann-Lyall and Juliana Watterston. This year's text has been fully revised and updated by Rebecca Cave and Iris Wünschmann-Lyall, and is up-to-date to the first two Finance Acts passed in 2010, which received Royal Assent 8 April 2010 and 27 July 2010.

Rebecca Cave
Rebecca@taxwriter.co.uk
August 2010

Contents

Table of statutes

[All references are to paragraph number]

Table of statutory instruments

[*All references are to paragraph number*]

Table of cases

[All references are to paragraph number]

F

G

H

I

List of abbreviations

ACT	advance corporation tax
ADP	acceptable distribution policy
AIM	alternative investment market
APA	advance pricing agreement
APR	agricultural property relief
ARC	Accounting Regulatory Committee
ASB	Accounting Standards Board
BA	balancing allowance
BES	business expansion scheme
BMT	bereaved minor trust
BPR	business property relief
CA 1985	Companies Act 1985
CAA 2001	Capital Allowances Act 2001
CFC	controlled foreign company
CIHC	close investment holding company
CTO	Capital Taxes Office
CVS	corporate venturing scheme
DOTAS	disclosure of tax avoidance schemes
EBT	employee benefit trust
EEA	European Economic Area
EIS	enterprise investment scheme
EMI	enterprise management incentive
ESC	Extra-statutory Concession
ESOP	employee share ownership plan
ESOT	employee share ownership trust
EUFT	eligible unrelieved foreign tax
FA	Finance Act
FHL	furnished holiday lettings
FII	franked investment income
FRS	Financial Reporting Standard
FRSEE	Financial Reporting Standard for Smaller Entities
FYA	first year allowance
GWR	gift with reservation
HMRC	HM Revenue and Customs
IA	initial allowance
IA 1986	Insolvency Act 1986
IAS	International Accounting Standards
IASB	International Accounting Standards Board
IBA	industrial buildings allowance

ICTA 1988	Income and Corporation Taxes Act 1988
IFRS	International Financial Reporting Standards
IHT	inheritance tax
IHTA 1984	Inheritance Tax Act 1984
IHTM	Inheritance Tax Manual
IPDI	immediate post-death interest
ITA 2007	Income Tax Act 2007
ITEPA 2003	Income Tax (Earnings and Pensions) Act 2003
ITTOIA 2005	Income Tax (Trading and Other Income) Act 2005
LLP	limited liability partnership
OECD	Organisation for European Co-operation and Development
PCTCT	profits chargeable to corporation tax
PET	potentially exempt transfer
POA	pre-owned asset
QCB	qualifying corporate bonds
R & D	research and development
RBC	remittance basis charge
SDLT	stamp duty land tax
SE	small enterprise
SI	Statutory Instrument
SME	small and medium-sized enterprise
SSAP	Statement of Standard Accounting Practice
SSCBA 1992	Social Security Contributions and Benefits Act 1992
SSE	substantial shareholdings exemption
TAAR	targeted anti-avoidance rule
TCGA 1992	Taxation of Chargeable Gains Act 1992
TIOPA 2010	Taxation (International and Other Provisions) Act 2010
TMA 1970	Taxes Management Act 1970
TSI	transitional serial interest
UITF	Urgent Issues Task Force
UK GAAP	UK Generally Accepted Accounting Principles
UTR	Unique Taxpayer Reference
VCT	venture capital trust
VOA	Valuation Office Agency
WDA	writing down allowance
WDV	written down value

Chapter 1

Introduction to capital gains tax

BASIS OF CHARGE

1.1 Capital gains tax (CGT) is charged on capital gains, defined as chargeable gains accruing to a person on the disposal of an asset (*Taxation of Chargeable Gains Act 1992* (*TCGA 1992*), *s 1*). Spouses and civil partners are chargeable separately, but where the members of such a couple are living together transfers of assets between them are deemed to take place for a consideration that gives rise to no gain and no loss. There is no CGT on death, and the deceased's assets are deemed to be inherited at their market value.

A 'person' may be an individual, a trustee or personal representative, or a company. However, companies are excluded from CGT and are chargeable to corporation tax on their chargeable gains instead (*Interpretations Act 1978, Sch 1*; *CTA 2009, s 2*).

In very broad terms, the chargeable gain arising on the disposal of an asset is the excess of the disposal value over the acquisition value. **Chapters 1** to **6** focus on rules as they apply to individuals only. There are special rules for personal representatives of a deceased person (see **Chapter 7**) and trustees of a settled property (see **Chapter 8**). The chargeable gains accruing to a company for an accounting period are included in the company's total profits for the accounting period and are chargeable to corporation tax (see **Chapter 9**). **Chapters 10** to **17** focus on the reliefs that can reduce, defer or eliminate CGT.

HISTORY OF CGT

1.2 CGT was introduced in 1965, at the same time as corporation tax. Previously, short-term gains on disposal of capital assets were chargeable but were taxed as income.

From its introduction, CGT taxed inflationary gains as well as real ones. Indexation allowance attempted to remove the effect of inflation from March 1982, but older assets were still taxed on pre-1982 inflation. From March 1988, taxpayers had the option of excluding pre-March 1982 gains from their capital gains calculations by rebasing the asset at its 31 March 1982 value. However, this rebasing was not universal, so taxpayers could still compare calculations using the asset's March 1982 value and the original cost, taking the lower gain or loss to be taxed. This was known as the kink test. All assets held by individuals and trustees were compulsorily rebased at 31 March 1982, with effect from 6 April 2008, so the kink test became irrelevant.

Indexation allowance was frozen for disposals made by individuals, personal representatives and trustees from 6 April 1998, so no further indexation could accrue from that date. Indexation allowance was finally abolished for these taxpayers from 6 April 2008, but it remains in place for companies.

Taper relief was introduced on 6 April 1998, partly to compensate for the freezing of the indexation allowance. However, when the indexation allowance was withdrawn completely on 6 April 2008, so was taper relief (see **Chapter 17**).

Special share identification rules were enacted from 6 April 1998, as it was necessary to identify a holding period for separate acquisitions of shares. These identification rules were simplified considerably from 6 April 2008 for individuals, trustees and PRs, but not for companies (see **Chapter 9**).

The rate of CGT has swung from a flat rate set below the top income tax rates, to the taxpayer's marginal income tax rate, back again to a single flat rate, and now to two rates as summarised below. Low flat rates tend to encourage the re-categorisation of income as capital, and that problem has been partially addressed by raising the rate of CGT for those in the higher tax brackets from 23 June 2010.

Period:	*Rate of CGT*
5 April 1965–6 April 1982	30%, no relief for inflation but with retirement relief for business assets.
6 April 1982–5 April 1987	30%, with relief for inflation.
6 April 1987–5 April 1998	Marginal income tax rate up to 40%, with relief for inflation.
6 April 1998–5 April 2008	Marginal income tax rate up to 40%, taper relief gives enhanced relief for business assets.
6 April 2008–22 June 2010	18%, no relief for inflation, entrepreneurs' relief gives limited relief for certain business assets.
From 23 June 2010	18% for gains falling in basic rate band, 28% for gains falling in higher or additional rate bands. 28% for all gains made by trustees and PRs. No relief for inflation.

Trustees and personal representatives have paid CGT at different rates to individuals for many years (see **Chapter 8**).

The *Taxation of Chargeable Gains Act 1992*, as amended by subsequent Finance Acts, now contains the main provisions concerning taxation of chargeable gains.

Changes from 23 June 2010

1.3 The first Budget of the coalition government introduced some significant changes to capital gains tax that came into effect for disposals made on and after 23 June 2010. These are:

- Individuals pay CGT at 18% or 28%, or possibly at both rates, depending on the level of their total income and gains for the tax year (see **1.23**).
- Trustees and personal representatives pay CGT at 28% (see **Chapter 8**).
- Gains which are included in a successful claim for entrepreneurs' relief, and which fall within the lifetime cap for that relief, are taxed at 10%.
- The lifetime cap for entrepreneurs' relief is increased to £5 million (see **Chapter 11**).

These changes, which effectively divide the tax year at 22 June 2010, make the calculation of the CGT liability for 2010/11 quite complex. The determination of the exact disposal date for the transaction will be crucial, as this can vary according to the type of asset disposed of (see **Chapter 2**). There are a number of transitional provisions designed to simplify the computations required for the 2010/11 tax year:

- Taxpayers are permitted to off-set allowable losses and their annual exemption in the way that produces the lowest possible tax charge (see **1.23**).
- Where a taxpayer who has been temporarily non-resident resumes UK residence in 2010/11, any gains that become chargeable under *TCGA 1992, s 10A* are treated as arising before 23 June 2010 (see **5.29**).
- Where gains are charged on the settlor of a non-UK resident trust under *TCGA 1992, s 86,* those gains are deemed to arise before 23 June 2010.
- Where the UK-resident beneficiaries of a non-UK resident trust receive capital payments from that trust, the gains taxable on the beneficiaries under *TCGA 1992, ss 87(2), 89(2)* and *Sch 4C, para 8(1),* are deemed to accrue to the beneficiaries at the dates that those capital payments are made.

- Where gains are remitted to the UK by an individual who claims the remittance basis those gains are deemed to arise in the UK on the date the remittance is made (see **5.37**).
- Where an individual pays the remittance basis charge for the year, and as a result gains are deemed to be remitted under *ITA 2007, s 809J*, those gains are deemed to arise in the UK before 23 June 2010 (see **5.40**).

CHARGEABLE PERSONS

1.4 A person is chargeable to CGT in respect of chargeable gains accruing to him in a year of assessment, ie a 'tax year' ending on 5 April:

- during any part of which he is 'resident' in the UK; or
- during which he is 'ordinarily resident' in the UK (*TCGA 1992, ss 1, 2, 288*).

'Accruing' means realised or deemed to be realised, rather than accumulated over a period. Anti-avoidance rules provide for a person to be chargeable to CGT on gains accruing to others in certain circumstances. For example, the gains of a non-resident trust or company may be attributed to a UK-resident individual. Residence and other international issues are discussed in detail in **Chapter 5**.

Territorial limits

1.5 The UK comprises Great Britain and Northern Ireland. It includes the UK's territorial seas, but excludes the Isle of Man and the Channel Islands. A person who is a 'temporary non-resident' may also be chargeable to CGT. A non-resident person carrying on a business in the UK through a branch or agency (or through a permanent establishment, in the case of a company) is chargeable to CGT (or corporation tax) on gains arising from assets in the UK that are used for the purposes of the business (*TCGA 1992, ss 10, 10A, 276*).

CGT is not limited to gains on disposal of UK assets. However, an individual who is not domiciled in any part of the UK may not be chargeable on gains arising on non-UK assets if that individual has claimed, or has the automatic right to, the remittance basis and those overseas gains are not remitted to the UK. See **Chapter 5** regarding residence, etc and the location of assets.

Beneficial ownership

1.6 The beneficial owner of the asset disposed of is normally the chargeable person in relation to the disposal. There is no disposal where an asset is transferred between a beneficial owner and a nominee for him (*TCGA 1992, s 60*).

CHARGEABLE GAINS V INCOME

1.7 Every gain accruing on the disposal of an asset is a chargeable gain, but it should only be chargeable to CGT if it is not taxed by income tax. *TCGA 1992, s 37* expressly excludes from the chargeable gains calculation amounts charged to income tax or corporation tax as income. However, this rule does not prevent the same sum from being subject to two different taxes as HMRC may raise alternative assessments on that sum under income tax and CGT (*IRC v Wilkinson* [1992] STC 454, 65 TC 28 and *Bye v Coren* [1986] STC 393, 60 TC116).

There are a number of types of transaction that may result in the profits being taxed as income rather than as capital due to the impact of anti-avoidance legislation. For example an artificial transaction in land may give rise to an income tax or corporation tax charge on the profit under *ITA 2007, s 775* (*CTA 2010, ss 818–822* for corporation tax).

It is difficult, but not impossible, to convert income (taxed at 50% or more) into capital (taxed 18% or 28% for 2010/11). For example, a high earner may decide to invest in bonds that provide a return in the form of capital redemptions subject to CGT, rather than investments that return dividends or interest that are subject to income tax. Schemes that seek to convert employment income into an asset that would be subject to CGT on disposal, will have to be reported to HMRC under the DOTAS regulations with effect from a date to be announced (see **10.5**).

Capital losses are computed, as a general rule, in the same way as gains. If a gain accruing on an asset would be exempt from CGT, a loss accruing on the same disposal cannot generally be an allowable loss. Gains and losses can arise from the relative movement in exchange rates in respect of sums held in foreign currency bank accounts. A withdrawal of funds from such a bank account can be a disposal for CGT, creating a gain or a loss. The taxation of that gain or loss will depend on whether the taxpayer claims the remittance basis and how those funds are remitted to the UK (see **Chapter 5**).

EXEMPT ASSETS OR GAINS

1.8 The main exemptions applied to particular assets or gains by virtue of *TCGA 1992* are set out in **Table 1.1**, in the order in which they appear in the legislation. Exemptions provided elsewhere in the tax legislation are set out in **Table 1.2**. There are also a number of special rules relating to particular assets (see **Chapter 4**) and a variety of reliefs which either provide a reduction in the CGT liability or defer it until a later date (see **Chapters 11** to **17**).

Exemptions provided by TCGA 1992

1.9

Table 1.1

Exempt assets or gains	***TCGA 1992***
Foreign assets: CGT is not charged on gains from the disposal of assets situated outside the UK, accruing to non-UK domiciled individuals who are resident or ordinarily resident in the UK, if the remittance basis applies to those individuals for the relevant tax year. Where amounts are remitted to the UK in respect of such gains, CGT is charged on the amounts received in the UK, even if the remittance is in a later tax year (see **Chapter 5**).	*s 12*
Sterling is not an asset for CGT purposes (but currency other than sterling is an asset).	*s 21(1)(b)*
Wasting assets: No chargeable gain accrues on a disposal of tangible movable property that is a wasting asset as defined, subject to certain exceptions (see **Chapter 4**).	*s 45*
Winnings from betting, lotteries or games with prizes are not chargeable gains.	*s 51*
Compensation or damages for any wrong or injury suffered by an individual in his person or in his profession or vocation are not chargeable gains.	*s 51*
Death: The assets of which a deceased person was competent to dispose are deemed not to be disposed of by him on his death (see **Chapter 7**).	*s 62*
Interests in settled property: No chargeable gain accrues on the disposal of an interest in a settlement by the original beneficiary or by any other person except one who bought the interest. The trustees must be resident in the UK. There are also other exceptions (see **Chapter 8**).	*s 76*
Government stock and qualifying corporate bonds (QCB): A gain accruing on a disposal of government-issued securities known as gilts, or any QCB whoever issued it, or of any option or contract to acquire or dispose of such assets is not a chargeable gain.	*s 115*

Exempt assets or gains	***TCGA 1992***
Savings certificates and certain government securities are not chargeable assets, so that no chargeable gain accrues on a disposal.	*s 121*
Business expansion scheme (BES) shares: A gain accruing to an individual on disposal of shares issued after 18 March 1986 for which tax relief was given under the BES and has not been withdrawn is not a chargeable gain. Special rules apply to losses on disposal of such shares.	*s 150*
Enterprise investment scheme (EIS) shares: Gains accruing on the disposal after the end of the 'relevant period' of shares for which income tax relief under the EIS regime has been given (and not withdrawn) are not chargeable gains. Partial CGT exemption is available where income tax relief was restricted. Special rules apply to losses on disposal of such shares (see **Chapter 16**).	*ss 150A–150C, Sch 5B*
Individual Savings Accounts and Personal Equity Plan investments: No tax is chargeable on either the investor or the account manager in respect of gains arising on ISAs or PEPs provided certain conditions are met.	*s 151*
Venture capital trusts: A gain accruing to an individual on a 'qualifying disposal' of ordinary shares in a venture capital trust is, subject to certain conditions, not a chargeable gain. Special rules apply to losses on disposal of such shares (see **Chapter 17**).	*s 151A*
Companies – substantial shareholdings in trading companies: A gain on a disposal of a 'substantial shareholding' (broadly, an interest of at least 10%) that has been held for at least 12 months is not a chargeable gain provided various conditions are met (see **Chapter 9**).	*s 192A, Sch 7AC*
Life insurance and deferred annuities: A gain accruing on a disposal of (or of an interest in) rights conferred by a policy of insurance or contract for a deferred annuity is not a chargeable gain unless the policy, etc (or the interest in it) has been acquired for actual (not deemed) consideration.	*ss 204, 210*
Private residences: All or part of a gain on the disposal of a dwelling house which has been the individual's only or main residence at some time in the period of ownership, will be exempt from CGT (see **Chapter 12**).	*s 223*

Exempt assets or gains *TCGA 1992*

Pension funds, purchased annuities, and superannuation funds: *ss 237, 271*

Gains on the disposal of investments held for the purposes of a registered pension scheme are not chargeable to CGT. No chargeable gain accrues on the disposal of a right to payment out of a qualifying superannuation fund. This covers the majority of occupational pension schemes. Also the disposal of rights to payments under purchased annuities or covenants not secured on property is exempt.

Agricultural grants, etc: A sum receivable under the *Agriculture Act 1967, s 27* in return for relinquishing occupation of an uncommercial agricultural unit is not treated as part of the consideration on the disposal of any asset. *s 249*

Woodlands: Any part of the consideration for a disposal of woodland in the UK that is attributable to trees (including saleable underwood) growing on the land is excluded from the CGT computation together with the related costs. Where the occupier of woodlands manages them on a commercial basis with a view to the realisation of profits, consideration for the disposal of trees standing or felled or cut on the woodlands is excluded from the computation. Any capital sum received under an insurance policy relating to the destruction of (or damage to) trees or saleable underwood by fire or other hazard is also excluded. *s 250*

Debts: Where a person (A) incurs a debt to another person (B), no chargeable gain accrues to the original creditor (B) on a disposal of the debt, except in the case of (i) a debt on a security, and (ii) money held in a foreign currency bank account that does not represent currency acquired for personal expenditure outside the UK. *ss 251, 252*

Works of art, etc: A gain is not a chargeable gain if it accrues on the disposal of assets such as works of art, historical building, etc to which a conditional exemption from inheritance tax could or does apply. *s 258*

Chattels: A gain accruing on a disposal of tangible movable property is not a chargeable gain if the amount or value of the consideration for the disposal is not more than £6,000 (see **Chapter 4**). *s 262*

Exempt assets or gains	***TCGA 1992***
Motor cars: Vehicles which are commonly used as private motor cars are not chargeable assets, which means no chargeable gain or loss can accrue on their disposal. This exemption covers vintage cars, but not vehicles of a type not commonly used as a private vehicle and unsuitable to be so used.	*s 263*
Renewables obligation certificates: Where an individual disposes of a renewables obligation certificate in relation to an electricity generation system installed at their home and other conditions apply, there is no chargeable gain.	*s 263AZA*
Decorations for valour or gallant conduct: A gain accruing on the disposal of a decoration awarded for valour or gallant conduct is not a chargeable gain unless the taxpayer acquired it for a consideration in money or money's worth.	*s 268*
Foreign currency for personal expenditure: A gain accruing on the disposal by an individual of currency acquired for his own or his family's or his dependants' personal expenditure outside the UK is not a chargeable gain.	*s 269*
SAYE savings schemes: Interest on certified SAYE savings arrangements within *ITTOIA 2005, s 702* is disregarded for all purposes of CGT.	*s 271(4)*

Other exemptions

1.10

Table 1.2

Exempt assets or gains	**Source**
Cashbacks: These are lump sums received by a customer as an inducement for entering into a transaction for the purchase of goods, investments or services and received as a direct consequence of entering into the transaction (eg a mortgage). HMRC consider that a cashback does not derive from a chargeable asset for CGT purposes so that no chargeable gain arises. This practice does not extend to a cash payment by a building society to members, etc on a takeover by, or conversion to, a bank; or a payment by other mutual organisations such as insurance companies or friendly societies on demutualisation.	SP 4/97, para 35

Exempt assets or gains	**Source**
Child Trust Funds: Assets held by a named child as account investments are regarded as held by him in a separate capacity from that in which he holds similar assets outside the CTF. The child will be treated as selling the account investments and reacquiring them in his personal capacity at their market value on attaining the age of 18. Losses accruing on account investments are disregarded for CGT purposes.	*Child Trust Funds Act 2004, s 13*; *SI 2004/1450*
Compensation paid by foreign governments: By concession, and subject to conditions, certain capital sums paid as compensation by a foreign government for the confiscation or expropriation of property outside the UK are not treated as giving rise to a chargeable gain.	ESC D50
Lloyd's underwriters' special reserve funds: Profits and losses arising from disposal of assets forming part of a special reserve fund are excluded from CGT.	*FA 1993, Sch 20, para 9*
Compensation for bad pensions advice: compensation for misleading pensions advice given between 29 April 1988 and 30 June 1994 is not a chargeable gain.	*FA 1996, s 148*

Exempt persons

1.11 The main exemptions likely to be met in practice are set out in **Table 1.3**. Others include full or partial exemptions for the Crown, local authorities, health service bodies, friendly societies, certain museums, housing associations, self-build societies, pension schemes, trades unions, scientific research associations, certain central banks, visiting forces and diplomats.

Table 1.3

Exempt person(s)	**Source**
Nominees and bare trustees: Where assets are held by a person (A) as nominee or bare trustee for another person (B), the property is treated as vested in B and acts of the nominee or bare trustee are treated as acts of B, so that there is no occasion of charge where the bare trustee, for example, passes assets to B.	*TCGA 1992, s 60*
Charities: A gain is not a chargeable gain if it accrues to a charity and is applicable and applied for charitable purposes (subject to restrictions found in *ITA 2007, part 10*).	*TCGA 1992, s 256*

Exempt person(s)	**Source**
Community amateur sports clubs: A gain accruing to a registered club is not a chargeable gain if the whole of it is applied for qualifying purposes and the club makes a claim.	*FA 2002, Sch 18, para 7*

THE CAPITAL GAINS TAX CALCULATION

1.12 Individuals, trustees and personal representatives pay CGT at the rate or rates applying in the relevant tax year (see **1.23**).

See **Chapter 3** for a discussion of the detailed computation of chargeable gains. **Chapter 11** deals with entrepreneurs' relief and the complications that arise when qualifying gains are made both before and after 23 June 2010.

The amount chargeable

1.13 Once the gains have been computed as set out in **Chapter 3**, several adjustments may be required before the taxpayer can ascertain the taxable amount and then apply the appropriate rates of CGT.

CGT is charged on the total amount of chargeable gains accruing in the tax year, after deducting:

- any allowable losses accruing to the taxpayer in that tax year; and
- any allowable losses accruing to him in a previous tax year (not earlier than 1965/66) that have not already been allowed as a deduction from chargeable gains.

An allowable loss cannot be carried back to an earlier tax year, except where the loss has been sustained by an individual in the tax year in which he died (see **Chapter 7**). However, for entrepreneurs' relief losses must be aggregated with gains from a single business disposal, which could conceivably straddle two tax years (see **Chapter 11**). Relief cannot be given twice for the same loss under *TCGA 1992* and is not available for a capital loss that has been, or may be, relieved under the income tax legislation (*TCGA 1992, s 2(2), (3)*).

Gains accruing to others

1.14 This general rule is modified where gains have accrued to others but are attributed to the taxpayer, as settlor or beneficiary of a trust, under any of the following provisions (read, where appropriate, along with the rules in *TCGA 1992, s 10A* relating to temporary non-residents):

(a) *TCGA 1992, s 77* – charge on settlor with interest in settlement;

(b) *TCGA 1992, s 86* – attribution of gains to settlor with an interest in a non-resident or dual resident settlement;

(c) *TCGA 1992, s 87* – attribution of gains to a beneficiary; and

(d) *TCGA 1992, s 89(2)* – migrant settlements etc.

The effect of these special rules, examined further in **Chapter 8**, is that the taxpayer's own capital losses cannot be set against such gains (*TCGA 1992, s 2(4)–(8)*).

Taper relief

1.15 Taper relief was automatically given against gains arising on disposals made by individuals and trustees between 6 April 1998 and 5 April 2008. Losses were deducted before the net gain was tapered by a percentage dependent on the type of asset and the period the asset had been held. The taxpayer had the choice of which gain to set against any available loss (*TCGA 1992, s 2A*). For further discussion of taper relief see **17.22**.

Entrepreneurs' relief

1.16 Entrepreneurs' relief may be claimed where certain qualifying shares or business assets are disposed of after 5 April 2008. The relief reduces the effective rate of CGT to 10% on qualifying gains which are within the lifetime cap for the relief. Entrepreneurs' relief is examined in detail in **Chapter 11.**

Annual exemption

1.17 Most individuals are entitled to an annual exemption, the effect of which is to provide that a slice of the 'taxable amount' (see **1.19**) for a tax year is not chargeable to CGT. Any unused part of the annual exemption is lost – it cannot be carried forward to the following tax year. Spouses and civil partners are entitled to their own annual exemption, which is not transferable. Non-UK domiciled individuals are not entitled to an annual exemption where they claim or are entitled to use the remittance basis, subject to certain exceptions, see **Chapter 5**.

The amount of the annual exemption is as set out in **Table 1.4** (*TCGA 1992, s 3*).

Table 1.4

Tax year	Individuals, certain trustees (see **1.22**) and personal representatives	Other trustees
2010/11	£10,100	£5,050
2009/10	£10,100	£5,050
2008/09	£9,600	£4,800
2007/08	£9,200	£4,600
2006/07	£8,800	£4,400
2005/06	£8,500	£4,250

Indexation of the annual exemption

1.18 The annual exemption is increased each year in line with inflation as measured by the change in the retail prices index (RPI) in the year to September in the previous tax year, unless Parliament decides otherwise. For the 12 months to September 2009 the RPI was a negative figure, so the annual exemption was not increased for the tax year 2010/11. The new annual exemption is specified each year in a Treasury order (*TCGA 1992, s 3(3), (4)*).

The 'taxable amount'

1.19 The taxable amount is usually the amount of chargeable gains accruing to the taxpayer for a tax year after deduction of losses and reliefs. In some cases, gains accruing to others but chargeable on the taxpayer under anti-avoidance rules will be added at this stage in arriving at the taxable amount (see **1.14**) (*TCGA 1992, s 3(5)*).

Losses and the annual exemption

1.20 Allowable losses must be set against chargeable gains arising in the same tax year, even if this means reducing the taxable amount below the annual exemption. In other words, the set-off of current-year losses cannot be restricted in order to utilise the exemption and preserve some of those losses for future use. However, in 2010/11 the taxpayer does have the freedom to set-off losses against gains arising before or after the change in the CGT rate on 23 June 2010 (see **1.23**).

Allowable capital losses carried forward from an earlier year (or carried back from the year of the taxpayer's death) need not be deducted where the 'adjusted net gains' (see below) of the current tax year are covered by the annual exemption (*TCGA 1992, ss 2(2), 3(5A)*).

If the taxpayer's adjusted net gains exceed the annual exemption, then the amount set off in respect of losses carried forward (or back) is restricted to the excess. For this purpose the 'adjusted net gains' are, in most cases:

- the chargeable gains accruing to him for the year, before deduction of losses and reliefs, less
- allowable losses arising in the current year (*TCGA 1992, s 3(5B), (5C)*).

However, where gains have accrued to others but are attributed to the taxpayer as beneficiary of a settlement under the rules mentioned in (c) or (d) of **1.14**, then the smaller of the following amounts is added in arriving at the adjusted net gains:

- the amount of gains so attributed to him; and
- the amount of the annual exemption (*TCGA 1992, s 3(5C)*).

Personal representatives

1.21 The CGT treatment of personal representatives is considered in **Chapter 7**. Personal representatives of a deceased individual are entitled to the same annual exempt amount as an individual for:

- the tax year in which the individual died; and
- the next two following tax years (*TCGA 1992, s 3(7)*).

Trustees

1.22 The CGT treatment of trustees is considered in **Chapter 8**. Two sets of rules, set out in *TCGA 1992, Sch 1*, fix the annual exemption. Broadly, trustees generally are entitled to an annual exemption equal to one-half of the exemption available to an individual, but trustees of settled property held for people with disabilities and others are entitled to the full annual exemption (*TCGA 1992, s 3(8); Sch 1, para 2*).

Rates of tax

Individuals

1.23 The rate of CGT was set at a single rate of 18% from 6 April 2008 to 22 June 2010. During this period this flat rate of CGT applies irrespective of the level of other income taxed in the same tax year (*TCGA 1992, s 4*). However, for disposals made, and deemed to be made, on and after 23 June

2010 there are three possible tax rates of CGT that apply depending on the taxpayer's level of income and gains, and whether entrepreneurs' relief applies to the gain:

Taxpayer or gains:	*Rate of CGT*
Individuals with income and gains up to basic rate band:	18%
Individuals with income and gains at or above the basic rate band:	28%
All trustees and personal representatives:	28%
Gains subject to entrepreneurs' relief:	10%

The higher rate of CGT at 28% applies where the taxpayer's total taxable income and post-22 June 2010 gains is equal to or exceeds the basic rate threshold of £37,400. That sum includes the taxpayer's total income for the full tax year less personal allowances and all allowable deductions, less any part of the annual CGT exemption and losses set against those gains. The taxpayer can choose where to set their annual exemption and capital losses, including capital losses that arise in the tax year and losses which are brought forward from an earlier tax year.

Example 1.1

Sid's taxable income for 2010/11 is £27,400 after his personal allowance and all tax-allowable expenses have been deducted. He sold a property in May 2010 that made a gain of £17,000, and sold another property in November 2010 for a gain of £25,100. Neither disposal qualifies for entrepreneurs' relief or for the main residence exemption (see **Chapter 12**). Sid has no capital losses to use in 2010/11. The CGT on those gains is calculated as follows:

	May 2010 gain	*CGT payable*	*November 2010 gain*	*CGT payable*
Taxable income	N/A		£27,400	
Higher rate threshold	N/A		£37,400	
Available basic rate band			£10,000	
Gross gains	£17,000		£25,100	
Less annual exemption			£10,100	
Net taxable gains	£17,000		£15,000	
Gain taxed at 18% (using basic rate band)	£17,000	£3,060	£10,000	£1,800
Gain taxed at 28%			£5,000	£1,400
Total CGT payable		£3,060		£3,200

Sid has chosen to set his annual exemption of £10,100 against his later gain as that gives him tax relief at 28%. His total CGT liability for 2010/11 is £6,260 (£3,060 + £3,200) which is payable by 31 January 2012.

For the tax years 1988/89 to 2007/08 the rate of CGT paid by individuals was dependent on the amount of taxable income for the tax year (see **1.24** for trustees). Gains were treated as though they were the top slice of the individual's income, after allowing for deductions against income, and the relevant income tax rates (10%, 20% or 40%) were applied to those gains. For further discussion of the interaction of income tax thresholds and CGT rates see *Capital Gains Tax 2007/08* (Tottel Publishing).

Trustees and personal representatives

1.24 For disposal made from 6 April 2008 to 22 June all trustees pay CGT at 18%. For disposals made on and after 23 June 2010 all trustees pay CGT at 28%.

For the tax years 1988/89 to 2007/08 the rate of CGT was the same as the 'trust rate' under *ITA 2007, s 9,* where the gains accrue to either the trustees of a settlement or the personal representatives of a deceased person. This rate was increased from 34% to 40% from 6 April 2004.

Companies

1.25 Companies do not pay CGT. They are chargeable to corporation tax on their chargeable gains instead (see **Chapter 9**) (*TCGA 1992, s 1(2)*; *CTA 2009, s 2*). There were no changes to the taxation of chargeable gains for companies from 23 June 2010.

SELF-ASSESSMENT

1.26 The self-assessment system has applied to individuals, trustees and personal representatives, broadly, since 1996/97. An individual's tax return must include a self-assessment of income tax and CGT liabilities. The taxpayer is required to pay the tax on or before the due date, based on that self-assessment.

Self-assessment and related matters, including compliance with the regime for disclosure of tax avoidance schemes, are examined in detail in Chapter 2 of *Income Tax 2010/11* (Bloomsbury Professional). This chapter focuses on the fundamental aspects of self-assessment relating to capital gains.

HMRC provide general guidance on CGT at www.hmrc.gov.uk/cgt/index.htm. More detailed guidance can be found in the HMRC Capital Gains manual: www.hmrc.gov.uk/manuals/CG1manual/index.htm.

From the 2009/10 tax year HMRC also provide 'toolkits' (see: www.hmrc.gov.uk/agents/prereturn-support-agents.htm). These are interactive checklists covering the most difficult or problematic areas of tax returns. There are two toolkits that deal with capital gains issues:

- capital gains tax for land and buildings;
- capital gains tax for trusts and estates.

The use of the toolkits is completely optional when preparing the tax return. The 2009/10 Trust and Estate tax return does include a tick-box to confirm whether the relevant toolkit has been used, but the completion of this box is optional. However, if the relevant toolkit is used HMRC will regard the tax return preparer as having taken reasonable care in preparing the return. This could be a significant factor if errors are subsequently discovered on that return and penalties are imposed (see **1.48**).

Tax returns

1.27 Taxpayers may file their tax return online via the HMRC website, in which case a paper return form is not required. Where the taxpayer has not been sent a tax return form they may request one from their local tax office. Alternatively, all the tax return forms may be downloaded from the HMRC website: www.hmrc.gov.uk/cgt/forms.htm. The capital gains summary pages are required if an individual taxpayer answers 'yes' to question seven in the section entitled 'What makes up your Tax Return' on page TR2 of the 2009/10 form SA100. Page TRG5 of the Tax Return Guide sets out in greater detail the circumstances in which the capital gains summary pages (SA108) should be completed. Trustees and personal representatives need to complete the SA900 Trust and Estate tax return, with supplementary pages SA905 to report capital gains and losses.

HMRC provide notes to the capital gains pages (SA108 Notes for individuals, SA905 Notes for trustees), including examples. It also provides detailed helpsheets on various topics as set out in **Table 1.5**. These are available from the HMRC orderline on 0845 9000 404 or via the HMRC website: www.hmrc.gov.uk/cgt/forms.htm

Table 1.5

HS261	Foreign tax credit relief: capital gains
HS275	Entrepreneurs' relief
HS276	Incorporation relief
HS278	Temporary non-residents and Capital Gains Tax
HS281	Husband and wife, civil partners, divorce, dissolution and separation
HS282	Death, personal representatives and legatees
HS283	Private residence relief
HS284	Shares and Capital Gains Tax
HS285	Share reorganisations, company take-overs and Capital Gains Tax
HS286	Negligible value claims and Income Tax losses
HS287	Employee share and security schemes and Capital Gains Tax
HS288	Partnerships and Capital Gains Tax
HS290	Business asset roll-over relief
HS292	Land and leases, the valuation of land and Capital Gains Tax
HS293	Chattels (assets you can touch and move) and Capital Gains Tax
HS294	Trusts and Capital Gains Tax
HS295	Relief for gifts and similar transactions
HS296	Debts and Capital Gains Tax
HS297	Enterprise Investment Scheme and Capital Gains Tax
HS298	Venture Capital Trusts and Capital Gains Tax
HS299	Non Resident Trusts and Capital Gains Tax
HS301	Calculation of capital gains from non-resident trusts, dual resident and immigrating trusts

Notice to deliver a return

1.28 An officer of HM Revenue and Customs may give notice to the taxpayer requiring him to make and deliver a return to enable the officer to establish the amount of any income tax or CGT liability. The notice may request such accounts, statements and documents, relating to information contained in the return, as may reasonably be required (*TMA 1970, ss 8, 12*).

Information required to be sent with the return

1.29 The notice may require different information, accounts and statements for different periods or different sources of income. While there is no statutory authority for HMRC to require a taxpayer to provide a list of investments or other assets held at a particular date, HMRC guidance indicates that they may possibly ask for such a list if they are aware that one exists (CG20224). The return includes a declaration by the person making it to the effect that the return is, to the best of his knowledge, correct and complete.

The capital gains summary pages must be submitted together with detailed computations of each gain made. HMRC do not prescribe a format for the CGT computation, but it does include a worksheet for simple disposals in the notes to the capital gains pages (SA108 Notes).

For online submission the tax return must include an entry in the 'any other information' space (box 35) on page CG2, or an electronic file sent as a pdf attachment, if a capital gain is reported for the year. The data limit for box 35 is 20,480 characters, so a complex calculation will not fit, in which case the computation will need to be submitted as a pdf attachment.

Reporting limits

1.30 A return of capital gains is required only if certain reporting limits, set out below in relation to individuals, personal representatives and trustees respectively, are exceeded. However, the capital gains pages should be completed if there are allowable losses or the taxpayer wishes to make a claim or election for the year (see **1.46**).

Individuals

1.31 HMRC do not require the taxpayer to complete the capital gains summary pages where any of the following apply:

- the taxpayer's chargeable gains accruing in a tax year do not exceed the amount of the annual exemption (see **1.17**);
- the aggregate amount or value of the consideration for all 'chargeable disposals' (see below) that he made in the year does not exceed four times that annual exemption (ie £40,400 for 2010/11 and 2009/10), and the chargeable gain arising was less than the annual exemption; or
- the gain is on a residence and is wholly relieved by main residence relief.

For this purpose, the amount of chargeable gains accruing in the year is taken to be:

- the amount of overseas gains remitted; and
- the amount before any deduction for allowable losses.

'Chargeable disposals' for the purpose of these reporting limits exclude both disposals on which any gain accruing is not a chargeable gain and 'no gain, no loss' disposals between spouses or civil partners (*TCGA 1992, s 3A(1), (2), (3)*).

Personal representatives

1.32 The above reporting limits are applied to personal representatives for the tax year in which the individual concerned died and for the next two tax years (*TCGA 1992, s 3A(4)*).

Trustees

1.33 The rule in **1.31** also applies to trustees of a settlement but the reporting limits are calculated by reference to the reduced annual exemption available to the trustees where appropriate (see **1.17** and **Chapter 8**) (*TCGA 1992, s 3A(5); Sch 1, para 2(6A)*).

Estimates

1.34 A taxpayer who has used estimated figures to calculate gains or losses should:

- tick the relevant boxes on page CG1 or CG2 of the capital gains pages; and
- identify and give reasons for the estimates, either in the detailed computations or in box 35, the 'any other information' box on page CG2 as appropriate.

Valuations

1.35 The use of any valuation in a CGT computation should be indicated in the detailed computations. HMRC Statement of Practice 1/06 recommends that the following details should be given in the white space on the tax return:

- which firm or named individual carried out the valuation; and
- the basis on which the valuation was carried out (eg a 31 March 1982 value).

HMRC may check the valuation and in the absence of any agreement the valuation may be referred to the Tax Tribunal.

Before finalising the tax return the taxpayer may ask HMRC to carry out a 'post-transaction valuation check', by using the form CG34. This form can be downloaded from the HMRC website at www.hmrc.gov.uk/forms/cg34.pdf, and in most cases it should be submitted, together with all supporting documents, to the central CGT team rather than to the taxpayer's local office as it says on the form. The address for the CGT team is:

The Capital Gains Team (Individuals & Public Bodies)
16 West Government Buildings
Ty Glas Road
Llanishen
Cardiff
CF14 5FP

Tel: 0117 907 2466

If the taxpayer's tax office is Public Department 1, the High Net Worth unit or a Trust Office, the form CG34 should be submitted to the tax office that deals with the taxpayer's tax return.

The processing of the CG34 forms has been centralised to provide a consistent quality of service to all taxpayers, but HMRC expect the approval process for each form to take at least 56 days. Use of the CG34 procedure to ask for a valuation check does not change the filing date for the tax return, so the form CG34 should be submitted at the earliest opportunity.

The advantage of using the CG34 procedure is that if HMRC agree a valuation they will not challenge the use of that valuation in the return. This does not mean the final gain or loss is agreed, as factors other than the valuation may be relevant. If HMRC cannot agree the valuation as suggested on CG34 they will use specialist valuers to suggest alternatives.

The taxpayer should indicate in the detailed computation of the gains or losses submitted with the tax return, which transactions are, or have been, the subject of a CG34 valuation check.

It is possible to request a post-transaction ruling on the application of tax law to a transaction under Code of Practice 10 (COP10). However, HMRC will only devote resources to answering such queries where the tax treatment of the particular transaction is in doubt. They will not give post-transaction rulings on asset valuations that do not involve the interpretation of tax law or its application to the taxpayer's particular circumstances. The COP10 procedure should not be used in place of the CG34 procedure. Further details are set out in COP10, available at www.hmrc.gov.uk/pdfs/cop10.htm.

Provisional figures

1.36 HMRC advise taxpayers not to delay filing a tax return just because some of the required information is not available. Provisional figures should be provided and identified in the main pages of the return (by putting a cross in box 20 on page TR6 and a note in box 19 to indicate which figures are provisional). HMRC also want to be told why final figures could not be given and when those final figures will be provided.

The tax return guide (SA150) warns that a taxpayer may be liable to a penalty if they do not have good reasons for supplying provisional figures, or provide unreasonable figures. Pressure of work, or the complexity of the individual's tax affairs, are not good reasons to provide provisional figures. A taxpayer who uses provisional figures must ensure that the final figures are submitted as soon as they are available.

Filing date

1.37 The return must be delivered to HMRC by the filing date, which for electronically submitted returns will normally be 31 January following the end of the relevant tax year, ie 31 January 2011 for the year ended 5 April 2010. Taxpayers filing a paper return must do so by 31 October following the end of the tax year, or be subject to a late filing penalty where tax for year remains unpaid by the following 31 January. Tax returns for certain individuals such as MPs and members of the security forces cannot be submitted electronically, so may be submitted on paper up until 31 January with no late filing penalties. Where a notice to deliver a return is given after 31 July following the end of the tax year, the filing date is three months after the date of the notice.

Where a paper tax return is submitted on time HMRC undertake to calculate the tax liability, and adjust the PAYE notice of coding for the following tax year to include underpaid tax of up to £2,000 if this is requested. Electronic filing provides users with a tax calculation whenever the tax return is submitted (*TMA 1970, s 8(1A)*).

Payment of tax

1.38 CGT for a tax year is payable in one sum by 31 January following the end of the tax year for which the liability arose. Unlike the combined income tax and Class 4 national insurance liability, the CGT is not payable as part of the on-account payments due on 31 January in the tax year, and 31 July after the end of the tax year. See Chapter 2 of *Income Tax 2010/11* (Bloomsbury Professional), for details of how payments on account are calculated.

Where CGT is unpaid more than 28 days after the due date, a 5% surcharge is imposed, with a further 5% surcharge added to the liability if the tax remains unpaid six months after the due date.

COMPLIANCE ASSURANCE AND PENALTIES

HMRC's new powers

1.39 HMRC now have a single set of powers in order to monitor the accuracy of all tax returns, documents and information submitted to them, and to check the taxpayer's tax position at any time (**1.41**). A new power to publish the details of deliberate tax defaulters was introduced from 1 April 2010 (**1.47**).

The system of penalties has been aligned and modernised across all taxes, with a number of new penalties introduced to encourage timely filing and payment. The reform of the penalty regime is not complete and further categories of penalties are expected to be introduced in 2011. The old penalty system continues to apply to errors and mistakes in tax returns submitted before 1 April 2009 so will run in parallel with the new system for some years (**1.47**).

Interest rates on the late payment or over payment of tax have been harmonised across all taxes from September 2009. However, the circumstances in which interest will be paid or charged have not yet been aligned across all of HMRC's responsibilities.

The time periods in which HMRC are permitted to raise assessments have been largely aligned with the periods available to taxpayers to make certain claims and elections (**1.46**). Alongside these new HMRC powers the system of tax appeals has been completely reformed (**1.55**).

All of these changes collectively amount to a fundamental alteration in the compliance regime for UK taxes.

Training and guidance

1.40 The HMRC internal guidance on all the new powers and penalties has been brought together in the Compliance Handbook (www.hmrc.gov.uk/manuals/chmanual/Index.htm). A series of 13 compliance factsheets have been produced for taxpayers to explain their rights and those of the Tax Inspector during a compliance check (www.hmrc.gov.uk/compliance/factsheets.htm). These factsheets also cover the penalties that can be imposed.

There are a number of training packages available on the HMRC website designed to inform HMRC staff of the changes, but which can equally be used by tax practitioners and their staff (www.hmrc.gov.uk/about/hmrc-learning.htm). In addition, HMRC have organised a number of workshops on the new compliance powers to which both HMRC staff and tax agents are invited.

Compliance checks

1.41 From 1 April 2009 HMRC can use the information and inspection powers introduced by *FA 2008, Sch 36*, to undertake compliance checks on individuals and businesses for PAYE, VAT, CGT, income tax and corporation tax. In this section, references to paragraphs are to paragraphs of *FA 2008, Sch 36*. These powers were extended to other taxes such as IHT, SDLT and environmental taxes from 1 April 2010, and will cover excise and other duties from 1 April 2011.

A compliance check includes carrying out an investigation or enquiry of any kind (*para 58*), but it will not necessarily develop into a full-blown tax investigation. Tax advisers should note that HMRC now have the power to request information ahead of the submission of any tax return.

The new compliance powers can be used by HMRC officers to obtain information and documents from the taxpayer and third parties which are reasonably required for the purpose of checking the tax position of the taxpayer. The 'tax position' is defined in *para 64* as the person's past, present or future liability to pay any tax. This includes:

- UK taxes: income tax, CGT, corporation tax, VAT, NIC and relevant foreign taxes;
- penalties paid or payable in respect of any tax; and
- claims, elections, applications and notices that have been made or may be made or given in connection with any tax.

Visits by HMRC

1.42 As part of the compliance check HMRC may visit business premises to inspect the premises, business assets and statutory records. 'Business premises' means any premises or any part of them that HMRC think are used in connection with the carrying on of a business, so includes homes that are partly used for business purposes. However, HMRC officers do not have the power to enter or inspect any part of the premises that is used solely as a dwelling. The Compliance Handbook instructs HMRC officers only to arrange to visit a person's home if it is essential to checking the person's tax position, and they must get their manager's agreement first (CH254510).

The HMRC officer will normally give at least seven days' notice of an inspection, or will arrange the inspection at a time which is reasonable with agreement of the occupier. HMRC can make unannounced visits, when the HMRC officer must still give a notice to the occupier of the premises if he is there when they arrive; or to someone who appears to be in charge of the premises; in any other case, the notice must be left in a prominent place on the premises. In each case the notice must state the possible consequences of obstructing the officer in the exercise of his power. If the notice was given with the approval of the Tribunal, it must say so.

HMRC officers do not have the power to force entry to the premises or to search the premises (para CH25100). *Paras 15–17*, give HMRC powers to copy documents, to remove them and to mark assets and record information. HMRC are liable to pay the owner reasonable compensation should they lose or damage the document (*para 16*). HMRC officers may also inspect any computer used by the business (*FA 2008, s 114*), but the officer must first seek the advice of a HMRC data handling specialist (para CH23360).

Information notices

1.43 The HMRC officer will normally ask informally, either orally or in writing, for the information he requires. However, if this does not produce the required result he can issue a formal taxpayer's notice, or a third-party notice or an identity unknown notice. A 'third party notice' is one issued under *para 2* by an HMRC officer to check the tax position of someone whose identity is known to the officer and which names that taxpayer, except where approval has been obtained from the First-tier Tribunal to the issuing of the third-party notice without the requirement to name the taxpayer.

The notice will usually specify or describe the information or documents to be provided or produced and stipulate a time limit for production. If the notice is given with the approval of the tribunal this must be stated in the notice. Where a tax return has been submitted, *para 21* only permits an HMRC officer to issue a taxpayer notice if one of the following conditions applies:

(a) the enquiry window for the return is still open, or an enquiry into that return is still open; or

(b) HMRC have reason to suspect tax has been over- or underpaid or too much tax relief has been given for the period; or

(c) information is needed to check the taxpayer's VAT position; or

(d) information is needed to check the taxpayer's PAYE position.

Situation (b) is similar to the old discovery assessment position where an HMRC officer could make an assessment to tax if he discovered some relevant information or facts that were not disclosed in the tax return. However, the hurdle for this condition is much lower. The HMRC officer only needs to have suspicion of tax irregularities not the actual evidence (see para CH23560). Having said that, the HMRC officer should not make random requests for information; he needs to identify a specific risk that tax was under- or overpaid.

Safeguards

1.44 The taxpayer can only appeal against the taxpayer notice if it asks for something that is not part of the taxpayer's statutory records. Statutory records are very loosely defined as any information or document required to be kept by the *Taxes Act* or *VAT Act* (*para 62*).

HMRC may also ask for what it calls supplementary information that does not comprise statutory records, such as appointment diaries, correspondence and employment contracts. However, if this information concerns a person's physical, mental, spiritual or personal welfare, the taxpayer or third party cannot be required to produce it (CH22180).

There are also restrictions on the power of HMRC officers to inspect documents in the following categories (*paras 18–28*):

- information older than six years;
- relating to the conduct of tax appeals;
- journalistic material;
- legally privileged information or documents;
- auditors' statutory audit papers; and
- tax advisers' papers giving advice.

Where the taxpayer has died, an information notice may not be given more than four years after the death (*para 22*).

Partnerships

1.45 For CGT purposes the tax practitioner should particularly be aware of *FA 2008, Sch 38, para 37* relating to partnerships. The restriction in *para 21* on taxpayer notices where a return has already been filed, described at **1.41** applies, as if the partnership return had been made by each of the partners with extension where an enquiry is open in relation to any partner. Notice to one partner may effectively be notice to all, and, see *para 37(6)*. An information notice given to one of the partners to check the position of one or more of the other partners whose identity is not known does not require approval of the First-tier Tribunal.

Time limits

1.46 It was noted at **1.41** that time limits have changed for claims and elections, and for the periods available to HMRC to asses taxes. The new time limits for direct taxes, including CGT, generally came into effect for all tax assessments, claims or elections submitted after 31 March 2010 (*SI 2009/ 403*).

However, there is a transitional period for taxpayers who were not within self-assessment for the tax year for which the claim or election is made. For those taxpayers the new time limits apply for claims and elections submitted on or after 1 April 2012 (*SI 2009/403, reg 10*), until that date the old time limits for claims apply. Not being within self-assessment is defined as not being given notice to complete either an individual SA return, partnership SA return, or trustee return within one year of the end of the relevant tax year. This extension of the old time limits does not apply to companies.

Tax practitioners should pay particular attention to the tax periods covered by assessments raised by HMRC officers on and after 1 April 2010, to ensure that the periods assessed are not time-barred. The following table summarises the changes to claims and assessment periods introduced by *FA 2008, Sch 39*.

Table 1.6

Statutory Provision	*Description*	*Old period*	*New period*
TMA 1970, s 28C(5)(a)	Determination of tax where no return delivered	5 years from filing date	3 years from filing date
TMA 1970, s 33(1)	Error or mistake claim	5 years from 31 January after end of tax year	4 years from the end of tax year
TMA 1970, s 33A(2)	Error or mistake claim – partnership	5 years from 31 January after end of tax year	4 years after the end of the tax year
TMA 1970, s 34	Ordinary time limit for individuals	5 years from 31 January after end of tax year	4 years from the end of tax year
TMA 1970, s 35	Disclosure of late receipts of income	Within 6 years after year received	4 years after year received
TMA 1970, s 36(1)	Assessment to make good loss of tax through carelessness	20 years	6 years

Statutory Provision	*Description*	*Old period*	*New period*
TMA 1970, s 36(1A)	Assessment to make good loss of tax through fraud	20 years	20 years
TMA 1970, s 40	Assessment on personal representatives	3 years from 31 January after end of tax year.	4 years from the end of tax year of death
TMA 1970, s 43	Claims	5 years from 31 January after end of tax year	4 years after the end of the tax year
TCGA 1992, s 203(2)	Capital losses	6 years	4 years
TCGA 1992, s 253(4A)	Loans to traders	5 years from 31 January after end of tax year	4 years from the end of the tax year
TCGA 1992, s 279(5)	Foreign disposal, delayed remittance	5 years from 31 January after end of tax year	4 years from the end of the tax year
FA 1998, Sch 18 para 36(5)	Determination of tax for companies	5 years from end of accounting period	3 years from end of accounting period
FA 1998, Sch 18 para 46	General time limit for assessment for companies	6 years from end of accounting period	4 years from end of accounting period
FA 1998, Sch 18 para 51(1) (c)	Relief for mistake by companies	6 years from end of accounting period	4 years from end of accounting period
FA 1998, Sch 18 para 55	General time limit for claims by companies	6 years from end of accounting period	4 years from end of accounting period

The new penalty regime

1.47 HMRC may now impose penalties in the following circumstances:

- failure to notify certain tax-related events, such as becoming chargeable to tax;

- failure to provide information, or concealing or destroying documents requested in an Information Notice;
- obstructing an inspection approved by the First-tier Tribunal;
- inaccuracies or errors in returns/information given to HMRC (see **1.48–1.54**);
- VAT and Excise wrongdoing;
- failure to pay on time;
- failure to submit a return on time.

From 1 April 2010 HMRC may publish details of deliberate tax defaulters who have incurred penalties for deliberate or deliberate or concealed actions, where the potential lost revenue is £25,000 or more, and the penalty has not been subject to full mitigation.

This section examines the penalty provisions for errors contained in *FA 2007, Sch 24.*

Penalties for errors

1.48 The new penalty regime for errors applies to documents or returns concerning VAT, NIC, PAYE, CIS, income tax, CGT, or corporation tax submitted to HMRC on or after 1 April 2009 which relate to a return period that commenced on or after 1 April 2008. The old penalty rules continue to apply to tax returns or information submitted for earlier periods.

The basis of the new penalties is the taxpayer's behaviour, which is categorised as falling into one of four categories in relation to each particular error or inaccuracy. The penalty charged is a percentage of the 'potential lost revenue' (see **1.49**). The range of penalties which can be imposed for each category of taxpayer behaviour is summarised in the following table:

Table 1.7

Type of taxpayer behaviour	*Maximum penalty*	*Minimum penalty – unprompted disclosure*	*Minimum penalty – prompted disclosure*
Took reasonable care	0%	0%	0%
Careless action	30%	0%	15%
Deliberate but not concealed	70%	20%	35%
Deliberate with concealment	100%	30%	50%

If the taxpayer took reasonable care, but nevertheless made a mistake there is no penalty under the new regime.

If several errors or inaccuracies are discovered each error must be categorised separately according to the taxpayer's behaviour. *Sch 24, para 6* requires careless inaccuracies to be taken as corrected before deliberate inaccuracies. Deliberate inaccuracies that were not concealed are taken to be corrected before those that have been concealed. However, these rules do not apply to the new penalties imposed on third parties.

Potential lost revenue

1.49 The 'potential lost revenue' is defined by *Sch 24, para 5* as the additional amount due or payable in respect of tax as a result of correcting the inaccuracy or understatement. This includes an inaccuracy that is attributable to the supply of false information or the withholding of information. To summarise, the potential lost revenue can be:

(a) the additional tax due and payable;

(b) any excessive repayment of tax made by HMRC;

(c) 5% of the tax delayed for each year of the delay; or

(d) 10% of any unused loss.

Point (b) can include the situation where HMRC make an assessment that the taxpayer knows is too low, but where the taxpayer does not, within a reasonable time, tell HMRC of their error. This could also trigger a penalty.

Disclosure

1.50 Disclosure (whether of an inaccuracy, the supply of false information, or of withholding of information, or failure to disclose) is achieved by taking three measures:

- telling HMRC;
- giving HMRC reasonable help in correcting the error; and
- allowing HMRC access to the records.

By *Sch 24, para 9(2)* disclosure is 'unprompted' and therefore qualifies for a greater reduction in penalty if it is made at a time when the person who makes it has no reason to believe that HMRC have discovered, or are about to discover, the inaccuracy, the supply of false information, the withholding of information or the underassessment. In all other situations disclosure is 'prompted' and the minimum penalty which can be imposed is defined in **Table 1.7** above.

Multiple penalties

1.51 The complexity of the new penalty regime is such that it is quite possible for the same situation to generate multiple penalties. *Paragraph 12* of *Sch 24* prescribes that where a penalty becomes payable both by the taxpayer and by a third party in respect of the same inaccuracy, the result is that the total penalty may not exceed the potential revenue that has been lost (see **1.49**).

Third-party documents

1.52 *FA 2007, Sch 24, para 1A* can impose a penalty on the taxpayer where the error in the taxpayer's document is attributable to another person, where:

- a third-party gives HMRC a relevant document which contains an inaccuracy; and
- that inaccuracy is attributable to false information that was attributable to the taxpayer;
- who supplied the third party with that false information or who deliberately withheld information from the third party;
- intending that the document sent to HMRC would be wrong.

For this purpose the 'relevant inaccuracy' is one that leads to an understatement of the tax liability or a false or inflated loss claim or repayment claim. A penalty becomes due under this paragraph in respect of the inaccuracy whether or not the person who supplies the document to HMRC is also liable to a penalty under the main provision in *Sch 24, para 1*.

Suspension of penalties

1.53 HMRC may agree to suspend the whole or part of a penalty for up to two years to encourage the taxpayer to improve his systems, so that a further similar mistake could not occur. Only penalties imposed as a result of careless inaccuracies can be suspended. Penalties that relate to CGT errors will not generally be suitable for suspension due to the one-off nature of the tax (see CH83130).

Tax agents

1.54 The taxpayer cannot escape penalties completely by engaging an agent to help prepare his tax return. If the tax agent makes a mistake in the return, the taxpayer is still liable unless he can show HMRC that he took reasonable care to avoid the inaccuracy (see CH84520).

It is possible for the tax agent to suffer a penalty where that tax agent has deliberately supplied false information or has withheld information, and that action has resulted in an understatement of tax liability, a false or inflated loss, or a false or inflated repayment of tax.

Tax appeals system

1.55 Where a taxpayer disagrees with an appealable decision made by an HMRC officer he can submit a written appeal, stating the grounds of the appeal within 30 days. HMRC may accept a late appeal where there is a reasonable excuse for the delay.

Once an appeal has been submitted the taxpayer can ask for the decision to be reviewed by the HMRC internal review panel, or HMRC may offer a review. The taxpayer needs to accept the HMRC offer of the review within 30 days or it will lapse. The taxpayer can reject the offer of a review and take the case directly to the First-tier Tribunal.

The review is undertaken by HMRC staff who have not been involved in the original case. The review team should produce a decision within 45 days, or such longer time as agreed. The taxpayer then has 30 days to ask the Tax Tribunal to consider the appeal if they disagree with the result of the review. If the taxpayer does not respond to the review decision within 30 days he is deemed to have accepted the HMRC decision.

Tax disputes are referred to the First-tier Tribunal (tax chamber) and then on to the Upper Tribunal. Some cases may go directly to the Upper Tribunal. An appeal from the Upper Tribunal will go to the Court of Appeal in England, Northern Ireland or Wales, or the Court of Session in Scotland. For further discussion of the new tax appeals system see chapter 2 of *Income Tax 2010/11* (Bloomsbury Professional). Guidance on the tax appeals system is also provided in the HMRC Appeals, reviews and tribunals manual.

Chapter 2

Disposals

INTRODUCTION

2.1 Every gain accruing on the disposal of an asset is a chargeable gain, unless otherwise expressly provided – see the exemptions listed in **1.8–1.11** (*TCGA 1992*, *ss 1, 15*)).

The date of the disposal determines which period the gain is to be taxed in. It will be particularly important to pin down this date for gains falling in the tax year 2010/11, as the change of rates of CGT on 23 June 2010 mean there are two distinct periods for CGT in that tax year (see **1.23**). The rules for determining the date of disposal vary according to the nature of the disposal, for example by gift, under contract, or by deemed disposal.

Meaning of 'asset'

2.2 All forms of property, wherever they are situated, are assets for CGT purposes, although there are special rules for assets owned by persons who are not domiciled in the UK (see **5.5**). Assets include options, debts, intangible property, and currency other than sterling. Property that has been created by the person disposing of it, or has otherwise come to be owned without being acquired, is also an asset (*TCGA 1992, s 21(1)*).

Meaning of 'disposal'

2.3 *TCGA 1992* does not define 'disposal'. HMRC guidance indicates that the word takes its natural meaning and that a disposal is 'an occasion when you sell an asset or give it away' (CG10242). A disposal for CGT purposes can include all of the following:

- sale, gift or exchange of assets;
- part disposal (see **2.4**);
- the entire loss or destruction of an asset (see **2.10**);

- repayment of a debt (see **4.34**);
- grant of an option (see **4.7**);
- receipt or entitlement to receive capital distribution in respect of shares (see **2.23**);
- transfer into a settlement (see **2.21**);
- money or money's worth received in respect of an asset (see **2.14**);
- deemed disposal (see **2.6**).

HMRC may contend that a series of transactions is so closely linked that, as a matter of legal construction, the transactions should be regarded as a single disposal (CG12700).

Part disposals

2.4 Any 'part disposal' of an asset is a disposal for CGT purposes. A part disposal occurs where a person makes a disposal and any description of property derived from the asset remains undisposed of. There is also a part disposal of an asset where the disposal itself creates an interest in, or a right over, the asset (eg where a lease is granted by the person holding the freehold interest in land) as well as in the case where the interest or right existed before the disposal (*TCGA 1992, s 21(2)*).

Where there is a part disposal, any allowable costs of acquisition and improvement which cannot be wholly attributed to either the part retained or the part disposed of are apportioned by reference to the following formula (*TCGA 1992, s 28(2)*; see also **Chapter 3**):

$$\frac{A}{A + B}$$

Where:

A is the proceeds received (actual or deemed); and

B is the market value of the part retained.

Example 2.1—Part disposal

Robert buys a piece of land in April 1998 for £182,000. He subsequently sells half of it to Lesley in May 2010 for £150,000. The remainder of the land, because of its better position, is estimated to be then worth £200,000. Robert's capital gain is computed as follows:

A = £150,000

B = £200,000

The cost attributable to the part disposed of is:

$$\frac{150{,}000}{150{,}000 + 200{,}000} \times £182{,}000 = £78{,}000$$

2010/11	£
Proceeds of land sold to Lesley	150,000
Less: Cost allocated to the part disposed of	78,000
Less: Annual exemption	10,100
Robert's chargeable gain is	£61,900

The cost allocated to the remaining land, when that is disposed of, will be:

	£
Original cost of all the land	182,000
Less: Cost of part disposal	78,000
Cost of remaining land	£104,000

'Small disposal' proceeds

2.5 Where a capital sum is received for an asset which is not lost or destroyed, the receipt is not treated as a disposal if certain conditions are satisfied (eg where the proceeds are small compared with the value of an asset). The capital sum is instead deducted from the allowable expenditure on a subsequent disposal.

In practice, 'small' for these purposes means the higher of the following (*Tax Bulletin, Issue 27*, February 1997):

- 5% of the value of the asset; or
- £3,000.

There are special rules for part disposals of land. Where certain conditions are satisfied, the taxpayer may claim that the part disposal of land does not constitute a disposal for capital gains tax purposes. The disposal proceeds are instead deducted from the cost of the land when calculating a gain on its subsequent disposal. The qualifying conditions are as follows (*TCGA 1992, s 242*):

(1) The proceeds on the part disposal of land is:

   - not more than 20% of the land's market value; and
   - not more than £20,000; or

(2) the land is subject to compulsory purchase by an authority and the proceeds received are small (*TCGA 1992, s 243*). The definition of 'small' is:

- not more than 5% of the market value of the entire land; or
- £3,000 or less (irrespective of whether the 5% test is satisfied).

Whilst these limits will stand, the taxpayer can also argue that larger amounts should also be considered as 'small' for a particular case, or that smaller receipts should be treated as a full disposal. In both of the above cases, a claim must be made within one year of 31 January following the tax year in which the transfer is made, or for corporation tax purposes within two years following the accounting period of transfer (*TCGA 1992, ss 242(2A), 243(2A)*).

Example 2.2—Part disposal of land

Cuniliffe owns farmland which cost £134,000 in May 1988. In February 1997, a small plot of land is exchanged with an adjoining landowner for another piece of land. The value placed on the transaction is £18,000. Cuniliffe makes a claim for this transaction not to be treated as a disposal for capital gains tax purposes.

The value of the remaining estate excluding the new piece of land is estimated at £250,000 in February 1997. In May 2010, Cuniliffe sells the whole estate for £500,000.

	£	£
Small land swap in February 1997		
Allowable cost of original land		134,000
Less: Disposal proceeds		18,000
Adjusted allowable cost		£116,000
Allowable cost of additional land		£18,000
Disposal in May 2010		
Disposal proceeds		500,000
Allowable cost:		
Original land	116,000	
Additional land	18,000	134,000
Net gain		366,000
Annual exemption		10,100
Chargeable gain 2010/11		£355,900

If Cuniliffe had not claimed that the small disposal should be ignored for capital gains tax purposes, the capital gain in 1997 would be:

Disposal in February 1997	£
Disposal proceeds	18,000
Allowable cost:	
$\frac{18{,}000}{18{,}000 + 250{,}000} \times £134{,}000 =$	9,000
Unindexed gain	9,000
Indexation allowance (£9,000 × 0.46)	4,140
Chargeable gain 1996/97	£4,860

The above rules for small part disposals of land do not apply if the allowable expenditure is less than the part disposal proceeds. However, the taxpayer may elect that the costs are deducted from the part disposal proceeds, with none of the expenditure being an allowable deduction on subsequent part disposals. In other words, the gain is treated as in the same way as a disposal of the whole asset. A claim must be made within one year of 31 January following the tax year of the part disposal, or for corporation tax purposes within two years following the accounting period of transfer (*TCGA 1992, s 244*).

Deemed disposals

2.6 The legislation treats assets as having been disposed of in certain circumstances, including the following:

(a) *Capital sums derived from assets.* A deemed disposal for capital gains tax purposes can arise where a capital sum is derived from an asset, even where the person who pays the capital sum does not acquire the asset (subject to the small disposal exception). The time of disposal in this context is when the capital sum is received (see **2.16**).

(b) *Negligible value.* Where the value of an asset has become negligible, the owner may claim to be treated as having sold and immediately reacquired it at market value, in order to realise an allowable loss (see **2.10**).

(c) *Death.* The assets of a deceased individual's estate are deemed to be acquired by the personal representatives at market value on death but are not deemed to be disposed of by the deceased (see **2.9**).

(d) *Trusts.* Trustees are deemed to dispose of and immediately reacquire assets at market value in certain circumstances, eg where a person becomes absolutely entitled to assets as against the trustees, or if the trustees cease to be resident in the UK (see **2.21**).

(e) *Migration of trade, or company*. See **2.22** for deemed disposals which can arise when chargeable assets are transferred abroad.

(f) *Value shifting*. A disposal or a part disposal of land or shares may be deemed to have to take place if certain conditions are satisfied (*TCGA 1992, s 29*). In this case there is a corresponding acquisition by the person or persons who receive the value. These anti-avoidance rules are broadly designed to prevent value passing from one holding or interest into another without there being any disposal for capital gains purposes, see **Chapter 10**.

Deemed disposals between spouses or civil partners are exempt even where the value shifting rules apply (*TCGA 1992, s 58*). Relief may also be available under other capital gains tax provisions if the relevant conditions are satisfied, for example relief for gifts of business assets within *TCGA 1992, s 165* (see **Chapter 13**).

No gain, no loss disposals

2.7 Certain disposals are treated as giving rise to neither a gain nor a loss, known as no gain, no loss disposals:

- disposals between husband and wife or civil partners (*TCGA 1992, s 58(1)*) (see **3.62**);
- disposals within the same 75% group of companies (*TCGA 1992, s 171) (1)*) (see **9.28**);
- disposals of business assets where a claim is made to roll over the gain against a replacement asset (*TCGA 1992, s 152(1)(a)*) (see **Chapter 14**);
- transfers on a company reconstruction (*TCGA 1992, s 139(1)*) (CG52800);
- on the termination of pre-22 March 2006 (and certain other) interests in possession in settled property by reason of the death of the person so entitled, if the property reverts to the settlor (*TCGA 1992, s 73(1)(a)*) (see **8.12**); and
- gifts to charities (*TCGA 1992,s 257(2)(a)*) (see **2.22**).

The deemed disposal consideration (and the transferee's acquisition cost) is an amount equal to the original cost plus indexation allowance (if applicable).

Disposals under contract

2.8 Where an asset is disposed of and acquired under a contract, the time of the disposal and acquisition is the time when that contract is made, ie the date contracts are exchanged. It is not the date of the completion of the contract, or time of the conveyance or transfer of the asset (if different). However, if the contract is never completed the disposal never takes place (CG14261).

In the case of a conditional contract, the time of disposal and acquisition is the time when the condition is satisfied. This applies in particular to a contract that is conditional on the exercise of an option (*TCGA 1992, s 28*).

There is no statutory definition of what a 'conditional' contract is, and the meaning of the term varies according to context. However, for capital gains tax purposes, a contract is only conditional if:

- the condition has to be satisfied before the contract becomes binding; and
- it is not something that one of the parties has agreed to bring about, such as fence a plot of land.

A condition which must be satisfied before the contract becomes legally binding is termed a 'condition precedent'. Such a condition must be distinguished from a 'condition subsequent', which is broadly a condition that is not fundamental to the immediate performance of the contract. In such cases, the contract continues to be legally binding. The Capital Gains Manual (at CG14270) gives an example of a conditional contract, based on the comments of Walton J in *Lyon v Pettigrew* (1985) 58 TC 452:

> 'It would, for example, be possible for a hotelier to make a booking with a tour operator conditionally upon the next Olympic Games being held in London. Then, until it had been decided that the next Olympic Games were going to be held in London, there would be no effective contract: the whole contract would be conditional, the whole liabilities and duties between the parties would only arise when the condition was fulfilled.'

See **2.18** to **2.23** for special circumstances where the date of disposal may be different.

Disposals on death

2.9 The assets which the deceased was competent to dispose of are deemed not to be disposed of, whether or not they are the subject of a will. The deceased's personal representatives are deemed to acquire the assets at their market value at the date of death.

A disposal by way of *donatio mortis causa* is a lifetime gift that will take effect only if the donor dies. When the donor dies he is not competent to dispose of the relevant assets, so the above rule cannot apply and there is a disposal at the time of death. However, it is provided separately that no chargeable gain accrues on a disposal by way of *donatio mortis causa* (*TCGA 1992, s 62*). See also **Chapter 7**.

ASSETS LOST, DESTROYED OR BECOMING OF NEGLIGIBLE VALUE

2.10 There is generally a disposal of an asset on the occasion of the entire loss, destruction, dissipation or extinction of the asset. This applies whether or not a capital sum is received by way of compensation or otherwise. If a gain arising on the disposal would have been a chargeable gain, any loss arising will be an allowable loss (*TCGA 1992, ss 16(2), 24(1)*).

The owner of an asset that has become of negligible value cannot claim relief for a capital loss under the normal rules, because he has not disposed of the asset. However, the taxpayer may claim to be treated as having sold and immediately reacquired the asset, either at the time of the claim or at some earlier time (see below). It is up to the taxpayer who makes the claim to prove that the value of the asset has become negligible during the taxpayer's period of ownership, and this may be difficult. In *David Harper v CRC* [2009] UKFTT 382, the taxpayer claimed the shares became of negligible value at 5 April 2004 (the time of the claim), but the tribunal found that the shares were of negligible value when they were acquired. To support the claim the taxpayer needs to provide evidence of the asset's value at the time of acquisition. If unquoted shares have become of negligible value it may be possible to make a claim for share loss relief against income (see **17.16**).

A negligible value claim can also be made when the taxpayer acquired the asset by way of a no gain, no loss transfer (see **2.7**). The asset must have been of negligible value at the time of that transfer and there have been no other transfers of that asset since it became of negligible value, other than no gain, no loss transfers (*TCGA 1992, s 24 (1A)–(1C)*).

The deemed consideration for both the deemed disposal and the deemed reacquisition is the value specified in the claim. The legislation does not define 'negligible', but HMRC regard it as meaning 'next to nothing' (*TCGA 1992, s 24(2)*; CG13124).

The claim may specify an earlier time for the deemed disposal if the taxpayer owned the asset at that time and it had become of negligible value at that time. The earlier time must not be more than two years before the beginning of the tax year in which the claim is made. In the case of a company chargeable to corporation tax, the earlier time must fall within the earliest accounting period ending not more than two years before the date of the claim.

For these purposes a building may be regarded as an asset separate from the land on which it stands. The taxpayer is treated as if he had sold and immediately reacquired the site at its market value (*TCGA 1992, s 24(3)*).

HMRC operate a post-transaction valuation service for capital gains, which is accessed by submitting form CG34 to the HMRC CGT team (see **1.35**). This service can also be used to check if an asset has become of negligible value. The form CG34 should be submitted at the same time as the negligible value claim, or shortly after that claim has been made (CG13130). Acceptance by HMRC that the value of the asset is negligible should not be taken as agreement that all of the conditions for the negligible value claim are met.

HMRC maintain a list of the dates they have agreed that quoted shares became of negligible value see: www.hmrc.gov.uk/cgt/negvalist.htm.

Asset lost or destroyed: replacement asset acquired

2.11 If the asset is lost or destroyed, a capital sum received in compensation for the loss or destruction, or under an insurance policy against the risk of such loss or destruction, gives rise to a disposal as described in **2.12**. However, a form of roll-over relief is available where the taxpayer applies the capital sum in acquiring a replacement asset within one year of receiving that sum, or within a longer period allowed by HMRC. The taxpayer is treated as if:

(a) the consideration for the disposal of the old asset was reduced to an amount giving rise to no gain and no loss on the disposal; and

(b) the consideration for the acquisition of the new asset was reduced by the excess of the capital sum received and any residual or scrap value over the reduced consideration in (a).

Partial relief is available where only part of the capital sum is reinvested in this way. As long as the part of the compensation not applied is less than the gain deemed to accrue on the disposal of the old asset, the owner can claim to reduce the gain arising to the amount not spent on the new asset.

Where the assets concerned are buildings, and the old building is destroyed or irreparably damaged, then for these purposes the old building is treated as lost or destroyed and each building is regarded as an asset separate from the land on which it is stands (or stood) (*TCGA 1992, s 23(4)–(7)*). For a detailed discussion of the capital gains treatment of compensation see chapter 12 of *Capital Gains Tax: Roll-over, Hold-over and Deferral reliefs 2010/11* (Bloomsbury Professional).

Example 2.3—Treatment of compensation

Arthur bought a Hockney painting for £50,000 in February 1991. It was destroyed by fire in October 2009 and Arthur receives £900,000 compensation in December 2009. Arthur buys a Hirst painting to replace the Hockney in May 2010 for £1,000,000. Arthur makes a claim that the disposal of the Hockney painting should be treated as at no gain, no loss and the allowable expenditure on the Hirst painting should be reduced by the amount of excess capital received.

2009/10	£
Compensation received	900,000
Cost of destroyed asset	50,000
Excess gain to be rolled over (ie the gain otherwise accruing)	£850,000
2010/11	
Consideration for acquisition of new painting	1,000,000
Excess gain rolled into this cost	850,000
Reduced allowable expenditure on new asset	£150,000

If Arthur only spends £800,000 on the replacement Hirst painting, he can make a claim to reduce the capital gain arising to the amount of compensation not applied.

2009/10	£	£
Excess gain on disposal (as above)		850,000
Compensation monies received	900,000	
Compensation monies reinvested	800,000	
Amount not reinvested in a new asset (being less than the gain of £840,000)	£100,000	
Chargeable gain (the compensation not reinvested)		100,000
Net chargeable gain 2009/10		£100,000
The chargeable gain to be rolled over is reduced to: (£850,000 – £100,000)		£750,000
The allowable expenditure on the new asset is:		
Actual expenditure on new Hirst painting		800,000
Gain rolled over into cost of new asset, being amount of chargeable gain not already assessed.		750,000
Total allowable expenditure		£50,000

Capital sums derived from assets

2.12 There is a disposal of assets by their owner where a capital sum (which may include 'money's worth', see **2.14**) is derived from assets, whether or not the person paying the capital sum acquires an asset (*TCGA 1992, s 22(1)*; CG12940–12999). This general rule is applied in particular to the following receipts:

(a) compensation for damage or injury to assets, or for the loss, destruction or dissipation of assets or for any depreciation (or risk of depreciation) of an asset, including infringement of copyright and 'injurious affection' of land;

(b) capital sums received under an insurance policy against risk of damage or injury to (or loss or depreciation of) assets;

(c) capital sums received in return for forfeiture or surrender of rights (or for refraining from exercising rights) such as an amount paid on the release of a person from a contract or restrictive covenant; and

(d) capital sums received as consideration for use or exploitation of assets, such as a lump sum paid to a farmer in return for the granting of easements.

Incentive payments and inducements offered by financial institutions, such as free shares on demutualisation of a building society, can potentially fall within (b) and will be chargeable to CGT (CG13028). However, a cash-back offered to encourage a person to take on a mortgage is not treated as a capital sum derived from an asset and is not chargeable to CGT (CG13027).

Capital or revenue?

2.13 Any sum received that is chargeable as income is excluded from CGT. In *Lang v Rice* [1984] 57 TC 80, CA (NI) the taxpayer carried on business in two rented bars in Belfast. They were both destroyed by bombs and neither business was restarted. He claimed compensation from the Northern Ireland Office (NIO) under the *Criminal Injuries to Property (Compensation) Act (Northern Ireland) 1971*. Although the claim referred to 'loss of profit, ie goodwill, 1.5 years' purchase of net profit', in making the payment the NIO specified a sum as 'in respect of the temporary loss of profit for … the length of time allowed for the … business to resume normal trading'. The Inspector of Taxes raised an assessment to CGT on the basis that these were capital sums in respect of compensation for loss of goodwill. The Court of Appeal in Northern Ireland held that there was no reason not to accept at face value the revenue nature of the sums paid, as stated by the NIO.

This case and others relevant to the treatment of compensation receipts as income are discussed in HMRC's Business Income Manual at BIM40101–40140 (*TCGA 1992, s 37(1)*).

Money's worth

2.14 HMRC regard this phrase (see CG12950) as taking its ordinary meaning, ie 'anything which … can be recognised as equivalent to, or can be converted to, money'. HMRC will ask whether it can be turned into money, and whether its value can be expressed in money terms. There does not actually have to be a conversion into money, but it must be possible. The writing off of a debt cannot be turned into money so it is not money's worth.

Capital sum derived from rights

2.15 Compensation may be derived from rights such as statutory rights, contractual rights or rights to take action for compensation or damages, rather than directly from the asset itself.

The decision in *Zim Properties Ltd v Proctor* (1984, 58 TC 371, Ch D) established the general principle that the right to take court action for compensation or damages is an asset for capital gains tax purposes, the disposal of which (eg by negotiated settlement) could result in a capital gain. In that case, a company brought an action against its solicitors alleging that the solicitors had drawn a contract for the sale of land negligently. A compromise agreement was subsequently reached, resulting in a payment to the company by the solicitor's insurers. The court held that the capital sum was derived from an asset, ie not the land but Zim's right to take action against the solicitors for compensation or damages. The receipt of that capital sum for disposing of the right was therefore taxable.

HMRC subsequently introduced an Extra-statutory Concession (ESC D33) to remove some of the unintended consequences of this decision. The effect of ESC D33 is broadly that, although the receipt of damages and compensation payments can strictly give rise to a CGT liability, by concession the damages will be treated as derived from the underlying asset if there is one. Hence the receipt will be taxable if the underlying asset is taxable, or exempt if the underlying asset is exempt. Alternatively, the damages will be treated as exempt if there is no underlying asset (CG13010–13024).

Time of disposal

2.16 In the four cases (a) to (d) in **2.12**, the time of the disposal is the time when the capital sum is received. In other cases where the capital sum is paid under a contract, the agreement of the contract will set the date of disposal. Where there is no such contract, HMRC regard the date on which the sum is received as the time of disposal (CG12941).

The full disposal proceeds must be brought into account at the time of disposal. There must be no reduction for postponement of the right to receive any part of it, or to allow for the risk of any part of the sum being irrecoverable, or any discount because part of the consideration may be contingent (*TCGA 1992, s 48*). However, there is effectively an entitlement to a form of 'bad debt relief' if a claim is made on the basis that any part of the consideration brought into account has subsequently become permanently irrecoverable (CG14930–14933).

Capital sum applied in restoring the asset

2.17 The taxpayer can elect for the receipt of a capital sum not to be treated as a disposal where the whole or a part of a capital sum within (a) to (d) in **2.12** is used to restore the asset. Instead, the consideration that would have been taken into account on that deemed disposal is deducted from the allowable expenditure on a later disposal of the asset (*TCGA 1992 s 23(1)*), where:

(a) the whole of the capital sum is applied in restoring the asset;

(b) all but a part of the capital sum is applied in this way, and that part is not reasonably required for the purpose and is small compared to the capital sum received; or

(c) the amount of the capital sum is small in relation to the value of the asset.

The allowable expenditure is fixed by reference to *TCGA 1992, s 38* (see **3.36**). These rules are modified in relation to wasting assets.

Where there is no such allowable expenditure, or the consideration for the deemed disposal is greater than the allowable expenditure, then (b) and (c) above do not apply. This means that the deduction from allowable expenditure on a later disposal applies only if the whole of the capital sum is applied in restoring the asset.

Where there is allowable expenditure the taxpayer may elect for the amount of the consideration for the disposal to be reduced by the amount of the allowable expenditure. This would result in none of that expenditure being deducted in computing the gain accruing on a future disposal (*TCGA 1992, s 23(2)*).

In a case where the taxpayer makes no such election and applies in restoring the asset a part of a capital sum within (a) or (b) in **2.12** that has been derived from an asset that is not lost or destroyed, then he may make a claim for that part of the capital sum not to be treated as consideration for the disposal as provided by *TCGA 1992, s 22*. Instead, the capital sum is deducted from any allowable expenditure deducted in computing a gain on a future disposal of the asset (*TCGA 1992, s 23(3)*).

SPECIAL SITUATIONS

Mortgages and charges

2.18 The following transfers are not treated as involving any acquisition or disposal of an asset:

- the conveyance or transfer of an asset (or of an interest or right in or over the asset) by way of security; and
- the transfer of a subsisting interest or right by way of security in or over an asset (including a retransfer on redemption of the security).

A lender enforcing the security and selling the mortgaged property is treated as acting as nominee for the borrower (*TCGA 1992, s 26(1), (2)*).

Hire-purchase transactions

2.19 Under a hire-purchase transaction a person obtains the use of an asset for a period, and at the end of that period the property in the asset will (or may) pass to him. The hire-purchase transaction is treated as the entire disposal of the asset to that person at the beginning of the hire period. An adjustment will be required if the hire period ends without ownership passing to him (*TCGA 1992, s 27*).

Gifts

2.20 A gift is treated as having been made when the donor has done everything within his power to transfer the property to the donee (*Re Rose, Rose and Others v CIR* CA [1952] 1 All ER 1217). However, general law principles will determine whether that transfer is effective. For example contracts in respect of land must be evidenced in writing, so the disposal date will be the date of exchange of those contracts. In the case of shares the disposal date will be when the share transfer form is sent to the company. In the case of a gift of a chattel, the gift is effective when the chattel is delivered.

Settlements

2.21 A transfer into a trust or settlement is a disposal of the property that becomes settled property, even if that transferor is a trustee of the settlement or has some interest as a beneficiary (*TCGA 1992, s 70*). The trust deed itself may transfer the legal title of the property to the trustees, so the date of the deed will be the disposal date (CG35730). In other cases the disposal date of the gift into the settlement will follow the rules set out in **2.20**.

See **Chapter 8** regarding this and other rules relating to settled property, including:

- person becoming absolutely entitled to settled property (*TCGA 1992, s 71*);
- termination of life interest on death of the person entitled (*TCGA 1992, s 72*);
- death of life tenant: exclusion of chargeable gain (*TCGA 1992, s 73*);
- disposal of interests in settled property (*TCGA 1992, ss 76, 76A, 76B*);
- trustees ceasing to be resident in UK (*TCGA 1992, s 80*).

Nominees or bare trustees may hold assets for beneficiaries who are absolutely entitled to those assets (or would be entitled but for being an infant or a disabled person). For capital gains tax purposes, disposals by nominees or bare trustees are treated as having been made by the beneficiary for whom they act (*TCGA 1992, s 60*).

Deemed disposal by non-resident

2.22 There is a deemed disposal and reaquisition of assets at their market value where 'chargeable assets' (see below) that have been used in a business carried on through a UK branch or agency (or a permanent establishment in the case of a company) are transferred abroad, unless the transfer occurs on the occasion of the cessation of the business (*TCGA 1992, s 25(1), (2)*).

Assets are 'chargeable assets' for this purpose if a chargeable gain on their disposal would be chargeable under *TCGA 1992, s 10(1)* or *s 10B* (non-residents with a UK branch, agency or permanent establishment). For further details, and the situation where the business ceases or is transferred overseas, see **Chapter 5**.

Receipt of capital from shares

2.23 Many small companies are wound up informally without a liquidator being appointed. If clearance is obtained from HMRC under Extra-statutory Concession C16, the funds distributed to the shareholders are treated as capital receipts, as if they were capital distributions made in the course of a formal winding-up. The disposal date for such a capital receipt is the date the capital is received. Any capital gain arising on such a distribution may qualify for entrepreneurs' relief (see **11.32**).

For a detailed discussion of the tax and legal issues related to the winding up of small companies see *Dissolving the Family Company* (Tottel Publishing).

Chapter 3

Computation of gains and losses

INTRODUCTION

3.1 The general rules governing the computation of gains and losses accruing on the disposal of assets are set out *TCGA 1992, Pt II*. Every gain is a chargeable gain except where provided otherwise – see **1.7** (*Taxation of Chargeable Gains Act 1992* (*TCGA 1992, ss 1, 15*)). This chapter summarises the general rules for computing chargeable gains and losses. **Chapter 4** deals with special rules applying to particular assets, and **Chapter 9** discusses the specific computational rules and reliefs that only apply to companies.

In particular the indexation allowance, designed to compensate the taxpayer for the effect of inflation, only applies to corporate disposals from 6 April 2008 (see **3.60**). The calculation of indexation allowance is discussed at **9.12**.

From 6 April 2008 assets held by individuals and trustees are automatically rebased to 31 March 1982, meaning the value at that date is used in place of the original cost where the asset was acquired earlier (see **3.59**). Assets held by companies are not automatically rebased, unless a global rebasing election has been made. Rebasing to 31 March 1982 simplifies the calculation of gains on long-held assets for non-corporate taxpayers as the kink test and halving relief are removed. These tests and the rebasing election are discussed in **Chapter 9** as they now only apply to companies.

Example 3.1

Colin inherited a cottage in April 1980 when it was worth £12,000. Its value on 31 March 1982, after some improvements had been made, was £40,000. Colin sold the cottage on 21 June 2010 for £310,000, and thus benefits from the lower rate of CGT for sales made before 23 June 2010. The legal and estate agents' fees associated with the purchase and sale were £5,000. Entrepreneurs' relief does not apply as the cottage had not been let commercially as a furnished holiday lettings for the last year up to the date of sale (see **11.15**). Colin has a capital loss brought forward of £15,000 and makes no other disposals in 2010/11. His CGT liability for 2010/11 is £43,182:

2010/11	£
Proceeds	310,000
Rebased value at 31 March 1982	(40,000)
Legal and estate agents' fees	(5,000)
Gross gain	265,000
Loss brought forward	(15,000)
Net chargeable gain	250,000
Annual exemption	(10,100)
Taxable gain	239,900
CGT due at 18%	43,182

Interaction with VAT

3.2 The acquisition and enhancement costs of an asset for CGT purposes exclude any VAT, where the VAT represents deductible input tax and thus can be reclaimed by the VAT-registered taxpayer. In any other case the cost for CGT purposes includes the VAT suffered.

If the taxpayer charges VAT on the proceeds of disposal of a chargeable asset, the consideration for the disposal (see **3.4**) excludes the VAT. The treatment of any VAT suffered on expenses relating to the disposal follows the treatment of acquisition and enhancement costs (HMRC Statement of Practice D7).

Exceptions for corporate transactions

3.3 A company generally calculates its chargeable gains on the same basis as individuals although indexation allowance is deductible for all periods an asset has been held since 31 March 1982 (see **9.12**), and assets held on that date are not automatically rebased (see **9.4**). The company pays corporation tax rather than CGT on those gains. There are a number of special corporation tax rules that treat gains falling in the following regimes as income for corporation tax rather than as gains:

- loan relationships (*CTA 2009, part 5*);
- derivative contracts (*CTA 2009, part 7*); and
- intangible fixed assets (*CTA 2009, part 8*).

See **Chapter 9**.

CONSIDERATION FOR THE DISPOSAL

3.4 The first step in the computation is to determine the consideration for the disposal. The consideration may be receivable some time after the date of the disposal, but the full amount must be brought into account without any discount for postponement of the right to receive it or for the risk that not all of the consideration may be recovered (see **3.21**).

Consideration includes money or money's worth (see **2.14**) and any assumption by the purchaser of a liability of the person making the disposal. The items listed in **3.5** as receipts can also be taken into account for CGT, regardless of the exclusion for sums chargeable as income. Consideration also includes the value of any asset received in exchange for the asset disposed of, and the capitalised value of:

- the right to receive income or payments in the nature of income;
- relief from liability, eg to repay a loan;
- the benefit of loans on non-commercial terms; and
- the benefit of rights to obtain goods or services on favourable terms.

Sums chargeable as income

3.5 Sums that are chargeable to tax as income, or taken into account in computing income or profits or gains or losses for income tax purposes, are excluded from CGT. Income or profits taxable by deduction at source are treated as chargeable to income tax for this purpose (*TCGA 1992, s 52(2), (3)*). This rule does not preclude the following receipts being taken into account for CGT:

- receipts giving rise to balancing charges or certain other adjustments to income tax capital allowances;
- the capitalised value of a rent charge, or ground annual, or feu duty;
- the capitalised value of a right of any other description to income, or to payments in the nature of income over a period, or to a series of such payments (*TCGA 1992, s 37*); and
- amounts charged to income under profit-sharing schemes (*TCGA 1992, s 238*).

A profit on the disposal of trading stock is included in trading profits and charged to income tax. HMRC consider that the disposal of an asset not normally regarded as trading stock may mark the end of 'an adventure in the nature of trade', in which case any profit is chargeable to income tax. However, see **4.36** regarding assets appropriated to or from trading stock.

An income tax liability may arise under anti-avoidance rules on the disposal of land, including buildings, or an interest in land, or assets such as shares which derive their value from land; or on the sale by an individual of income derived from personal activities (*ITA 2007, ss 755, 756*). In such a case the gain is not charged to CGT. See also **2.13** regarding the question whether compensation received is chargeable to income tax (*TCGA 1992, ss 15, 16; ITA 2007, s 778*; CG10260, CG14340, CG14342).

Other amounts excluded from consideration for CGT purposes are grants for giving up uncommercial agricultural land and profits made from woodlands managed on a commercial basis (*TCGA 1992, ss 249, 250*).

Market value rule for disposals

3.6 The market value (see **3.7**) of an asset is substituted for the actual consideration for the disposal where the taxpayer disposes of the asset:

(a) otherwise than by way of a bargain made at arm's length (see below), and in particular where he disposes of it by way of gift, or on a transfer into a settlement by the settlor, or by way of distribution from a company in respect of shares in the company; or

(b) wholly or partly for a consideration that cannot be valued; or

(c) in connection with his own or another's loss of office or employment or diminution of emoluments; or

(d) otherwise in consideration for (or in recognition of) his or another person's services or past services in an office or employment, or any other service rendered to another person (*TCGA 1992, s 17(1)*).

The market value may be substituted even if there is no corresponding acquisition, eg when a debt is repaid. HMRC regard a bargain as made 'at arm's length' if it is a normal commercial transaction in which all of the parties involved try to obtain the best deal for themselves in their particular circumstances. They accept that both a 'bad bargain' and a deal that is made when one party to the transaction has better information than another party can be a bargain made at arm's length. HMRC provide the following examples at CG14541:

- Mr A may wish to sell his property quickly so that he can go and live in Malta. Mr B knows that Mr A wants to sell his property quickly so he offers him a low price for a quick sale. No-one else makes an offer. Mr A accepts the price Mr B has offered. This may not have been the best possible price which Mr A could have achieved if he had left the property on the market for longer, but he was still trying to achieve the best deal possible for himself. It was a bargain made at arm's length.

- Mrs S sells a picture from her attic to Mr T for £500. Mr T, who is an art dealer, knows that the picture is worth £5,000. There has been a bargain with both people trying to get the best deal for themselves. Again, this is a bargain made at arm's length, even if the price paid is not the 'market value' of the asset.

A disposal is treated as made not at arm's length – so that the market value rule above applies – if the person acquiring the asset is 'connected' with the person making the disposal (see **3.11**). Other disposals are treated as made not at arm's length, where there is some gratuitous intention on behalf of one of the parties to the bargain (CG14542).

Ascertaining market value

3.7 It is the taxpayer's responsibility to obtain a valuation of market value if one is required, in order to complete a return of chargeable gains. See **1.35** regarding the valuation checking service provided by HMRC, and the information that needs to be provided with the tax return concerning the valuation.

The general rule is that the 'market value' of an asset is the price that it might reasonably be expected to fetch on a sale in the open market. No reduction is made to take account of the possible impact of all of the assets concerned (eg a holding of shares) being placed on the market at one time.

Where the value of an asset has been ascertained for inheritance tax purposes, that valuation fixes its market value for CGT as at the date of death. HMRC consider that a value has been ascertained only if their Capital Taxes Office has used a valuation to arrive at the final inheritance tax liability, and the amount of that liability was dependent on that valuation (*TCGA 1992, ss 272(1), (2), 274*; CG32224). The probate value put forward by the executors is not necessarily the 'ascertained value', particularly where no IHT was payable for the estate (CG32222).

Quoted shares and securities

3.8 The market value of shares or securities quoted on the Stock Exchange Daily Official List is generally taken to be the lower of the figures found in (a) and (b) below, or the figure found in (a) where there were no recorded bargains on the relevant date:

(a) the 'quarter-up value', ie the lower of the two prices quoted on the relevant date plus a quarter of the difference between them;

(b) the midpoint between the highest and lowest prices at which bargains were recorded for that date, ignoring bargains at special prices.

This measure of market value does not apply where 'special circumstances' have affected the quoted prices. If the London Stock Exchange is closed on the relevant date, the above exercise is to be done for both the latest previous date and the earliest subsequent date on which it is open. The lower of the two measures found in this way is taken to be the market value (*TCGA 1992, s 272(3), (4)*).

Example 3.2

Sarah gifts 1,000 quoted shares on 8 June 2010. The price of the shares quoted on the Stock Exchange daily list for that day are 100 – 120 pence and bargains are marked at 98p (special), 102p, 118p, 115p, and 109p. The market value for CGT purposes is the lower of:

- ¼ up rule: 100 + ¼ (120 – 100) = 105p
- average of highest and lowest bargains ignoring the 'special': ½ (102 + 118) = 110p

The value is 105p × 1,000 shares = £1,050.

Unit trust holdings

3.9 Where the buying and selling prices of units in unit trusts are published regularly, the market value is the lower published price (ie the price that the managers will pay to someone wishing to sell units). If no prices were published on the relevant date, the lower of the latest prices published before the disposal is taken (*TCGA 1992, s 272(5)*).

Unquoted shares and securities

3.10 The market value of shares and securities that are not listed on a 'recognised stock exchange' (see below) when their value is to be fixed is the price that the shares, etc might reasonably be expected to fetch on a sale in the open market. For this purpose it is to be assumed that, in such an open market, any prospective buyer would have available all the information that a prudent prospective buyer might reasonably require if he were proposing to buy it from a willing vendor by private treaty and at arm's length (*TCGA 1992, s 273*).

The shares valuation division of HMRC Capital Taxes is responsible for checking and negotiating the valuation of unquoted shares and certain other assets including the goodwill of a business. The District Valuer at the Valuation Office Agency deals with the valuation of land and buildings in the UK.

A 'recognised stock exchange' means any stock exchange which is designated as a recognised stock exchange by HMRC for the purpose of *ITA 2007, s 1005* (*TCGA 1992, s 288(1)*). The London Stock Exchange and PLUS-listed markets have been designated as recognised stock exchanges. There are also a number of overseas stock markets that are recognised stock exchanges as listed on the HMRC website at www.hmrc.gov.uk/fid/rse.htm.

Disposals to connected persons

3.11 A disposal is treated as made otherwise than by way of a bargain made at arm's length – so that the market value rule in **3.7** applies – if the person acquiring the asset is 'connected' (see **3.16**) with the person making the disposal.

See **3.63** regarding the special rules for transactions between spouses and civil partners and **3.12** regarding assets disposed of in a series of transactions.

There must be both a disposal and a corresponding acquisition for this rule to apply. It cannot apply, for example, to an issue of shares by a company, or the purchase by a company of its own shares (*TCGA 1992, s 18(1), (2)*; CG14570).

The market value of the asset, to be used in place of the actual consideration, is adjusted where the asset is subject to a right or restriction such as a restrictive covenant (*TCGA 1992, s 18(6)–(8)*).

Assets disposed of in a series of transactions

3.12 If assets are disposed of in a series of transactions to one or more connected persons, anti-avoidance rules may operate to increase the deemed consideration for one or more of the disposals. The rules are designed to prevent an advantage being gained where the total value placed on a number of separate gifts of shares to relatives, for example, would be less than the value that would apply to a single gift of all of the shares (*TCGA 1992 ss 19, 20*).

The rules apply where:

- a person disposes of assets, to a person (or persons) connected with him, by means of a series of linked transactions, ie two or more 'material transactions' that are linked; and

- the 'original market value' of the assets disposed of by any of those transactions is less than the 'appropriate portion' of the 'aggregate market value' of the assets disposed of by all the transactions – all of these terms are defined below.

In these circumstances, the consideration for the disposal effected by any linked transaction is deemed to be equal to the appropriate portion of the aggregate market value. However, this rule does not affect the operation of the no gain, no loss rule for transfers between spouses or civil partners (see **3.62**) (*TCGA 1992, s 19(1), (2)*).

A 'material transaction' is a transaction by way of gift or otherwise, and two or more material transactions are linked if they occur within a period of six years ending on the date of the last transaction (*TCGA 1992, s 19(3)*).

This rule applies when a series of linked transactions is created by a second material transaction and it applies again, with any necessary adjustments being made, when an existing series is extended by a further material transaction. An adjustment may be required if an earlier transaction ceases to form part of the series because of the six-year rule (*TCGA 1992, s 19(4)*).

Original market value

3.13 The original market value is determined as follows where there is a series of linked transactions:

(a) if the transaction is the most recent in the series of transactions, the 'original market value' of the assets disposed of is the market value that would be deemed to be the consideration in the absence of *TCGA 1992, s 19*; and

(b) for any other transaction in the series, the original market value of the assets disposed of is the value which, prior to the transaction in (a), was (or would have been) deemed to be the consideration for that transaction, whether as a result of *TCGA 1992, s 19* applying or under any other provision (*TCGA 1992, s 20(3)*).

Appropriate portion

3.14 The 'appropriate portion' of the aggregate market value (see **3.15**) of the assets disposed of by all the transactions in a series is the portion of that value that it is reasonable to apportion to the assets actually disposed of by the particular transaction (*TCGA 1992, s 20(4)(b)*).

Aggregate market valuc

3.15 The aggregate market value of the assets disposed of by all the transactions in a series of linked transactions is the market value that would have been attributed to all of those assets if, considering all of them together, they had been disposed of by one disposal occurring at the time of the transaction (*TCGA 1992, s 20(4)(a)*).

When the assets are considered 'together' they are considered as a group, holding or collection of assets each of which retains its separate identity. However, they are also considered as brought together to form a single asset (or number of assets) distinct from the assets comprised in the individual transactions, where this would give a higher market value (*TCGA 1992, s 20(5)*).

Some of the assets disposed of in a series of linked transactions may have been acquired after the time of the first transaction. In such a case the aggregate market value is apportioned to each transaction without regard to assets acquired after the time of that transaction, unless the assets were acquired by means of a no gain, no loss transfer within *TCGA 1992, s 171*.

The number of assets taken into account is limited to the maximum number held by the taxpayer at any time in the period covered by the series, ie beginning immediately before the first of the transactions and ending immediately before the last. This is modified where a company disposed of any assets on a no gain, no loss transfer to a company in the same group before the time of the first transaction in the series. In that event the maximum number of assets taken into account is determined as if that transfer had occurred after the first transaction in the series (*TCGA 1992, s 20(6), (7)*).

If the assets disposed of are securities – including any assets of a nature to be dealt in without identifying the particular assets disposed of or acquired – they are identified with assets acquired on an earlier date (rather than with assets acquired on a later date) on the occasion of each disposal (*TCGA 1992, s 20(8), (9)*).

Example 3.3

Richard owned 10,000 shares in an unquoted company. He made two gifts of shares to his son over three years which in total amounted to 6,000 shares. The market value of each gift is calculated as follows:

Transferred in	*Number of shares gifted*	*Value of 6,000 shares at date of gift*	*Portion of market value at date of gift*
October 2007	2,000	£12,000	£4,000
October 2010	4,000	£36,000	£24,000
Total	6,000		

The appropriate portion of the aggregate market value is computed thus:

October 2007: 2,000 / 6,000 × £12,000 = £4,000

October 2010: 4,000 / 6,000 × £36,000 = £24,000

If the company is Richard's personal company he may be able to claim hold-over relief against the gains arising on the gifts to his son, (see **Chapter 13**). The gift made in October 2010 may also qualify for entrepreneurs' relief (see **Chapter 11**).

Connected persons

3.16 The rules for determining whether one person is connected with another (so that those persons are 'connected with one another') are set out in *TCGA 1992, s 286* and are summarised below.

Individuals

3.17 A person is connected with an individual if that person is:

- the individual's spouse or civil partner;
- a relative of the individual (see below);
- the spouse or civil partner of a relative of the individual;
- a relative of the individual's spouse or civil partner;
- the spouse or civil partner of a relative of the individual's spouse or civil partner.

A 'relative' for this purpose is a brother, sister, ancestor or lineal descendant. The term excludes, for example, uncles, aunts, nephews and nieces (*TCGA 1992, s 286(2)*).

HMRC's Capital Gains Manual provides a diagram showing all of the people who are connected with an individual. It points out that death, divorce or the dissolution of a civil partnership can lead to persons other than the former spouse or civil partner ceasing to be connected with an individual (CG14583).

Trustees

3.18 The trustees of a settlement are connected with:

- any individual who is a settlor in relation to the settlement;
- any person connected with such an individual; and
- any body corporate that is connected (see below) with that settlement.

A body corporate is connected with a settlement if it is a close company (or would be a close company if it were UK resident) and its participators include the trustees of the settlement; or it is controlled by such a company. Any connection between the trustee and the settlement other than in his capacity as trustee is ignored (*TCGA, s 286(3), (3A)*).

The trustees are treated as a single and continuing body, distinct from the persons who are actually serving as trustees, so the identity of the trustees is disregarded. Settlements do not include will trusts or approved or registered pension funds (CG14590, CG14596).

A person who transfers assets into a registered pension fund is not regarded as connected with that pension fund, even if that person is also a beneficiary of the fund. However, HMRC require the transfer to be valued at open market value for CGT purposes, as the bargain may not have been made at arm's length (see **3.6**). In any case the pension scheme rules would normally demand the contribution of an asset to be independently valued at the open market value.

Business partners

3.19 A person is connected with:

- any person with whom he is in partnership; and
- the spouse or civil partner or a relative of any individual with whom he is in partnership.

However, this rule does not apply in relation to acquisitions or disposals of partnership assets pursuant to bona fide commercial arrangements (*TCGA 1992, s 286(4)*). Partnerships are examined further in **Chapter 6**.

Companies

3.20 A company is connected with another company:

- if the same person has control of both companies, or a person has control of one and persons connected with him (or he and persons connected with him) have control of the other company; or
- if a group of two or more persons has control of each company, and the groups either consist of the same persons or could be regarded as consisting of the same persons by treating (in one or more cases) a member of either group as replaced by a person connected with him.

A company is connected with another person if that person has control of it, or that person and persons connected with him together have control of it.

In addition, any two or more persons acting together to secure or exercise control of a company are treated as connected with one another in relation to that company, and connected with any person acting on the directions of any of them to secure or exercise control of the company. HMRC consider that it is not sufficient for the persons to have control of the company – they have to 'act in some way' to control it – but exercising control could include refraining from voting in a particular way. Directors who are connected with each other under this rule are 'connected persons' only in relation to their transactions with the company. The question whether they are connected in relation to transactions between themselves is a separate issue (*TCGA 1992, s 286(5), (6), (7)*; CG14622–14623).

Losses between connected parties

3.21 A loss accruing on the disposal of an asset by the taxpayer (A) to a connected person (B) is not deductible from chargeable gains generally, under the normal rules for allowable losses (see **3.47**). It is deductible only from a chargeable gain accruing to A on another disposal to B at a time when A and B are connected. HMRC guidance refers to such losses as 'clogged losses' (*TCGA 1992, s 18(3)*; CG14561).

This restriction is waived for a gift into a settlement if the gift – and the income from it – is wholly or primarily applicable for educational, cultural or recreational purposes, so long as the persons benefiting are confined to members of an association and most of them are not connected persons. The restriction does not affect the transfer of trustees' unused losses to a beneficiary on the occasion of the beneficiary becoming absolutely entitled to the settled property (*TCGA 1992, s 18(4)*; CG37207).

If A's first disposal to B in the above scenario is the grant of an option to enter into a sale or other transaction, and the option holder (B) disposes of the option, any loss accruing to B on the disposal of the option is allowable only if the disposal is made at arm's length to a person who is not connected with B (*TCGA 1992, s 18(5)*).

Delayed or irrecoverable consideration

3.22 The consideration for a disposal is taken into account:

- without any discount for postponement of the right to receive any part of it; and
- in the first instance, without regard to either a risk of any part of the consideration being irrecoverable, or the right to receive any part of it being contingent.

An adjustment is made, by way of discharge or repayment of tax or otherwise, if any part of the consideration taken into account in this way proves later to be irrecoverable (*TCGA 1992, s 48(1)*; CG14933).

Contingent liabilities

3.23 When an asset (typically, a holding of shares in a company) is sold, the vendor may provide warranties or representations to compensate the purchaser if, for example, there are tax liabilities in addition to those disclosed to the purchaser at the time of the disposal. The liability is contingent on there being a breach of the warranty, etc. It is specifically provided that no allowance is made to the vendor in the first instance, when the gain is computed, for:

(a) any liability, remaining with or assumed by the person (B) assigning a lease, that is contingent on the assignee's (C's) default in respect of liabilities assumed by C either at the time of the assignment or subsequently – eg where the original lessee B may remain liable to account to his immediate lessor (A) in the event of a breach of covenant by C;

(b) any contingent liability of the person making the disposal in respect of a covenant for quiet enjoyment or other obligation as vendor of land (or of any estate or interest in land) or as a lessor;

(c) any contingent liability in respect of a warranty or representation made on a disposal (by way of sale or lease) of any property other than land.

If such a contingent liability is enforced, the payment made is deducted from the consideration for the disposal and the vendor must make a claim for the appropriate adjustment to his CGT computation. This claim must be made within four years of the end of the tax year in which the disposal was made, or four years from the end of the accounting period that contained the disposal for corporate taxpayers.

If the contingent liability ultimately paid exceeds the consideration received on the disposal, the consideration is reduced to nil and no relief is available to the vendor for the excess. In practice, HMRC accept that this treatment may be extended to a payment made under an indemnity (as opposed to a warranty or representation) given by the vendor to the purchaser (*TCGA 1992, s 49*; ESC D33, para 13; CG14805, CG14807).

By concession, where the disposal is a sale of shares in exchange for an issue of shares or debentures other than qualifying corporate bonds and the new asset is treated as acquired at the same time as the old asset, HMRC allow the vendor to treat his payment as consideration given for the new shares or debentures. The purpose of the concession, which applies only to cases within (c) above, is to provide relief for the payment where there is no disposal of the old asset because of the way in which the rules concerning share reorganisations in *TCGA 1992, ss 135* and *136* operate (ESC D52; CG14818–14821).

Example 3.4

David sold all the shares in his own software company for £555,000 on 22 July 2010. The disposal qualifies for entrepreneurs' relief (see **11.9**). Under an indemnity included as part of the deal he agrees to pay the purchaser £250,000 if the main software product produced by the company proves to be defective within two years. David's shares have a base cost of £1,000. His CGT liability before and after the indemnity comes into effect is calculated as:

2010/11	£	£
Disposal proceeds		555,000
Less cost		(1,000)
Gain		554,000
CGT payable at entrepreneurs' relief rate of 10%:		55,400
After indemnity is paid:		
Disposal proceeds	555,000	
Less indemnity payment	(250,000)	305,000
Less cost		(1,000)
Gain		304,000
CGT payable at entrepreneurs' relief rate of 10%		30,400

No adjustment for other contingent liabilities

3.24 Where the disposal is made subject to a contingent liability to which (a) to (c) in **3.23** above do not apply, the consideration for the disposal is reduced by the value of the contingent liability and there is no adjustment if and when the liability is enforced. This was established in *Randall v Plumb* (1975) 50 TC 392, Ch D.

The purchaser

3.25 So far as the purchaser is concerned, his receipt under the terms of the warranty, etc represents a capital sum derived from an asset (see **2.12**). HMRC guidance indicates that in practice the purchaser's acquisition cost may be reduced by the amount received, but any excess over that cost will be taxable (CG14807).

Deferred or contingent consideration

3.26 As indicated in **3.23**, the consideration for a disposal must be brought into account without any discount for postponement of the right to receive it. The first step to consider, in the event that part of the consideration is to be deferred, is whether the amounts to be received by the vendor in the future are 'ascertainable'.

Ascertainable deferred consideration

3.27 The full amount of any deferred consideration, the amount of which can be ascertained, is treated as part of the consideration for the disposal, without any discount for postponement of payment (*TCGA 1992, s 48(1)*). However, the CGT may be paid in instalments where the consideration is payable over a period exceeding 18 months (beginning not earlier than the time of the disposal) (see **3.35**).

The amount of any deferred consideration is ascertainable if it is either known at the time of disposal, or is capable of being calculated by reference to information known and events that have occurred by that time. HMRC provide the following examples of ascertainable deferred consideration:

- The agreement for the disposal provides for a consideration of £300,000, of which £100,000 is payable on completion and £200,000 will be payable in four annual instalments of £50,000.

- The agreement for the disposal of a business provides for a consideration of £100,000 and a sum equal to half of the taxable profits of the business for the year ended on the date of disposal payable nine months after the date of the contract (CG14882).

Payments that are ascertainable but contingent, ie they depend on the occurrence of some future event, are treated in the same way as ascertainable amounts that are not contingent (*TCGA 1992, s 48(1)*). Terms stipulating a ceiling on the amount of deferred consideration do not make the amount of that consideration ascertainable (CG14883, CG14889).

Unascertainable deferred consideration

3.28 Where the amount of deferred consideration cannot be ascertained, the value of the right to receive that consideration is treated as part of the consideration for the disposal, as established in *Marren v Ingles* (1980) 54 TC 76, HL. The House of Lords held that the right to the deferred consideration was a chose in action and that when the deferred consideration was received there was a disposal of an asset, namely the chose in action, within *TCGA 1992, s 22* (capital sums derived from assets, see **2.12**). The amount of any deferred consideration is unascertainable if the events or circumstances fixing that amount do not occur or exist at the time of the disposal.

The *Marren v Ingles* treatment may be found when a business is sold and part of the consideration is received as a deferred 'earn-out'. The earn-out the vendor receives is based on the post-sale profits of the business, and it may be paid in the form of cash, shares or loan notes issued by the purchasing company. The net present value of the earn-out is taxed upfront with the sale of the business and the disposal of the earn-out right is taxed when the earn-out is received. If the disposal of the business or shares qualifies for entrepreneurs' relief, the present value of the deferred consideration taxed at the time of the disposal, will also qualify for the relief, subject to the life-time cap (see **11.5**).

Example 3.5

Ben sold his company B&J Ltd for £750,000 on 1 July 2008, which he formed in 1990 and subscribed £1,000 for the shares at that time. This disposal qualifies for entrepreneurs' relief. Ben was also entitled to a deferred earn-out consideration based on the profits for the two years to 30 June 2010 payable on 31 October 2010. The value of this earn-out as at 1 July 2008 has been agreed at £250,000 with HMRC shares valuation office. Ben's initial gain taxable in 2008/09 and the final gain taxable in 2010/11, are calculated as follows:

2008/09	£
Sale proceeds	750,000
Present value of earn-out	250,000
Total assessable proceeds	1,000,000
Less original cost of shares	(1,000)
Taxable gain	999,000
Entrepreneurs' relief: 4/9th × £999,000	444,000
Chargeable gain before annual exemption	555,000
2010/11	
After the earn-out is paid:	
Earn-out consideration paid in cash	700,000
Less cost assessed in 2008/09	(250,000)
Chargeable gain before annual exemption.	450,000

The earn-out right disposed of in 2010/11 in **Example 3.5** is not a disposal of shares, so it does not qualify for entrepreneurs' relief. Where the earn-out is paid in the form of shares or loan-notes (commonly QCBs), the upfront taxation of the earn-out right can be avoided, if the exchange of the original shares for the new shares or loan notes can meet the conditions for a share exchange in *TCGA 1992, s 135*. For a further discussion of the application of entrepreneurs' relief to gains deferred on share for share exchanges or share for QCB exchanges see **Chapter 11**.

The earn-out payment may be made in stages, in which case each separate payment occasion gives rise to a part disposal of the right to future consideration. The value of the right acquired at the time of the original disposal is taken to be the acquisition value for the purpose of the CGT computation, and in the case of any part disposal it is necessary to value the right to the remaining future consideration (following the rules for part disposals described in **2.4**).

If any part of the unascertainable deferred consideration becomes 'irrecoverable', no relief is available under *TCGA 1992, s 48(1)* (see **3.21**) because, instead of receiving quantifiable consideration at the time of the disposal, the vendor in this situation received a right which was valued at that time in computing the gain on that disposal. However, a loss may arise on the disposal of the right (see **3.29**).

Election to carry back loss on disposal of a right

3.29 A loss may accrue on the disposal of the right to unascertainable deferred consideration (see **3.28**), where the value of the right – which forms the acquisition value in the CGT computation – exceeds the consideration ultimately received. Where such a loss accrues after 9 April 2003, the taxpayer may elect to carry it back for set-off against the gain accruing on the disposal of the asset in return for which the right was received. This option is only available to taxpayers within the charge to CGT; it is not available to companies subject to corporation tax (*TCGA 1992, s 279A*).

The form of the election, which is irrevocable, is set out in *TCGA 1992, s 279D*. In many cases the effect of an election will be reasonably straightforward, but several complications can arise and detailed guidance is provided in HMRC's Capital Gains Manual at CG15083–15130. The election is available if:

(a) the right was acquired wholly or partly by the taxpayer as the whole or part of the consideration for a disposal (the 'original disposal') by him of another asset (the 'original asset');

(b) the year of the original disposal was earlier than the year of disposal of the right;

(c) when the taxpayer acquired the right there was no corresponding disposal of it; and

(d) the right is a right to unascertainable consideration (*TCGA 1992, s 279A(2)*).

Where the taxpayer disposes of the right and an allowable loss accrues (under the normal rules) on that disposal, and the disposal takes place in a tax year in which the taxpayer is within the charge to CGT (the 'year of loss'), then – subject to the two conditions described in **3.30** and **3.31** – he may elect for the loss to be treated as accruing in the year of the earlier disposal (*TCGA 1992, s 279A(1)*).

Condition 1

3.30 The first condition is that a chargeable gain accrued to the taxpayer (or would have accrued to him but for a claim to deferral relief under either the enterprise investment scheme or the venture capital trust scheme) on any one or more of the following events:

- the original disposal;
- an earlier disposal of the original asset by the taxpayer in the year of the original disposal;
- a later disposal of the original asset by the taxpayer in a year earlier than the year of disposal of the right to future consideration.

This condition is modified where the right was acquired in consideration for more than one disposal (*TCGA 1992, s 279A(3), (4)*).

Condition 2

3.31 The second condition is that a chargeable gain accrued to the taxpayer as described in either (a) or (b) below in the 'eligible year' (ie a tax year earlier than the 'year of loss' but not earlier than 1992/93), and a residual amount of gain remains chargeable to CGT for that year:

(a) a chargeable gain meeting condition 1 above; or

(b) a chargeable gain that would have met condition 1 if it had not been deferred under the reliefs for investment in the enterprise investment scheme or the venture capital trust scheme, where that gain was treated as accruing at a later time by virtue of a chargeable event – such a gain is called, for this purpose, a 'revived gain'.

There is a residual gain remaining for a tax year if there remains (ignoring the effect of the election) an amount on which the taxpayer is chargeable to CGT after taking account of any previous elections made by the taxpayer and after excluding certain trust gains assessed on the taxpayer (against which losses cannot be set) (*TCGA 1992, s 279A(5), (6), (7)*).

Definitions

3.32 Various definitions and further conditions are set out in *TCGA 1992, s 279B*. A key condition is that a right is a right to unascertainable consideration if, and only if:

- it is a right to consideration the amount or value of which is unascertainable at the time when the right is conferred; and
- that amount or value is unascertainable at that time because it is referable, wholly or partly, to matters which are uncertain at that time because they have not yet occurred.

Effect of election

3.33 The rules surrounding the election are designed to ensure that any losses already set against gains accruing in the earlier year are not disturbed. The taxpayer cannot elect to carry back only part of the losses even if this results in a loss of the annual exemption for the earlier year. All of the loss must go back and if this exceeds the chargeable gain in the earlier year the unused loss is carried forward. This carried-forward loss is then set against the next eligible tax year, as described in condition 2 above. If there is no other eligible year, the loss is carried forward to be used in the year after the year of the loss, or a later year (*TCGA 1992, s 279C*). The election must be made by the first anniversary of 31 January following the end of the tax year in which the loss occurred.

Example 3.6

Sandra sold all the shares in her own soft toy company in July 2007, and realised a gain before taper relief of £90,000. The company was formed in May 1998 and Sandra has always owned all of the shares. Sandra had losses brought forward of £55,000 to set against her gains in 2007/08. In July 2010 she disposed of a right connected with the sale of her company in 2007 which generated a capital loss of £12,000. Sandra made no other capital gains in 2010/11 so elects under *TCGA 1992, s 279A* for the loss to be set against her gains in 2007/08.

2007/08	£
Gains before losses and taper relief	90,000
Less losses brought forward:	(55,000)
Gain	45,000
Taper relief: £45,000 × 75% (see **17.22**)	(33,750)
Chargeable gain after taper relief	11,250
After loss from 2010/11 is carried back:	
Gains before losses	90,000
Less losses brought forward:	(55,000)
	45,000
Less loss carried back:	(12,000)
Gain before taper relief:	33,000
Taper relief: £33,000 × 75% (see **17.22**)	(24,750)
Chargeable gain after taper relief	8,250

Payment of CGT in instalments

3.34 The general rules for payment of CGT are set out in **1.38**. However, CGT may be paid in instalments if all or part of the consideration taken into account in the computation of the gain is payable by instalments over a period longer than 18 months and beginning not earlier than the time of the disposal. If the taxpayer opts for payment by instalments, HMRC may allow payment of CGT over a period of up to eight years, ending not later than the time when the last of the instalments of consideration is payable. The taxpayer does not need to demonstrate hardship in order to pay CGT in instalments (*TCGA 1992, s 280*).

Due dates for payment

3.35 HMRC normally expect the vendor to pay instalments of CGT equal to 50% of each instalment of consideration due (without any deduction for incidental costs of disposal) until the total CGT liability has been paid.

- Where instalments of consideration fall due on or before the normal due date for the payment of the tax, the corresponding instalments of tax are payable on that normal due date.
- The instalments of tax relating to later instalments of consideration will be payable at the time when the vendor is contractually entitled to receive that consideration, but HMRC are likely to seek to agree a schedule whereby the instalments of tax are paid at intervals of at least six months (CG14912).

Example 3.7

Simon enters into a contract for the sale of the rights to the format of a successful TV programme on 1 May 2009. The consideration is £3.6 million payable in six annual instalments of £600,000 commencing 1 August 2009. This consideration represents the full gain as there is no base cost. The total CGT payable on the deal is £648,000 which would normally all be due to be paid by 31 January 2011. Simon asks for *TCGA 1992, s 280* to apply. Using this instalment option the tax is payable on the following dates:

		£
	Payable:	Tax
50% of the consideration due on 1 August 2009	31 January 2011	300,000
50% of the consideration due on 1 August 2010	31 January 2011	300,000
Balance of tax due from the consideration payable on 1 August 2011	1 August 2011	48,000
		648,000

ALLOWABLE EXPENDITURE

3.36 Three categories of expenditure are allowable as a deduction from the consideration in computing a chargeable gain or loss. These are:

- the costs of acquiring (or providing) the asset, including certain incidental costs (see **3.38**);
- the costs of enhancing the asset's value, and any costs of establishing, preserving or defending title to it (see **3.39**); and

- certain incidental costs of disposal (see **3.40**).

No payment of interest may be deducted. Any deemed disposal and reacquisition of an asset cannot give rise to a deduction for assumed incidental costs. No deduction is allowed more than once in the computation of a gain (*TCGA 1992, ss 38(1), (3), (4), 52(1)*).

Expenditure that is, or would be, allowable in computing trading income chargeable to income tax is not allowable (see **3.41**). Special rules apply to 'wasting assets' (see **4.27**).

Costs of acquisition

Consideration for the acquisition

3.37 This is the amount or value of the consideration, in money or money's worth, given by the taxpayer, or on his behalf, wholly and exclusively for the acquisition of the asset. If the taxpayer created rather than purchased the asset, for example, where goodwill or copyright is created, the allowable expenditure is any expenditure wholly and exclusively incurred by him in providing the asset (*TCGA 1992, s 38(1)(a)*).

Confusion arose in 2003 concerning the base cost for shares acquired by way of unapproved share options. The case, *Mansworth v Jelley* [2003] STC 53, was interpreted by HMRC as meaning that the base cost of such shares was the market value of the shares at the date when the shares were acquired, plus the amount charged to income tax when the option was exercised and the shares were acquired. For example share options exercised for £100 would incur an income tax charge on £100. When the shares were sold shortly after exercise for £100 a capital loss of £100 would be created.

This interpretation meant that many shares acquired through unapproved share options stood at a loss for CGT purposes. This situation applied for all unapproved share options exercised before 10 April 2003, when *TCGA 1992, ss 144ZA–144ZD* were introduced to change the position back to what most people thought applied all along (CG56305).

On 12 May 2009 HMRC changed their opinion about the base cost of shares acquired through pre-10 April 2003 share options (HMRC brief 30/09). This brief asserts that the base cost for such shares comprises only the market value of those shares at the date they were acquired, so no capital loss would generally arise. Any capital losses already claimed by taxpayers under the previous HMRC guidance should stand, but taxpayers submitting loss claims on or after 12 May 2009 need to consider the new HMRC guidance on this matter.

Incidental costs of acquisition

3.38 These are the incidental costs to the taxpayer of the acquisition, as specified below:

(a) expenditure wholly and exclusively incurred by him for the purposes of the acquisition, being the costs (including stamp duties) of the transfer or conveyance of the asset, and any fees, commission or remuneration paid for professional services of a surveyor, valuer, auctioneer, accountant, agent or legal adviser; and

(b) the costs of advertising to find a seller (*TCGA 1992, s 38(1)(a), (2)*).

Reasonable costs incurred in ascertaining the market value of the asset for CGT purposes can be deducted, for example where the asset was acquired before 31 March 1982. No deduction is allowed for expenditure by the purchaser in transporting assets from the point of acquisition (CG15260).

Costs of enhancement, etc

3.39 These are the amounts of:

(a) expenditure wholly and exclusively incurred on the asset, by the taxpayer or on his behalf, for the purpose of enhancing its value, so long as the asset's state or nature at the time of the disposal reflects that expenditure (see below); and

(b) expenditure wholly and exclusively incurred by the taxpayer in establishing, preserving or defending his title to, or to a right over, the asset (*TCGA 1992, s 38(1)(b)*).

With regard to (a) above, Lord Emslie observed in *Aberdeen Construction Group Ltd v CIR* (1978) 52 TC 281, HL that what the provision was looking for, as the result of relevant expenditure, was 'an identifiable change for the better in the state or nature of the asset'. This change must be a change distinct from the enhancement of value, he added. HMRC regard the time of the disposal for this purpose as the date of completion and not the date of the contract (CG15185), although the disposal date for calculating the CGT due would be the date contracts were agreed or exchanged (see **2.8**).

TCGA 1992, s 38(1)(b) does not refer (in the way that *TCGA 1992, s 38(1)(a)* refers) to consideration in money or money's worth, but the High Court held in *Chaney v Watkis* (1986) 58 TC 707, Ch D that money's worth given (in the form of an agreement to provide a tenant with rent-free accommodation) for the purpose of enhancing the value of an asset was allowable as a deduction.

However, HMRC may seek to challenge a deduction for money's worth where the recipient is connected with the taxpayer or there are other grounds for suspecting that enhancing the asset's value may not have been the only purpose of the transaction. *Oram v Johnson* (1980) 53 TC 319, Ch D established that 'expenditure' means money, or money's worth, in the sense of something which diminishes the total assets of the person making the expenditure. It does not, therefore, include the value of an individual's own skill and labour (CG15211).

Incidental costs of disposal

3.40 These are the incidental costs to the taxpayer of the disposal, as specified below:

(a) expenditure wholly and exclusively incurred by him for the purposes of the disposal, being the costs (including stamp duties) of the transfer or conveyance of the asset, and any fees, commission or remuneration paid for professional services of a surveyor, valuer, auctioneer, accountant, agent or legal adviser;

(b) the costs of advertising to find a buyer; and

(c) costs reasonably incurred in making any valuation or apportionment required in computing the gain, including establishing market value where required for the purposes of *TCGA 1992* (*TCGA 1992, s 38(1)(c), (2)*).

The cost of the transfer or conveyance of an asset would include the vendor's costs of transporting it to the point of sale (CG15260). The costs mentioned in (c) include costs incurred for the purposes of rendering a tax return or for the purposes of a post-transaction valuation check (see **1.35**) in advance of submission of the return, but they exclude costs of resolving valuation disputes with HMRC (CG15261).

Expenditure allowable in computing income

3.41 No deduction is available, in computing chargeable gains, for any of the following expenditure, irrespective of how the benefit of the expense mentioned is (or would be) obtained:

(a) expenditure allowable as a deduction in computing the profits or losses of a trade, profession or vocation for income tax purposes;

(b) expenditure allowable as a deduction in computing any other income or profits or gains or losses for income tax purposes; or

(c) expenditure that would be allowable as a deduction in computing any losses but for an insufficiency of income or profits or gains (*TCGA 1992, s 39(1)*).

Expenditure that would have been deductible in computing the profits or losses of a trade, had the asset disposed of been a fixed asset used for that trade, is not deductible in computing a chargeable gain (*TCGA 1992, s 39(2)*).

Example 3.8

Mrs Gold inherited two cottages in 1981. In 1985 she converted the properties into one house and she let the house until August 2010, when it was sold. She incurred the following expenses which are treated as deductions from the rental income (for income tax purposes) or from the proceeds of the sale (for CGT purposes) as shown:

Expenditure	Income tax	CGT
	£	£
Market value at 31 March 1982		1,000
Legal costs to establish the property boundary		2,500
Planning permission to convert cottages to one		200
Conversion costs		40,000
Drawing up tenancy agreements	500	
Commission to letting agent	25,000	
Decoration of interior	4,000	
Replacement of front door (a repair)	400	
New conservatory (an improvement)		10,000
New carpets and curtains (sold with the property)		3,000
Estate agents' fees and commission on sale		5,000
Replacement of central heating boiler (a repair)	1,400	

In *Emmerson v Computer Time International Ltd (in liquidation)* (1977) 50 TC 628, CA, a payment of arrears of rent, made in order to obtain the landlord's consent to an assignment of a lease, was held to be rent paid in respect of a fixed asset of the trade and was not deductible in computing the chargeable gain.

Sums are regarded for this purpose as chargeable to (or taken into account for) income tax if they would be so chargeable (or taken into account) but for the fact that the profits or gains concerned are not chargeable to income tax or that losses are not allowable. Income or profits taxable by deduction at source are treated as chargeable to income tax (*TCGA 1992, s 52(2), (3)*).

These rules do not deny a deduction for expenditure qualifying for capital allowances, but any capital loss arising may be restricted by reference to such allowances (see **3.56**).

Expenditure reimbursed out of public funds

3.42 Any expenditure met (or to be met) directly or indirectly by the Crown or UK or other government, public or local authority is to be excluded from the computation of a gain (*TCGA 1992, s 50*). If, on a disposal of the asset, the taxpayer is required to repay all or part of a grant out of the proceeds of sale, or can demonstrate that there has been a corresponding reduction in the amount of a later grant, then by concession (ESC D53) HMRC allow the consideration received on the disposal to be reduced by the amount of the repayment (CG15289).

Market value rule for acquisitions

3.43 The market value of an asset (determined as set out in **3.7**) is substituted for the actual consideration given for the acquisition where the taxpayer acquires the asset:

(a) otherwise than by way of a bargain made at arm's length (see **3.6**), and in particular where he acquires it by way of gift, or on a transfer into a settlement by a settlor, or by way of distribution from a company in respect of shares in the company;

(b) wholly or partly for a consideration that cannot be valued;

(c) in connection with his own or another's loss of office or employment or diminution of emoluments; or

(d) otherwise in consideration for (or in recognition of) his or another person's services or past services in an office or employment, or any other service rendered to another person (*TCGA 1992, s 17(1)*).

However, market value is not substituted on an acquisition if there is no corresponding disposal of the asset and:

- there is no consideration in money or money's worth; or
- the amount or value of the consideration is less than the asset's market value (*TCGA 1992, s 17(2)*).

Where a company issues its own shares, there is no disposal corresponding to the shareholder's acquisition. The above exception applies only if no consideration is given or the consideration is less than market value. The market value is substituted, therefore, if the consideration given is higher than the market value. The effect of this rule is that the lower of the actual consideration and market value is taken in a case where there is an acquisition but no corresponding disposal (CG14550).

Acquisitions from connected persons

3.44 Where the person acquiring the asset is 'connected' with the person making the disposal, the acquisition is treated as made otherwise than by way of a bargain made at arm's length, so that the market value rule in **3.43** applies. See **3.16** as to whether persons are connected with one another; **3.21** regarding restrictions on the use of losses accruing on transactions between connected persons; and **3.62** regarding the special rules for transactions between spouses and civil partners (*TCGA 1992, s 18*).

Part disposals

3.45 Part disposals are discussed in **2.4.** A part disposal may occur where the disposal itself creates an interest in, or a right over, the asset. For example, the grant of a lease by the person who holds the freehold interest in land. Other part disposals involve the grant of a licence to exploit a copyright, or a patent, or to remove minerals from land, tip rubbish, cut down trees or exercise sporting rights over a particular piece of land, or simply the disposal of part of a large plot of land (*TCGA 1992, s 21(2)*).

Special rules apply to part disposals of land and small disposals. See examples at **2.4** and **2.5**.

This apportionment of allowable expenditure is made before applying any restriction of capital losses by reference to capital allowances (provided by *TCGA 1992, s 41*). On a subsequent disposal of the part of the asset retained, the capital allowances to be taken into account (in the event that a loss accrues on that disposal) include such allowances relating to expenditure both before and after the part disposal, but in order to avoid double counting they exclude any allowances that were applied in restricting the capital loss on the first part disposal (*TCGA 1992, s 42(3)*).

This apportionment (and all similar apportionments of expenditure provided for elsewhere) is also made before – and without regard to – any of the following rules in *TCGA 1992*:

- transfers between spouses and civil partners – *s 58*;
- transfers within a group of companies – *s 171*;
- roll-over relief on replacement of business assets – *ss 152–158*;
- any other rule providing for neither a gain nor a loss to accrue on the disposal (*TCGA 1992, s 42(5)*).

Assets derived from other assets

3.46 The value of an asset may be derived from another asset in the same ownership where:

- assets have been merged or divided or have changed their nature; or
- rights or interests in or over assets have been created or extinguished.

In such a case it is necessary to apportion the allowable expenditure incurred on the 'old' asset and then apply the appropriate proportions to the old asset (if it is retained) and the new asset. The apportionment is to be made on a 'just and reasonable' basis (*TCGA 1992, ss 43, 52(4)*).

LOSSES

3.47 Where a particular type of transaction will produce a chargeable gain, it will also produce an allowable capital loss. The loss is computed in the same way as gains, but the indexation allowance cannot increase or create a loss (see **3.60**). If a gain that arises on a disposal would not be chargeable because it is exempt from CGT, any loss arising from the disposal is not allowable (*TCGA 1992, s 16(1), (2)*).

A loss would not normally arise on the non-recovery or write-off of a debt or unsecured loan (see **4.35**), but a capital loss may be available under the loan to trader provisions, see **17.11** to **17.15**.

There are special rules for the use of capital losses arising in the following circumstances:

- in the tax year the taxpayer dies (see **7.3**);
- between connected persons (see **3.21**);
- on the disposal of a right to unascertainable deferred consideration (see **3.29**);
- incurred outside the UK by UK resident non-dom (see **3.51**);
- where the asset disposed of is a chattel (see **4.25**);
- on the deemed disposal of assets to a beneficiary (see **8.19**)
- where arrangements exist to create a tax advantage (see **10.2**);
- as part of the disposal of a business qualifying for entrepreneurs' relief (see **11.6**);

In addition a capital loss sustained by the subscriber of certain unquoted trading company shares on the disposal or loss of those shares may be set off against that taxpayer's income (see **17.16**). In certain circumstances a trading income loss may be treated as a capital loss (see **3.52** and **3.53**).

Order of set-off of losses

3.48 The allowable capital losses arising in the tax year are normally set off against any capital gains arising in the same tax year, before the annual exemption is deducted (see **1.20**). However, in 2010/11 and in subsequent years where the taxpayer has gains that are chargeable to CGT at more than one rate, the taxpayer can choose which gains their losses are set against, such that the CGT liability for the year is reduced to the lowest possible charge (*TCGA 1992, s 4B*) (see **1.23**).

Allowable losses brought forward from an earlier tax year are set against the taxpayer's adjusted net gains, which are broadly the gains for the current tax year less the allowable losses for that year. However, the allowable brought-forward losses can be restricted to preserve the annual exemption. It appears that the brought-forward losses may also be allocated against gains for 2010/11 and in any subsequent years, in such a way that minimises the tax charge for the year.

A peculiar feature of entrepreneurs' relief is that it demands aggregation of all the gains and losses arising from a qualifying business disposal, before entrepreneurs' relief for that disposal is calculated (*TCGA 1992, s 169N(1)*) (see **11.7**). The change in the way entrepreneurs' relief is calculated from 23 June 2010 affects the value of any losses that are set against the net gains that qualify for entrepreneurs' relief. Losses set off against such qualifying gains made before 23 June 2010 will achieve tax relief at 18%, losses set off against later gains qualifying for entrepreneurs' relief will only achieve tax relief at 10%.

Under taper relief due on gains made before 6 April 2008, losses had to be set off against untapered gains before the taper relief was deducted, which allowed the taxpayer to set off the loss against the gain which would attract the minimum of taper relief (see **17.40**).

Claims

3.49 A loss must be 'claimed' before it can be set against gains. It is not an allowable loss unless the taxpayer gives a notice to HMRC for the tax year in which the loss accrued. The notice, which must quantify the amount of the loss, is treated as a claim within *Taxes Management Act 1970* (*TMA 1970*), *ss 42* and *43* (*TCGA 1992, s 16(2A)*).

Where the taxpayer is required to submit an SA tax return, he or she should include the allowable capital losses on the capital gains pages of that return. A computation of the loss must be attached to the return as the tax return pages only have room for a summary. The HMRC notes to the capital gains pages (SA108 – notes) advise the taxpayer to make it clear on the computation that a claim for losses is being made.

Claims under *TMA 1970, ss 42* and *43* must be submitted by non-corporate taxpayers no more than four years after the end of the tax year to which the claim relates, and for companies four years after the end of the relevant accounting period. For example, an individual taxpayer must claim capital losses that arose in 2006/07 by 5 April 2011. However, taxpayers who were not within self-assessment for the year of the claim have until 1 April 2012 to claim such losses (see **1.46**).

Non-residents

3.50 If the taxpayer is not resident or ordinarily resident in the UK at all during any part of the tax year, a loss accruing to him in that year is not an allowable loss. There is an exception where a gain accruing on the relevant disposal would be chargeable on the non-resident taxpayer under *TCGA 1992, ss 10* or *10B* (non-residents with a UK branch, agency or permanent establishment) (*TCGA 1992, s 16(3)*).

Non-domicile UK residents

3.51 Where an individual is resident or ordinarily resident, but not domiciled in the UK (a 'non-dom'), and has gains accruing from the disposal of assets situated outside the UK those gains can escape CGT if the individual claims the remittance basis, and those gains are *not* remitted to the UK. Not all non-dom individuals will want to claim the remittance basis, see **5.32**.

From 6 April 2008, non-domiciled individuals who claim the remittance basis can make a one-off irrevocable election to obtain UK tax relief for losses realised on foreign-situated assets (see **5.43**) (*TCGA 1992, s 16ZA(2)*). The election will be effective for first tax year for which the taxpayer claims the remittance basis, and all subsequent tax years. Non-domiciled individuals who do not claim the remittance basis are taxed on all their worldwide gains and losses just like other UK residents, so do not need to make an election in respect of foreign losses.

Trading losses set against chargeable gains

3.52 Where the taxpayer makes a claim under *Income Tax Act 2007* (*ITA 2007*), *s 64* or *s 128* to set trading or employment losses against income for income tax purposes, he may also make a claim for an amount – the 'relevant amount' – to be treated as an allowable loss for CGT purposes (*TCGA 1992, s 261B*).

The relevant amount for the tax year to which the claim relates is the part of the trading loss that cannot be set off against his income for the year and has not already been relieved for any other year under *ITA 2007, s 64,* or otherwise. However, if the relevant amount exceeds the 'maximum amount' (see below), the excess is not treated as a capital loss.

The 'maximum amount' is the amount on which the taxpayer would be chargeable to CGT disregarding the annual exemption (see **1.17**), and the loss to be relieved under *TCGA 1992, s 261B*. It is calculated without regard to any event occurring after the relevant amount has been determined, which would otherwise reduce the maximum amount.

In the absence of this limitation, a claim to CGT roll-over relief on the replacement of business assets, for example, could reduce the maximum amount so that part of the trading loss could no longer be treated as a capital loss. Instead, the maximum amount is unchanged and the effect of the roll-over relief claim is to create unrelieved losses available to carry forward and set against future chargeable gains.

Post-cessation expenditure

3.53 Where the taxpayer claims relief for post-cessation expenditure under *ITA 2007, s 96* or *s 125* he may specify that any amount of that expenditure that cannot be set off against his income is to be treated for CGT purposes as an allowable loss (*TCGA 1992, ss 261D–261E*). This relief is not available to companies within the charge to corporation tax as the relief only applies to income tax losses.

Former employees: employment-related liabilities

3.54 Where income tax relief is available for liabilities related to a former employment and the deduction exceeds the taxpayer's total income, the excess relief may be treated as an allowable loss accruing to the former employee (*TCGA 1992, s 263ZA*).

Restriction by reference to capital allowances

3.55 Although expenditure allowable as a deduction in computing trading profits, etc is not deductible in computing chargeable gains (see **3.41**) there is no general exclusion of expenditure for which a 'capital allowance' or 'renewals allowance' (see **3.56**) is made. However, if a loss accrues on the disposal it may be restricted by reference to those allowances. The restriction is applied by excluding from the sums allowable as a deduction in the CGT computation any expenditure to the extent that a capital allowance or renewals allowance has been – or may be – made for that expenditure. This rule can have the effect of reducing the capital loss to nil, but it cannot turn that loss into a gain (*TCGA 1992, s 41(1), (2), (4), (5)*).

It is important to determine exactly which asset the loss arises on. In *Revenue & Customs v Smallwood* [2007] EWCA Civ 462 the taxpayer invested £10,000 in 1989 in an Enterprise Zone Property Unit Trust. In 1999 he realised a loss on a part disposal of his investment. During that ten-year period the trustees of the unit trust invested in buildings in the Enterprise Zone that attracted Industrial Buildings Allowances (IBAs). The taxpayer received the benefit of a portion of those IBAs, but HMRC argued that the loss he made on his investment should be restricted by the benefit of the capital allowances he enjoyed. The Court of Appeal held that the loss arose on the disposal of the units in the Property Unit Trust, and not the disposal of the buildings the trustees had invested in, and thus the loss was allowed to stand.

What capital allowances are taken into account

3.56 A 'capital allowance' is any allowance under the *Capital Allowances Act 2001* (*CAA 2001*) or certain provisions relating to expenditure on sea walls and cemeteries. A 'renewals allowance' is a non-statutory deduction allowed in computing trading income, for the cost of a replacement asset for the purposes of the trade. For the purpose of this restriction, the renewals allowance given on the acquisition of the replacement asset is regarded as an allowance for expenditure incurred on the old asset (*TCGA 1992, s 41(3)*; CG15404).

The capital allowances to be taken into account include the addition of any balancing allowances and the deduction of any balancing charges available on the disposal (*TCGA 1992, s 41(6)*).

If the taxpayer acquired the asset on a transfer treated for capital allowances purposes as made at its written-down value, this restriction takes account of capital allowances made to the transferor (and the previous transferor in relation to any earlier transfers) as well as the taxpayer (*TCGA 1992, s 41(3)*; CG15411).

Similarly, capital allowances made to the previous owner (or owners) of the asset may be taken into account where the taxpayer acquired the asset on a transfer to which either of the following provisions applied:

- *TCGA 1992, s 140A* – transfer of a UK trade between EU member states; or

- *TCGA 1992, s 171*, ignoring for this purpose the exceptions in *s 171(2)* – transfers within a group of companies (*TCGA 1992, s 41(8)*).

On a disposal of plant or machinery that has attracted allowances under *CAA 2001, Pt 2* without restriction for either non-qualifying use or partial depreciation subsidies (*CAA 2001, ss 205–212*), the allowances taken into account for the purpose of this restriction are taken to be the difference between the capital expenditure incurred (or treated as incurred) on providing the asset and the asset's disposal value for capital allowances purposes (*TCGA 1992, s 41(7)*).

Example 3.9

Keynes Ltd bought a printing press to use in its trade in April 1998 for £220,000. In May 2010 Keynes Ltd sold the printing press for £20,000 to an unconnected person. The capital gain is calculated as follows:

Capital allowances calculation:		£
Cost of the asset		220,000
Less disposal proceeds		20,000
Capital allowances to be taken into account		200,000
Gains calculation:		
Disposal proceeds		20,000
Deduct cost of asset	220,000	
Less capital allowances:	200,000	20,000
Net gain:		Nil

ENTREPRENEURS' RELIEF

3.57 Entrepreneurs' relief is available for certain gains made on or after 6 April 2008 by individuals and trustees of interest in possession trusts where there is also a qualifying beneficiary. The relief is restricted to the net gains made on the disposal of a business, shares in a personal company, or business assets that are disposed of after the cessation of a business, or in association with the disposal of a business. Entrepreneurs' relief is examined in detail in **Chapter 11**.

TAPER RELIEF

3.58 Taper relief was available for eligible gains made in the tax years from 1998/99 to 2007/08 by individuals, trustees and personal representatives.

Gains made on the disposal of business assets with a qualifying holding period of at least one year; or non-business assets with a qualifying holding period of at least three years were eligible for different rates of taper relief – see **17.22**.

ASSETS HELD ON 31 MARCH 1982

3.59 Assets held by individuals and trustees on 31 March 1982 and disposed of on or after 6 April 2008 are automatically rebased to their value at 31 March 1982 by *TCGA 1992, s 35*. The effect is to substitute the 31 March 1982 value for the actual cost of the asset and any enhancement expenditure incurred prior to that date. If the value of the asset being disposed of is derived from another asset held on 31 March 1982 rebasing may apply by reference to the original asset's value on that date (*TCGA 1992, s 35(1), (2), Sch 3, para 5*).

Rebasing to 31 March 1982 eliminates all the inflationary gains made prior to that date, and this was achieved by a rebasing election made prior to 6 April 2008. In some cases, the March 1982 value would be lower than the original cost of the asset, so a rebasing election would not be advantageous. Where the asset has been rebased to 31 March 1982, the indexation allowance (see **3.60**) is based on the market value at that date.

Companies can still choose whether to have their assets rebased to 31 March 1982 by making a rebasing election. The rebasing election, the exceptions and exclusions are discussed in **Chapter 9**.

INDEXATION ALLOWANCE

3.60 The indexation allowance was introduced in 1982 in order to eliminate 'paper gains' attributable to inflation. Combined with the rebasing of CGT by reference to 31 March 1982 values (see **3.59**) with effect from April 1988, indexation provided 'inflation-proofing' of gains.

The allowance was frozen with effect from April 1998 for individuals, trustees and personal representatives, and was withdrawn completely for these taxpayers from 6 April 2008. The allowance could be obtained in addition to taper relief (see **17.22**) where appropriate.

Companies chargeable to corporation tax continue to be eligible for indexation allowance (*TCGA 1992, s 52A*)). The calculation of indexation allowance is discussed in **Chapter 9.**

Assets disposed of on a no gain, no loss transfer

3.61 Where the indexation allowance is available (see **3.60**) and the disposal treated as a disposal on which neither a gain nor a loss accrues, then the consideration for the disposal is taken to be the amount that would give rise to an unindexed gain equal to the indexation allowance available on the disposal. The effect of this rule is that after deducting the indexation allowance there is no chargeable gain and no allowable loss. An adjustment to the deemed consideration may be required in some cases, to prevent a loss accruing on a subsequent disposal by the transferee (*TCGA 1992, s 56*).

Example 3.10

Elton bought an investment property in May 1982 for £100,000, which he transferred to his civil partner David in February 2008. David acquires the property as a no gain, no loss transfer after deducting the indexation allowance, which at that time amounts to a factor of 1.59. David sold the property in May 2010, and the capital gain was calculated as follows:

2010/11		£
Proceeds from sale of property		350,000
Original cost in 1982	100,000	
Add indexation at 1.59 to April 1998:	159,000	
Cost acquired for no gain, no loss		259,000
Net gain before annual exemption:		91,000

Spouses and civil partners

3.62 Transfers of assets between spouses or registered civil partners living together are treated as 'no gain, no loss' transfers.

Where an individual is living with their spouse or civil partner in a tax year and during that year one of them disposes of an asset to the other, both the transferor and transferee are treated as if the asset was transferred for a consideration that would give rise to neither a gain nor a loss in the hands of the transferor (*TCGA 1992, s 58(1)*).

Spouses or civil partners are treated as living together unless they are either:

- separated under an order of a court of competent jurisdiction, or by deed of separation; or
- in fact separated in such circumstances that the separation is likely to be permanent (*TCGA 1992, s 288(3)* applying *ITA 2007, s 1011*).

The no gain, no loss rule described above applies regardless of the rules substituting market value for transfers between connected persons (see **3.11**) and appropriations to and from trading stock (see **4.36**) and regardless of any other rule fixing the amount of the consideration deemed to be given on the disposal or acquisition of an asset.

However, it does not apply if:

- the asset formed part of the taxpayer's trading stock until the disposal;
- the asset is acquired, by a person carrying on a trade, as trading stock; or
- the disposal is by way of *donatio mortis causa* (see **2.9**) (*TCGA 1992, s 58(2)*).

ASSETS HELD ON 6 APRIL 1965

3.63 The rules for assets held on 6 April 1965 only apply to companies in respect of disposals made on or after 6 April 2008, as all assets held by individuals and trustees are automatically rebased to 31 March 1982 (see **3.59**). The rules for assets held at 6 April 1965 will also only apply where a universal rebasing election has not been made, so in practice will be very rarely encountered.

The special rules that apply for different types of assets held at 6 April 1965 are discussed at **9.18** to **9.21**.

DOUBLE TAX RELIEF

3.64 Relief for foreign tax suffered on gains that are chargeable to UK CGT or corporation tax may be obtained under the terms of a double taxation agreement between the UK and the relevant overseas territory (see **3.65**); or by means of a 'unilateral' tax credit granted under UK domestic tax law (see **3.66**); or by means of a deduction in computing the gain chargeable to UK tax (see **3.69**). See **5.55** with regard to the application of double tax relief where gains are assessed on the remittance basis. Anti-avoidance provisions were introduced in 2005 to counter schemes designed to create tax credit relief (*TIOPA 2010, ss 83–88*)

Double taxation agreements

3.65 The UK has more than a hundred double tax agreements or treaties with overseas territories, designed to limit the taxing rights of the contracting states in order to prevent double taxation, and to assist in countering evasion by means of exchange of information between tax authorities. The agreements contain articles to determine the residence status of persons who are resident in both territories under their respective domestic tax law. Many agreements have articles setting out how capital gains are to be taxed. Where a UK-resident taxpayer suffers foreign tax on a gain that is subject to CGT or corporation tax, the agreement itself may provide for a credit in respect of the foreign tax to be given against any UK liability (*TIOPA 2010, s 6*).

Unilateral foreign tax credit relief

3.66 Where chargeable gains are subject to tax in a territory that has no double taxation agreement with the UK, credit for any foreign tax liability is given 'unilaterally' unless the taxpayer elects for a deduction instead (see **3.69**) (*TIOPA 2010, s 18*). The provisions are also applied to corporation tax on chargeable gains (*TIOPA 2010, s 42*).

The UK tax and the foreign tax must be chargeable on the same chargeable gain, although there is no requirement that the respective liabilities arise at the same time or are charged on the same person (*TIOPA 2010, s 9*). A liability may arise in the UK, but not in the overseas territory.

In some cases it may be difficult to ascertain the amount of the gain that is subject to 'double taxation' in the absence of any relief. HMRC practice in this regard is set out in the Capital Gains Manual at CG14380–14427 and summarised below.

(a) Where the whole period of ownership of the asset is considered in arriving at both the UK assessment and the foreign assessment and the amount of the UK assessment is equal to or greater than the foreign assessment, the whole of the foreign tax is allowable for foreign tax credit relief. However, the credit cannot exceed the amount of the UK tax liability arising on the gain and no deduction is available in the computation for any foreign tax that is not allowed as a tax credit.

(b) Where the whole period of ownership is considered for both assessments as stated in (a), but the amount of the UK assessment is less than the foreign assessment, the whole of the gain is treated as doubly taxed, but the foreign tax credit is restricted to the fraction A/B, where A is the amount of the UK assessment and B is the amount of the foreign assessment.

(c) Relief for the foreign tax paid is restricted when the same period of ownership is considered in arriving at both assessments but the amount of the UK assessment is less than the foreign assessment, and when the foreign assessment relates to a longer period of ownership than the period forming the basis of the UK assessment (eg as a result of the March 1982 rebasing of UK CGT, see **3.59**).

HMRC also provide a working sheet to assist taxpayers to calculate their UK tax liability, which is contained within the tax return helpsheet HS261: Foreign tax credit relief: capital gains.

3.67 HMRC consider that foreign tax credit relief is available in the following circumstances:

- the foreign tax liability charges capital gains as income;
- foreign tax is payable on a no gain, no loss disposal between group companies (within *TCGA 1992, s 171*) and a UK tax liability arises on a subsequent disposal;
- an overseas trade carried on through a branch or agency or permanent establishment is domesticated (ie transferred to a non-resident subsidiary), relief is given under *TCGA 1992, s 140*, a later event gives rise to a UK liability, and foreign tax is charged wholly or partly by reference to the gain accruing at the date of domestication; or
- foreign tax is payable by reference to increases in the value of assets, although there is no disposal for UK tax purposes, and a UK liability arises on a later disposal (HMRC Statement of Practice 06/88).

HMRC have listed in their Double Taxation Relief Manual (at DT2140 onwards) the double taxation agreements for each country which in turn list the taxes that they consider to be admissible (or inadmissible) for tax credit relief. New agreements or treaties are added or revised at regular intervals and the latest information can be found on the Tax Treaty News section of the HMRC website: www.hmrc.gov.uk/si/tax-treaty-news.htm.

Statement of Practice 07/91 (revised in August 2005) sets out how HMRC interpret the requirement in *TIOPA 2010, ss 8, 9, 29, 30* and *129* (previously *ICTA 1988, s 790(12)*) that the foreign tax must 'correspond' to the UK tax in order for relief to be available. Broadly, the question is to be determined by examining the tax within its legislative context in the foreign territory and deciding whether it serves the same function as the UK tax.

EU savings directive: special withholding tax

3.68 Where the consideration for the disposal of an asset giving rise to a chargeable gain, consists of or includes an amount of 'savings income', and 'special withholding tax' is levied in respect of that consideration (or a part of it), then credit relief is available for the amount found by the formula:

$$SWT \times [GUK/(G - SWT)]$$

where:

- SWT is the special withholding tax levied;
- GUK is the amount of the chargeable gain received in the UK; and
- G is the amount of the chargeable gain accruing on the disposal.

'Special withholding tax' means a withholding tax (however described) levied under the law of an EU member state territory outside the UK implementing *article 11* of the *EU Savings Directive*, or levied under a 'corresponding provision of international arrangements' in the case of a territory other than an EU member state (*TIOPA 2010, s 32*).

'Savings income', in the case of special withholding tax levied under the law of an EU member state, has the same meaning as 'interest payment' has for the purposes of the *EU Savings Directive*. If the tax is levied elsewhere, 'savings income' has the same meaning as the corresponding expression has for the purposes of the relevant international arrangements. To the extent that it cannot be set off, special withholding tax is repayable (*TIOPA 2010, s 135(2)*).

Relief by deduction

3.69 Relief for foreign tax may be given by deduction if no foreign tax credit relief is available, or the taxpayer elects to forego any credit (as provided in *TIOPA 2010, s 27*). The effect of the election may be to create or increase an allowable loss. Where foreign tax is suffered on a gain that is the subject of a UK roll-over relief claim (see **Chapter 14**), no foreign tax credit relief is available because there is no UK liability, but relief by deduction reduces both the gain accruing and the amount to be deducted from the acquisition cost of the replacement asset as a result of the roll-over relief claim (*TIOPA 2010, s 113*).

ALTERNATIVE FINANCE ARRANGEMENTS

3.70 'Alternative finance' is the term used in the Finance Act provisions which define the tax treatment for specific types of Islamic finance arrangements that generally avoid the payment or receipt of interest. Under many of these arrangements an asset is sold from one party to another and the return on the deal is taxed as if it were interest rather than a capital gain.

There are alternative finance arrangements defined in *TCGA 1992, Part IV, ch IV*, which deal with transactions that broadly reflect the following Islamic finance structures:

- purchase and resale (*Murabahah*);
- deposit arrangements (*Modaraba*);
- profit-share agency (*Wakala*);
- diminishing share ownership (diminishing *Musharaka*); and
- investment bond (*Sukak*).

Chapter 4

Particular assets

WHAT IS COVERED HERE

4.1 This chapter discusses particular types of asset to which special rules apply:

- shares and securities – **4.2**
- options and deposits – **4.7**
- land – **4.11**
- furnished holiday lettings – **4.22**
- chattels – **4.24**
- wasting assets – **4.26**
- debts – **4.34**
- assets appropriated to and from trading stock – **4.35**.

Various exemptions for certain assets, gains or persons are examined in **Chapter 1**. Private residences are examined in **Chapter 12**.

SHARES AND SECURITIES

4.2 The taxation of gains arising on the disposal of shares has been considerably simplified for disposals made after 5 April 2008 by individuals, trustees and personal representatives. The 'pooling' rules for identifying shares continue to apply for companies, and these are discussed in **Chapter 9**. For illustrations of how the identification rules applied to shares and securities disposed of by non-corporate taxpayers between 5 April 1998 and 6 April 2008, please refer to *Capital Gains Tax 2007/08* (Tottel Publishing).

'Securities' means shares or securities (ie loan capital) of a company and any other assets (eg units in a unit trust) that are dealt in without identifying the particular assets concerned. These are 'fungible' assets in that they all answer to the same definition; the separate components of a holding cannot be identified and distinguished from each other. (This definition of 'securities' is separate from – and wider than – the definition in *TCGA 1992, s 132*, which determines whether loan capital is a chargeable asset.)

Shares or securities of a company are treated as being of the same class only if they are treated as such by a recognised stock exchange, or would be so treated if they were dealt in on a recognised stock exchange (*TCGA 1992, s 104(3)*).

Securities held by a person who acquired them as an employee (of any company) on terms that restrict his right to dispose of them are treated as being of a different class from other securities (*TCGA 1992, s 104(4)*), which do not have such restrictions. Shares with these restrictions are known as 'clogged shares' by HMRC (CG50575).

Share identification: general rules for CGT

4.3 The general rules that apply for CGT (not corporation tax) purposes are summarised below. These rules apply to disposals after 5 April 2008, when all assets held at 31 March 1982 are automatically rebased to their market value at that date (see **3.59**). As indexation allowance and taper relief have been abolished for these taxpayers, it is no longer necessary to compute values for separate pools of shares held on 6 April 1965 and 31 March 1982. All shares of the same company and class, held by the same person in the same capacity, are now generally treated as a single pool of shares that expands or contracts with additions and disposals. This is known as the *section 104* pool or holding. The base cost of each share contained in the *section 104* pool is calculated as an average cost for the entire holding.

Special rules apply to shares acquired through:

- the enterprise management incentive scheme or other approved share option scheme (see **4.4**);
- enterprise investment scheme (see **16.6**); and
- venture capital trusts (see **17.4**).

'Shares' in the following summary includes securities that are within the definition 'securities' set out in **4.2**. Shares disposed of are identified with shares of the same class acquired by the person making the disposal. The shares disposed of are identified with acquisitions in the following order:

(a) any shares acquired on the same day as the disposal (*TCGA 1992, ss 105(1)(b), 106A(9)*);

(b) any shares acquired in the period of 30 days after the disposal, taking earlier acquisitions first (*TCGA 1992, s 106A(5)*);

(c) all other shares in the *section 104* pool which are not acquisitions under (a) or (b) (*TCGA 1992, s 106A(6)*).

With regard to (a), shares of the same class that are acquired (or disposed of) by the same person on the same day and in the same capacity are treated as acquired (or disposed of) in a single transaction. The 30-day rule in (b) was introduced in March 1998 to remove the tax advantage gained by 'bed and breakfasting' shares (see **10.20**) in order to realise losses or utilise the CGT annual exemption.

If there are more shares or securities disposed of that are identified using the rules in (a) to (c) above, the excess is identified with the acquisitions made after the disposal and after the 30-day rule in (b), taking earlier acquisitions in priority to later ones. This could happen where shares have been sold 'short', ie sold before they are acquired.

The date of disposal for share transactions will normally be clear from the broker's statement. In the case of a private sale the principles discussed in **Chapter 2** should be referred to.

Example 4.1

Judith sold 500 ordinary shares in BBH Ltd on 1 December 2010 for £68,000 and had the following share history for ordinary shares in that company:

Date	Transaction	Holding	Cost
1 May 1998	bought	5,000	£5,000
1 September 2007	bought	500	£50,000
	Total:	5,500	£55,000

The 500 shares disposed of on 1 December 2010 are assumed to be 500/5500 of the complete holding of her BBH shares, which collectively has a base cost of £55,000. The gain on the disposal of 500 shares is calculated as:

2010/11		£
Proceeds		68,000
Cost	(500 / 5,500) × £55,000	(5,000)
Taxable gain		63,000

To summarise the *section 104* pool may contain shares of the same class from the same company from the following former share pools and holdings:

- the existing *section 104* pool from 6 April 2008;
- the old 1982 pool;
- shares acquired between 6 April 1998 to 5 April 2008 which were not previously pooled;
- shares acquired prior to 6 April 1965.

EMI and approved share schemes

4.4 The taxpayer may elect for rule (a) in **4.3** to be modified, for acquisitions made after 5 April 2002, where shares are acquired under an approved employee share option scheme or an enterprise management incentive scheme (EMI). The approved share scheme shares are then treated as a separate acquisition, and are treated as disposed of after the non-scheme shares. This election may be beneficial if the allowable expenditure relating to the scheme shares is higher than the average cost computed under the 'same day' rule (*TCGA 1992, ss 105(1)(a), 105A, 105B*).

Reorganisations and stock dividends

4.5 There are special rules to cater for reorganisations and stock dividends (*TCGA 1992, s 127*). Broadly, shares issued on the occasion of a bonus or rights issue are treated as acquired at the same time as the original shares. Where a disposal after a bonus or rights issue gives rise to taper relief, the holding period for the new holding begins with the later of the date of acquisition of the original holding, and 6 April 1998, when taper relief was introduced.

Where a company offers its shareholders (after 5 April 1998) a dividend in the form of additional shares (ie a stock or scrip dividend) as an alternative to cash, the new shares are treated as a free-standing acquisition – they are not related back to the time when the original shares were acquired (*TCGA 1992, s 142*).

Example 4.2

Duncan bought 500 shares in Anybank Plc for £5,000 on 17 May 2000. Anybank Plc announced a one-for-one rights issue of new ordinary shares at £1 each in April 2010. Duncan sold his rights when they were worth £600 and the original holding of 500 shares was worth £8,000.

	Total	Sold	Retained
	£	£	£
Proceeds of sale of rights	600	600	
Market value of shares retained	8,000		8,000
	8,600		
Cost allocated in proportion: (600 / 8,600) × £5,000	(5,000)	(349)	(4,651)
	3,600		
Gain on disposal of rights		251	

The realised gain of £251 is chargeable to CGT.

Relevant securities

4.6 There is a further exception to the general pooling rule for relevant securities. Relevant securities are:

- securities and loan stock identified by the accrued income scheme rules (*ITA 2007, part 12, ch 2*);
- qualifying corporate bonds; and
- securities which represent material interests in non-qualifying offshore collective investment schemes or funds (*ICTA 1988, part 17, ch 5*).

These relevant securities are matched with other relevant securities of the same company, type and class acquired at a later time rather than at an earlier time (*TCGA 1992, s 106A(6)*).

OPTIONS AND DEPOSITS

4.7 An option is an offer to acquire, or dispose of, an asset, which is the subject of the option. It is made clear in *TCGA 1992, s 21* that options are also assets in their own right. When an option is granted the grantor has disposed of an asset (ie the option itself) and the person who acquired the option (the grantee) has acquired an asset. This applies even in the case where the option is abandoned. In many cases the grant of the option will be treated as part of a larger transaction (see below). The basic rules relating to the grant, exercise and abandonment of options are set out below (*TCGA 1992, s 144(1)*).

So far as the person who granted the option is concerned, the time of the asset's disposal for CGT purposes is the time of the following disposal:

- if the option binds the grantor to sell, the disposal made in fulfilment of the grantor's obligations under the option; or
- if the option binds the grantor to buy, the disposal made to the grantor in consequence of the exercise of the option.

The date the option is exercised a separate contract is made in relation to the asset under the option, and the actual option is disposed of. The date of exercise of the option is thus the disposal date for the option.

There was an exception for share options granted under an enterprise management incentive (EMI) scheme, where the qualifying holding period for taper relief on the shares acquired under the option began on the date the option was granted (*TCGA 1992, Sch 7D, para 15*). The holding period for entrepreneurs' relief in respect of shares acquired under EMI begins when the option is exercised and the shares are acquired, not when the option is granted. Most employees who acquire shares in their employing company under EMI will not qualify for entrepreneurs' relief as they will not hold at least 5% of the ordinary voting shares of the company (see **11.10**).

Exercise of an option

4.8 If an option is exercised, the grant of the option and the transaction taking place on its exercise are merged into a single transaction. Where the option binds the grantor (A) to sell, the consideration for the grant is added to the sale consideration in A's CGT computation. Where the option binds the grantor (A) to buy, then the consideration received by A for that option is deducted from the cost of A's acquisition (*TCGA 1992, s 144(2)*).

Where the person (B) who is entitled to exercise an option does so, there is no disposal by him. The acquisition of the option and the transaction taking place on its exercise are treated as a single transaction. Where the option binds the grantor (A) to sell, the cost of acquiring the option forms part of B's allowable expenditure on acquisition of the asset. Where the option binds the grantor (A) to buy, the cost of the option is treated as a cost incidental to B's disposal to A (*TCGA 1992, s 144(2)*).

Abandonment of an option

4.9 The abandonment of an option by the person entitled to exercise it is not generally a disposal of an asset by him (*TCGA 1992, s 144(4)*). However, in the following situations the abandonment of the option is a disposal when the option is:

- a quoted option which is listed on a recognised stock exchange, to subscribe for shares in a company;

- a traded option or financial option, which is an option listed on a recognised stock exchange or recognised futures exchange; or
- an option to acquire assets exercisable by a person intending to use them, if acquired, for the purpose of a trade that he carries on.

Forfeited deposits

4.10 Where a deposit of purchase money for a prospective purchase is forfeited because the transaction is abandoned, there is no disposal by the prospective purchaser and no capital loss can arise. The prospective seller, however, is treated as disposing of an option (*TCGA 1992, s 144(7)*).

LAND

4.11 Land (including any building situated on it), or an interest in or right over land, is an asset for CGT purposes. However, in certain circumstances land transactions can give rise to a charge to income tax (or corporation tax) as trading or other income. This may apply where the land is acquired with the intention of selling it for profit, or holding it as trading stock, or developing it prior to disposal at a profit. See Chapter 7 of *Income Tax 2010/11* (Bloomsbury Professional) for a discussion of the relevant anti-avoidance provisions.

The legal owner of land will not always be the person who has the beneficial interest in it. In most cases it is the beneficial owner who is chargeable to CGT. HMRC regard the following factors as indicative of beneficial ownership, although each case is considered on its particular facts:

- legal title (in the absence of any contrary evidence the legal owner will normally also be the beneficial owner);
- occupation of the land;
- receipt of any rental income from the land;
- provision of the funds used to purchase the land; and
- receipt of the sale proceeds from a disposal of the land (CG70230).

Part disposals of land

4.12 The special rules that apply to small part disposals of land are discussed in **2.5**. Where the conditions are satisfied, the taxpayer may claim that the part disposal does not constitute a disposal for CGT purposes. The disposal proceeds are instead deducted from the cost of the land when calculating a gain on its subsequent disposal.

The grant of a lease is a part disposal and the CGT treatment depends on the term of the lease (see **4.17**).

Leases of land

4.13 It is important to distinguish between the grant of a new lease by a landlord, and the assignment of an existing lease. A leasehold interest entitles the holder to exclusive possession of the property for a fixed term. A lease includes, for this purpose:

- an underlease, sublease, tenancy or licence;
- an agreement for a lease, underlease, sublease, tenancy or licence; and
- a corresponding interest in land outside the UK (*TCGA 1992, Sch 8, para 10(1)(a)*).

There are special rules to determine the duration of a lease for these purposes, for example, where the terms of the lease include a provision that either allows the landlord to terminate the lease before the end of the stated term, or allows the tenant to extend the term.

Any term of a lease that makes it unlikely that it will continue beyond a certain time – for example, a provision for an increase in rent to an amount greatly in excess of a commercial rent – is treated as granted for a period ending at that time (*TCGA 1992, Sch 8, para 8*).

Assignment of a lease

4.14 The assignment of a lease is treated as a disposal (not a part disposal) of an interest in the property. The CGT treatment depends on how long the lease has to run at the time of the assignment:

- the assignment of a long lease is subject to the normal CGT rules;
- the assignment of a short lease (ie one that has no more than 50 years to run at the time of the disposal) is a disposal of a 'wasting asset', and only a percentage of the original cost is allowable for CGT purposes, as set out below.

A lease does not become a wasting asset until its duration does not exceed 50 years. Once it has become a wasting asset, its value does not waste away at a uniform rate (as described in **4.27** in relation to other wasting assets). The rate of decline in the value of the lease increases towards the end of its term and the allowable expenditure is restricted by reference to the table in *TCGA 1992, Sch 8, para 1*, as explained below.

Exclusion from acquisition expenditure

4.15 A fraction of the acquisition expenditure (within *TCGA 1992, s 38(1)(a)*) that is equal to:

$$\frac{P(1) - P(3)}{P(1)}$$

is excluded, where:

- P(1) is the percentage shown in the table for the duration of the lease at the beginning of the period of ownership; and
- P(3) is the percentage shown in the table for the duration of the lease at the time of the disposal (*TCGA 1992, Sch 8, para 1(4)*).

Exclusion from enhancement expenditure

4.16 A fraction of the enhancement expenditure (within *TCGA 1992, s 38(1)(b)*) that is equal to:

$$\frac{P(2) - P(3)}{P(2)}$$

is excluded, where:

- P(2) is the percentage shown in the table for the duration of the lease at the time when the expenditure is first reflected in the nature of the lease; and
- P(3) is the percentage shown in the table for the duration of the lease at the time of the disposal (*TCGA 1992, Sch 8, para 1(4)*).

Grant of a lease

4.17 The owner of a freehold interest may grant a lease, or a leaseholder may grant a sublease for all or a part of the remaining term of his leasehold interest. The grant of a lease out of a freehold or longer lease is treated as an asset derived from another asset (see **3.46**).

The grant of a lease or sublease is a part disposal because the taxpayer retains an interest in the property. Part of the lease premium is chargeable to income tax as additional rent if the lease is for 50 years or less (see **4.19** and **4.20**). The part that is not treated as rent represents the proceeds of a part disposal for CGT purposes.

If a lease is granted to a connected person, or otherwise granted in a transaction not made at arm's length (see **3.6**), the market value is taken to be the premium received (*TCGA 1992, s 17, 18*).

Grant of a long lease

4.18 Where a long lease is granted out of either a freehold interest or a long lease, the computation of the gain accruing follows the normal part disposal rules, using the formula [A/(A + B)] (*TCGA 1992, s 42*), as described in **2.4**. In this situation:

- A is the amount of the premium received; and
- B is the value of the interest retained by the landlord plus the value of the right to receive rents payable under the lease (*TCGA 1992, Sch 8, para 2*).

Grant of a short lease out of freehold or long lease

4.19 Where a short lease is granted out of a freehold interest, or a short sublease is granted out of a long lease, the following rules apply.

First, part of the premium is treated as rent and is chargeable to:

- income tax under *ITTOIA 2005, s 276*; or
- corporation tax under *CTA 2009, s 217.*

This amount is excluded from the consideration for the disposal (*TCGA 1992, Sch 8, para 5(1)*). It is calculated using the formula set out in the relevant income tax or corporation tax provision.

Secondly, the [A/(A+B)] part disposal formula in **4.18** is modified so that:

- A in the numerator is not the whole of the premium received but only the part of it that is not treated as rent, but
- A in the denominator (A + B) is unchanged because (A + B) has to represent the value of the whole interest before the lease was granted (*TCGA 1992, s 42(2)*; CG70961).

Grant of a short sublease out of a short lease

4.20 Where a short sublease is granted out of a short lease, the part disposal formula in *TCGA 1992, s 42* does not apply. A short lease is a wasting asset and the allowable expenditure to be set against the premium in computing the gain is restricted so as to allow, as a deduction, the expenditure that will waste away during the term of the sublease (*TCGA 1992, Sch 8, para 4*).

The amount of the premium that is treated as rent is, in this case, deducted in arriving at the chargeable gain. It is not excluded from the consideration for the disposal (as shown in **4.19**) (*TCGA 1992, Sch 8, para 5(2)*).

Exchange of joint interests in land

4.21 If the proceeds received on the compulsory acquisition of land by an authority are reinvested in acquiring new land, a form of CGT roll-over relief may be available – see **17.21**.

Relief is also given on similar lines where there is an exchange of interests in land that is in joint ownership (*TCGA 1992, ss 248A–248E*). Before 6 April 2010 this CGT relief was given under Extra-statutory Concession D26.

The relief is available where:

- a holding of land is held jointly and, as a result of the exchange, each joint owner becomes the sole owner of part of the land formerly owned jointly; or
- a number of separate holdings of land are held jointly and, as a result of the exchange, each joint owner becomes the sole owner of one or more holdings.

There are no restrictions on the use of the land, either before or after the exchange. However, the relief is denied or restricted where land acquired on the exchange is, or becomes subsequently, a dwelling house (or part of a dwelling house) eligible for the main residence relief within *TCGA 1992, ss 222–223* within six years of the date of the exchange (*TCGA 1992, s 248C*). See **Chapter 12** for a detailed discussion of the main residence relief.

However, the relief may be claimed where, as a result of the exchange, individuals who were joint beneficial owners of two or more main residences become sole owners of just one home each, providing that any gain accruing on a disposal of each dwelling house immediately after the exchange would be exempt by virtue of main residence relief (*TCGA 1992, s 248E*).

FURNISHED HOLIDAY LETTINGS

4.22 Letting property is not regarded as a trade for income tax purposes, so property used for a letting business does not qualify for the various capital gains and inheritance tax reliefs that apply to business assets that are used for a trade. However, from 6 April 1984 the 'commercial letting of furnished holiday accommodation' in the UK has been treated as a trade (*TCGA 1992, s 241*). This allows a number of special tax reliefs to apply (see **4.23**). For a discussion of the conditions that must be met for the letting of a property to qualify as commercial furnished holiday lettings (FHL) see Chapter 7 of *Income Tax 2010/11* (Bloomsbury Professional).

The requirement for the let property to be situated in the UK to qualify as FHL was found to be not compliant with European law, so on 22 April 2009 HMRC announced that property located in any EEA country could qualify as FHL, if the conditions were met, with retrospective effect. The EEA countries consist of all 27 member states of the EU plus Iceland, Norway and Liechtenstein. On the same date it was announced the FHL special treatment would be withdrawn in all cases from 6 April 2010 . However, due to some pre-election bargaining, the FHL abolition did not occur. The conditions for FHL treatment to apply are expected to be amended from 6 April 2011, (1 April 2011 for companies), but the FHL special treatment will remain in some form.

The CGT reliefs

4.23 A property business that consists of FHL properties is treated as a trade, and all such lettings made by a particular person (or partnership or body of persons) are treated as one trade, for all of the following purposes:

(a) roll-over relief on replacement of business assets (*TCGA 1992, s 152*);

(b) hold-over relief for gifts of business assets (*TCGA 1992, s 165*);

(c) relief for loans to traders (*TCGA 1992, s 253*);

(d) taper relief for disposals before 6 April 2008 (*TCGA 1992, Sch A1*);

(e) entrepreneurs' relief for disposals on or after 6 April 2008 (*TCGA 1992, ss 169H–169S*); and

(f) the substantial shareholdings exemption for companies (*TCGA 1992, Sch 7AC*).

As long as the FHL conditions are met for the tax year, or accounting period for a company, the accommodation is taken to be used only for the purposes of the lettings trade in that tax year. This applies even if the accommodation is let out of season for longer than the prescribed 31 days to one tenant.

However, if the property is neither let commercially nor available to be so let for a part of the period, and it is not prevented from being so let by construction or repair work, then the trade is not treated as carried on during that part of the period (*TCGA 1992, s 241(3)–(5)*).

A 'just and reasonable' apportionment is to be made where accommodation is let and only a part of it is holiday accommodation (*TCGA 1992, s 241(7)*).

Where roll-over relief is obtained on a disposal – by virtue of (a) above – and the main residence relief is available on a disposal of the replacement asset, the gain eligible for main residence relief is reduced by the amount of the reduction in allowable expenditure to take account of the roll-over relief claim. The effect is that the main residence relief is restricted to the part of the gain that exceeds the amount of the earlier gain that was rolled over (*TCGA 1992, s 241(6)*; CG61452).

CHATTELS

4.24 An asset is a chattel if it is tangible, moveable property, ie a physical object that is not permanently attached to land or a building and can be moved easily without damaging its surroundings. Examples would include paintings and small items of plant and machinery.

A gain accruing on the disposal of a chattel that is not a wasting asset (see **4.26**) is not a chargeable gain if the amount or value of the consideration is £6,000 or less (*TCGA 1992, s 262(1)*).

Where the consideration exceeds £6,000, a marginal relief is deducted in arriving at the chargeable gain. The chargeable gain is restricted to five-thirds of the amount by which the consideration exceeds £6,000 (*TCGA 1992, s 262(2)*).

If a loss accrues on the disposal and the consideration does not exceed £6,000, the allowable loss is restricted by substituting £6,000 for the actual consideration. There is no such restriction if the consideration exceeds £6,000 (*TCGA 1992, s 262(3)*).

The chattels exemption does not apply to disposals of currency of any description, or disposals of commodities dealt with on a terminal market (*TCGA 1992, s 262(6)*).

Example 4.3

Hannah sells a painting for £7,200. The gain accruing, before deduction of the chattels exemption, is £5,500. Marginal relief is available so that the chargeable gain is restricted to 5/3 × (£7,200 – £6,000) = £2,000.

Parts of a set

4.25 Special rules are designed to prevent the taxpayer splitting a set of articles worth more than £6,000 into individual assets and selling them for less than £6,000 in order to secure the chattel exemption.

They apply where the taxpayer has disposed of two or more assets that have formed part of a set of articles, all of which he has owned at one time, and the disposals were made (either on the same occasion or on different occasions) to:

(a) the same person;

(b) persons acting 'in concert' (see below); or

(c) persons who are connected persons (see **3.16**).

In these circumstances, the transactions are treated as a single transaction disposing of a single asset. The chattels exemption, as described in **4.24**, is applied to the deemed single transaction and apportioned accordingly among the various assets (*TCGA 1992, s 262(4)*).

HMRC take the view that a number of articles will form a set only if they are essentially similar and complementary and their value taken together is greater than their total individual value (CG76632).

With regard to (b) above, HMRC consider that if persons not connected with each other acquire assets forming part of a set, the fact that they have done so is not sufficient. There must be evidence that they have previously agreed to act together to acquire the assets, such as a number of dealers acting together at an auction (CG76634).

WASTING ASSETS

Exemption for wasting chattels

4.26 As a general rule, no chargeable gain accrues on a disposal of a 'wasting chattel', ie an asset that is both tangible moveable property (see **4.24**) and a wasting asset (see **4.27**). Where an asset has been used for business purposes and has qualified for capital allowances the gain may be taxable if the disposal consideration was more than £6,000, see **4.28** (*TCGA 1992, s 45(1)*).

Wasting asset: definition

4.27 A 'wasting asset' is generally an asset with a predictable life of no more than 50 years, as determined at the time the asset was acquired (CG76704). In the case of tangible moveable property, 'life' means useful life having regard to the taxpayer's purpose in acquiring or providing the asset. Freehold land is never a wasting asset, irrespective of the nature of the land itself or the buildings on it.

Plant and machinery is always regarded as having a predictable life of less than 50 years. It is assumed, in estimating its predictable life, that:

- the asset's life will end when it is finally put out of use as being unfit for further use; and
- the asset will be used in the normal manner and to the normal extent throughout its estimated life.

A life interest in settled property is not regarded as a wasting asset until the predicted life expectancy of the life tenant is 50 years or less. The HMRC Policy Business (Life Assurance) department will provide an estimate of the predictable life of such life interests (*TCGA 1992, s 44,* CG38022).

Wasting assets qualifying for capital allowances

4.28 All items of plant and machinery are wasting assets, but unless the item is also a chattel the wasting chattels exemption (see **4.26**) does not apply. However, the allowable expenditure deducted in the CGT computation may be restricted (see **4.29**) if the taxpayer:

(a) used the asset solely for the purposes of a trade, profession or vocation from the beginning of his period of ownership and either claimed or could have claimed capital allowances for expenditure that is also allowable expenditure in the CGT computation; or

(b) incurred any expenditure on the asset (or interest in it) that has otherwise qualified in full for capital allowances (*TCGA 1992, s 45(2)*).

Separate CGT computations are required where:

- the taxpayer has used the asset partly for the purposes of the business and partly for other purposes;
- he has used it for business purposes for only part of the period of ownership; or
- the asset has qualified in part only for capital allowances.

In these circumstances, both the consideration for the disposal and the allowable expenditure are apportioned by reference to the extent to which the expenditure qualified for capital allowances, and the exemption is not given for the part of the gain apportioned to the use or expenditure described in (a) or (b) above (*TCGA 1992, s 45(3)*).

The exemption does not apply to a disposal of commodities that is made by a person dealing on a terminal market (*TCGA 1992, s 45(4)*).

Example 4.4

Victor bought an aircraft on 31 May 2000 at a cost of £90,000 for use in his air charter business. It has been agreed that Victor's non-business use of the aircraft amounts to 1/10, on a flying hours basis, and capital allowances and running costs have accordingly been restricted for income tax purposes.

On 1 June 2010, Victor sells the aircraft for £185,000. The aircraft is agreed as having a useful life of 20 years at the date it was acquired. Only the business use part of the gain arising on the disposal of the aircraft is taxable.

2010/11	£
Relevant portion of consideration 9/10 × £185,000	166,500
Relevant portion of expenditure 9/10 × £90,000	(81,000)
Taxable gain	85,500

Restriction of allowable expenditure

4.29 The gain accruing on the disposal of a wasting asset that is not exempt (see **4.26**) is computed on the assumption that an equal amount of expenditure on the asset is written off every day. This restriction does not apply, however, to certain wasting assets qualifying for capital allowances (see **4.33**).

Acquisition costs

4.30 The asset's residual or scrap value is deducted from the amount of expenditure incurred on its acquisition (including incidental costs) and the balance remaining is written off – from its full cost down to nil – at a uniform rate from the time of the acquisition of the asset to the end of its life. The residual or scrap value in this calculation is adjusted for any enhancement expenditure (see below) that increases that value.

This writing down of the allowable expenditure is achieved by excluding from the acquisition costs the fraction:

$$\frac{T(1)}{L}$$

where

- L is the predictable life of the asset at the time when it was acquired or provided by the person making the disposal; and

- T(1) is the period from that time to the time of disposal (*TCGA 1992, s 46(2)(a)*).

Enhancement costs

4.31 Enhancement expenditure is written off, in the same way, from the time when it is first reflected in the asset's state or nature to the end of the asset's life (*TCGA 1992, s 46(1), (3)*).

The allowable expenditure to be excluded from the enhancement costs is given by the fraction:

$$\frac{T(2)}{L - [T(1) - T(2)]}$$

where

- L is the predictable life of the asset at the time when it was acquired or provided by the person making the disposal; and
- T(2) is the period from the time when the enhancement expenditure is first reflected in the state or nature of the asset to the time of disposal (*TCGA 1992, s 46(2)(b)*).

Residual or scrap value

4.32 The 'residual or scrap value' of a wasting asset is the value that the asset is predicted to have at the end of its predictable life. Where the nature of an asset does not determine immediately its predictable life and its residual or scrap value, such questions are determined on the basis of facts that were known or ascertainable at the time when the person making the disposal acquired or provided the asset (*TCGA 1992, s 44(2), (3)*).

Wasting assets qualifying for capital allowances

4.33 The restriction of allowable expenditure (see **4.29**) does not apply if the taxpayer:

(a) used the asset solely for the purposes of a trade, profession or vocation from the beginning of his period of ownership and either claimed or could have claimed capital allowances for expenditure that is also allowable expenditure for the purpose of the CGT computation (see **3.41**); or

(b) incurred any expenditure on the asset (or interest in it) that has otherwise qualified in full for capital allowances (*TCGA 1992, s 47(1)*).

Separate CGT computations are required where:

- the taxpayer has used the asset partly for the purposes of the business and partly for other purposes;
- he has used it for business purposes for only part of the period of ownership; or
- the asset has qualified in part only for capital allowances.

In these circumstances both the consideration for the disposal and the allowable expenditure are apportioned having regard to the extent to which the expenditure qualified for capital allowances. The consideration for the disposal is apportioned in the same proportions as the allowable expenditure is apportioned, except that any apportionment used in computing a balancing allowance or balancing charge by reference to the disposal is to be used for this purpose.

The restriction described in **4.29** does not apply to the part of the gain apportioned to the use or expenditure described in (a) or (b) above (*TCGA 1992, s 47(2)*).

DEBTS

4.34 A debt is an asset for CGT purposes. However, where a person (A) incurs a debt to another person (B), no chargeable gain accrues to the original creditor (B) on a disposal of the debt. Although a gain may arise where the disposal is of a debt on a security, or money held in a foreign currency bank account that does not represent currency acquired for personal expenditure outside the UK (*TCGA 1992, ss 21(1), 251, 252*).

For individuals, trustees and personal representatives, a debt is, therefore, not normally subject to CGT unless it is a 'debt on a security' (meaning, broadly, marketable loan stock) See *Taylor Clark International Ltd v Lewis* [1998] STC 1259, for a full definition of a debt on a security. Most loan stock is a type of 'qualifying corporate bond (QCB)', which is an exempt asset (*TCGA 1992, s 115*).

Gains on simple debts (which are not debts on securities) are exempt from CGT and no relief is available for losses. However, capital loss relief is available for losses incurred (or guarantee payments made) in respect of loans made after 11 April 1978 to UK traders, where the loan has become irrecoverable and certain conditions are met. This relief is discussed at **17.16**.

Profits and losses on loans by companies are generally dealt with under the 'loan relationship' rules. Corporate debt is, therefore, outside the scope of corporation tax on chargeable gains but is otherwise included in the calculation of profits chargeable to corporation tax. Refer to Chapter 14 of *Corporation Tax 2010/11* (Bloomsbury Professional) for a discussion of the loan relationship rules.

ASSETS APPROPRIATED TO OR FROM TRADING STOCK

Assets appropriated to trading stock

4.35 If the taxpayer appropriates a valuable asset he has owned personally into his business where it is categorised as a stock item, then in the absence of any election (see **4.36**) he is treated as if, at the time of the appropriation, he sold the asset for its market value. This is the case providing that a chargeable gain or allowable loss would have accrued on an actual sale at market value (*TCGA 1992, s 161(1)*).

Election

4.36 This deemed disposal rule does not apply where the asset is appropriated for the purposes of a trade carried on wholly or partly in the UK, the income of which is chargeable to income tax or corporation tax, and the taxpayer makes an election (*TCGA 1992, s 161(3)*).

The effect of the election is that the asset's market value at the time of the appropriation is treated as reduced, in computing the trading income, by the amount of the chargeable gain that would have accrued on the deemed sale mentioned in **4.35**. If an allowable loss would have arisen, then the market value is increased by the amount of that loss. An election made by a person carrying on a trade in partnership at the time of the appropriation is effective only if the other partners concur in the election (*TCGA 1992, s 161(3), (4)*).

The election must be made within the period that ends on the first anniversary of 31 January following the tax year in which the accounting period ended that contained the appropriation to stock. For corporation tax purposes the election must be made within two years after the end of the accounting period in which the appropriation took place (*TCGA 1992, s 161(3A)*).

Note this election apparently works independently of the requirement to value the stock item within the trade as if it had been acquired at market value (*ITTOIA 2005, s 172C* for income tax, *CTA 2009, s 158* for corporation tax). The combination of the capital gains and the income tax/corporation tax provisions could wipe out all the taxable profit on an item of stock.

Example 4.5

Trulove purchased an antique desk for his personal use some years ago for £600. In May 2010 he transfers the desk into his own business (Trulove Antiques) to sell at the market value of £1,600. The gain in Trulove's hands is £1,000, but as he has a number of other gains arising in 2010/11 he makes an election under *TCGA 1992, s 161(3)* to transfer the desk at a value of £600, reducing his taxable gain to nil. Trulove Antiques immediately sells the desk for £1,600. However, *ITTOIA 2005, s 172C* requires the desk to be valued at its market value of £1,600 as it enters the business, so the taxable profit on the salc of the desk is nil.

Assets appropriated from trading stock

4.37 If the taxpayer appropriates for another purpose an asset forming part of his trading stock, or he retains the asset on the cessation of his trade, he is treated as having acquired it at that time for a consideration equal to the amount brought into the accounts as a trading receipt (*TCGA 1992, s 161(2)*). The provisions in *ITTOIA 2005, s 172B* and *CTA 2009, s 157* require the amount brought into the accounts to be the open market value of the item, where the stock is appropriated on or after 12 March 2008.

Chapter 5

Foreign issues

This chapter focuses on the CGT implications of an individual's residence and domicile status. The residence status of trustees is examined in **Chapter 8**. See **Chapter 9** and *Corporation Tax 2010/11* (Bloomsbury Professional) regarding companies.

This Chapter is intended only to set out an initial guide to foreign issues. For a more detailed analysis on the treatment of foreign income and gains see *Booth: Residence, Domicile and UK Taxation*, 14th edition (Bloomsbury Professional).

BASIS OF THE CHARGE TO CGT

5.1 A person is chargeable to CGT in respect of chargeable gains accruing to him on the disposal of assets in a tax year:

- during any part of which he is 'resident' in the UK; or
- during which he is 'ordinarily resident' in the UK (*TCGA 1992, ss 1, 2(1)*).

'Accruing' here means realised or deemed to be realised, rather than accumulated over a period.

Where an individual is not domiciled in the UK but resident or ordinarily resident in the UK, the remittance basis applies for CGT (see **5.31**).

Anti-avoidance rules provide for a person to be chargeable to CGT on gains accruing to others in certain circumstances. For example:

- a non-resident person carrying on a business in the UK through a branch or agency (or through a permanent establishment, in the case of a company) is chargeable to CGT (or corporation tax) on gains arising from assets in the UK that are used for the purposes of the business (see **5.22**);

- a person who is a 'temporary non-resident' of the UK may be chargeable on gains accruing during years of non-residence (see **5.27**); and
- the gains of a non-resident trust (see **8.42**) or company (see **5.45**) may be attributed to a UK-resident individual.

LOCATION OF ASSETS

5.2 It is often unnecessary to establish the location of an asset for CGT purposes, but in some circumstances the asset's location will determine the extent of any liability. For example:

- non-residents are chargeable to tax on gains arising on the disposal or deemed disposal of UK assets used to carry on a business in the UK (see **5.22**); and
- a remittance basis applies to non-domiciled individuals, but only in relation to non-UK assets (see **5.27**).

The territorial limits of the UK are set out in **5.3**. Most of the rules fixing the location of assets for CGT purposes are contained in *TCGA 1992, s 275* and the main rules are summarised briefly in **Table 5.1**. Note also the changes enacted in *F(No 2)A 2005* as summarised below.

Table 5.1

Asset	*Location*
1. Immovable property	Where the property is situated
2. Tangible movable property or chattels	Where the property is situated
3. Debts (secured or unsecured)	Where the creditor resides
4. Shares or securities of a local or governmental authority	The country of that authority
5. Other shares or securities	See below
6. Ships or aircraft	The country in which the owner is resident
7. Goodwill	Where the trade, etc is carried on
8. Patents, trademarks and registered designs	Where they are registered
9. Copyright, design right and franchises	Where the right or design is exercisable
10. A judgment debt	Where the judgment is recorded
11. Futures, options and intangible assets	See below

With regard to item 5, anti-avoidance legislation applies to assets such as bearer shares in a UK company with effect from 16 March 2005. Shares in, or debentures of, a company incorporated in the UK (other than shares, etc within item 4) are treated as situated in the UK. Subject to that rule, registered shares or debentures are situated where they are registered. If they are registered in more than one register, they are situated where the principal register is situated (*TCGA 1992, s 275(1)* as amended by *F(No 2)A 2005, s 34* and *Sch 4, para 4).*

New rules for determining the location of futures, options and underlying intangible assets (item 11) were also introduced with effect from 16 March 2005. The basic rule is that such assets are located in the UK if they are subject to UK law (*TCGA 1992, ss 275A–275C* inserted by *F(No 2)A 2005, s 34* and *Sch 4, para 5).*

TERRITORIAL LIMITS OF CGT

5.3 The UK comprises Great Britain and Northern Ireland. It includes the UK's territorial seas but excludes the Isle of Man and the Channel Islands. However CGT is not limited to gains on the disposal of UK assets.

Meaning of residence and domicile since FA 2008

Overview

5.4 'Resident' and 'ordinarily resident' have the same meanings in *TCGA 1992* as they have in the *Income Tax Acts* (ie the enactments relating to income tax, including any provisions of the *Corporation Tax Acts* which relate to income tax) (*TCGA 1992, s 9(1)*; *ICTA 1988, s 831(1)*). In each case the legislation has been revised by *FA 2008, s 24*, as shown below. The interpretation of 'residence' and 'ordinary residence' is largely based on decisions made in the courts and the interpretation of these decisions adopted by HMRC, so uncertainty therefore prevails.

An individual's domicile is also a key factor in determining a person's liability to CGT. An individual who meets the residence tests outlined in **5.10** and is domiciled in any part of the UK is chargeable to CGT on gains accruing on the disposal of assets situated anywhere in the world. However, the liability of a non-domiciled individual in respect of gains accruing on the disposal of non-UK assets was formerly limited to gains remitted to the UK (see **5.31**), though that general rule has been severely cut down by *FA 2008, s 25*, which introduces *Sch 7*. In this chapter, any reference to *Sch 7* is to *FA 2008, Sch 7*.

HMRC's Centre for Non-Residents handles matters relating to a taxpayer's residence status: see www.hmrc.gov.uk/cnr. Detailed guidance is available in HMRC6 – Residence, Domicile and Remittance Basis (replacing IR20, which has ceased to apply from 6 April 2009.) HMRC6 was published to update guidance in light of the changes brought about by *FA 2008, s 24* and *Sch 7*. Following criticism from professional bodies Part 5 of HMRC6, which deals with the remittance basis, has been updated in February 2010. However caution still needs to be exercised in relation to HMRC6, which is couched in such general terms that it is difficult to apply to more complex situations. The residency rules are difficult to interpret. Careful consideration needs to be given to case law, established practice and HMRC6. The Treasury and stakeholders are currently working together to produce a statutory residence test.

Domicile

5.5 Under UK law, every individual has a domicile, but only one domicile. For capital gains tax purposes, a person is domiciled in the state in which he is domiciled under the general law. The deemed domicile rules for inheritance tax in *IHTA 1986, s 267* have no application to capital gains tax. It is difficult to acquire a domicile of choice which will displace a UK domicile of origin, difficult to know if this has indeed been achieved, and it requires fairly drastic lifestyle changes. Change of domicile is a matter of fact and generally requires a detailed analysis of the individual's circumstances. Those who do have, or can with determination acquire, a non-UK domicile could until recently use this to minimise the impact of capital gains tax on their estates, even whilst retaining some assets and presence here, but that has now changed.

HMRC6 on pages 24 to 30 includes a number of flowcharts and examples to assist the understanding of domicile.

5.6 There are three different types of domicile:

- domicile of origin;
- domicile of dependence; and
- domicile of choice.

They are described as different *types* of domicile because they can be acquired and lost in different ways. The country in which a person is domiciled is sometimes described as his permanent home (see *Winans v Attorney General* [1904] AC 287). This can be a useful description, and it is certainly true that domicile requires a degree of permanence which residence, by contrast, does not. Remember, though, that both domicile of origin and domicile of dependence are acquired by operation of law rather than by choice: it is possible for a person to be domiciled in a place where he has never been, let alone had a home or lived permanently.

Domicile of origin

5.7 Everyone acquires a domicile of origin at birth and this remains his domicile until it is replaced by a domicile of dependence or a domicile or choice. It is important to identify a person's domicile of origin because it can revive when a domicile of choice is lost. A person's domicile of origin is:

- his father's domicile at the time of his birth; unless
- his parents were not married; or
- his father died before he was born.

In those other cases, his domicile of origin will be his mother's domicile. Although as a matter of fact it will often be the country in which he was born, this need not be so.

Example 5.1

A child might be born in California to parents who had lived there for 20 years. Suppose that the father had an English domicile of origin and that this had not been displaced by a domicile of choice. In that case, the child would acquire an English domicile of origin at birth despite the fact that it might never come to England.

A domicile of origin is the most clinging, tenacious form and will be displaced only if a person acquires a domicile of choice or a domicile of dependence.

Domicile of dependence

5.8 Domicile of dependence now only affect children under 16 and persons of unsound mind. Prior to 1 January 1974, this category included married women. Before that date, a woman acquired her husband's domicile on marriage and her domicile changed when his did. This rule was abolished by the *Domicile and Matrimonial Proceedings Act 1973*, but has some relevance to women who were married before 1 January 1974. The rule has no relevance to women married on or after 1 January 1974.

Domicile of choice

5.9 A domicile of choice is acquired by both physical presence in another country *and* the intention of settling there permanently. It will not be acquired if, for example, that intention is conditional; nor will it be acquired by going to a country for work, even for an extended period, unless there is a definite intention to stay there permanently once the employment has ceased.

A domicile of choice can be lost by leaving the country without any definite intention of returning. A person will acquire a new domicile of choice if he goes to another country with the intention of settling there permanently. If no new domicile of choice is acquired, his domicile of origin will revive.

A person seeking to establish that a domicile of origin has been lost and a domicile of choice acquired has to discharge a heavy burden of proof. This is equally so whether it is the taxpayer whose domicile of origin is in the UK and who is arguing that it has been superseded by the acquisition of a domicile of choice; or HMRC arguing that a taxpayer whose domicile of origin is outside the UK has lost that domicile and acquired a domicile of choice in the UK.

For example, the Revenue argued in favour of acquisition of domicile of choice before the Special Commissioners in *F and another (personal representatives of F deceased) v IRC* [2000] STC (SCD) 1 but failed to prove that the deceased had lost his Iranian domicile of origin and acquired a UK domicile of choice. In *IRC v Bullock* [1976] STC 409, the taxpayer had been brought up in Canada but had come to live in England in 1932. He married in England and lived there virtually constantly thereafter but was held to have retained his Canadian domicile of origin because his intention, in the event of surviving his wife, was to return to Canada permanently. This meant that he could not be described as having a settled intention of remaining in England permanently.

In *Re Furse, Furse v IRC* [1980] STC 596, on the other hand, the taxpayer had been born in Rhode Island in 1883 and was a US citizen but had a close connection with England throughout his life. He and his wife had a family house in New York and visited it regularly but they also had a farm in Sussex. It had been bought by the wife in 1924 and the taxpayer lived there until his death in 1963. Unlike the taxpayer in *Bullock*, there was evidence that this taxpayer was happy in the Sussex farm. The only suggestion that he might ever leave England was if and when he was no longer fit enough to lead an active life on the farm. He did not really wish to leave and was quite settled in England. The court accordingly found that he died domiciled in England.

The case of *Re Clore (No 2)* [1984] STC 609 shows how important it is, if there is a settled intention of acquiring a domicile of choice in another jurisdiction, that there is plenty of clear written evidence of that intention and that matters are not just left to the recollections of friends and acquaintances after the death of the individual.

The effect on domicile, as it happens in a non-tax context, of the acquisition of British citizenship was illustrated in the case of *Re Bheekhun deceased* (CA, 2 December 1998, unreported). Mr Bheekhun had a domicile of origin in Mauritius. He came to the UK to find work in 1960 at the age of 29. When Mauritius became independent he had to choose whether to take British citizenship or Mauritian citizenship. He chose British citizenship, although he retained business links with Mauritius, acquired properties there and later acquired a Mauritian passport. At all times, he continued to live and work in the UK. When he renewed his UK passport, it described him as resident in the UK. After his death, his separated spouse claimed under the *Inheritance (Provision for Family and Dependants) Act 1975* and her claim depended upon establishing that he died domiciled in the UK. The Court of Appeal upheld the decision that he had acquired a domicile of choice in the UK by the time of his death.

We should not conclude from this decision that citizenship is a determinant of domicile. It is not. The case remains unreported, so we have to assume that Mr Bheekhun's choice of a UK passport was simply one fact taken into account as evidence of his intention to settle permanently in the UK. The question ultimately remains one of fact and that the weight attached to any particular fact will depend on all the circumstances.

Allen and Hateley (as executors of Johnson deceased) v HMRC [2005] STC (SCD) 614 concerned Mrs Johnson, who was born in England in 1922, but moved abroad with her husband in 1953. She was diagnosed as suffering from Parkinson's disease in 1975. The couple settled in Spain in 1982 and bought a house there. Following her husband's death in 1996, Mrs Johnson moved to England to live with family as a 'visitor' (as she described it) in order to receive the care and support her illness demanded. Apart from clothes and jewellery she left her possessions (including pets) in the Spanish property, which was maintained ready for her occupation. In 2001 she bought the house next door to the family residence, with the intention of renovating it for her needs. However, she was admitted to hospital and died in August 2002 without occupying the property. Mrs Johnson retained the property in Spain until her death, and regarded it as her home.

On the executors' appeal from the notice of determination by HMRC that Mrs Johnson was domiciled in the UK at the time of her death the Special Commissioner held that the Revenue had failed to establish that she ceased to intend residing permanently in Spain. Mrs Johnson had maintained her house there. The purchase of a UK property had been the alternative to moving into a residential care home. The appeal was allowed.

In *Mark v Mark* [2006] 1 AC 98, the House of Lords held, inter alia, that unlawful presence is not necessarily a bar to the establishment of a domicile of choice.

In *Cyganik v Agulian* [2006] EWCA Civ 129, the Court of Appeal held that an individual born in Cyprus but who had lived and worked in England for about 43 years between the age of 19 and his death at the age of 63, had not lost his Cypriot domicile of origin and had not acquired a domicile of choice in England.

Residence and ordinary residence

5.10 An individual can be resident in one or more countries for tax purposes. It is possible to be resident in the UK, but not ordinarily resident. Currently there is no statutory definition for residence or ordinary residence.

If an individual is in the UK for fewer than 183 days in the tax year and according to HMRC6 'his normal home' is outside the UK, he may be viewed as non-resident.

Ordinary residence, in contrast, is where an individual has resided in the UK for a sufficient period on a habitual basis. Following the case of *Genovese v Revenue and Customs Commissioners* [2009] SpC 741 that period was to be held three years. However this clarity was displaced by the First-tier Tribunal case of *Tuczka v HMRC* [2009] TC 366, which seems to indicate that if a person becomes resident in the UK and takes up employment in the UK, he will become ordinarily resident immediately on his arrival, even if his intention is not to stay very long. It is difficult to see how these two cases can be reconciled.

Further uncertainty was introduced by the recent case of *R (on the application of Davies, James & Gaines-Cooper) v HMRC* [2010] EWCA Civ 38 which suggests that mere day counting is not conclusive, but that other factors are taken into account. Mr Gaines-Cooper has been granted leave to take the case to the Supreme Court. Progress of the case will be keenly watched by non-UK resident individuals and tax advisers alike.

An obvious indication to a more subjective approach to determining residence – see **5.20**. This has to be contrasted with the decision in *Philip George Turberville v HMRC* [2010] UKFTT 69 (TC) which found in favour of the taxpayer, A great deal of uncertainty surrounds the concepts of 'residence' and 'ordinary residence' and the higher court authority rests with the *Gaines-Cooper* decision. A detailed statutory definition of residence would be welcome.

Presence in UK for temporary purposes only

5.11 As a general rule, an individual who is present in the UK for some temporary purpose only, and not with any intent to establish his residence here, is charged to CGT on chargeable gains accruing in a tax year if (and only) if he is resident in the UK in that tax year for a period (or periods) amounting to more than 183 days. The day-counting rules have been altered or clarified by *FA 2008, s 24(7)*. The new rules apply for 2008/09 and onwards. A day is spent in the UK if the person is present at the end of the day: see *TCGA 1992*, new *s 9(5)*. However, the day of arrival as a passenger 'just passing through' is ignored if the passenger leaves the next day and, in effect, does not use the time in the UK:

- for business; or
- to see friends; or
- to visit a property in the UK owned by that person.

See *TCGA 1992*, new *s 9(6)(b),* which refers to not engaging 'in activities that are to a substantial extent unrelated to the individual's passage through the United Kingdom'. It may prove difficult to police.

Any living accommodation available in the UK for the individual's use is disregarded for this purpose. For years prior to 1993/94, an individual who had living accommodation available to him in the UK was generally treated as UK resident in any tax year during which he visited the UK, regardless of the length of his visit (*TCGA 1992, s 9(3), (4)*).

In *HMRC v Grace* Ch D 2008 [2009] STC 213 it was decided that a South African airline pilot was not in the UK for only temporary purposes, as he fulfilled duties under an indefinite contract of employment in the UK.

Coming to the UK as a student

5.12 If an individual comes to the UK as a student and remains in the UK for less than four years, he will be resident in the UK, but not ordinarily resident if:

- he does not own or buy accommodation here; or
- he does not acquire accommodation on a lease of three years or more; and
- when leaving the UK he does not plan to return for regular visits which average 91 days or more in a tax year.

Calculation of average visits

5.13 The formula to be applied is (see HMRC6):

$$\frac{\text{Total days visiting the UK}}{\text{Tax years you have visited (in days)}} \times 365 = \text{annual average visits}$$

If the annual average visits exceed 91 days over a four-year period, the individual will become resident and ordinarily resident in the UK, even if he never exceeded the normal 183 days rule.

Visiting armed forces

5.14 A member of the visiting armed force of a designated country is not treated as resident in the UK for CGT purposes, and is not treated as changing his residence or domicile status, for any period to which the income tax exemption in *ITEPA 2003, s 303(1)* applies solely because he is a member of that force (*TCGA 1992, s 11(1)*).

Diplomatic staff

5.15 UK-resident 'agents-general' (representatives of certain foreign governments) and certain members of their staff are entitled to the same immunity from CGT as that conferred on a UK-resident head of a diplomatic mission under the *Diplomatic Privileges Act 1964* (*TCGA 1992, s 11(2)–(4)*).

Disputes as to residence, etc status

5.16 Any decision as to whether a person is (or has been) ordinarily resident or domiciled in the UK for CGT purposes can be appealed within 30 days. However, under the appeals procedure introduced on 1 April 2009, if a taxpayer disagrees with a decision, he should first write to the person who made the decision. If matters cannot be resolved, the taxpayer can request an internal review by the HMRC review team, or this can be offered by HMRC. Where the taxpayer does not agree with the conclusion of this review, or declines the offer of an internal HMRC review, he can ask the First–tier Tax Tribunal to determine the question. HMRC have no power to refer cases directly to the Tribunal.

ARRIVING IN OR LEAVING THE UK

Arriving in the UK

5.17 An individual who is not ordinarily resident in the UK and arrives in the UK with the intention of settling here is treated as UK resident from the date of arrival. He is, therefore, resident for a part of the tax year in which he arrives and is chargeable to CGT for that year (see **5.1**).

An individual who is present in the UK for a temporary purpose only (see **5.11**), but spends at least 183 days in the UK in a tax year becomes chargeable to CGT on the basis that he is resident for that part of the year in which he is present here.

The rule set out in **5.1** means that strictly speaking an individual who is resident in the UK during any part of the tax year is chargeable to CGT on all chargeable gains accruing during that year, including those accruing before he became resident.

By concession, however, for an individual (but not a trustee) HMRC will split the year in which UK residence begins, so that gains accruing before the change of status are not chargeable, so long as the taxpayer has not been resident or ordinarily resident here at any time during the five preceding tax years (HMRC concession ESC D2, reproduced below, CG25791).

HMRC will consider withholding the benefit of this concession where the taxpayer 'has entered into arrangements in an attempt to use the terms of ESC D2 to avoid liability to CGT which would otherwise arise'. See, for example, **5.19** with regard to *R v HM Inspector of Taxes, Reading ex parte Fulford-Dobson* ((1987) 60 TC 168) (CG25981).

> HMRC concession ESC D2
>
> Residence in the UK: year of commencement or cessation of residence: CGT
>
> '1. An individual who comes to live in the United Kingdom and is treated as resident here for any year of assessment from the date of arrival is charged to capital gains tax only in respect of chargeable gains from disposals made after arrival, provided that the individual has not been resident or ordinarily resident in the United Kingdom at any time during the five years of assessment immediately preceding the year of assessment in which he or she arrived in the United Kingdom.
>
> 2. An individual who leaves the United Kingdom and is treated on departure as not resident and not ordinarily resident here is not charged to capital gains tax on gains from disposals made after the date of departure, provided that the individual was not resident and not ordinarily resident in the United Kingdom for the whole of at least four out of the seven years of assessment immediately preceding the year of assessment in which he or she left the United Kingdom.
>
> 3. This concession does not apply to any individual in relation to gains on the disposal of assets which are situated in the United Kingdom and which, at any time between the individual's departure from the United Kingdom and the end of the year of assessment, are either:
>
> (i) used in or for the purposes of a trade, profession or vocation carried on by that individual in the United Kingdom through a branch or agency; or
>
> (ii) used or held for, or acquired for use by or for the purposes of, such a branch or agency.
>
> 4. This concession does not apply to the trustees of a settlement who commence or cease residence in the United Kingdom or to a settlor of a settlement in relation to gains in respect of which the settlor is chargeable under Sections 77–79 TCGA 1992, or Section 86 and Schedule 5 TCGA 1992.

5. This revised concession applies to any individual who ceases to be resident or ordinarily resident in the United Kingdom on or after 17 March 1998, or becomes resident or ordinarily resident in the United Kingdom on or after 6 April 1998.'

The split-year treatment provided by paragraph 1 of the concession does not apply, therefore, where a taxpayer arriving in the UK was previously resident here and there are less than five complete tax years between the time of his departure and his return to the UK. In this situation, gains accruing at any time in the tax year of arrival are chargeable.

Leaving the UK

5.18 An individual leaving the UK during a tax year may be treated as not resident and not ordinarily resident in the UK from the day after his departure. However, his UK-resident status for the period up to the date of departure means, as indicated in **5.1**, that strictly speaking he is chargeable to CGT on all chargeable gains accruing during the year, including those accruing after he became not resident and not ordinarily resident.

By concession, HMRC will split the year of departure so that gains accruing after the change of status are not chargeable, so long as the taxpayer has been not resident and not ordinarily resident in the UK for the whole of at least four out of the seven preceding tax years (HMRC concession ESC D2, reproduced in **5.17**).

The split-year treatment provided by paragraph 2 of the concession does not apply, therefore, where a taxpayer leaving the UK has been UK resident or ordinarily resident in any part of four or more of the seven preceding tax years. In this situation, gains accruing at any time in the tax year of departure are chargeable.

HMRC guidance indicates that cases will be examined where the date of disposal of an asset appears to be soon after the date of emigration, with a view to establishing whether a CGT liability arises, because:

- there was a binding agreement or contract for sale on or before the date of emigration;
- a business was carried on in the UK through a branch or agency in the period from the date of emigration to the date of disposal; or
- an attempt has been made to use ESC D2 for tax avoidance (CG25805).

See **5.24** regarding the exception in paragraph 3 of the concession for gains on the disposal of assets used in or for the purposes of a trade, etc carried on in the UK through a branch or agency.

5.19 As indicated above, HMRC may seek to withhold the concession if the taxpayer tries to use it for tax avoidance purposes. In *R v HM Inspector of Taxes, Reading ex parte Fulford-Dobson* (1987) 60 TC 168 (QB), the taxpayer's wife (W) inherited a farm in 1977. She was considering selling it during 1980, at a time when the taxpayer (H) was negotiating employment with a German firm. H's contract of employment was signed on 18 August, requiring him to live and work in Germany and to commence work on 15 September. W transferred the farm to H by deed of gift on 29 August; H left for Germany on 13 September; and the farm was sold by auction on 17 September.

H admitted that one of the reasons for W's transfer of the farm to him was to ensure that the sale would be outside the scope of CGT by virtue of ESC D2, because at the time of the sale he would not be UK resident. HMRC took the view that there was an attempt to use the concession for tax avoidance and denied the benefit of the concession. The taxpayer sought a judicial review of that decision and the High Court held that:

- concession D2 was lawful, falling within the proper exercise of managerial discretion;
- HMRC were entitled, in giving a concession, to take reasonable steps to prevent its abuse; and
- the transactions undertaken by the taxpayers amounted to tax avoidance within the terms of HMRC's general 'health warning' about the use of concessions for tax avoidance.

HMRC do not regard a genuine postponement of the disposal on its own as an attempt to use the concession for avoidance, although they may regard it as such if it is combined with other arrangements (CG25982).

They accept that the benefit of the no gain, no loss rule for transfers between spouses and civil partners (under *TCGA 1992, s 58*, see **3.61**) is available on the transfer to a non-resident spouse or civil partner (i) after that spouse or civil partner has become non-resident, and (ii) in a year throughout the whole of which that spouse or civil partner is non-resident. This reflects the majority decision of the House of Lords in *Gubay v Kington* (1984) 57 TC 601, HL. HMRC guidance says (CG22300):

> 'There is no longer any authority to treat a non-resident spouse as separated from a resident spouse merely because of their residence status. Similarly a non-resident civil partner may not be treated as separated from a resident civil partner merely because of their residence status. So the possibility of passing assets outside the UK tax net remains.'

A taxpayer who becomes neither resident nor ordinarily resident in the UK may become chargeable to CGT, as a result of his change of status, on a gain that was held over following a claim to hold-over relief for gifts of business assets (see **13.2**) or gifts immediately chargeable (or exempt from) inheritance tax (see **13.37**).

'Clean-break'

5.20 The decision in *Gaines-Cooper* seems to confirm that a mere day-counting test is not sufficient. The case determined that the act of leaving indefinitely will not automatically lead to non-resident status because HMRC will look, among other factors, at the connections that are retained with the UK. Severing of ties sufficient to divest a taxpayer of residence status will remain a key factor.

In the case of Mr Gaines-Cooper the fact that his wife and son remained living in the UK and that his son attended school in the UK determined that he did not leave the UK 'permanently or indefinitely'. Mr Gaines-Cooper has now been granted leave to take the case to the Supreme Court. It will be interesting to see if the day-counting rule will prevail.

Practicalities

5.21 If leaving the UK, individuals, in addition to day-counting, may wish to consider any of the following actions to show that they are leaving indefinitely:

- File P45 and P85 to obtain a tax refund for year of departure and inform HMRC of their intention of leaving the UK.
- Sever all ties with the UK, for example cease employment, move family abroad and change postal address.
- Sell accommodation or lease it on a long lease to convince HMRC that there is no intention to return in the near future.
- Generate permanent ties with their new home country: buy a house, open bank accounts and join local clubs.
- Remain outside the UK for a full tax year or make sure that over a four-year period no more than 90 days are spent in the UK;
- Obtain an overseas employment contract covering at least a whole tax year.

HMRC will look at all the facts and the settled pattern of an individual's life.

NON-RESIDENTS DOING BUSINESS IN THE UK

5.22 Non-residents are, broadly, chargeable to tax on gains arising (i) on the disposal of UK assets used to carry on a business in the UK (see **5.24**), or (ii) on a deemed disposal when the assets are removed from the UK or the business ceases (see **5.25**).

Individuals

5.23 A person who is neither resident nor ordinarily resident in the UK in a tax year remains chargeable to CGT in respect of certain gains accruing to him in that year if he is carrying on a trade, profession or vocation in the UK through a branch or agency in that year. See **5.26** regarding companies chargeable to corporation tax.

Disposal of assets

5.24 The charge applies to gains accruing on the disposal of any of the following assets, where the disposal is made at a time when the person is carrying on the trade, etc in the UK through a branch or agency:

- assets situated in the UK and used in, or for the purposes of, the trade, etc either at the time when the capital gain accrued or before that time;
- assets situated in the UK and used, or held, for the purposes of the branch or agency either at or before that time; and
- assets situated in the UK and acquired for use by, or for the purposes of, the branch or agency (*TCGA 1992, s 10(1), (2), (5)*).

'Branch or agency' means any factorship, agency, receivership, branch or management. There is no charge under this rule if the taxpayer is exempt from income tax on the profits or gains of the branch or agency by virtue of double tax relief arrangements (*TCGA 1992, s 10(4), (6)*).

The split-year concession ESC D2, discussed in **5.18**, does not apply (see paragraph 3 of the concession) to an individual in relation to gains on the disposal of assets situated in the UK that are used as set out in (a) or (b) below at any time between his departure from the UK and the end of the tax year:

(a) used in or for the purposes of a trade, profession or vocation carried on by that individual in the UK through a branch or agency; or

(b) used or held for, or acquired for use by or for the purposes of, such a branch or agency.

For an individual seeking to sell a UK business as a going concern and emigrate from the UK, the combined effect of *TCGA 1992, s 10* and HMRC's denial of concession ESC D2 is broadly as set out below:

- Delaying the contract until after the taxpayer's departure is likely to involve making arrangements for the business to continue in his absence – HMRC consider that in most cases such as this they could argue that the activity is carried on in the UK through a branch or agency in the period between departure and the date of the contract.
- A disposal after the date of emigration but before the end of the tax year would be within the charge to CGT as set out in *TCGA 1992, s 2* and ESC D2 would not apply (as already indicated).
- A disposal in the tax year following the year of emigration would also be within the charge to CGT, by virtue of *TCGA 1992, s 10* (CG25900–25903).

Deemed disposals

5.25 A chargeable gain is deemed to accrue in the circumstances described below. This rule was introduced to prevent a taxpayer avoiding the charges on an actual disposal, described in **5.24**, by (i) transferring assets abroad before the disposal, or (ii) discontinuing the branch activities in one tax year and disposing of the assets in the following tax year.

There is a deemed disposal and reacquisition at market value where 'chargeable assets' (see below) are:

(a) transferred abroad (*TCGA 1992, s 25(1)*); or

(b) cease to be 'chargeable assets' because the individual ceases to carry on the trade, etc in the UK through a branch or agency (*TCGA 1992, s 25(3)*).

For this purpose, assets are 'chargeable assets' only if the individual is not resident and not ordinarily resident in the UK and a chargeable gain on their disposal would be chargeable under *TCGA 1992, s 10(1)* as described above (*TCGA 1992, s 25(7)*).

There is no deemed disposal within (a) if:

- the transfer occurs on the cessation of the trade, etc; or
- the asset is an exploration or exploitation asset, as defined (*TCGA 1992, s 25(2)*).

There is no deemed disposal within (b) if the asset is used, before the end of the chargeable period in which the cessation occurs, in another trade, etc carried on by the same individual in the UK through a branch or agency (*TCGA 1992, s 25(5)*).

Companies

5.26 A company that is not resident in the UK is nonetheless chargeable to corporation tax in respect of chargeable gains accruing to it if the company is carrying on a trade (including for this purpose a vocation, office or employment) in the UK through a permanent establishment in the UK (*TCGA 1992, s 10B*). See **Chapter 9** and *Corporation Tax 2010/11* (Bloomsbury Professional).

TEMPORARY NON-RESIDENCE

5.27 Special rules apply to individuals who realise capital gains during a period of temporary absence from the UK, during which their residence status would otherwise mean that they escaped CGT (*TCGA 1992, s 10A*). Broadly, an individual who leaves the UK and subsequently returns is chargeable to CGT on gains arising during his absence on the disposal of assets owned prior to departure, if:

- he was UK resident for at least four of the seven tax years prior to departure; and
- the period of non-residence is less than five complete tax years.

Gains arising in the year of departure are chargeable in that year and gains arising during the period of absence are chargeable in the year in which UK residence is resumed (*TCGA 1992, s 2*). Gains on assets acquired abroad that are realised in the intervening years of non-residence are outside the charge, subject to certain anti-avoidance provisions.

The following summary relates to the provisions of *TCGA 1992, s 10A* as amended by *F(No 2)A 2005*. These apply, broadly, where the 'year of departure' (see below) is 2005/06 or later (or, in some cases, 2004/05).

5.28 The charge arises in the following circumstances, a 'year' being a tax year:

(a) the taxpayer satisfies the 'residence requirements' (ie broadly speaking, he is resident or ordinarily resident in the UK, see below) for a year (the 'year of return');

(b) he did not satisfy the residence requirements for one or more years immediately preceding the year of return, but there are prior years for which he did satisfy them;

(c) there are fewer than five 'intervening years', ie years falling between the year of departure (see below) and the year of return; and

(d) he satisfied the residence requirements for at least four out of the seven years immediately preceding the year of departure (*TCGA 1992, s 10A(1)*).

All of these conditions must be met before the charge can arise. If any of these conditions is not met, no charge arises on any gains accruing in the intervening years (and any losses accruing in those years are not allowable).

With regard to (a), the taxpayer satisfies the residence requirements for a tax year:

- if he is resident in the UK and not 'treaty non-resident' (see below) during any part of that year; or
- if he is ordinarily resident in the UK during that year (unless he is treaty non-resident during that year) (*TCGA 1992, s 10A(9)*).

The 'year of departure' in (c) is the last tax year, before the year of return, for which the taxpayer satisfied the residence requirements. An 'intervening year', where conditions (a) to (d) above apply, is a tax year falling between the year of departure and the year of return (*TCGA 1992, s 10A(8)*).

An individual is 'treaty non-resident' at any time if, at that time, he is regarded as resident in a territory outside the UK for the purposes of double taxation relief arrangements (*TCGA 1992, s 10A(9A)*; *s 288(7B)* inserted by *FA 2006, s 74 (3), (4)* with effect from 22 March 2006).

Gains, etc treated as accruing in year of return

5.29 In the circumstances outlined above, the taxpayer is chargeable to CGT as if the following gains or losses accrued to him in the year of return:

(a) all the chargeable gains and losses which, apart from this rule, would have accrued to him – had he been resident and ordinarily resident in the UK – in an intervening year;

(b) all the chargeable gains which, under *TCGA 1992, s 13* or *TCGA 1992, s 86* (see **8.1**), would be treated as accruing to him in an intervening year if he had been resident in the UK throughout that intervening year; and

(c) any losses which, by virtue of *TCGA 1992, s 13(8)*, would have been allowable in an intervening year if he had been resident in the UK throughout that intervening year (*TCGA 1992, s 10A(2), (6)*).

Chargeable gains and allowable losses are not to be brought into account in the year of return if they are gains or losses accruing in an intervening year and they fall to be taken into account under *TCGA 1992, s 10* or *s 16(3)* (non-residents carrying on a trade, etc through a UK branch or agency, see **5.22**) (*TCGA 1992, s 10A(5)*).

In order to simplify computations for 2010/11, transitional provisions were introduced in the *Finance (No 2) Act 2010*. Therefore were a taxpayer has been temporarily non-resident, but resumes UK residence during 2010/11, any gains that become chargeable under *TCGA 1992, s 10A* are treated as arising before 23 June 2010.

The normal time limits for assessments are modified where *TCGA 1992, s 10A* applies. Any assessment for the year of departure may be made at any time up to two years after the 31 January following the year of return (*TCGA 1992, s 10A(7)*).

Exclusion for assets acquired after departure from UK

5.30 The legislation must be read with care, to take account of double negatives. The gains and losses treated as accruing to the taxpayer in the year of return (see **5.29**) exclude (except as mentioned below) any gain or loss accruing on his disposal of an asset if:

(a) he acquired the asset at a time in the year of departure or any intervening year when (i) he was neither resident nor ordinarily resident in the UK, or (ii) he was resident or ordinarily resident in the UK but was 'treaty non-resident' (see below);

(b) the acquisition did not take place by means of a 'relevant disposal' (see below) treated as a no gain, no loss transfer by virtue of *TCGA 1992, ss 58, 73* or *258(4)* (transfers between spouses or civil partners, property reverting to settlor on the death of a life tenant, and transfers of heritage property);

(c) the asset is not an interest created by or arising under a settlement; and

(d) the amount or value of the consideration for the taxpayer's acquisition of the asset is not reduced by any of the CGT roll-over reliefs provided by *TCGA 1992, ss 23(4)(b), (5)(b), 152(1)(b)*,or *153(1)(b)* (with effect for disposals after 15 March 2005), *162(3)(b), 247(2)(b)* or *247(3)(b).*

The 'relevant disposal' above is a disposal of an asset acquired by the person making the disposal at a time when he was resident or ordinarily resident in the UK and was not 'treaty non-resident' (*TCGA 1992, s 10A(3), (8)*).

However, a gain is not excluded from the charge (ie it is chargeable as described in **5.29**) if:

- it has accrued or would have accrued on the disposal of any asset (the 'first asset');
- it is treated as accruing on the disposal of the whole or part of another asset (the 'other asset') by virtue of *ss 116(10), (11), 134* or *154(2), (4)* (reorganisations, compensation stock and roll-over relief for depreciating assets); and
- paragraphs (a) to (d) above apply to that other asset but not to the first asset (*TCGA 1992, s 10A(4)*).

The exclusion for assets acquired after departure from the UK applies only to the special charge under *TCGA 1992, 10A*. It does not have any bearing on any liability under the basic charging provision of *TCGA 1992, s 2*, which may give rise to a liability in the year of departure or the year of return to the UK where the split-year concession (ESC D2) is not available.

Nothing in any double tax relief treaty is to be read as preventing the taxpayer from being chargeable to CGT in respect of chargeable gains treated as accruing to him in the year of return (*TCGA 1992, s 10A(9C)*).

Example 5.2

Sergio came to live permanently in the UK on 5 January 1995. He left the UK to live in Cuba on 1 April 2006 and returned on 16 March 2010. During the period of absence he sold shares he acquired in a UK company in 1996 and made a gain of £40,000. Sergio is treated as being a temporary non-resident as the period of non-residence amounted to less than five complete tax years, and he was UK resident for at least four of the seven tax years before he left on 1 April 2005. The gain of £40,000 realised while he was living in Cuba is chargeable to CGT in 2009/10 and the CGT due is payable on 31 January 2011.

FOREIGN ASSETS OF NON-UK DOMICILED TAXPAYERS

The remittance basis

5.31 Until enactment of *FA 2008*, CGT was not charged (except as stated below) on gains accruing on the disposal of assets situated outside the UK to an individual who was:

- resident or ordinarily resident in the UK (ie within the charge to CGT); but
- not domiciled in any part of the UK.

Where this exemption applied but amounts were remitted to the UK in respect of such gains, CGT was charged on the amounts received in the UK. Remittances were treated as gains accruing when they were received in the UK. The remittance basis did not apply, however, to remittances of gains that accrued before the individual became resident or ordinarily resident in the UK (*TCGA 1992, s 12(1)*).

HMRC take the view that if a non-domiciled individual acquires a UK domicile, the remittance basis applies to gains accruing before the change of domicile that are remitted to the UK after the change (CG25311).

A non-domiciled individual who meets the residence tests in **5.1** remains chargeable on all gains accruing on the disposal of UK assets. The location of assets is examined in **5.3**.

This structure has been overhauled by *Sch 7*, which taxes the gains of non-UK domiciliaries even if not remitted to the UK and which tightens up considerably the meaning of remittance. Following representations by various professional bodies, amendments were made to the remittance basis in *Finance Act 2009*.

Remittances

5.32 For years up to 5 April 2008 the remittance basis applies by default. From 6 April 2008 it applies only by election. The entitlement to the remittance basis has not changed by *FA 2008*, but it is now available only on the making of an annual claim and payment of the new remittance basis charge (RBC).

The general rule is that an amount is treated as received in the UK in respect of a gain if it is:

- an amount paid, used or enjoyed in the UK; or
- an amount transmitted or brought in any manner or form to the UK.

It is also provided that the anti-avoidance rules in *ITTOIA 2005, ss 833* and *834* (dealing with the repayment of UK-linked debts) apply as they would apply for the purpose of *ITTOIA 2005, s 832* if the gain were 'relevant foreign income' (*TCGA 1992, s 12(2)*). These rules are designed to counter arrangements involving loans, the proceeds of which are used or enjoyed in the UK, that are repaid out of gains that are not otherwise remitted to the UK.

There is no CGT charge on a gain that is remitted before the person making it comes to the UK. Where a gain is not remitted directly but is invested in other assets, the gain is traced through those assets in order to establish whether the gain has been remitted to the UK. HMRC take the view that such tracing can take place through 'any number of investments, deposits to bank accounts, transfers between accounts, etc' (CG25352).

Whether to choose the remittance basis or pay CGT on an arising basis will very much depend on the scale of the unremitted gains an individual made during the period in question.

'Small income or gains' rule

5.33 If a taxpayer has a combined total of unremitted offshore income and gains of less than £2,000 in a tax year, the old rules still apply and tax will be charged only on UK gains and on any offshore gains that are remitted in the UK (*ITA 2007, s 809D*). Such a person will keep the advantages of the annual exempt allowance (£10,100 for 2010/11) and need not pay the RBC. No remittance basis claim will need to be made in such circumstances.

If the offshore income and gains exceed £2,000 and the taxpayer does not wish to pay the RBC he must pay UK tax on the offshore gains (and income) on an arising basis.

Unremitted gains of more than £2,000

5.34 If the unremitted gains (and income) exceed £2,000 a claim has to be made if the taxpayer wishes to rely on the remittance basis. Care needs to be taken, as in addition to the RBC the taxpayer may lose his entitlement to UK personal allowances including the annual exempt amount for CGT. There are double taxation agreements with the UK and a number of countries (like France, Germany, Sweden and Switzerland, among others) which allow UK personal allowances to be used for dual residents who rely on the remittance basis. Any decision will turn on the facts of each individual case and it is important to see whether any double taxation agreements apply.

'Stay away' rule

5.35 If a person has no UK income or gains, has remitted neither income nor gains to the UK, and has not been resident in the UK either in the year under consideration or in at least seven of the last nine years; he need not complete a self-assessment return even if the offshore income and gains that year exceed £2,000. See *ITA 2007, s 809E*: in the seventh year of residence in the UK the remittance basis must be claimed under *ITA 2007, s 809B*.

Election for the remittance basis

5.36 The claim may be made, under *ITA 2007, s 809B*, by a person resident in the UK who is either not ordinarily resident or who is not domiciled here. If the claimant:

- is over 18 in the tax year; and
- has been resident in the UK for at least seven of the last nine tax years,

the RBC is due and the taxpayer must nominate the income, or the gains that are subject to the RBC. These are the 'nominated gains' and will usually be of at least £166,667 so that, ignoring the annual exempt amount, which by *ITA 2007, s 809H* is not available, the tax on the gains is at least £30,000.

The intended structure of the RBC is that it franks the tax on the relevant income or gains, which can thereafter be remitted in the UK free of a further tax charge. This may also help the taxpayer to claim double taxation relief but there is no guarantee of that. Payment of the RBC is not itself a remittance of income or gains. Once the claim is made *TCGA 1992, s 12* operates to tax on the remittance basis any gains over the nominated gains that are brought to the UK. CGT adopts the income tax rules as to what constitutes a remittance. As always, there are exceptions: offshore life bonds are taxed on the arising basis and gains from offshore companies and trusts attract special rules.

In order to simplify computations for 2010/11, transitional provisions were introduced in the *Finance (No 2) Act 2010*. Therefore where an individual pays the remittance basis charge for the year and as a result gains are deemed to be remitted under *ITA 2007, s 809J*, those gains are deemed to arise in the UK before 23 June 2010.

'Remittance' under the new rules

5.37 Gains are remitted to the UK where conditions A and B are met, or where condition C or D is met: see *ITA 2007, s 809L*.

- A: money etc is brought to the UK; or received in the UK; or used in the UK; or services are bought in the UK; and is so brought, or is received by a 'relevant person'.
- B: the property or value involved is:
  - part of the gain; or
  - belongs to a 'relevant person' or is consideration given by such a person and is derived in some way from the gains; or

  - the gains are used outside the UK in connection with a 'relevant debt'; or
  - anything derived from the gains is used in some way in connection with a relevant debt.
- C: a gift is enjoyed by the relevant person, being property that would have been within A or B above but is remitted in the UK by way of gift. (This closes a long-established loophole, illustrated by *Carter v Sharon* [1936] 1 All ER 720.)
- D: there is a remittance by connected operations as defined in *ITA 2007, s 809O(3).*

Where a transaction is caught by C or D, it is remitted when the person first enjoys the benefit, so there are no ongoing charges: *ITA 2007, s 809L(6).*

Definitions for the remittance rules

5.38 'Relevant debt', see *ITA 2007, s 809L(7),* now means, in relation to the relevant person, any debt that relates to:

- money brought, received or used in the UK;
- services provided in the UK;
- qualifying property as a gift that is brought, received, used or enjoyed in the UK;
- the like property which is consideration for a service enjoyed in the UK;
- property of a third party, brought, received or enjoyed in the UK, where connected operations apply; or
- property of a third party where there are connected operations and a service is enjoyed in the UK.

Paying interest can be a remittance under these rules.

'Relevant person' now means (see *ITA 2007, s 809M*):

- the person himself;
- that person's spouse, civil partner or (see *ITA 2007, s 809M(3)(a)*) cohabitee;
- that person's child or grandchild, if under 18;
- the close company in which any person mentioned here is a participator;
- the trustees of a settlement that can benefit any person mentioned here; or

- a body connected with such a settlement.

The inclusion of cohabitees under *ITA 2007, s 809M(3)* is a bold step that some will welcome as tending to prevent avoidance. Few relatives escape the definition, but parents and adult children are unaffected by the new rules.

'Gift recipients' are defined by *ITA 2007, s 809N* as those to whom property (wholly or partly) derived from chargeable gains is given, so defined at the time the gift is made. If the recipient becomes a relevant person, as where she gives him a red sports car and he later moves in with her, he changes status. Gifts may be outright or transfers at an undervalue; if the latter, the remittance is of the discount only: *ITA 2007, s 809N(6)*. Where a gift is made from which the relevant person derives no benefit or enjoyment; or pays a high price to enjoy; or gets no greater benefit than any member of the public could; such enjoyment as he gets is disregarded. This overrules the decision in *Carter v Sharon* mentioned above.

How much is remitted?

5.39 The proceeds of sale will usually include the original cost as well as the gain. The old rule was usually that any remittance was pro rata the gain. The new rule is harsher: the remittance is first of any gain, see *ITA 2007, s 809P*, but limited to gains that are subject to the remittance basis, so pre-residence gains are not taxable when brought in the UK. That makes it important for taxpayers to keep such funds separate from gains realised after they reach the UK.

It may even be wise to keep each gain separate from others, especially where losses have been made. The proceeds of a small gain on a large sum allow greater sheltered remittances of the original stake than where a small investment has done very well; but beware remittances of small gains that are derived from earlier, larger, unremitted gains. The proceeds of any nominated gains should sit in a 'tax paid' fund so that they can be remitted later. Note, however, the effect of anti-avoidance legislation in *ITA 2007, s 809S*, described in the next paragraph.

Order of remittances

5.40 Although this account of the changes introduced by *FA 2008* is concerned with capital gains, the treatment of sums remitted must be put in the context of income as well. Where the taxpayer has already nominated either income or gains but over and above that has both income and gains offshore that have not yet been remitted, once there is a remittance *ITA 809I* and *809J* set out this deemed order, see *ITA 2007, s 809J(2):*

(1) foreign earnings not subject to foreign tax;

(2) foreign specific employment income not taxed offshore;

(3) foreign income not taxed overseas;

(4) foreign gains not taxed offshore;

(5) foreign earnings subject to foreign tax;

(6) foreign specific employment income taxed overseas;

(7) foreign income taxed overseas; and finally

(8) foreign gains taxed abroad.

Previously the approach of HMRC to remittances from 'mixed' funds was set out in CG25380–25440. It was not statutory. With effect from 6 April 2008, *ITA 2007, ss 809Q* and *809R* now deem remittances from a mixed fund to be broadly as set out below. Where an item falls within two categories it may be allocated on a 'just and reasonable' basis, see *ITA 2007, s 809R(3)*:

(1) employment income, unless within (2), (3) or (6) below;

(2) 'relevant foreign earnings', unless within (6) below;

(3) foreign specific employment income, unless within (6) below;

(4) relevant foreign income, unless within (7) below;

(5) foreign gains, unless within (8) below;

(6) employment income taxed abroad;

(7) relevant foreign income taxed abroad;

(8) foreign gains taxed abroad; then

(9) any other income or capital.

ITA 2007, ss 809R and *809S* will require detailed examination in difficult cases. They trace indirect payments and seem to override careful bank account planning so as to treat the fund, not as containing, say, a foreign tax credit, or some other non-taxable item but as subject to the allocation rules just described. Some property is exempt, to keep the rules slightly simpler than they would otherwise have been. There are six categories, see *ITA 2007, s 809X*:

- heritage items;
- personal items;
- items for repair;
- temporary imports;

- items under £1,000; and
- certain foreign services.

Heritage items must meet the rules as to public access, viz:

- works of art, antiques or *objets de vertu*;
- access at an approved establishment such as a museum or gallery;
- transit to or from storage at an approved establishment, or available on request for educational use;
- in the UK for at least two years; and
- they qualify for relevant VAT relief.

Personal items such as clothing and jewellery must belong to a 'relevant person' and be for the use of a 'relevant individual': see *ITA 2007, ss 809M* and *809Z2*.

Restoration items must be at, or in transit to or from, defined premises: see *ITA 2007, s 809Z3*.

Temporary importation means in the UK for 275 days or fewer, including any public access days, see *ITA 2007, s 809Z4*.

For items to come within the 'under £1,000' rule the test is the amount of income that would be caught under the remittance rules. Cash never comes within this rule. The import of only part of a set of items triggers an apportionment based on what actually comes to the UK.

The 'foreign services' exception, see *s 809W*, arises where the service, though provided in the UK, relates mainly to property abroad, and is paid for from foreign income or gains. This could relate to legal fees for advice on foreign assets and may thus protect a niche sector of the UK economy.

Anti-avoidance: temporary non-residence

5.41 A rule similar to that described at **5.27** is introduced by *TCGA 1992, s 10A(9ZA)* to catch the non-UK domiciled taxpayer living here who wishes to go offshore briefly so as to set up pre-entry tax free remittances. The new subsection deems the remittances made in the 'year away' to be made in the year of return, catching any gains made during the period of non-residence on assets that had been held at the time of departure if those gains are remitted in the UK, either whilst the taxpayer is still abroad or after return. This is slightly harsher than the income tax treatment of short absences; but it mirrors the previous difference between income and gains in this respect.

Remittance basis: computation of gains

5.42 Once gains remitted to the UK have been identified, the computation of the chargeable gain (in sterling) follows the normal rules applying at the time of the disposal, with indexation allowance (frozen at April 1998) being given where appropriate. Any delay between the time of the disposal and the remittance to the UK does not change the qualifying holding period for taper relief (see **Example 5.3**). HMRC practice regarding the application of double tax relief where gains are assessed on the remittance basis is explained at CG14385–14427.

Example 5.3

Arno is a non-domiciled but UK-resident taxpayer. He acquired shares in ABN, a foreign quoted company, in May 2003 and disposed of them in August 2007. The gain was remitted to the UK in January 2010. Depending on the amount of capital gain, Arno now needs to decide whether to pay the £30,000 RBC, or pay CGT on an arising basis. Detailed calculations are required.

A loss accruing on the disposal of non-UK assets to an individual who is resident or ordinarily resident but not domiciled in the UK was not formerly an allowable loss (*TCGA 1992, ss 12(1), 16(4)*). That now changes. If a non-UK domiciliary never claims the new remittance basis, he is effectively taxed in the UK like a UK taxpayer; he should enjoy the use of losses. *TCGA 1992, s 16(4)* is altered to achieve this. Foreign losses can from 6 April 2008 be set against any gain but subject to anti-avoidance carry-forward rules as for UK losses. There is no need to remit anything: this might not always be possible anyway.

It is more complicated where the taxpayer claims the remittance basis after 6 April 2008. The rules look at the year to which the claim relates and depend on whether, in that year, the remittance basis or the arising basis applied (*ITA 2007, s 809B*). As might be expected, allowance of losses is less generous in years to which the remittance basis applied. The first claim under *ITA 2007, s 809B* to the remittance basis closes the door forever to the use of losses as they arise, even though there may later be a year when the remittance basis no longer applies.

The rules for making an election to offset losses under *TCGA 1992, s 16ZA* are strict. Often the taxpayer will not wish to claim, as where relief is available under *TCGA 1992, s 16* as revised. Where the new election is in force, there are difficult identification rules: see *TCGA 1992, ss 19ZB* and *ZC,* which are beyond the scope of this book.

Losses and the remittance basis

5.43 An individual who claims the remittance basis can make a one-off irrevocable election to obtain UK tax relief for losses realised on foreign situated assets (*TCGA 1992, s 16ZA*). The election will be effective for the first tax years for which the taxpayer claims the remittance basis and all subsequent tax years. As this election will impact on both UK and foreign losses, detailed advice should be taken.

If no such election is made 'foreign losses' are not allowable losses.

Detailed rules on how to determine the capital gain chargeable to capital gains tax can be found in the legislation:

Step 1

Deduct any allowable losses from the chargeable gains in the following order:

(1) foreign chargeable gains accruing and remitted to the UK in that year

(2) foreign chargeable gains accruing but not remitted in that year

(3) all other chargeable gains arising in that year (other than gains treated as accruing on the remittance to the UK of foreign chargeable gains arising in a previous year).

Chargeable gains accruing under *TCGA 1992, ss 87* or *89(2)* ie gains treated as accruing to the beneficiary are not taken into account.

If the losses do not exhaust the available chargeable gains within (2) above, the losses are deducted first from the last of the gains to accrue.

Step 2

Therefore the actual chargeable gain will be all the gains arising within that year, less the losses mentioned in step 1 from the gains within (1) and (3), but not (2).

Where a loss has been deducted from an unremitted foreign chargeable gain, the loss relief will continue if the gain is subsequently remitted to the UK.

Liability to CGT on the remittance basis

5.44 **Table 5.2**, based on HMRC6, para 5.4 summarises the effect of an individual's residence, ordinary residence and domicile status and the location of assets in determining CGT liability. It is necessarily of general application and the detailed provisions should be examined in each case.

Table 5.2

Residence and domicile	*UK resident and domiciled*	*UK resident but not domiciled*
UK ordinarily resident	Not eligible to the remittance basis ('RB') All UK and foreign income and gains are liable to UK tax on the arising basis ('AB')	Eligible to use RB If RB used all UK income and gains are liable to UK tax on the AB Foreign income and gains are liable to UK tax on the RB.
UK not ordinarily resident	Eligible to use RB If RB is used all UK income and gains are liable to UK tax on AB Foreign gains are liable to UK tax on AB Foreign income is liable to UK on the RB	Eligible to use RB If RB is used all UK income and gains are liable to UK tax on the AB Foreign income and gains are liable to UK tax on the RB

APPORTIONMENT OF NON-RESIDENT COMPANY'S GAINS

5.45 Chargeable gains accruing to certain non-UK resident companies may be treated as accruing to UK-resident individuals who have an interest in the company. The rules in *TCGA 1992, s 13* apply to chargeable gains accruing to a company that is not resident in the UK but would be a close company if it were UK resident. Gains apportioned to participators in this way are not eligible for taper relief (see **11.35**) (*TCGA 1992, s 13(10A)*). HMRC guidance on the application of these rules is set out in CG57200–57411, but will need revision in the light of *FA 2008* and therefore needs to be treated with care.

Apportionment to UK-resident participator

5.46 When a chargeable gain accrues to the company, a part of it is treated as accruing to every person who:

- is resident or ordinarily resident in the UK when the chargeable gain accrues to the company;

- is (in the case of an individual) domiciled in the UK; and
- is a participator in the company.

There is no 'motive test': the rules are absolute. The company's gain is computed as if the company were within the charge to corporation tax on capital gains. Transfers between members of a group of non-resident companies are treated as if the group was UK resident for this purpose. The part of the gain that is attributed to each participator is based on the extent of his interest as a participator in the company. However, there is no charge where the amount apportioned to the taxpayer and to persons connected with him is not more than 10% of the gain (*TCGA 1992, ss 13(1)–(4), 13(11A), 14*).

If the company to which the gain accrues pays the participator's tax liability, that payment is ignored for the purposes of income tax, CGT and corporation tax but is not allowable as a deduction in computing the participator's gain on a disposal of shares (*TCGA 1992, s 13(11)*).

'Participator' and 'close company' take their meaning from *ICTA 1988, ss 417* and *414* respectively (*TCGA 1992, ss 13(12)* and *288(1)*), but see also **5.52** regarding participators.

Exceptions

5.47 There is no charge in respect of a chargeable gain:

- accruing on the disposal of an asset used only for the purposes of (i) a trade carried on by the company wholly outside the UK, or (ii) the part carried on outside the UK of a trade carried on by the company partly within and partly outside the UK;
- accruing on the disposal of either currency or a debt within *TCGA 1992, s 252(1)*, where the currency or debt is (or represents) money in use for the purposes of a non-UK trade carried on by the company; or
- in respect of which the company is chargeable to tax under *TCGA 1992, s 10B* (see **5.26**) (*TCGA 1992, s 13(5)*).

The assets of a pension scheme are ignored in determining a person's interest as participator for this purpose, if a gain accruing on disposal of the scheme's assets would be exempt from CGT (*TCGA 1992, s 13(10B)*).

Set-off on distribution of gain

5.48 Where a charge arises (see **5.46**) and tax is paid accordingly, and there is a distribution in respect of the chargeable gain within a specified period (see below), the tax is set against the taxpayer's liability to income tax, CGT or corporation tax on the distribution.

The distribution may be made by means of a dividend or distribution of capital, or on the dissolution of the company. The set-off is reduced to the extent that the tax is reimbursed by the company or applied as a deduction (see below).

The specified period is the period of three years from the earlier of:

- the end of the company's period of account in which the chargeable gain accrued; or
- the end of the period of 12 months from the date when the chargeable gain accrued (*TCGA 1992, s 13(5A), (5B)*).

Deduction on disposal of interest in the company

5.49 If the taxpayer pays the CGT charged as mentioned in **5.46** and the tax is neither reimbursed by the company nor set off as mentioned in **5.48**, it is allowable as a deduction in computing a gain accruing on his disposal of any asset representing his interest as a participator in the company (*TCGA 1992, s 13(7)*).

Calculation of the income tax or CGT chargeable

5.50 For the purpose of calculating any income tax or CGT chargeable for any year on the distribution or disposal, the following rules apply:

(a) a distribution treated as the person's income for that year forms the highest part of his chargeable income;

(b) a gain accruing in that year on the person's disposal of any asset representing his interest as a participator forms the highest part of his chargeable gains;

(c) where a distribution falls to be treated as a disposal giving rise to a chargeable gain, the gain forms the next highest part of his chargeable gains, after any gains within (b); and

(d) a gain apportioned to him as mentioned in **5.46** and treated as accruing to him in that year is regarded as the next highest part of his chargeable gains, after any gains within (c) (*TCGA 1992, s 13(7A)*).

Losses

5.51 Losses accruing to the non-resident company are not attributed to participators. However, in arriving at the amount of gains accruing to a company that can be apportioned to participators, a loss may be deducted if it would be an allowable loss in the hands of a UK-resident company (*TCGA 1992, s 13(8)*).

Participators

5.52 'Participator' takes its meaning from *CTA 2010, s 454*. Broadly, any person who has a share or interest in the capital or income of the company is a participator. However, it is also provided for the purpose of the apportionment of gains under *TCGA 1992, s 13*, that:

(a) a person's interest as a participator in a company is the interest in the company that is represented by all the factors contributing to his treatment as a participator; and

(b) the 'extent' of that interest is the proportion of all participators' interests that the person's interest represents.

The apportionment in (b) is made on a just and reasonable basis and takes account of interests of participators who are neither resident, nor ordinarily resident in the UK (*TCGA 1992, s 13(13)*).

Any appeal as to the extent of a person's interest as a participator for this purpose is made to the First-tier Tax Tribunal (*TCGA 1992, s 13(15)*).

If a person's beneficial interest under a settlement is a factor in determining whether he has an interest as a participator in a company, the interest as a participator is deemed to be the trustees' interest to the extent that it is represented by the beneficial interest (*TCGA 1992, s 13(14)*).

Corporate participators

5.53 If the participator (A) in the non-UK resident company (B) is itself a non-UK resident company, but would be a close company if it were UK resident, then the amount apportioned to A is further apportioned among A's participators according to the extent of their respective interests as participators. Since A's participators may include companies, and those companies' participators may also include companies, the rule is applied through any number of companies (*TCGA 1992, s 13(9)*).

Trustees

5.54 Gains may be attributed to trustees of a settlement who are participators in the company, even if they are neither resident nor ordinarily resident in the UK. Such gains may be attributed to UK-resident beneficiaries under the provisions of *TCGA 1992, Ch II* (see **8.1**) (*TCGA 1992, s 13(10)*; *FA 2006 Sch 12, para 8*).

DOUBLE TAX RELIEF

5.55 Double tax relief is described in detail at **3.64**.Relief may be available by virtue of double tax relief arrangements to taxpayers who are not resident in the UK but are chargeable to UK tax under any of the provisions discussed in this chapter. See, however, **5.30** regarding double tax relief arrangements to be disregarded in relation to gains accruing in a period of temporary non-residence, and **5.42** regarding the application of double tax relief where gains are assessed on the remittance basis.

Chapter 6

Partnerships

INTRODUCTION

6.1 Partnerships, including limited liability partnerships, and Scottish partnerships are treated as transparent entities for CGT purposes. This means that:

(a) a disposal of a chargeable asset owned by the partnership is treated as a disposal by the partners, and not as a disposal by the partnership itself; and

(b) CGT is charged on each partner separately in respect of any chargeable gain accruing to him on the disposal of a partnership asset, and that gain is charged in the same way as other chargeable gains accruing to him in the same chargeable period (and if a loss accrues on the disposal each partner's share of the loss becomes an allowable loss which he can set against his own chargeable gains) (*TCGA 1992, s 59*).

A partner making such a disposal may be eligible for hold-over relief (see **Chapter 13**) or roll-over relief for replacement of business assets (see **Chapter 14**). If the disposal was made before 6 April 2008 he may be entitled to taper relief (see **17.22**). A disposal of a partnership share, or asset used by the partnership after 5 April 2008 may be eligible for entrepreneurs' relief (see **11.23**).

A partner treated as disposing of a partnership asset (or a share in it) can roll over a chargeable gain accruing against the acquisition of an asset for the purpose of another trade, whether that trade is carried on by him as a sole trader or by a partnership in which he is a partner.

What is a partnership?

6.2 The CGT legislation does not define 'partnership' but the *Partnership Act 1890* defines it as 'the relationship which subsists between persons carrying on a business in common with a view to profit'. A partnership is a separate legal person in Scotland, but this rule is overridden for CGT purposes so that there is no difference in treatment between, for example, a Scottish partnership and an English one (*TCGA 1992, s 59(1)(a)*).

Although a partnership's dealings are treated as dealings by the partners and not by the partnership itself, the partnership is required to provide details of disposals of partnership property. For this purpose the partnership tax return is to include the particulars that would be required if the partnership itself were liable to tax on a chargeable gain accruing on the disposal (*TMA 1970, s 12AA(7)*).

It may not always be clear whether, for CGT purposes, arrangements amount to a partnership or merely joint ownership of the assets concerned. HMRC provide guidance on this issue in their Business Income Manual (BIM72005–72015).

Legislation and HMRC practice

6.3 The only tax legislation, which is specifically written for dealing with the capital gains of partners and partnerships, is contained in *TCGA 1992, ss 59* and *59A* (for LLPs). This is inadequate to deal with all the complexities that can arise with partnership gains, so HMRC issued Statement of Practice D12 (reproduced in the appendix to this chapter), in 1975. This was supplemented by Statements of Practice 1/79 and 1/89. These apply in principle to corporate partners as well as individuals, although companies are chargeable to corporation tax on their chargeable gains (see **Chapter 9**). SP D12 was extended following the creation of limited liability partnerships as bodies corporate in 2001 (see **6.20**). See **6.21** regarding partnerships residing outside the UK or carrying on a business controlled and managed outside the UK.

In January 2008, HMRC issued Revenue & Customs Brief 3/08 dealing with the contribution of assets to a partnership. This Brief overrules the previous understanding presented in SP D12 para 4, of how gains on assets should be taxed when a partnership is established (see **6.17**). In March 2009, HMRC issued Revenue & Customs Brief 9/09 which deals with the rebasing rules as they apply to partnership assets (see **6.11**). Guidance on the taxation of partnership gains and gains made by partners, is found in the HMRC Capital Gains manual at paras CG27000–CG28420.

The operation of CGT for partners thus relies on HMRC practice rather than legislation and without a legislative framework this practice can be changed at any point, sometimes with retrospective effect.

PARTNERSHIP ASSETS AND 'OTHER' ASSETS

6.4 A 'partnership asset' is an asset owned by all of the partners. An asset that is owned by only some of the partners but used by the partnership is not a partnership asset – HMRC guidance refers to such assets as 'other assets'. It may be difficult to determine whether an asset is a partnership asset, in which case the intentions of the partners will be taken into account (CG27200).

Roll-over relief for replacement of business assets (see **Chapter 14**) is available to the owner of assets that are let to a partnership in which he is a partner, if those assets are used for the purposes of the partnership's trade or profession and the other conditions for the relief are met (Statement of Practice D11). Entrepreneurs' relief is available on the disposal of a share in the partnership assets, either on the introduction of a partner or when a partner reduces their interest in the partnership (see **Chapter 11**).

FRACTIONAL SHARE IN A PARTNERSHIP ASSET

6.5 When a partnership buys an asset, each partner is treated as acquiring a fractional share in it. In order to compute the gain or loss accruing to a partner on either the disposal of a chargeable asset owned by the partnership (see **6.8**) or a change in asset surplus-sharing arrangements (see **6.12**), it is necessary to calculate each partner's disposal consideration and allowable expenditure by reference to his fractional share in the partnership asset.

HMRC guidance sets out a series of tests to determine a partner's fractional share of a partnership asset. Where there is actual consideration for the disposal, HMRC will apply the following tests in the order shown:

- any specific written agreement setting out the allocation of capital assets;
- any agreement or other evidence setting out how capital profits are to be shared; and
- any agreement or other evidence setting out how income profits are to be shared.

If none of the above evidence exists (eg treatment in the accounts) the assets should be treated as held in equal proportions by all the partners as provided for by the *Partnership Act 1890, s 24(1)* (CG27220).

Where the market value of a partner's share in a partnership asset is to be ascertained for CGT purposes it is taken as a fraction of the value of the partnership's entire interest in the asset. There is no discount to take account of the size of the partner's share. For example, if a partner has a one-tenth share in the partnership assets and the partnership owns all of the shares in a company, the value of the partner's interest in the shareholding is one-tenth of the partnership's interest (Statement of Practice D12, para 1).

Allowable expenditure: multiple acquisitions

6.6 Where a partner has built up his fractional share in the partnership assets (including goodwill) in stages since 6 April 1965, his acquisition cost of the latest fractional share of those assets is calculated by pooling the expenditure relating to each acquisition (CG27300).

Where all or a part of the partner's share was acquired before 6 April 1965 the disposal will normally be identified with shares acquired on a 'first in, first out' basis, but HMRC may accept a different approach where this produces an unreasonable result (eg where there is a temporary change in the shares in a partnership due to a delay between the departure of one partner and the arrival of a new one) (Statement of Practice D12, para 10).

Partnership goodwill

6.7 The value of goodwill generated by a partnership is not generally recognised in the balance sheet, and it is customary not to place a value on that goodwill in dealings between the partners. In such cases the HMRC practice on a disposal of a partner's interest in that goodwill for actual consideration, is to regard that interest as the same asset as was acquired by the partner when he first became entitled to a share in it (CG68100).

Where the partnership goodwill was previously recognised in the accounts but the value has been written down to zero for whatever reason, HMRC will resist claims for a share of that goodwill to be treated as becoming of negligible value (*TCGA 1992, s 24(2)*). Such a claim, if successful, would create a capital loss for the claimant partner (see **2.10**). HMRC will only accept a capital loss on goodwill has arisen where the entire goodwill of the partnership has become of negligible value (CG28000).

Purchased goodwill may also not be recognised in the balance sheet at a value greater than cost, and may not otherwise be taken into account in dealings between partners. However, this purchased goodwill is treated as a separate asset for CGT purposes from the partnership's self-generated goodwill for the purpose of computing CGT taper relief (see **17.22**). The interest in purchased goodwill is, therefore, treated as acquired on the later of:

- the date of purchase by the partnership; or
- the date when the disposing partner first became entitled to a share in that purchased goodwill (Statement of Practice D12, para 12).

DISPOSAL OF PARTNERSHIP ASSETS

6.8 When a partnership disposes of an asset to an outside party, each partner is treated as making a disposal of his fractional share (see **6.5**) in that asset. The proceeds of disposal are allocated to the partners in the ratio of their share in asset surpluses at the time of disposal.

If this ratio is not specifically laid down, the allocation follows the destination of the surplus as shown in the partnership accounts but regard is also had to any agreement outside the accounts. If the surplus is put to a common reserve, the asset surplus-sharing ratio is used to divide the proceeds. If no such ratio is specified, the ordinary profit-sharing ratio will be used (Statement of Practice D12, para 2).

Example 6.1

Each of the following partnerships disposes of its chargeable asset to outside parties at arm's length, realising a gain of £90,000. The gain is apportioned among the partners as follows:

Arthur & Co

The partnership agreement states that each of the three partners shall be entitled to share equally in any surplus arising from assets disposed of by the partnership. Each partner is therefore treated as if he had made a gain of £30,000.

Binder & Co

The three partners in Binder & Co have no formal agreement, but interest on capital contributed to the partnership is shown in the accounts at the same sum for each. The inference is that the capital has been equally contributed and can be equally withdrawn, so that the apportioned gain is £30,000 to each partner.

Cooper & Co

The three partners, Abby, Chris and Kate, have no formal agreement and the capital is shown in the accounts as a global sum. The profit-sharing ratio is 3:2:1. Thus the gain is apportioned:

Abby	£45,000
Chris	£30,000
Kate	£15,000

Part disposals

6.9 If a partnership makes a part disposal, the part disposal rules (see **2.4**) are applied before the gain is divided among the partners. Where the relief for small part disposals of land is available (see **2.5**), the conditions are applied separately in relation to each partner. However, the normal part disposal rules do not apply to changes in fractional partnership shares between the partners (see **6.14**).

Partnership assets distributed in kind

6.10 Where a partnership asset is distributed to one or more partners (eg on a dissolution of the partnership), the disposal is treated as being made for a consideration equal to the market value of the asset. Partners who do not receive a share of the asset are treated as having disposed of their fractional share in the asset at the time of the distribution (CG27400).

The gain accruing to each individual partner is computed but the gain accruing to the partner receiving the asset is deducted from his allowable expenditure on a subsequent disposal of the asset. The same principle applies where a loss arises (Statement of Practice D12, para 3).

Rebasing rule for disposal of partnership assets

6.11 All assets held by individual partners at 31 March 1982 which are disposed of after 5 April 2008 are rebased at the March 1982 value for CGT purposes. Statement of Practice 1/89 deals with the indexation allowance in relation to no gain, no loss transfers between partners (CG28100–28180). For disposals made after 5 April 2008 SP 1/89 only applies to corporate partners whose capital gains are subject to corporation tax (see **Chapter 9**).

Where an individual partner has previously acquired an asset on a no gain, no loss basis, the base cost of that asset may include indexation allowance from 31 March 1982 or the month in which the partner acquired the asset, to the date of disposal or April 1998 if earlier (*TCGA 1992, s 35A*). This will occur in the following circumstances:

- the partner acquired the asset between 31 March 1982 and 5 April 1998 as a no gain, no loss transaction;
- any previous disposal and acquisition of the asset since 31 March 1982 has been on a no gain, no loss basis; and
- the asset was not rebased on the transfer to the partner.

Example 6.2

Alistair and Tony formed a partnership in March 1979 sharing all profits equally. They immediately acquired a building for use in the partnership business for £100,000. This building was valued at £120,000 on 31 March 1982. On 1 May 1999 Gordon joined the partnership and the profit-sharing ratios were changed to: Alistair 25%, Tony 50%, Gordon 25%, although Gordon made no payment towards his acquisition of a share in the partnership owned building. This building was not revalued in partnership accounts from the historical cost of £100,000 and the partners did not make rebasing elections in their capacity as partners. The building was sold on 4 June 2010 for £660,000.

Alistair is treated as disposing of 25% of the value of the partnership building to Gordon in 1999/00 at a no gain, no loss transfer. When the building is sold in 2010 all three partners are treated as disposing of their fractional shares in the property. The gains are calculated as follows:

Alistair: 1999/2000	£	£
Deemed disposal value	100,000 × 25%	25,000
Indexation allowance to April 1998 on 1982 value of £120,000	120,000 × 25% = 30,000 × 1.047	31,410
		56,410
Less cost – historical		(25,000)
Unindexed gain		31,410
Indexation allowance		(31,410)
No gain, no loss:		Nil

Under the practice set out in SP 1/89 Gordon acquires his share in the building for £56,410 (see **6.14**).

All partners: 2010/11	£	£
Alistair		
Disposal consideration	25% × 660,000	165,000
Less 1982 value	25% × 120,000	30,000
Gain:		135,000
Tony		
Disposal consideration	50% × 660,000	330,000
Less 1982 value:	50% × 120,000	60,000
Gain:		270,000

Gordon

Disposal consideration	25% × 660,000	165,000
Less cost per *TCGA 1992, s 35A*	25% × £120,000 =	30,000
Market value at 31 March 1992 plus indexation from 1992 to 1998	+ 30,000 × 1.047 =	31,410
		61,410
Gain:		103,590

Under *TCGA 1992, s 35A* Gordon acquires his interest in the partnership building at the indexed cost of the 1982 value. The provisions in *s 35A* supersede the result of the capital gains calculation in 1999/2000 based on SP 1/89 (see Revenue & Customs Brief 9/09).

CHANGE IN FRACTIONAL SHARE OF ASSETS

6.12 A reduction in an individual partner's fractional share of a partnership asset is a disposal for CGT purposes, and an increase in that share is an acquisition. Such a change can arise from:

- the actual disposal or acquisition of a partnership asset (see **6.8**);
- the partners varying the terms of the partnership agreement or reaching a separate agreement with regard to the asset concerned (see **6.13**); or
- a partner joining or leaving the partnership (see **6.16**).

Transfers of fractional shares between spouses or civil partners living together are, however, subject to the no gain, no loss rule laid down for such transfers and outlined in **3.62** (*TCGA 1992, s 58*).

Change in asset surplus-sharing ratios

6.13 An individual may introduce capital when joining a partnership, which is credited to his capital account (see **6.17**). The partnership's retained profits may subsequently increase his capital account balance. No CGT liability arises when those amounts of capital are subsequently withdrawn, for example, on retirement.

However, if consideration in money or money's worth passes between the partners on a change in asset surplus-sharing ratios, that consideration represents:

- the disposal consideration received by the partner whose share is reduced; and
- acquisition expenditure incurred by the partner whose share is increased.

The CGT treatment of a merger of two or more partnerships to form one partnership follows the treatment for a change in partnership asset surplus-sharing ratios. Roll-over relief on replacement of business assets (see **Chapter 14**) may be available where a partner disposes of part of his share in the assets of the old partnership and acquires a share in other assets put into the merged partnership (Statement of Practice D12, paras 4, 9).

Consideration within the accounts

6.14 If there is no direct payment of consideration outside the partnership, then the consideration for the disposal is the fraction of the asset's current balance sheet value that corresponds to the fractional share passing between the partners. The normal part disposal rule (see **2.4**) is not applied in this situation.

If the firm's assets have not been revalued, a reduction in an existing partner's capital profit-sharing ratio is treated as a disposal on which no gain or loss arises. No taper relief is available on such a disposal (where made before 6 April 2008), and the acquiring partner's qualifying holding period for taper relief begins on the date of his acquisition (CG27600).

HMRC have agreed that such a disposal may be treated as a no gain, no loss disposal for the purpose of the 31 March 1982 rebasing rules (*TCGA 1992, Sch 3*) and the partial relief for deferred charges on gains accrued before 31 March 1982 (*TCGA 1992, Sch 4*). Where indexation allowance is available the consideration for the disposal is calculated on the assumption that an unindexed gain equal to the indexation allowance accrued, so that there is no gain and no loss after deducting the indexation allowance (Statement of Practice 1/89).

Example 6.3

Ben and Jerry are in partnership and the only chargeable asset is a property. If the fractional shares change from 50:50 to 40:60, Ben has disposed of a 10/50 of his share in the assets and Jerry has acquired a 10/50 share.

The current balance sheet value of the property is £50,000. Ben's disposal proceeds, and Jerry's acquisition cost, will be (10/50 × £50,000) × 1/2 = £5,000.

Ben's disposal gives rise to no gain and no loss so long as the asset has not been revalued – see below – because his acquisition cost is also (10/50 × £50,000) × 1/2 = £5,000.

If assets (such as land and buildings) are revalued to a higher amount, the surplus is credited to the existing partners' capital accounts. No chargeable gain accrues on that event. However, the partner has effectively realised a proportion of the partnership's assets. A chargeable gain therefore arises upon a subsequent disposal (which results in all or part of the capital account being paid to him).

In summary, an upward revaluation of the partnership asset in the balance sheet gives rise to a potential gain on a future change in asset surplus-sharing ratios, although the revaluation itself does not represent a disposal for CGT purposes (CG27650 and Statement of Practice D12, para 5).

Consideration outside the accounts

6.15 Any payment made outside the partnership accounts on a change of asset surplus-sharing ratios represents consideration for the disposal of the whole or part of a partner's share in partnership assets. This consideration is in addition to the consideration by reference to balance sheet value (see **6.14**). It may be paid directly to the partners or via a transfer between capital accounts.

Such a payment may represent consideration for goodwill that is not included in the balance sheet. In such cases:

- the partner receiving the payment will have no allowable expenditure to set against it unless he made a similar payment for his share in the asset; and
- the partner making the payment will only be allowed to deduct it in computing gains or losses on a subsequent disposal of his share in the asset (CG27660 and Statement of Practice D12, para 6).

Example 6.4

David, Edward and Fiona are partners in a firm of accountants who share all profits in the ratio 7:7:6. George is admitted as a partner in May 2010 and pays the other partners a total of £10,000 for the partnership goodwill. The new partnership shares are: David 3/10, Edward 3/10, Fiona 1/4 and George 3/20. The book value of goodwill is £18,000, being its cost on acquisition of the practice from the predecessor in 1990. The table below shows the calculation of the chargeable gains accruing to David, Edward and Fiona and George's acquisition costs. The capital gains accruing to David, Edward and Fiona could be reduced by entrepreneurs' relief if the other conditions for that relief also apply (see **Chapter 11**).

David		£	£
Fractional share disposed of 7/20 – 6/20 = 1/20			
Disposal consideration for partnership goodwill:			
Notional reduction in book value: 1/20 × £18,000		900	
Actual disposal paid by new capital: 7/20 × £10,000		3,500	
			4,400
Allowable expenditure, reduction in book value 1/20 × £18,000			(900)
Gain			3,500
Edward			
Fractional share disposed of 7/20 – 6/20 = 1/20			
Gain (computed as for David)			3,500
Fiona			
Fractional share disposed of 6/20 – 5/20 = 1/20			
Disposal consideration for partnership goodwill:			
Notional reduction in book value: 1/20 × £18,000		900	
Actual disposal paid by new capital: 6/20 × £10,000		3,000	
			3,900
Allowable expenditure, reduction in book value 1/20 × £18,000			(900)
Gain			3,000
George			
Allowable expenditure on share of goodwill:			
Actual consideration paid			10,000
Notional consideration transferred:	from David: 1/20 × £18,000	900	
	from Edward: 1/20 × £18,000	900	
	from Fiona: 1/20 × £18,000	900	
			2,700
Total consideration			12,700

Partners joining and leaving the partnership

6.16 Until 21 January 2008, it was thought that changes in asset surplus-sharing arrangements on the occasion of one or more partners joining or leaving the partnership would be treated for CGT purposes in a similar way to the changes outlined in **6.12**. However, the Revenue & Customs Brief 3/08 changed the approach where capital is contributed to the partnership (see **6.17**).

The CGT treatment is different where a partner leaves the partnership and reduces his share to nil. The capitalised value of an annuity paid to a retiring partner may represent consideration in money's worth but HMRC practice is to disregard annuities meeting certain conditions (see **6.18**).

Capital introduced to a partnership

6.17 On 21 January 2008 (the date of publication of Revenue & Customs Brief 03/08) HMRC clarified their practice in relation to capital gains arising on the introduction of a capital asset to a partnership. When the asset is introduced on forming a new partnership, or where a new partner joins an existing partnership, this can generate a chargeable gain (CG27900).

Example 6.5

Martin owns music rights worth £600,000, which he has acquired from various music creators over time. He joined the B&H partnership as an equal one-third partner and introduced the music rights to the partnership by way of his capital contribution. Martin is treated as making a disposal of two-thirds of the music rights at their current value: £600,000 × 2/3 = £400,000. Martin's gain could be reduced by entrepreneurs' relief (see **Chapter 11**).

When a new partner introduces cash as his capital contribution to the partnership, rather than an asset, no gain can arise, as the gift or transfer of cash into the partnership is not a disposal for CGT purposes.

The application of the ruling in Revenue & Customs Brief 3/08 may not be entirely clear for every situation. Where genuine uncertainty exists and the issue is commercially significant, the taxpayer can apply to HMRC for a ruling using the non-statutory business clearance process as detailed in the HMRC non-statutory business clearance guidance manual.

Where advice has previously been given by HMRC based on the pre-21 January 2008 interpretation of Statement of Practice D12, HMRC will stand by that advice, and not disturb the agreed tax treatment. Where no ruling was given on the case, which has not been finalised through the self-assessment system, the tax treatment could be disturbed and a gain may arise where none was thought to exist. In these cases it may also be prudent to seek a ruling from HMRC under the clearances procedure mentioned above.

Annuities to retiring partners

6.18 The capitalised value of an annuity paid to a retiring partner represents consideration in money's worth for the disposal of the retiring partner's share of the partnership assets. This is the case whether or not the partnership buys a life annuity for the benefit of the retiring partner. The potential CGT charge on this consideration is not precluded by the general exclusion of money or money's worth charged to income tax from the consideration for a disposal of assets (*TCGA 1992, s 37(3)*).

However, HMRC practice is to treat that capitalised value as consideration only if the amount of the annuity is 'more than can be regarded as a reasonable recognition of the past contribution of work and effort made by the partner to the partnership', (CG28400). HMRC's measure of 'reasonable' recognition is based on a fraction of the partner's share of the partnership's profits. That fraction depends on how long the taxpayer has been a partner, as indicated below. See **6.21** regarding the treatment of a lump sum paid in addition to an annuity.

Partner for at least ten years

6.19 A reasonable recognition of the partner's contribution will be no more than two-thirds of their average share of profit in the 'best three' of the last seven years of assessment in which he devoted substantially the whole of their time to acting as a partner. The share of profit is computed before deducting any capital allowances, charges, or losses (CG28400).

Partner for less than ten years

6.20 If the retiring partner was a partner for less than ten years, the fraction of his average share of profit – to be used instead of two-thirds in **6.19** – is set out in the table in para 8 of Statement of Practice D12 (see **6.25**). The annuity may be stated as a percentage of future partnership profits. HMRC guidance indicates that they are unlikely to spend time enquiring about the level of future payments in cases that are 'clearly marginal'. In most cases, a reasonable estimate of the amount likely to be paid would fall within the above limits (CG28400).

However, the full capitalised value of the annuity is taken as consideration for the partner's disposal (and will represent allowable acquisition expenditure on the part of the remaining partners) if it exceeds the limits. HMRC will take advice from the HMRC Actuarial Team where necessary, but their guidance indicates that the response to any request from the taxpayer for an advance clearance will be limited to providing a general outline of their published practice (CG28400).

Lump sum paid in addition to annuity

6.21 Where a lump sum is paid in addition to an annuity:

- the lump sum is treated as consideration for the disposal; and
- one-ninth of the lump sum is added to the capitalised value of the annuity and if the total exceeds the fraction of the retired partner's average share of the profits (ie the fraction given in either **6.19** or **6.20**) then the capitalised value of the annuity is treated as additional consideration (Statement of Practice 1/79; CG28420).

MARKET VALUE RULE

6.22 Partners are connected persons (see **3.19**) for CGT purposes. However, where an interest in a partnership asset is transferred between partners on a commercial basis, market value is not substituted for the actual consideration passing unless the partners are otherwise connected.

HMRC guidance makes it clear that this practice applies to:

- 'normal disposals and acquisitions' of fractional shares in partnership assets between partners who are otherwise acting at arm's length and connected solely by partnership; and
- acquisitions made by an incoming partner and disposals made by the existing partners (*TCGA 1992, s 286(4)*; CG27800).

HMRC may seek to apply the market value rule where the partners are connected otherwise than by partnership, or where they are not so connected but may not be acting at arm's length. HMRC will consider whether any consideration passing is of an amount that might reasonably have been expected to pass had they been unconnected except by partnership, and acting at arm's length (CG27800; HMRC Statement of Practice D12, para 7).

LIMITED LIABILITY PARTNERSHIPS

6.23 A limited liability partnership (LLP) carrying on a trade or business with a view to profit is treated in the same way as a conventional partnership for CGT purposes, ie it is 'fiscally transparent'. Although an LLP is a corporate body, for CGT purposes its assets are treated as held by its members as partners and the LLP's dealings are treated as dealings by the members in partnership rather than by the LLP itself. Tax is charged on the members of the LLP separately, in respect of chargeable gains accruing to them as members, on a disposal of any of the LLP's assets (*TCGA 1992, s 59A(1)*).

The CGT provisions applying to partnerships other than LLPs are generally extended to LLPs and it is provided that references to members of a partnership include members of an LLP. However, references to a company or its members do not include an LLP or its members (*TCGA 1992, s 59A(2)*).

The members of an LLP are entitled to the same reliefs as partners in a conventional partnership. All HMRC concessions and statements of practice apply to an LLP in the same way as they apply to a conventional partnership while it is carrying on a trade or business. However, they do not apply to the members of an LLP that has ceased to be 'fiscally transparent' (see below) (Statement of Practice D12, introduction; CG27050).

The 'transparency' treatment outlined above continues on the temporary cessation of a trade or business carried on with a view to profit. It also continues during a period of winding-up following a permanent cessation of the trade or business, so long as that period is not unreasonably prolonged and the winding-up is not done for reasons connected with tax avoidance. Transparency ceases to apply, however:

- on the appointment of a liquidator; and
- where a court makes a winding-up order or there is a corresponding event under the law of an overseas territory (*TCGA 1992, s 59A(3), (4)*).

Where transparency does end, and tax is charged on the LLP as a company in respect of chargeable gains accruing on a disposal of its assets (or on the members in respect of chargeable gains accruing on a disposal of their capital interests in the LLP) then the liability is computed and tax is charged as though the rules outlined above never applied (*TCGA 1992, s 59(5)*).

There is no deemed disposal of assets by the LLP or any member as a result of transparency beginning or coming to an end (*TCGA 1992, s 59(6)*).

However, when transparency ends and a member of the LLP holds an asset that he acquired for a consideration that was treated as reduced by virtue of a claim to roll-over relief (under *TCGA 1992, s 152* or *s 154*) he is treated as if a gain equal to the amount of that reduction accrued at that time. There is a similar provision for clawback of hold-over relief on gifts under *TCGA 1992, s 165* or *s 260* (*TCGA 1992, ss 156A, 159A*).

RESIDENCE AND DOMICILE

6.24 A partnership's fiscal transparency (see **6.1**) means that special rules applying to partnerships controlled abroad are (with the exception mentioned below) no longer relevant. Each partner's CGT position depends on his own residence and domicile status (see **Chapter 5**). For example:

- a partner who is resident, ordinarily resident and domiciled in the UK is chargeable on gains accruing to him on the disposal of partnership assets irrespective of where they arise; and
- a partner who is neither resident nor ordinarily resident in the UK is chargeable only in relation to gains accruing on the disposal of assets used for the purpose of a trade carried on via a UK branch or agency (see **5.24**).

Any double taxation agreement providing relief from CGT in the UK for a partnership's capital gains does not affect the CGT liability on a UK-resident partner's share of those gains where the partnership carries on a trade, profession or business whose control and management are situated outside the UK (*TCGA 1992, s 59(2), (3)*).

APPENDIX: HMRC STATEMENT OF PRACTICE D12

6.25 *The full text of the statement of practice is reproduced below.*

This statement of practice was originally issued by the Commissioner for Her Majesty's Revenue and Customs on 17 January 1975 following discussions with the Law Society and the Allied Accountancy Bodies on the capital gains tax treatment of partnerships. This statement sets out a number of points of general practice which have been agreed in respect of partnerships to which *TCGA 1992, s 59* applies.

The enactment of the *Limited Liability Partnership Act 2000*, has created, from April 2001, the concept of limited liability partnerships (as bodies corporate) in UK law. In conjunction with this, new capital gains tax provisions dealing with such partnerships have been introduced through *TCGA 1992, s 59A*. *TCGA 1992, s 59A(1)* mirrors *TCGA 1992, s 59* in treating any dealings in chargeable assets by a limited liability partnership as dealings by the individual members, as partners, for capital gains tax purposes. Each member of a limited liability partnership to which *s 59A(1)* applies has therefore to be regarded, like a partner in any other (non-corporate) partnership, as owning a fractional share of each of the partnership assets and not an interest in the partnership itself.

This statement of practice has therefore been extended to limited liability partnerships which meet the requirements of *TCGA 1992, ss 59, 59A(1)*, such that capital gains of a partnership fall to be charged on its members as partners. Accordingly, in the text of the statement of practice, all references to a 'partnership' or 'firm' include reference to limited liability partnerships to which *TCGA 1992, ss 59, 59A(1)* applies, and all references to 'partner' include reference to a member of a limited liability partnership to which *TCGA 1992, ss 59, 59A(1)* applies.

For the avoidance of doubt, this statement of practice does not apply to the members of a limited liability partnership which ceases to be 'fiscally transparent' by reason of its not being, or its no longer being, within *TCGA 1992, ss 59, 59A(1)*.

1 Valuation of a partner's share in a partnership asset

Where it is necessary to ascertain the market value of a partner's share in a partnership asset for capital gains tax purposes, it will be taken as a fraction of the value of the total partnership interest in the asset without any discount for the size of his share. If, for example, a partnership owned all the issued shares in a company, the value of the interest in that holding of a partner with a one-tenth share would be one-tenth of the value of the partnership's 100% holding.

2 Disposals of assets by a partnership

Where an asset is disposed of by a partnership to an outside party each of the partners will be treated as disposing of his fractional share of the asset. In computing gains or losses the proceeds of disposal will be allocated between the partners in the ratio of their share in asset surpluses at the time of disposal. Where this is not specifically laid down the allocation will follow the actual destination of the surplus as shown in the partnership accounts; regard will of course have to be paid to any agreement outside the accounts. If the surplus is not allocated among the partners but, for example, put to a common reserve, regard will be had to the ordinary profit sharing ratio in the absence of a specified asset-surplus-sharing ratio. Expenditure on the acquisition of assets by a partnership will be allocated between the partners in the same way at the time of the acquisition. This allocation may require adjustment, however, if there is a subsequent change in the partnership sharing ratios (see paragraph 4).

3 Partnership assets divided in kind among the partners

Where a partnership distributes an asset in kind to one or more of the partners, for example on dissolution, a partner who receives the asset will not be regarded as disposing of his fractional share in it. A computation will first be necessary of the gains which would be chargeable on the individual partners if the asset has been disposed of at its current market value. Where this results in a gain being attributed to a partner not receiving the asset the gain will be charged at the time of the distribution of the asset. Where, however, the gain is allocated to a partner receiving the asset concerned there will be no charge on distribution. Instead, his capital gains tax cost to be carried forward will be the market value of the asset at the date of distribution as reduced by the amount of his gain. The same principles will be applied where the computation results in a loss.

4 Changes in partnership sharing ratios

An occasion of charge also arises when there is a change in partnership sharing ratios including changes arising from a partner joining or leaving the partnership. In these circumstances a partner who reduces or gives up his share in asset surpluses will be treated as disposing of part of the whole of his share in each of the partnership assets and a partner who increases his share will be treated as making a similar acquisition. Subject to the qualifications mentioned at 6 and 7 below the disposal consideration will be a fraction (equal to the fractional share changing hands) of the current balance sheet value of each chargeable asset provided there is no direct payment of consideration outside the partnership. Where no adjustment is made through the partnership accounts (eg by revaluation of the assets coupled with a corresponding increase or decrease in the partner's current or capital account at some date between the partner's acquisition and the reduction in his share) the disposal is treated as made for a consideration equal to his capital gains tax cost and thus there will be neither a chargeable gain nor an allowable loss at that point. A partner whose share reduces will carry forward a smaller proportion of cost to set against a subsequent disposal of the asset and a partner whose share increases will carry forward a larger proportion of cost.

The general rules in *TCGA 1992, s 42* for apportioning the total acquisition cost on a part-disposal of an asset will not be applied in the case of a partner reducing his asset-surplus share. Instead, the cost of the part disposed of will be calculated on a fractional basis.

5 Adjustment through the accounts

Where a partnership asset is revalued a partner will be credited in his current or capital account with a sum equal to his fractional share of the increase in value. An upward revaluation of chargeable assets is not itself an occasion of charge. If, however, there were to be a subsequent reduction in the partner's asset-surplus share, the effect would be to reduce his potential liability to capital gains tax on the eventual disposal of the assets without an equivalent reduction of the credit he has received in the accounts. Consequently at the time of the reduction in sharing ratio he will be regarded as disposing of the fractional share of the partnership asset represented by the difference between his old and his new share for a consideration equal to that fraction of the increased value at the revaluation. The partner whose share correspondingly increases will have his acquisition cost to be carried forward for the asset increased by the same amount. The same principles will be applied in the case of a downward revaluation.

6 Payments outside the accounts

Where on a change of partnership sharing ratios payments are made directly between two or more partners outside the framework of the partnership accounts, the payments represent consideration for the disposal of the whole or part of a partner's share in partnership assets in addition to any consideration calculated on the basis described in 4 and 5 above. Often such payments will be for goodwill not included in the balance sheet. In such cases the partner receiving the payment will have no capital gains tax cost to set against it unless he made a similar payment for his share in the asset (eg on entering the partnership) or elects to have the market value at 6 April 1965 treated as his acquisition cost. The partner making the payment will only be allowed to deduct the amount in computing gains or losses on a subsequent disposal of his share in the asset. He will be able to claim a loss when he finally leaves the partnership or when his share is reduced provided that he then receives either no consideration or a lesser consideration for his share of the asset. Where the payment clearly constitutes payment for a share in assets included in the partnership accounts, the partner receiving it will be able to deduct the amount of the partnership acquisition cost represented by the fraction he is disposing of. Special treatment, as outlined in 7 below, may be necessary for transfers between persons not at arm's length.

7 Transfers between persons not at arm's length

Where no payment is made either through or outside the accounts in connection with a change in partnership sharing ratio, a CGT charge will only arise if the transaction is otherwise than by way of a bargain made at arm's length and falls therefore within *TCGA 1992, s 17* extended by *TCGA 1992, s 18* for transactions between connected persons. Under *TCGA 1992, s 286(4)* transfers of partnership assets between partners are not regarded as transactions between connected persons if they are pursuant to genuine commercial arrangements. This treatment will also be given to transactions between an incoming partner and the existing partners.

Where the partners (including incoming partners) are connected other than by partnership (eg father and son) or are otherwise not at arm's length (eg uncle and nephew) the transfer of a share in the partnership assets may fall to be treated as having been made at market value. Market value will not be substituted, however, if nothing would have been paid had the parties been at arm's length. Similarly if consideration of less than market value passes between partners connected other than by partnership or otherwise not at arm's length, the transfer will only be regarded as having been made for full market value if the consideration actually paid was less than that which would have been paid by parties at arm's length. Where a transfer has to be treated as if it had taken place for market value, the deemed disposal will fall to be treated in the same way as payments outside the accounts.

8 Annuities provided by partnerships

A lump sum which is paid to a partner on leaving the partnership or on a reduction of his share in the partnership represents consideration for the disposal by the partner concerned of the whole or part of his share in the partnership assets and will be subject to the rules in 6 above. The same treatment will apply when a partnership buys a purchased life annuity for a partner, the measure of the consideration being the actual costs of the annuity.

Where a partnership makes annual payments to a retired partner (whether under covenant or not) the capitalised value of the annuity will only be treated as consideration for the disposal of his share in the partnership assets under *TCGA 1992, s 37(3)* if it is more than can be regarded as a reasonable recognition of the past contribution of work and effort by the partner to the partnership. Provided that the former partner had been in the partnership for at least ten years an annuity will be regarded as reasonable for this purpose if it is no more than two-thirds of his average share of the profits in the best three of the last seven years in which he was required to devote substantially the whole of this time to acting as a partner. In arriving at a partner's share of the profits regard will be had to the partnership profits assessed before deduction of any capital allowances or charges. The ten-year period will include any period during which the partner was a member of another firm whose business has been merged with that of the present firm. For lesser periods the following fractions will be used instead of two-thirds:

Complete years in partnership	*Fraction*
1–5	1/60 for each year
6	8/60
7	16/60
8	24/60
9	32/60

Where the capitalised value of an annuity is treated as consideration received by the retired partner, it will also be regarded as allowable expenditure by the remaining partners on the acquisition of their fractional shares in partnership assets from him.

9 Mergers

Where the members of two or more existing partnerships come together to form a new one, the capital gains tax treatment will follow the same lines as that for changes in partnership sharing ratios. If gains arise for reasons similar to those covered in 5 and 6 above, it may be possible for roll-over relief under *TCGA 1992, ss 152–158* to be claimed by any partner continuing in the partnership insofar as he disposes of part of his share in the assets of the old firm and acquires a share in other assets put into the 'merged' firm. Where, however, in such cases the consideration given for the shares in chargeable assets acquired is less than the consideration for those disposed of, relief will be restricted under *TCGA 1992, s 153*.

10 Shares acquired in stages

Where a share in a partnership is acquired in stages wholly after 5 April 1965, the acquisition costs of the various chargeable assets will be calculated by pooling the expenditure relating to each asset. Where a share built up in stages was acquired wholly or partly before 6 April 1965 the rules in *TCGA 1992, Sch 2, para 18* will normally be followed to identify the acquisition cost of the share in each asset which is disposed of on the occasion of a reduction in the partnership's share; that is, the disposal will normally be identified with shares acquired on a 'first in, first out' basis. Special consideration will be given, however, to any case in which this rule appears to produce an unreasonable result when applied to temporary changes in the shares in a partnership, for example those occurring when a partner's departure and a new partner's arrival are out of step by a few months.

11 Elections under TCGA 1992, Sch 2, para 4

Where the assets disposed of are quoted securities eligible for a pooling election under *TCGA 1992 Sch 2, para 4* partners will be allowed to make separate elections in respect of shares or fixed interest securities held by the partnership as distinct from shares and securities which they hold on a personal basis. Each partner will have a separate right of election for his proportion of the partnership securities and the time limit for the purposes of *Schedule 2* will run from the earlier of:

(a) the first relevant disposal of shares or securities by the partnership; and

(b) the first reduction of the particular partner's share in the partnership assets after 19 March 1968.

12 Partnership goodwill and taper relief

This paragraph applies where the value of goodwill which a partnership generates in the conduct of its business is not recognised in its balance sheet and where, as a matter of consistent practice, no value is placed on that goodwill in dealings between the partners. In such circumstances, the partnership goodwill will not be regarded as a 'fungible asset' (and, therefore, will not be within the definition of 'securities' in *TCGA 1992, s 104(3)*) for the purpose of capital gains tax taper relief under *TCGA 1992, s 2A*. Accordingly, on a disposal for actual consideration of any particular partner's interest in the goodwill of such a partnership, that interest will be treated as the same asset (or, in the case of a part disposal, a part of the same asset) as was originally acquired by that partner when first becoming entitled to a share in the goodwill of that partnership.

The treatment described in the preceding paragraph will also be applied to goodwill acquired for consideration by a partnership but which is not, at any time, recognised in the partnership balance sheet at a value exceeding its cost of acquisition nor otherwise taken into account in dealings between partners. However, such purchased goodwill will continue to be treated for the purpose of computing capital gains tax taper relief as assets separate from the partnership's self-generated goodwill. On a disposal or part disposal for actual consideration of an interest in such purchased goodwill by any particular partner, that interest shall be treated for taper relief purposes as acquired either on the date of purchase by the partnership or on the date on which the disposing partner first became entitled to a share in that goodwill, whichever is the later.

Chapter 7

Administration of an estate

INTRODUCTION

7.1 In the event of death, the property included in the deceased's estate does not automatically pass to the beneficiaries, but passes to the personal representatives or executors whose duty it is to administer the estate. The executors' or personal representatives' duty includes getting in the property, discharging the deceased's debts and finally distributing the assets to the beneficiaries under the will or according to the rules of intestacy.

In relation to CGT, the personal representative will be concerned with:

- capital gains arising in the period to the date of death; and
- capital gains arising in the administration of the estate.

Legislation is included in the *Finance (No 2) Act 2010* which introduces a new rate of 28% for personal representatives of deceased persons. This will have the effect that during 2010/11 there will be two rates of capital gains tax. Capital gains triggered prior to 23 June 2010 will be charged at 18%, while gains triggered on or after 23 June 2010 will be charged at 28%.

CAPITAL GAINS TAX IN THE PERIOD TO THE DATE OF DEATH

General provisions

7.2 Generally, the deceased will be liable to tax on any capital gains made in the period up to the date of death and it is the duty of the personal representative to ensure that this tax liability is discharged or provisions are made prior to the distribution of the estate. The normal self-assessment procedure has to be followed, however, *TMA 1970, s 40(1)* extends the self-assessment time limits and the assessment must now be made by the end of the third year after 31 January following the tax year in which the death took place. From 1 April 2010 the time limit will change to the end of four years.

Example 7.1—Time limits

John died on 1 July 2009. The tax return for the period from 6 April 2009 to the date of death has not yet been completed.

The date of death occurred in the tax year ending 5 April 2010, for which the filing date is 31 January 2011 for returns filed online. Paper returns need to be filed by 31 October 2010. Therefore, assessment in respect of the period to date of death may be made at any time up to 31 January 2014.

CGT losses of the deceased

7.3 Special provisions in relation to capital losses made in the tax year in which a person dies are introduced by *TCGA 1992, s 62(2)*. These rules provide that allowable losses sustained by an individual in the tax year in which he dies may, so far as they cannot be deducted from chargeable gains accruing in that year, be deducted from chargeable gains accruing to the deceased in the three tax years preceding the tax year in which his death occurs, taking chargeable gains accruing in a later year before those accruing in an earlier year.

Example 7.2—Capital losses

John (see **Example 7.1**), in the period 6 April 2009 to the date of death, made capital losses of £10,000. In 2008/09 he made capital gains of £12,000, on which CGT was paid.

His executors can make a claim under *TCGA 1992, s 62(2)* and obtain a tax refund, which will fall into John's estate for IHT purposes.

CAPITAL GAINS TAX IN THE ADMINISTRATION OF AN ESTATE

General provisions

7.4 The general rule is that the 'assets of which a deceased person was competent to dispose' are deemed to have been acquired by his personal representatives for a consideration equal to their market value at the date of death. These assets are not deemed to be disposed of by the deceased on death, and therefore there is no charge to CGT on the deceased's unrealised gains (*TCGA 1992, s 62(1)*).

'Assets of which the deceased was competent to dispose' are defined in *TCGA 1992, s 62(10)* as assets of the deceased, which he could, if of full age and capacity, have disposed of by will, assuming that the assets were situated in England, and, if he was not domiciled in the UK, that he was domiciled in England, and include references to his severable share in any assets to which, immediately before his death, he was beneficially entitled as joint tenant.

The provisions of *TCGA 1992, s 73* extend the general rule to settlements with an interest in possession created prior to 22 March 2006, immediate post death interests (IPDI), transitional serial interests (TSI), a disabled person's interest (DT) and bereaved minor trusts (BMT), in that on the death of a life tenant, the gains within the fund will be exempt from CGT. Following the *Finance Act 2006* these provisions will not apply to interest in possession settlements which fall under the relevant property regime, as the assets within such trusts will no longer form part of the estate of the deceased life tenant.

If on death the property within the trust reverts to the settlor, the disposal and reacquisition shall be deemed to be for such consideration so that neither a loss nor a gain accrues to the trustee (*see TCGA 1992, s 73(1)(b)*).

The exception to the rule in *s 73* is that, where gains were held over on the transfer of assets into a trust, such held-over gains will now be chargeable to CGT on the death of the life tenant (see *TCGA 1992, s 74*).

Example 7.3—Tax-free uplift on death

John's estate includes a seaside cottage, which he purchased in 1990 for £50,000. The property is now worth £250,000.

On John's death the gain of £200,000 on the seaside cottage is not chargeable to tax; instead John's executors acquire the seaside cottage at a new base value of £250,000.

John was also the life tenant of a pre-22 March 2006 interest in possession trust which was valued at £150,000 at date of his death. The settlor of the trust was John's father who transferred assets valued at £50,000 into the trust in 1982. The gain held over in 1982 was £20,000.

On John's death, the held-over gain of £20,000 becomes chargeable, unless it is possible to make another hold-over claim. John's estate, therefore, includes the value of the interest in possession trust at date of death less any held-over gain – £130,000 (£150,000 less £20,000).

Personal representatives

7.5 Personal representatives are treated as a single and continuing body of persons, and they are treated as having the deceased's residence, ordinary residence and domicile at the date of death (*TCGA 1992, s 62(3)*). They are liable to capital gains tax on disposals made by them during the administration of the estate. For the tax year in which the death occurs and the following two years of assessment, the personal representatives are entitled to the same annual exempt amounts as individuals with the same general provisions applying (*TCGA 1992, s 3(7)*).

As personal representatives are deemed to take the deceased's residence status, UK personal representatives of a non-resident deceased are not chargeable to CGT. However, this exception does not apply to trustees, and therefore if there are ongoing trusts, for example, because there are minor beneficiaries, the residence status of the trustees will determine whether the trust is UK resident for CGT purposes (see **8.43**).

Valuation of chargeable asset at the date of death

7.6 When considering a potential charge to CGT during the administration of an estate, any computation of a capital gain must start with a consideration of the market value, ie 'the price which the asset might reasonably be expected to fetch on a sale in the open market' (*TCGA 1992, s 272(1)*).

Where, on the death of any person, IHT was chargeable on the value of the estate immediately before death and where the value of an asset as part of that estate has been 'ascertained' for the purposes of IHT, that value is taken to be the market value for CGT purposes unless the value has only been ascertained to establish the amount of transferable nil rate band between spouses or civil partners from 9 October 2007 (*TCGA 1992, s 274*).

Care has to be taken in cases where the deceased's estate does not attract a charge to IHT, as the value of the asset will not be 'ascertained' for IHT, and so the personal representatives' base value will not be fixed. This can happen in the following situations:

- All the assets pass to a surviving spouse and the entire estate is IHT exempt.
- All the assets pass to charities or political parties and the estate is thus IHT exempt.
- The estimated value of the estate is well below the threshold on which tax is to be payable and therefore the estate is not subject to IHT charges.

- The assets of the estate are all subject to agricultural and business property relief for IHT at the rate of 100%.
- Some combination of the above factors and/or other exemptions makes the estate non-taxpaying.

If the value of an asset is not ascertained for inheritance tax, the normal rules of *TCGA 1992, s 272* will apply to determine the capital gains tax acquisition value of the beneficiary. The acquisition cost of each asset must be negotiated with HMRC when the asset is sold. The taxpayer *must* supply information about the transactions to which the valuations relate, as specified on CG34, together with any relevant tax computations. The taxpayer *may* use form CG34, but this is not mandatory. Costs *may* be subject to negotiations if HMRC decide to open an enquiry.

HMRC Capital Gains Manual in CG32210 to CG32271 explains the procedure to be adopted when either: values have been ascertained for IHT and there are queries; or the values have not been ascertained.

If it transpires during the administration of an estate that the market value on death of an asset for IHT is too high, relief from IHT may be available. The personal representatives may substitute a lower figure for the market value on death where property valued on death as 'related property' is sold within three years after the death (*IHTA 1984, s 161*), or if quoted securities are sold within 12 months of death for less than their market value on death (*IHTA 1984, ss 178* et seq) and land is sold within four years for less than its market value on death (*IHTA 1984, ss 190* et seq). See *Inheritance Tax 2010/11* (Bloomsbury Professional), Chapter 10. This lower figure will then also be used to form the personal representatives' base value for CGT.

Alternatively, it may be advantageous for the personal representatives to claim a CGT loss on the disposal. The example below illustrates this point:

Example 7.4—IHT revaluation

William died on 1 July 2010. His main asset is his home which is valued at £250,000. He also owns (quoted) shares in Green Ltd which on his death were valued at £100,000. His estate is worth £350,000 and the executors paid IHT of £10,000 ((£350,000 – £325,000) @ 40%).

During the first year of administration, it transpires that the shares in Green plc have fallen in value and are now only worth £35,000. The executors decide to sell. At the same time the value of the property, following a successful planning application, has increased by £110,000. The executors could consider claiming relief under *IHTA 1984, s 178* to reduce the estate below the nil rate band threshold for IHT of £325,000. A repayment of IHT would be £10,000, while at the same time a CGT charge of £27,972 (28% of £110,000 less annual exemption of £10,100) will be payable on the sale of the property.

This will result in an additional tax charge of £17,972 (CGT payment of £27,972 less repayment of IHT of £10,000).

Alternatively, the executors could claim the CGT loss of £65,000 on the sale of the shares against the £110,000 gain on the property, thereby returning a net taxable gain of £45,000. Taking into account the annual exemption of £10,100, an additional CGT charge of £9,772 will be due ((£45,000 – £10,100) @ 28%).

The executors, if they decide using the capital loss on the shares against the gain on the property rather than reclaiming IHT, save tax of £8,200 (£17,972 less £9,772).

Transactions during the administration period

7.7 Sales of assets comprised in the deceased's estate by the personal representatives are disposals for capital gains tax purposes. Capital gains tax, subject to the deductions and allowances mentioned below, will have to be paid on the difference between the sale consideration and the market value at the date of death. The rates of tax are as follows:

- Transactions until 5 April 2004 34%
- Transactions between 6 April 2004 and 5 April 2008 40%
- Transactions after 5 April 2008 but before 23 June 2010 18%
- Transactions on or after 23 June 2010 28%

Allowable expenses

7.8 Following the decision in *Richards' Executors HL* (1971) 46 TC 626, HL personal representatives can deduct an appropriate proportion of the cost of acquiring the assets from the testator (ie legal and accountancy costs that are involved in preparing the inheritance tax account and obtaining the grant of probate) from the sales proceeds.

HMRC Statement of Practice 02/04 has suggested a scale for deaths after 5 April 2004 (for deaths prior to 6 April 2004 see HMRC Statement of Practice 8/94).

Table 7.1—Statement of Practice 02/04 – Allowable expenditure

Gross value of estate	**Allowable expenditure**
A. Up to £50,000	1.8% of the probate value of the assets sold by the personal representatives
B. Between £50,001 and £90,000	A fixed amount of £900, to be divided between all the assets in the estate in the proportion to the probate values, and allowed in those proportions on assets sold by the personal representatives
C. Between £90,001 and £400,000	1% of the probate value of all assets sold
D. Between £400,001 and £500,000	A fixed amount of £4,000, divided as at B above
E. Between £500,001 and £1,000,000	0.8% of the probate value of the assets sold
F. Between £1,000,001 and £5,000,000	A fixed amount of £8,000, divided as at B above
G. Over £5,000,000	0.16% of the probate value of the assets sold, subject to a maximum of £10,000

Personal representatives may claim to deduct more, when higher expenses have been occurred. Note that this relief is available only to the personal representatives, and not, for example, to a beneficiary to whom the asset may have been appropriated.

Taper relief and indexation

7.9 The application of business asset taper relief and indexation allowance in relation to disposals by personal representatives prior to 6 April 2008 is explained in **Chapter 17**.

Following the *Finance Act 2008* disposals by personal representatives after 5 April 2008 but before 23 June 2010 are charged at the single rate of 18% irrespective of the type of asset disposed of. The single rate of 18% has been increased to 28% in the *Finance (No 2) Act 2010* for disposals on or after 23 June 2010.

Annual exemption

7.10 Personal representatives have the same annual exemption from CGT as individuals (£10,100 for 2010/11) in the tax year of death, and in each of the two following tax years *TCGA 1992* (*s 3(7)*).

With some foresight it may be advantageous to transfer assets to the legatees prior to a sale and use the legatees' annual exemptions to reduce the CGT burden. Personal representatives carefully need to consider the tax consequences of any sale (see **7.11**).

Example 7.5—Sale of property by personal representatives

Alice died on 29 June 2010 leaving a property worth £1,000,000. Alice's will leaves her estate to her six children Alfie, Ben, Claire, David, Emily and Freddie. The personal representatives now wish to sell the property.

	£
Sale proceeds	1,100,000
Probate value	1,000,000
Capital gain	100,000
Allowable expenses (0.8% of probate value)	8,000
Annual exemption	10,100
Taxable gain	81,900
Tax @ 28%	22,932

The personal representatives' liability to CGT will be £22,932 on the disposal of the property.

Transfers to legatees

7.11 Where a person disposes of an asset to which he became absolutely entitled as legatee, any incidental expenditure incurred by that person or by the personal representative in relation to the transfer of the asset to him is allowable as a deduction in the computation of the gain arising on the disposal (*TCGA 1992, s 64(1)*).

A 'legatee' includes any person taking under a testamentary disposition or on intestacy or partial intestacy, whether he takes beneficially or as trustee (*TCGA 1992, s 64(2)*).

On a transfer of an asset to a legatee, the personal representatives neither make a gain nor a loss for capital gains tax purposes. The legatee acquires the asset at the personal representative's base cost, which is usually the probate value. If there is more than one legatee receiving an asset, the base costs will have to be apportioned accordingly.

Where the asset disposed of is a dwelling house that has at some time in the period of administration been a residence of a person who is a legatee in respect of that dwelling house, private residence exemption may, in certain circumstances, be available under the terms of Extra-statutory Concession D5 and, for disposals after 9 December 2003, *TCGA 1992, s 225A*.

A *donatio mortis causa* (a gift in anticipation of death) is treated as a testamentary disposition and not a gift, so that the donee acquires the asset at its market value on the date of death and the asset therefore is subject to a tax-free uplift on death (*TCGA 1992, s 62(5)*).

CGT may be saved by using each legatee's annual exemption. In addition, further tax can be saved, if any of the legatees are not resident or ordinarily resident in the UK for tax purposes.

Example 7.6—Sale of property by legatees

The example is the same as in **7.5**, but the personal representatives recognise that a sale by the legatees may be advantageous.

Alfie and Ben live in Switzerland and are not resident nor ordinarily resident in the UK for tax purposes.

Claire and David's income is modest and is just above the personal allowance of £6,475 and they are both basic rate tax payers.

Emily's taxable income, after all allowable deductions and the personal allowance, is £35,000. The upper limit of the income tax basic rate band is £37,400 during 2010/11.

Freddie is a higher rate tax payer with taxable income of £90,000.

	£
1/6th share in sale proceeds	183,333
Proportionate probate value	166,667
Capital gain on 1/6th share	16,666
Alfie and Ben escape a charge to CGT, as they are not UK resident	
Claire and David's CGT position	
Capital gain	16,666
Annual exemption	10,100
Taxable gain	6,566
Tax @ 18%	1,182

Emily's CGT position	£
Capital gain	16,666
Annual exemption	10,100
Taxable gain	6,566
Tax @ 18% on £2,400 (£37,400 – £35,000)	432
Tax @ 28% on £4,166 (£6,566 – £2,400)	1,166
CGT payable by Emily	1,598

Freddie's CGT position	
Capital gain	16,666
Annual exemption	10,100
Taxable gain	6,566
Tax @ 28%	1,838
CGT payable by Freddie	1,838

The total CGT liability on the sale of the property by the legatees will be £5,800. This represents an overall tax saving of £17,132

Exempt legatees

7.12 As mentioned above, certain legatees are exempt from capital gains tax and the personal representative therefore has to consider carefully the capital gains tax position prior to selling any assets within the estate which are subject to a capital gain. The following legatees are exempt:

- UK charities under *TCGA 1992, s 256*;
- legatees who are not resident, nor ordinarily resident in the UK.

Problems may arise in situations where the estate is divided among several charities or where the personal representatives need part of the sale proceeds to cover administration expenses. In order for the *charity* exemption or the non-resident exemption to apply, the personal representatives should consider the following options:

- appropriate the assets to the charities or to the non-UK resident individual in partial or total satisfaction of their entitlement and then, having received instructions from the beneficiary, sell the assets as bare trustees for those charities; or

- appropriate the assets to charities or to the non-UK resident individual subject to a lien in favour of the personal representative.

LEGATEE OR BENEFICIARY

7.13 It is often difficult to determine whether someone receives assets as a legatee or as a beneficiary absolutely entitled under the terms of a trust. If assets are appointed by trustees of a trust, this will be a deemed disposal under *TCGA 1992, s 71* and a charge to CGT may arise (see **8.11**). In contrast, as explained above, there will not be any CGT consequences under *TCGA 1992, s 62* if personal representatives pass assets to legatees.

If a trust is created by a will or on intestacy, the trustees of that trust are legatees in precisely the same way as, for example, an individual taking an absolute interest in an asset. This is confirmed by *TCGA 1992, s 64(2)*. As a result the personal representatives are not liable to capital gains tax for disposals after assets have vested in the trustees, and the trustees acquire the assets at market value.

Problems often arise in situations where the same persons are appointed as executors and trustees under a will or on intestacy. The question then arises in what capacity those persons acted. In order to answer this question it is important to consider whether the administration period has come to an end. This will be the case once all the assets of the estate have been determined and the liabilities have been discharged or adequate provisions have been made. It will then be possible to ascertain the residue, ie the assets which will pass to the residuary beneficiaries, which signals the end of the administration period. Once the administration period has ended, it is likely that the beneficial interests have vested in trustees rather than being retained by the personal representatives. Any acts carried out after that time will therefore be carried out by those persons acting as trustees rather than the personal representatives (CG31123).

DEEDS OF APPOINTMENT, VARIATIONS OR DISCLAIMERS

7.14 The devolution of the estate may be varied in a number of ways:

- *Deeds of appointment*: if a will directs that after completion of the administration period, some or all of the assets of the estate are to be held on trust and that trust contains powers enabling the trustees to appoint assets out of the trust, a deed of appointment may be executed so that those assets pass direct to the appointee on vesting rather than entering the trust. For a discussion of the capital gains tax consequences of deeds of appointment see **8.11**.

- *Disclaimers*: if a legatee wishes to give up his or her entitlement to assets of the estate without directing how those assets should be dealt with thereafter, a deed of disclaimer may be executed.
- *Deeds of variation*: if a legatee wishes to give up his or her entitlement to certain assets of the estate but wishes to direct to whom those assets should devolve in place of that legatee, a deed of variation may be executed.

Disclaimers

7.15 A disclaimer operates in much the same way as a deed of variation, however, it is a much simpler document. A legatee can terminate his entitlement to an inheritance by executing a disclaimer. However, unlike with a variation, the legatee cannot redirect his interest. The benefit disclaimed will pass in accordance with the terms of the will relating to the residue in an estate or on intestacy.

Therefore, if the disclaimed interest was an absolute interest, either in specific assets or in residue, after the disclaimer those assets are added to the remaining residual entitlements. The residue is then distributed in accordance with the pre-existing terms of the will. If an interest in residue has been disclaimed, residue is divided between the other persons entitled to residue ignoring the bequest to the disclaimer, or if there are no other residuary beneficiaries, according to the rules of intestacy.

If under the terms of a will a person would have received a life interest, a disclaimer by that person will result in the acceleration of the interests of other persons having successive interests.

Example 7.7—Disclaimer

Alice's will leaves her husband William a pecuniary legacy of £50,000 with a life interest in the residue. The life interest will pass, on William's death, to their children Hannah and Imogen absolutely in equal shares.

William is elderly and financially secure, and he wishes to help Hannah and Imogen, who are both in the process of purchasing their first property. He therefore wishes to disclaim his interest in the pecuniary legacy and the life interest. If he executes such a disclaimer, the estate will pass to Hannah and Imogen in equal shares absolutely.

Deeds of variation

7.16 A person who executes a deed of variation gives up his or her rights to receive an interest that he or she would otherwise have received under the terms of a will or intestacy. However, in contrast to disclaimers, the person who decides to vary his interest gives directions as to how the assets subject to the variation shall devolve. Variations are very flexible tools which usually remove certain clauses from the will and replace them with other clauses redirecting the original legatee's interest. For intestacies, variations deem to pass assets under a will having clauses containing the new conditions.

A deed of variation may be used to:

- vary certain clauses in a will;
- create a trust that was not in the original will, which is often used in estate planning to create a nil rate band discretionary trust to utilise the IHT nil rate band of a deceased spouse;
- vary the terms of a trust created by the will without varying the assets passing from the estate to the trustees;
- delete a trust that was in the will; or
- sever a joint tenancy to allow jointly held assets to pass under the terms of the will or the variation.

Example 7.8—Deed of variation

Using the scenario in **Example 7.7**, William is worried about passing the assets to Hannah and Imogen absolutely. Hannah is about to get married. William does not like her future husband, who has poor job prospects and spends most of his spare time gambling. He is worried that Hannah's inheritance will rapidly be whittled away.

Under a deed of variation, William could consider passing some of the assets to the two daughters outright to help them to purchase a property, while leaving the remainder on trust to retain some control over the use of those assets.

Effect of disclaimers and deeds of variations

7.17 A variation or disclaimer shall not constitute a disposal for capital gains tax purposes and it will be treated as if the dispositions have been effected by the deceased if:

- the variation or disclaimer was made within the period of two years after a person's death; and

- the variation or disclaimer was made by an instrument in writing made by the persons who benefit or would benefit under the dispositions (*TCGA 1992, s 62(6)*).

In other words, the effects of the disclaimer or variation are treated as being retrospective to the date of death. The assets are therefore deemed to have been acquired by the person at market/probate value at the date of death. A future gain therefore is calculated by reference to the probate value and not to the value at the time the variation or disclaimer was executed. It may sometimes be beneficial not to elect for *s 62(6)* to apply, as is discussed at **7.18**.

The provisions of *s 62(6)* do not apply to a variation or a disclaimer that is made 'for any consideration in money or money's worth other than consideration consisting of the making of a variation or disclaimer in respect of another of the dispositions' (*TCGA 1992, s 62(8)*).

Finance Act 2002, s 52 amended *s 62(7)* in that for a variation to be effective for capital gains tax purposes, the deed of variation now has to contain a statement by the persons making the instrument to the effect that they intended *s 62(7)* to apply to the variation. This in effect means that for deeds executed after 31 July 2002, it will not be necessary to give notice to HMRC within six months of the date of execution of the instrument, for *s 62(6)* to apply. As long as the variation expressly states that the provisions of *s 62(6)* are to apply to the deed of variation, the provisions automatically apply without further notices to HMRC. Note, however, that although for the purposes of trust law a deed of variation may give effect to many changes, as described at **7.16**, it will be retrospective for CGT only if it varies the dispositions of the estate of the deceased.

Care has to be taken if the variation creates a settlement, as following the case of *Marshall v Kerr* [1994] 3 All ER 106, [1994] STC 638, HL the settlor for the purposes of CGT is the original beneficiary who made the variation and not the deceased. Prior to 6 April 2008, if the variation established a UK settlement *TCGA 1992, s 77* provided that if the settlor retains an interest he is taxed on all gains realised by the trustees. This would be the case where a surviving spouse executed a deed of variation to create a nil rate band discretionary trust to utilise the nil rate band of the deceased spouse, but is included in the list of beneficiaries. Following the introduction of a single CGT rate of 18% for individuals, trustees and personal representatives from 6 April 2008, *s 77* was no longer considered necessary, and was therefore abolished in *Finance Act 2008*. However, the corresponding anti-avoidance rule for non-UK resident settlements (*s 86*) continues to apply after 5 April 2008.

Finance Act 2006 inserted a new section to determine the identity of the settlor of a trust following a *s 62(6)* election. These new rules apply to variations occurring on or after 6 April 2006 irrespective of the date on which the deceased person died. Therefore, the person who gives up part or all of their entitlement to property under the will or intestacy will be regarded as a settlor for capital gains tax purposes (*TCGA 1992, s 68C*).

Advisers need to be aware of the recent case of *Mrs Margaret Lau (The Executor of Werner Lau Deceased) v Her Majesty's Revenue & Customs* [2009] UK VAT SpC 00740 (18 March 2009). The deceased left, among others, a legacy of £665,000 to his stepson with the residue passing to his widow. The stepson subsequently disclaimed this legacy but, following the administration of the estate, the widow paid £1 million to him. The widow contended that the payment of £1 million was unconnected with her son's disclaimer – the payment was made in fulfilment of an earlier promise to fund her son's business ventures. The Special Commissioner decided that evidence overwhelmingly demonstrated that the disclaimer was made in return for the payment of the £1 million and therefore it was ineffective for *Inheritance Tax Act 1984, s 142(3)*, as it was made for consideration.

To elect or not to elect?

7.18 As explained above, if the deed of variation or disclaimer expressly elects for *s 62(6)* to apply, the new beneficiaries are deemed to acquire the assets at market/probate value at the date of death. Sometimes, however, there may be capital gains tax advantages in not electing for *s 62(6)* to apply, and for the new beneficiary to acquire the assets based on the market value at the date of execution of the variation or disclaimer, rather than at probate value. This can best be illustrated with the following examples.

Example 7.9—To elect or not to elect?

Scenario 1

Isabella's will, among other assets, leaves shares worth £100,000 to her daughter Julie. Julie wishes to vary her mother's will and to pass the shares to her son Stuart. The value of the shares has now increased to £108,000.

If Julie decides not to elect for *s 62(6)* to apply, Julie will be subject to a capital gain of £8,000. This will be covered by her annual exemption and Stuart will acquire the shares at the higher base cost of £108,000, which may reduce a potential future capital gains tax liability when he decides to sell the shares.

Scenario 2

Alice's estate includes shares which have a probate value of £400,000. Alice's son James, the sole legatee, wishes to pass these shares to his daughter Isabella. In the meantime, the shares have risen in value to £440,000. James will have to decide whether to elect for *s 62(6)* to apply. If James elects for *s 62(6)* to apply, he will pass the shares to Isabella at the base cost of £400,000 and therefore will escape a charge to CGT on the capital gain of £40,000. If James has personal losses he may decide not to elect for *s 62(6)* to give Isabella a higher base value. This may be advantageous in a rising market if Isabella wishes to sell the shares in the near future.

SALES BY LEGATEES

7.19 During the administration period, until assets are vested in the beneficiaries or residue has been ascertained, the legatee only holds a 'chose in action' ie a right to have the estate properly administered (see *Cochrane's Executors v CIR* (1974) 49 TC 299 and *Prest v Bettinson* (1998) 53 TC 437, Ch D).

The disposal of such a 'chose in action' by the legatee is the same as when the legatee executes a deed of variation for full consideration which is not retrospective to the date of death. The disposal consideration is the price received rather than the market value of the expectation.

Chapter 8

Capital gains tax – settlements

INTRODUCTION

8.1 The *Finance Act 2008*, apart from introducing a single rate of CGT of 18%, made sweeping changes to CGT by abolishing indexation and taper relief. These new rules also apply to settlements.

The generous tax rate of 18% has increased to 28% in the *Finance (No 2) Act 2010* for disposals by trustees on or after 23 June 2010.

Trustees of certain settlements are liable to capital gains tax on disposals and deemed disposals. The legislation distinguishes between UK-resident trusts and non-resident trusts. In addition there are separate rules for bare trusts which charge any capital gain tax arising on the beneficiary.

The *Finance Act 2006* introduced a new tax regime for interest in possession trusts and accumulation and maintenance trusts with the effect that such settlements are now chargeable transfers for inheritance tax. Therefore, in relation to interest in possession trusts, it will be necessary to ascertain whether the settlement was created prior to 22 March 2006, or is an immediate post-death interest (IPDI), transitional serial interest (TSI), bereaved minor trust (BMT) or disabled trust. In relation to accumulation and maintenance trusts, it will be necessary to ascertain whether a beneficiary has become entitled to an interest in possession prior to 22 March 2006.

The *Finance Act 2006* also introduced changes to the definition of settlor-interested settlements in *TCGA 1992, s 169F* by extending these provisions to parental trusts for minor children who are unmarried, or not in a civil partnership. Capital gains tax hold-over relief for settlements where children or stepchildren are potential beneficiaries is not available from 22 March 2006.

The *Finance Act 2008* has removed some of the rules for settlor-interested trusts found in *TCGA 1992, ss 77–79*, because the new single rate of CGT means that these rules became superfluous.

When determining the tax position of a settlement, it is important to determine whether one deals with the creation of a settlement, a disposal or deemed disposal by the trustees. In addition it will be necessary to determine whether the trustees will be assessed on any capital gains tax arising or whether one of the special rules, listed below, apply:

- *TCGA 1992, s 60* provides for a number of situations in which the 'settled property' is treated for tax purposes as belonging to the beneficiary and taxed as such (see **8.2**).
- In settlor-interested settlements gains accruing to the trustees up to 5 April 2008 are not chargeable on them, but are treated as accruing to the settlor (see **8.39**).
- Special capital gains tax rules apply to overseas resident settlements (see **8.43**).
- The *Finance Act 2005* created a new trust tax regime for 'vulnerable persons' (see **8.45–8.48**).

DEFINITION OF 'SETTLEMENT' AND 'SETTLED PROPERTY'

General considerations

8.2 Prior to *FA 2006* the legislation did not define the term 'settlement'. *TCGA 1992, s 68* provided that 'settled' property meant any property held in trust other than property to which *s 60* applies. *Schedule 12* of *FA 2006* introduced a group of changes which had the effect that, from 6 April 2006, the definitions of 'settled property', 'settlement', 'settlor' and the tests as to residence of trustees are the same for income tax and CGT.

In outline:

- new *s 68A* defined 'settlor';
- new *s 68B* looked at transfers of property between settlements, to determine who is the settlor of them;
- new *s 68C* introduced new rules in relation to instruments of variation to determine who is the settlor;
- *s 69* was substantially revised by the insertion of subsections *(1), (2)* and *(2A)* to *(2E)* which address residence issues;
- *s 169F* was also substantially amended so as to widen the concept of 'settlor-interest' to include benefits for minor dependent children (including stepchildren) who are unmarried and do not have a civil partner.

'Bare trusts' and 'absolute entitlement'

8.3 *Section 60(1)* provides that, although there is a trust of property, the property is not 'settled property' and is treated as belonging to the beneficiary, where:

- assets are held by a person as nominee for another person, or as trustee for another person absolutely entitled as against the trustee, which includes nomineeships and simple or bare trusts;
- property is held on trust 'for any person who would be absolutely entitled but for being an infant or other person under a disability';
- property is held for two or more persons who are or would be jointly entitled, which, for example, includes joint ownership of land in England or Wales where trustees hold the legal title upon 'trust for sale' for the joint tenants or tenants in common (see *Kidson v Macdonald* [1974] STC 54).

If a person is 'absolutely entitled against the trustee' and he has the 'exclusive right' to direct how that asset shall be dealt with, the property will not be 'settled property' for capital gains tax and any gains will be assessed on the beneficiary personally (*TCGA 1992, s 60(2)*).

Example 8.1—Bare trust

Sven holds shares for his son Matthew who is 26 years old. As Matthew can direct Sven at any time either to transfer the shares to him or to sell the shares and to pass the proceeds to him, this is a bare trust.

For capital gains tax the shares will be treated as belonging to Matthew and a transfer of the shares to Matthew will not incur a charge to capital gains tax. Any capital gain on the sale of the shares will be attributed to Matthew personally.

Example 8.2—Minor beneficiaries

Scenario 1

Max is nine years old and therefore is not able to own property in his own name. His parents hold the property for him absolutely. As a minor cannot demand the property from his parents, the trust is not a bare trust. Nevertheless *s 60(1)* provides that for capital gains tax purposes he is treated as owning the asset absolutely. When he attains the age of 18 and his parents transfer the property to him, the transfer will not trigger a charge to CGT.

Scenario 2

The property was passed to Max under his father's will contingent upon Max attaining the age of 18. Max is only nine years old. As his entitlement is contingent upon his attaining the age of 18, the property will be settled property for capital gains tax purposes and *s 60(1)* does not apply. Therefore, when he attains the age of 18, there will be a disposal by the trustees under *s 71(1)* which will trigger a charge to CGT.

For a time it seemed that HMRC wished to challenge the status of a bare trust where its terms contained administrative powers, in particular the power to accumulate income. That was logical if the trustees did in fact have a discretion over the application of income, but the professions argued, eventually successfully, that a mere statutory power, such as in the *Trustee Act 1925*, did not turn what was otherwise a bare trust into a substantive trust. The point is more important for IHT than for CGT and is discussed in *Inheritance Tax 2010/11* (Bloomsbury Professional).

'Exclusive right'

8.4 'The exclusive right … to direct how that asset shall be dealt with' may cause problems where there is more than one beneficiary entitled to the fund and the assets within the fund are indivisible assets like land, a painting, an item of antique furniture or a single share in a company. Therefore, apart from the terms of the settlement, the type of property held will determine when a beneficiary can direct the trustees to deal with his or her share in the trust asset and when such assets may be assessed to capital gains tax. One has to look towards the judgment of Goff J in *Crowe v Appleby* [1976] 2 All ER 914 and HMRC Capital Gains Manual on CG37540 to find the answer to when a beneficiary becomes absolutely entitled in an indivisible asset as against the trustees.

The rule in *Crowe v Appleby* states that in relation to indivisible assets, a beneficiary, among a group of beneficiaries, might have to wait for his absolute entitlement until the last beneficiary has fulfilled a possible contingency, for example, reached a specified age.

Example 8.3—Absolute entitlement to trust assets

Under James' will his estate passes to his three children Sophie, Max and Saskia contingent upon them attaining the age of 21. James' estate comprises a property and 90,000 shares in Pharmaceuticals plc. Sophie has just turned 21 and the question arises whether she will be able to claim her one-third share in her father's estate and whether the trustees will be charged to capital gains tax.

Sophie now can claim her one-third share in the shares, as they are divisible assets and the trustees can pass these shares to her subject to any capital gains tax charges, which may arise.

Following the rule in *Crowe v Appleby*, however, she will only become entitled to her one-third share in the property, once all her siblings have turned 21 or die before they are 21. Any capital gain, therefore, will be assessed, once the last sibling has become absolutely entitled. The assessment will be on the market value of the property when the last beneficiary turned 21.

The rule in *Crowe v Appleby* ceases to apply if the trustees sell the land in question after the first contingency, even if the proceeds are used to buy further land. Once the sale has taken place the trust fund, or the relevant part, consists of cash and the beneficiaries with absolute interests can call upon the trustees to hand over their share of the money. If further land is bought, then there is a tenancy in common with the tenants in common being the trustees of the original settlement and the absolutely entitled beneficiaries.

THE CREATION OF A SETTLEMENT

General provisions

8.5 *Section 70* provides that a transfer into a settlement, whether revocable or irrevocable, is a disposal of the entire property thereby becoming settled property notwithstanding that the settlor has some interest as a beneficiary (ie the settlement is settlor-interested) and notwithstanding that he is a trustee, or the sole trustee of the settlement.

The transfer into the trust is made at market value. If the transfer is a chargeable transfer for inheritance tax purposes, or would be but for the annual inheritance tax exemption (of currently £3,000), the settlor can elect hold-over relief to hold any capital gain over as against the trustees under *s 260* or, in the case of business assets, under *s 165*, unless the trust is settlor-interested, which precludes the application of hold-over relief.

Example 8.4—Creation of a settlement

Alice decides to settle her shares in X plc on her son Boris, who is 19 years old. She acquired the shares in 2000 for £100,000. The market value of the shares now stands at £200,000.

Deemed disposal consideration:	£200,000
Cost	£100,000
Capital gain	£100,000

Alice will be subject to capital gains tax on her gain of £100,000 when she transfers the shares into the settlement. Alice can use her annual exemption to reduce her tax liability. Alternatively, since the creation of a lifetime settlement is now nearly always a chargeable transfer, Alice could elect for hold-over relief under *s 260*, as Boris is not a dependent child under *TCGA 1992, s 169F(4A).*

The 'connected persons' rule

8.6 If the settlor and the trustees are connected persons, any gains on a transfer from the settlor to the trustees of a settlement can only be offset against losses on a transfer to the same settlement *(TCGA 1992, s 81(3))*. This can best be illustrated by the following example:

Example 8.5—Connected persons

James wishes to benefit his two children Louis and Lily, who have three children each. Ideally, he would like to set up two trusts – one for each branch of the family. His assets include a property worth £200,000 which he acquired many years ago for £50,000 and a share portfolio which is also worth £200,000, but which he originally acquired for £250,000.

He discusses the capital gains tax position with his accountant. If James decides to create two new settlements, one which will receive the property, the other which will receive the share portfolio, he will not be able to offset the loss on the shares against the gain on the property.

His accountant therefore advises him to transfer his assets into the same settlement. Subsequently, it will be possible to create two sub-funds, one for each branch of the family, which will not be a disposal under *s 71(1)*, unless the trustees elect for the new sub-fund rules to apply (see **8.17**).

The issue of connected persons was examined recently by the Court of Appeal in *Foulser v MacDougall* [2007] STC 973 where the taxpayer had entered into the following complicated series of transactions designed to shelter from CGT a large gain in company shares.

- They set up trusts in the Isle of Man.
- The trustees bought shelf companies in the Isle of Man.

- The taxpayers took out a personal portfolio bond with an Irish company and assigned it to one of the shelf companies.
- The Irish bond provider bought two shelf companies within the personal portfolio bond.
- The taxpayers then gave their shares in the company that stood at a gain to the shelf companies, claiming hold-over relief under *TCGA 1992, s 165*.

The issue was whether the taxpayers were connected persons who were acting together to control the donee company, within *TCGA 1992, s 167(3)*. If they were, the scheme would fail. *Held*, they were, and it did fail.

ACTUAL AND DEEMED DISPOSALS BY TRUSTEES

General considerations

8.7 The general rule is that gains arising from a disposal, whether an actual disposal or a deemed disposal of trust assets, whether of assets originally settled or acquired subsequently by the trustees, are chargeable on the trustees. Exceptions to this rule apply to the disposal of trust assets of settlor-interested trusts prior to 5 April 2008 (see **8.39**), non-UK resident trusts (see **8.42–8.44**) and trusts for 'vulnerable persons' (see **8.45–8.48**).

Following *s 69(1)*, when new trustees are appointed, this is not treated as a disposal for capital gains tax, as trustees are treated as a single and continuing body. However, care has to be taken when appointing a non-UK resident trustee not inadvertently to export the trust, which may trigger a charge to capital gains tax. Following the *Finance Act 2006* changes to the residence rules of trusts, practitioners are advised to review certain offshore arrangements which may be affected (see **8.45**).

Person becoming absolutely entitled to settled property (s 71)

8.8 There are many ways in which a beneficiary may become absolutely entitled as against the trustee. The main examples are:

- the termination of the trust after a term of years;
- when a beneficiary reaches a particular age;
- the happening of any other contingency;
- the termination of a prior life interest;
- the exercise by the trustee of a discretionary power to release capital;

- an order of the court;
- an agreement by the beneficiaries to terminate the trust; and
- the merger of interests.

Termination of the trust after a term of years and/or happening of a contingency

8.9 *Section 71(1)* provides that there is a deemed disposal by the trustees when the beneficiary of a settlement 'becomes absolutely entitled to any settled property as against the trustees'. The trustees are treated as disposing of that property at market value and immediately reacquiring it for the same value. A charge to capital gains tax may arise on the capital gain.

After the reacquisition of the assets the trustees will hold the property in question at market value as bare trustees. The beneficiary is then treated as the owner of the property and anything done by the trustees afterwards is treated as if it had been done by the beneficiary. When the trustees actually transfer the property to the beneficiary entitled to it, this is disregarded for capital gains tax purposes. If they sell it on behalf of the beneficiary, that is treated as a disposal by him or her, and the gain or loss is the difference between the sale proceeds and the market value on the occasion of the deemed acquisition.

Example 8.6—See HMRC Capital Gains Manual at CG37040

The case of *Stephenson v Barclays Bank Trust Co Ltd* (1975) STC 151 illustrates the general principles for determining when absolute entitlement occurs.

The facts (simplified) are as follows. Under the will of W, his daughters C, D and E were entitled to annuities of £300 a year during widowhood. Subject to the annuities the property was to be held in trust for such of his grandchildren as should reach the age of 21. There were two grandchildren, A and B, who both reached 21 before CGT was introduced in 1965.

In 1969 the trustees, the daughters and the grandchildren entered into a deed under which specific funds should be set aside to meet the annuities and the rest of the property should be paid over to the grandchildren. In fact, however, the trustees held onto this property.

The Revenue argued that A and B became absolutely entitled only when the deed was executed.

The trustees' arguments were that an individual grandchild merely had to be entitled to specific property, not to possess it. The judge agreed: he considered that the two grandchildren together were entitled to the whole of the settled property prior to 1965. Therefore, they were 'jointly' absolutely entitled as against the trustees when the deed was executed. Thus, there was no charge to capital gains tax on the trustees when the property was handed over to the beneficiary some time later.

Where trustees sell assets after the occasion of charge under *s 71(1)* but before assets are appropriated to the beneficiaries, charges on the beneficiaries should be calculated under *s 60(1)* in proportion to their entitlement on the gain arising between absolute entitlement and sale by the trustees.

Life interest released in favour of remaindermen

8.10 It is very common for a deed to give a person a life interest, with the property going absolutely to one or more individuals, or to the members of a class of persons, on the death of the life tenant. Sometimes, the life interest can be contingent upon the happening of a certain event, ie until the life tenant remarries.

On the termination of the life interest, when the property passes absolutely to one or more beneficiaries (also called the 'remaindermen'), the trustees will be subject to capital gains tax charges on the gain arising on any assets which now pass absolutely to these beneficiaries. *Section 71(1)* also applies where a life tenant releases his or her interest in favour of any remainderman who then becomes entitled to an absolute interest as against the trustees.

If, however, the termination is due to the death of the person entitled to the life interest, which was created prior to 22 March 2006, or an IPDI, TSI, BMT or disabled trust, the trustees may, subject to certain exceptions, escape a charge to capital gains tax under s*s 72* and *73* (see **8.12**).

Exercise of power to advance or appoint capital

8.11 A beneficiary may become absolutely entitled as against the trustees on the following occasions:

- Following a power within the trust document, the trustees pay a capital sum (rather than interest) to a beneficiary of a discretionary trust or they use their overriding powers in an interest in possession trust.
- The trustees exercise their powers under the *Trustee Act 1925, s 32* (the statutory power of advancement for England and Wales) which permits trustees to pay or apply one half of a beneficiary's presumptive or vested share for his or her 'advancement' or benefit. In many cases, the deed

authorises payment of the full share instead of limiting it to the statutory one half.

Section 71(1) applies to such an advance and/or appointment and the trustees will be chargeable to any capital gains arising on the advanced/appointed assets.

A charge to capital gains tax under *s 71(1)* may also arise when the trustees, in the exercise of their express powers in the trust document, resettle property on a new, different settlement.

Termination of life interest on death of the person entitled (s 73)

8.12 For inheritance tax purposes, if a person has a life interest in possession in settled property, which was created prior to 22 March 2006 and this person dies, the value of the settled property in which he or she has the interest is treated as part of his or her property on death.

Section 73 was amended by *FA 2006* to include a new *s 73(2A)*, so that from 22 March 2006 the capital gains tax-free uplift on death applies only to an interest in possession that is:

- immediate post-death interest (IPDI);
- transitional serial interest (TSI);
- bereaved minor trust (BMT); or
- disabled trust.

The expressions IPDI, TSI, BMT and disabled trust refer to categories of trusts that were formerly treated as interests in possession prior to the coming into force of *FA 2006* and which are still so treated. For a full exposition of the subject the reader is referred to *Inheritance Tax 2010/11* (Bloomsbury Professional), Chapters 7 and 8.

Therefore, if a life interest settlement has been created after 22 March 2006 and does not fall into one of the four categories of trusts mentioned above, the *Finance Act 2006* provides that the settled property will not be treated as part of the deceased's estate, as the creation of such a life interest is now treated as a chargeable event for inheritance tax.

Following *s 72* for life interests created prior to 22 March 2006, IPDIs, BMTs, TSIs or disabled trusts, no chargeable gain accrues on the death of the life tenant, unless there was a hold-over election on the acquisition of the property by the trustees (**8.28**), or where the property reverts to the settlor.

Example 8.7—Death of life tenant (I)

Alice has an interest in possession in her husband's estate for life or until she remarries. The remainderman is her son William.

Scenario 1

Alice's husband died on 5 June 2005 which was prior to the changes introduced by the *Finance Act 2006*.

On Alice's death, there will not be a charge to capital gains tax following *s 73*, but the value of the assets subject to the life interest will form part of her estate for inheritance tax.

If Alice's interest is terminated following remarriage *s 73* will not apply, and there will be a charge to capital gains tax on William's absolute entitlement following *s 71(1)*.

Scenario 2

Alice's husband died on 5 June 2006 which was after the changes introduced by the *Finance Act 2006*. Her life interest therefore will be an 'immediate post-death interest'. Unfortunately, Alice dies a month later so William becomes absolutely entitled to the trust assets.

On Alice's death there will not be a charge to capital gains tax (*TCGA 1992, s 73(2A)(a)*). As in Scenario 1, the value of the assets subject to the life interest will form part of Alice's estate for inheritance tax.

Example 8.8—Death of a life tenant (II)

Alice is the life tenant of an interest in possession trust, which was created by her father during his lifetime on 1 May 2006, which was after the introduction of the *Finance Act 2006* changes. Alice, unfortunately, dies a few weeks later. The fund now passes to William.

Section 73(2A) applies here. Alice's interest in possession does not fall within the restricted class of interests in *s 72(1B)*. As a result, the charge that would have applied under *s 73(1)* or *73(2)* is disapplied. Therefore, on her death there will be no capital gains tax-free uplift. If the trust had continued there would have been no disposal for CGT; however as the trust now comes to an end on the vesting of William's interest, any capital gains within the fund will be subject to a charge under *s 71(1)* because the remainderman now becomes absolutely entitled. As the termination of the life interest will be a chargeable transfer for IHT, the trustees ought to consider a hold-over election under *s 260* (see paras **8.28–8.29** and **Chapter 13** for a discussion on hold-over relief).

Termination of life interest on death of the person entitled (s 72), where settlement continues

8.13 The rule prior to 22 March 2006 was that if the life interest on the death of the life tenant was terminated and the property continued to be settled property, the trustees were treated as disposing of the settled property and reacquiring it at market value on the date of death, but without any charge to capital gains tax.

In relation to settlements created after 22 March 2006, the rule is that, as noted above, the tax treatment will depend on whether the fund remains with the trustees. The ending of the prior (post-*FA 2006*) life interest is not treated as an occasion of charge, see *s 72(1A)*, because it is not an interest within *s 72(1B)*, ie not an IPDI, a TSI, a BMT, or a disabled trust.

DISPOSAL OF INTERESTS IN SETTLED PROPERTY

General considerations

8.14 The general rule is that there is no charge to CGT when a beneficial interest in trust property is disposed of and the disposal was made:

- by the person for whose benefit the interest was created; or
- by any other person except one who acquired the interest for a consideration in money or money's worth (*TCGA 1992, s 76(1)*).

However, once a beneficial interest has been purchased, a future disposal is chargeable to CGT.

The capital gains tax exemption in *s 76(1)* used to offer CGT planning opportunities for individuals who placed assets in trust subject to a CGT hold-over election, but retaining an interest in the trust asset which was subsequently sold. The sale of the interest did not attract a charge to CGT. However, as of 21 March 2000 trustees of settlor-interested trusts will be treated as disposing of the asset and re-acquiring it at market value. As of 5 April 2008, any CGT will be charged on the trustees at the trust tax rate. The trustees can then recover the tax charge from the beneficiary who sold his interest (*TCGA 1992, s 76A* and *Sch 4A*).

Example 8.9—Disposal of beneficial interest

William is the remainderman in a life interest trust set up under his father's will. He sells his interest to his friend Fred. Under the rule in *s 76(1)* there is no charge to CGT.

However, Fred's subsequent sale of the beneficial interest in the trust is outside the protection of the rule in *s 76(1)* and any capital gain therefore will be taxable under general principles.

Purchase by one beneficiary of other interest

8.15 The general rule in *s 76(1)* does not apply where an original life tenant of settled property makes a payment to the original remainderman for the sale of his or her interest to the original life tenant, as the life tenant now becomes absolutely entitled to the property as against the trustees. The gain will be chargeable under *s 71(1)* and the property is deemed to have passed to the original life tenant at market value.

The same applies if the original remainderman acquires a life interest from the original life tenant.

Purchase of life interest and reversion

8.16 Where a person acquires a life interest or remainder in settled property for a consideration in money or money's worth and subsequently also acquires the other interest and therefore becomes absolutely entitled as against the trustees to the settled property, a charge to CGT will occur on the trustees under both *s 71(1)* and a charge under *s 76(2)* will occur.

Example 8.10—Purchase of life interest and reversion

Alice has a life interest in a trust and William is the remainderman; both are original beneficiaries. Fred buys Alice's life interest and, before this interest terminates, he also buys the remainder interest from William.

Fred therefore becomes absolutely entitled to the settled property as against the trustees and a charge to CGT will arise on the trustees. As Fred is not the original life tenant, a charge under *s 76(2)* will arise on him.

SUB-FUND ELECTIONS

8.17 Where a settlement has been divided into one or more sub-funds which are administered by either the same, or different, trustees for different beneficiaries, the main settlement and any sub-funds are treated as a single settlement for capital gains tax purposes.

The *Finance Act 2006* introduced provisions which allow trustees of a settlement to elect that a sub-fund or portion of the settlement shall be treated as a separate settlement, called a 'sub-fund' settlement for capital gains tax purposes as of 6 April 2006 (*TCGA 1992, Sch 4ZA*).

Making a sub-fund election will give rise to a charge to capital gains tax, as it is considered to be a deemed disposal under *s 71(1)* (*TCGA 1992, Sch 4ZA, para 20).* This single factor is likely to deprive the facility of any practical use for trustees: see below.

In order to make the election, a number of conditions have to be satisfied:

- Condition 1 is that the principal settlement is not itself a sub-fund (*TCGA 1992, Sch 4ZA, para 4*).
- Condition 2 is that the sub-fund does not comprise the whole of the property of the principal settlement (*TCGA 1992, Sch 4ZA, para 5*).
- Condition 3 is that, if the sub-fund election had taken effect, the sub-fund settlement would not consist of or include an interest in an asset which would be comprised in the principal settlement (*TCGA 1992, Sch 4ZA, para 6*).
- Condition 4 is that, once the sub-fund election had taken effect, no person would be a beneficiary under both the sub-fund settlement and the principal settlement.

As making the election gives rise to a disposal for capital gains tax purposes, the trustees would be in the same position as trustees who had used their powers to transfer property out of the principal settlement into a new settlement, thereby triggering a charge to capital gains tax. A sub-fund election therefore will only be useful in relation to settlements which were drafted without wide powers of advancement. A sub-fund election is unlikely to be attractive where trust assets are subject to substantial gains.

RATES OF TAX

General considerations

8.18 The rate of capital gains tax applicable to the trustees of any settlement who are liable in respect of disposals of settled property is as follows:

From 6 April 1998 to 5 April 2005	34%
From 6 April 2005 to 5 April 2008	40%
From 6 April 2008 to 22 June 2010	18%
From 23 June 2010	28%

Trustees are treated as a single and continuing body of persons regardless of any changes in the persons acting. Assessments are to be made on those in office at the time of the assessment, not those in office when the gain is made.

If tax assessed on the trustees of a settlement in respect of a chargeable gain accruing to the trustees is not paid within six months from the date when it becomes payable by the trustees, and the asset in respect of which the chargeable gain accrued, or any part of the proceeds of sale of that asset, is transferred by the trustees to a beneficiary, that person may at any time within two years from the time when the tax became payable be assessed and charged (in the name of the trustees) to capital gains tax (*TCGA 1992, s 69(4)*).

Actual disposals and losses

8.19 Where a beneficiary becomes absolutely entitled to settled property as against the trustees, any allowable loss which arises on the deemed disposal by the trustees on the asset transferred and which cannot be deducted from gains accruing to the trustees, is treated as a loss of the beneficiary (*TCGA 1992, s 71(2)*).

Where the beneficiary has become absolutely entitled to an asset on or after 16 June 1999, and he is treated as if he had incurred an allowable loss on that occasion, that loss can only be set against chargeable gains accruing on the same asset or, where the asset is an estate, interest or right in or over land, that asset or any asset deriving from that asset.

Example 8.11—Allowable losses

William becomes absolutely entitled to a trust set up by his late father. The trust assets are a portfolio of shares. The trustees have unused trust losses of £15,000. The share portfolio to which William becomes absolutely entitled to is worth £25,000 less than when it was acquired.

The unused losses of £15,000 belong to the trustees and cannot be passed on to William.

The capital loss of £25,000 on the share portfolio can only be used by William on a future gain of the disposal of the same share portfolio, unless the trustees can use it against gains realised earlier or gains arising on William's absolute entitlement.

Allowable expenditure by trustees

8.20 *TCGA 1992, s 38* sets out the basic types of expenditure regarded as 'incidental costs … of making and acquisition or disposal' (see **3.38**), which can be deducted from capital gains. *Section 38* also applies to trustees.

In addition, there are a number of cases which directly refer to allowable expenses by trustees:

- Expenses in varying and/or ending settlements are allowable and they may include the costs of legal and actuarial services including stamp duty on transfers and ancillary expenses incurred in varying or ending a settlement (see *CIR v Chubb's Trustee* 1972 SLT 81).
- Fees in respect of discharges and commission on the transfer of assets to beneficiaries, but not insurance premiums, see *Allison v Murray* [1975] 3 All ER 561.

Where property is transferred to a person absolutely entitled to that property as against the trustees of a settlement, then, on any subsequent disposal of that property, the person to whom the property is transferred may be allowed a deduction for the expenses involved in the transfer of this asset.

The issue of deductibility of trust expenses was considered by the Special Commissioners in some detail in *Clay v HMRC* [2007] STC (SCD) 362. The case was concerned with the rate of income tax applicable to trusts, but has implications for the allocation of costs to capital. It decided that, in order to achieve a fair balance between income and capital beneficiaries, a proportion of all the expenses that were in issue, with the exception of the investment management fees, was attributable to income for the purposes of what was then *TA 1988, s 686(2AA)*, but is now *ITA 2007, s 484*; and that the accruals basis that had been adopted by the trustees was a proper way of allocating expenses to a particular tax year. As is explained in Annex 1, change 87, the law as redrafted does now adopt the accrual basis and to that extent adopts the decision in *Clay*.

It was clear in that case that the fees of investment managers were attributable to capital: yet after such costs have been so allocated it does not follow that they may be set against any gains arising on sale of the investments. Such expenditure is not set against income and is therefore not excluded from offset by *TCGA 1992, s 39*. Can a gain therefore be reduced by a proportion of the manager's fee? It is arguable that the work of an investment manager does not enhance the value of any individual asset, even though it may have a profound influence on the value of the portfolio as a whole. The advisory element of the manager's fee is therefore probably not deductible; but custody fees (which were substantial in *Clay*) should be claimable as incurred for preserving the title to the trust assets.

HMRC Statement of Practice 2/04, updating Statement of Practice 8/94, lists the amount of expenditure allowable to be deducted for expenses incurred by personal representatives and corporate trustees. Note, however, that this allowance is not available to a beneficiary to whom an asset has been appropriated or assented, because the expenses in question were incurred not by the beneficiary but by the personal representative/trustee, even though in reality it may be the beneficiary who eventually foots the bill.

The deductibility of valuation costs and costs of appeal was reviewed in *Caton's Administrators v Couch* [1997] STC 970 and disallowed by the Court of Appeal, affirming the judgment of the High Court. The costs of the initial valuation were allowable but not the litigation costs, since that would deter taxpayers from 'reaching a sensible agreement with the Revenue as to the quantum of liability'.

Trust insurance policy gains

8.21 Trustees may decide to invest in a policy so as to avoid both the complication of receipt of income, and having to account for it to the beneficiaries, and its taxation under *ITA 2007, s 493* (formerly *ICTA 1988, s 687*). However, if the trustees encash the policy they may trigger a chargeable event gain for income tax and if they do, the question arises what part, if any, of the resultant tax liability goes into the tax pool in *ITA 2007, s 497*. This has been addressed by *FA 2007, s 56*, inserting into *ITA 2007, s 498* an extra category, or type, of income, being the tax arising on life insurance contracts. What goes into the pool is:

- the tax deemed to be paid under *ITA 2007, s 482*, less
- the savings rate under *ITTOIA 2005, s 530*.

Therefore, the tax deducted at source and certified to the trustees at the rate of 20% together with the additional tax paid by the trustees (30% from 5 April 2010) will not enter the tax pool.

A chargeable event gain is not a capital gain for tax purposes but will be treated as income and taxed accordingly.

Care needs to be taken when taking out such policies within interest in possession trusts. The income tax rates for such trusts are 10% for dividend income and 20% for all other income. Chargeable event gains however are charged on trustees at the income tax rate applicable to trusts, which is 50% from 5 April 2010. As interest in possession trusts do not have tax pools, the additional income tax payable by the trustees (30% from 5 April 2010) will not enter a tax pool, and therefore is not reclaimable by the beneficiaries.

PARTICULAR TRANSACTIONS AFFECTING TRUSTS

Capital receipts on company purchase of own shares

8.22 *FA 2006* provided, in *Sch 13, para 3*, amendments to *ICTA 1988, s 686A*, which applies on the purchase by a company of its own shares where a trust is involved. In trust law, ie disregarding any tax treatment, such a purchase is a capital transaction, and the problem for HMRC was that *s 686* caught only income that was subject to the discretion of the trustees. However, the 2006 amendment did not hit its target accurately, making it necessary to amend in *FA 2007*. The change, backdated to 6 April 2006, is in *FA 2007, s 55* and amends both *TA 1988, s 686A* and *ITA 2007, s 482* as necessary.

Single farm payment and 'old' quota entitlements

8.23 Many trusts of farming interests will be affected by the introduction of the entitlement to Single Farm Payment, which has superseded entitlements under 'old' quota arrangements, as for milk, etc, making them valueless. Although some were acquired by allocation, some may have been purchased and where this has happened, and the quota in question has ceased to exist, an opportunity may now arise to make a 'negligible value' claim under *TCGA 1992, s 24*, especially when realising a capital gain on the disposal of other assets.

Identifying the source of distributions from a trust IRS

8.24 Although the tax treatment of offshore trusts is outside the scope of this book, cases occasionally throw up principles of wider application. In *Herman v HMRC* (2007) SpC 609, the Special Commissioner had to review a scheme that attempted to deal with stockpiled gains that they were not treated as capital payments for the purpose of the charging regime under *TCGA 1992, s 87*. The case is important because the taxation of stockpiled gains troubles many families who perhaps now regret that their wealth is tied up in an offshore structure that is becoming increasingly expensive to maintain.

The precise facts may now be academic; they concerned a 'Mark II flip-flop' scheme, use of which has been curtailed by subsequent legislation: see *TCGA*

1992, Sch 4C. What is still relevant is the way the Commissioners applied the phrase 'directly or indirectly' in *TCGA 1992, s 97(5)(a)*. They decided to work back to see exactly where the money had come from. Had the receipt resulted by accident or through circumstances not originally envisaged, the linkage might not be there; but on the facts there was here a comprehensive tax plan. The husband taxpayer knew exactly what was going on; he was consulted at every stage; on the facts, what they received was indirectly received from the trustees, so it was taxable under *TCGA 1992, s 97*.

Tax advantages using a trust in the light of FA 2007

8.25 What is 'normal' tax planning and what is 'objectionable' tax avoidance? A few years ago 'bed and breakfast' transactions were considered to be no more than good housekeeping, but were outlawed by the identification rules in *TCGA 1992, s 104* et seq. Continuing this trend, *FA 2006* introduced targeted anti-avoidance rules (TAARs) for corporation tax to prevent some losses from being allowable. The trend has continued by the anti-avoidance rules in *FA 2007, s 25* et seq and in particular by *FA 2007, s 27* which inserts into *TCGA 1992* new *s 16A,* bringing general practitioners into the frame. With effect from 6 December 2006 a loss is not allowable if:

- there are 'arrangements';
- the loss accrues to a person directly or indirectly from those arrangements; and
- the main purpose or one of the main purposes of the arrangements was to secure a tax advantage.

'Arrangements' is very widely drawn so as to include:

- agreements;
- understandings;
- schemes; and
- transaction or series of transactions

whether or not any such are legally enforceable.

'Tax advantage' means:

- tax relief, or extra tax relief;
- tax refunds or bigger tax refunds;
- avoiding tax or paying less of it; and
- managing to avoid a possible assessment to tax.

It does not matter whether the loss accrues at a time when there happen not to be any gains to set against it; nor whether the tax advantage is for the person who has suffered the loss or someone else.

Naturally, there has been much comment in the professional press and by the learned societies as to the scope of the rules. HMRC have been mildly reassuring: transfers between spouses, where one had made a large gain and the other had the potential to transfer loss-making assets, might not always be caught. What of the situation where a beneficiary of an estate has losses brought forward and stands to inherit a house which has appreciated since it was valued for probate, where that value is fixed under *TCGA 1992, s 274*? It would be standard practice to appropriate the house to the beneficiary, so that he may set his loss against his new gain. Is that 'normal' tax planning, and as such not caught by the new rule? It probably is, but we must await the clarification of seeing tax returns go through unchallenged before we can be sure.

EXEMPTIONS AND RELIEFS

Annual exemption

8.26 *TCGA 1992, Sch 1*, modified by the *Finance Act 2009*, determines the level of the annual exemption.

Trustees of a settlement are entitled to one-half of the annual exemption available to an individual for any tax year during the whole or part of which any property is 'settled property' as defined in *TCGA 1992, s 68*. Thus, the trustees' exemption for 2010/11 is £5,050. Trustees of settled property held for people with disabilities and others are entitled to the full annual exemption.

Where two or more 'qualifying settlements' comprise a 'group' (see definitions below) then each qualifying settlement is entitled to an annual exemption equal to the greater of:

- one-tenth of the annual exemption for an individual (ie £1,010 for 2010/11); or
- one-half of that exemption divided by the number of settlements in the group.

For these purposes:

- a 'qualifying settlement' is any settlement (other than an 'excluded settlement', see below) made after 6 June 1978 where these rules apply to the trustees for the tax year; and

- all qualifying settlements that have the same settlor (see below) comprise a group.

A settlement may feature in more than one group by virtue of having more than one settlor. In such a case the number by which one-half of the annual exemption for an individual is to be divided is the number of settlements in the largest group.

Following the new sub-fund election rules, *Finance Act 2006* introduced *TCGA 1992, Sch 1, para A1*, which states that in relation to the annual exemption, the principal settlement and its sub-fund settlements shall be treated as if no sub-fund election has been made.

8.27 'Settlor' has the meaning given by *ITTOIA 2005, s 620* and includes the testator in the case of a settlement arising under a will and the intestate under an intestacy. Thus a settlor, in relation to a settlement, is any person by whom the settlement was made. A person is treated as having made a settlement if he has made or entered into it directly or indirectly. In particular, he is treated as having made the settlement if he has:

- provided funds directly or indirectly for the purpose of the settlement;
- undertaken to provide funds directly or indirectly for the purpose of the settlement; or
- made a reciprocal arrangement with another person for the other person to make or enter into the settlement.

'Excluded settlement' means:

- any settlement where the trustees are not, for the whole or any part of the tax year, treated under *TCGA 1992, s 69(1)* as resident and ordinarily resident in the UK;
- any settlement where the property comprised in it is held for charitable purposes only and cannot become applicable for other purposes;
- with effect from 6 April 2006, subject to transitional rules, any settlement where the property comprised in it is held for the purposes of a registered pension scheme, a superannuation fund to which *ICTA 1988, s 615(3)* applies or an occupational pension scheme within the meaning of *FA 2004, s 150(5)* that is not a registered pension scheme; and
- prior to 6 April 2006, any settlement where the property comprised in it is held for the purposes of a fund to which *ICTA 1988, s 615(3)* applies, schemes and funds approved under *ICTA 1988, s 620* or *s 621*, sponsored superannuation schemes as defined in *ICTA 1988, s 624* and exempt approved schemes and statutory schemes as defined in *ICTA 1988, Pt XIV, Ch I*.

Hold-over relief

8.28 Hold-over relief may, subject to the exceptions discussed below, be available in two circumstances:

- On a transfer of assets into a trust, it may be possible to make a claim for gifts hold-over relief under *TCGA 1992, s 260* where, for the purposes of inheritance tax, there is a chargeable transfer or there would be a chargeable transfer but for the application of an inheritance tax exemption or the availability of the nil rate band.
- Hold-over relief also applies to gifts of business assets to a settlement under *s 165(1)(b)*.

Where both reliefs are available, *s 260* takes priority. A claim has to be made on helpsheet HS 295.

Hold-over relief under *s 260*

8.29 Prior to 22 March 2006, hold-over relief under *s 260* used to be available only for:

- gifts to discretionary trusts;
- when a discretionary trust was terminated; or
- when assets were appointed/advanced to beneficiaries of discretionary trusts.

Gifts to accumulation and maintenance trusts and interest in possession trusts used to be potentially exempt transfers rather than chargeable transfers for inheritance tax, therefore *s 260* hold-over relief did not apply.

The *Finance Act 2006* changed the inheritance tax treatment of interest in possession trusts and accumulation and maintenance trusts in that transfers into such settlements are now treated as chargeable transfers for inheritance tax. Therefore all transfers into trusts, whether discretionary or not, now allow the election of *s 260* hold-over relief.

A planning opportunity existed for accumulation and maintenance trusts where a beneficiary became entitled to income at the age of 18 and capital at the age of 25. If the beneficiary, once he turned 18, but before the age of 25, resettles his interest away from himself so that he will not become entitled to capital until the age of 25, capital gains tax hold-over relief under *s 260* will be available when he becomes absolutely entitled. Despite the changes introduced by the *Finance Act 2006*, this planning opportunity is still available for beneficiaries who have obtained an interest in possession in the accumulation and maintenance trust prior to 22 March 2006. All other beneficiaries are subject to the new inheritance tax charging regime for accumulation and maintenance trusts in any event, which allows for the application of *s 260* hold-over relief, when a beneficiary becomes absolutely entitled to trust assets.

The *s 260* relief extends to actual and deemed disposals of trustees of settlements which are subject to ongoing inheritance tax charges or exit charges, or would be if the value of the assets were above the nil rate band for inheritance tax. Such settlements are as follows:

- discretionary settlements, whether created prior to 22 March 2006 or afterwards; and
- interest in possession trusts and accumulation and maintenance trusts created after 22 March 2006.

Hold-over relief under *s 165*

8.30 *Section 165(1)(b)* extends the application of hold-over relief for business assets (as discussed in detail in **Chapter 13**) to settled property.

Anti-avoidance measures

8.31 There are two main anti-avoidance provisions:

- The first can be found in *TCGA 1992, ss 169B–169G* on a transfer into settlor-interested settlements. For this purpose a settlor has an interest in a settlement where any property within the settlement may be used for the benefit of the settlor or his spouse. *TCGA 1992, s 169F* extends the settlor-interested definition further to include minor unmarried children who are not in a civil partnership, which also includes stepchildren. Hold-over relief under *s 260* or *s 165* will not be available for trusts set up by a parent where minor children and/or stepchildren are potential beneficiaries. Hold-over relief remains available for grandparents' trusts.
- *Section 226A* has been introduced by the *Finance Act 2004* and prevents the application of principal private residence relief under *TCGA 1992, s 223* in cases where hold-over relief has been claimed under *s 260*, when property was transferred into the settlement. This measure applies from 9 December 2003 and principal private residence relief is not available from this date, and any subsequent gains will have to be apportioned.

For a case that turned on the meaning of this legislation, especially *s 167(3)*, see *Foulser v MacDougall* at **8.6** above.

Taper relief

8.32 Taper relief was abolished by the *Finance Act 2008*, however the rules still apply for transactions completed prior to 6 April 2008. **Chapter 17** discusses the operation of taper relief on disposals by individuals with reference to disposals by trustees. While the same principles and definitions apply to taper relief on disposals by trustees, when determining whether business asset taper applies, the rules vary from those applying to individuals.

Disposals of assets after 5 April 2008

8.33 The *Finance Act 2008* abolished taper relief and indexation relief for transactions completed after 5 April 2008. Irrespective of the type of asset disposed of, a flat rate of CGT of 18% for disposals prior to 23 June 2010 and 28% thereafter will apply replacing the complex taper relief rules outlined above.

Entrepreneurs' relief

8.34 Entrepreneurs' relief may apply to disposals of the whole or part of a business and in some circumstances, disposals of shares. For disposals prior to 23 June 2010 entrepreneurs' relief reduced qualifying gains by 4/9ths and the remaining 5/9ths were then charged at the single rate of 18%. This resulted in qualifying gains being taxed at the effective CGT rate of 18%. The amount of an individual's gain that can qualify for entrepreneurs' relief was subject to a lifetime limit of £2 million from 6 April 2010 to 23 June 2010 (£1 million prior to 6 April 2010).

The increase of the capital gains tax rate for trustees from 18% to 28% means that the 4/9ths reduction will not achieve an effective tax rate of 10%. The *Finance (No 2) Act 2010* amended these provisions in that capital gains on disposals which qualify for entrepreneurs' relief will be charged at a rate of 10%. The lifetime limit has been increased to £5 million.

This relief applies to disposals by trustees of interest in possession trusts, but not discretionary trusts, as outlined below:

TCGA 1992, s 169J applies to disposals of trust business assets. Entrepreneurs' relief will apply where three conditions are satisfied:

- The trustees of a settlement dispose of 'settlement business assets', which are defined as shares in or securities of a company, or interests in such shares or securities, or assets that have been used for the purposes of a business, or interests in such business; and

- The individual is a 'qualifying beneficiary' of the settlement. This means that the individual must have an interest in possession in the whole of the settled property or in part of the settled property that contains the settlement business asset; and
- One of two conditions, called the 'relevant conditions' are satisfied:
  - The relevant condition, that must be satisfied, if the settlement business assets are shares in or securities of a company, or interests in such shares or securities, is that throughout a period of one year ending within three years up to the date of disposal (defined as 'material time'):
    - the company is the qualifying beneficiary's personal company; see **11.10** for a definition of 'personal company';
    - the company is a trading company or the holding company of a trading group; see **11.12** and **11.19** for a definition of 'trading company' and 'holding company'; and
    - the qualifying beneficiary is an officer or employee of the company or of one or more companies that are members of the group.
  - If the settlement business assets are assets that have been used for the purposes of the business, the relevant condition is that:
    - throughout the period of one year ending with the three years up to the date of disposal, the settlement business assets are used for the purposes of a trade carried on by the qualifying beneficiary; and
    - the qualifying beneficiary ceases to carry on the business some time during that three-year period.

Trustees are advised to consider the application of entrepreneurs' relief, if the trust assets include business assets, especially if a sale of these assets is anticipated in the future. The relief does not apply to assets held subject to the discretion of the trustees and in some situations it may be beneficial to consider appointing these assets on interest in possession trusts which will allow the application of this relief.

The relief has to be applied for jointly by the 'qualifying beneficiary' and the trustees. In effect the beneficiary will transfer the unused portion of his lifetime allowance up to a maximum of £5 million to the trustees.

Section 169O introduces special provisions where on a disposal of trust business assets there is in addition to the qualifying beneficiary at least one other beneficiary who, at the material time, has an interest in possession in all the trust assets or the part now disposed of. In such situations the aggregated gains and losses are apportioned by reference to the qualifying beneficiary's interest, at the material time, in the income of that part of the settled property that includes the settlement business assets. The relevant proportion of the aggregated gains and losses so calculated is to be taken into account for entrepreneurs' relief and the remainder of the amount which does not qualify for relief is a chargeable gain.

These special provisions will restrict the availability of entrepreneurs' relief where there is more than one beneficiary in an interest in possession trust.

Roll-over relief

8.35 Trustees may claim reinvestment roll-over relief to roll the gain realised on a business asset into the purchase of another asset (*TCGA 1992, ss 152–158*). The rules are explained in detail in **Chapter 14**.

However, as one of the requirements for the application of roll-over relief is that the asset on which roll-over relief is to be claimed, and the trade in which the asset is used, must be within the same ownership, the availability of roll-over relief to the trustees is likely to be rare. It would only apply where a trust owns the asset and is a partner in the trade.

Example 8.12—Roll-over relief

Julian is a life tenant in a settlement and runs a restaurant from premises owned by the trust. If the premises were sold to purchase bigger premises, roll-over relief will not be available.

Roll-over relief would only be available if the trust was a partner in the restaurant.

Principal private residence relief

8.36 The disposal by trustees of a dwelling house which has been the only or main residence of a beneficiary or beneficiaries entitled to occupy it under a settlement may well give rise to a chargeable gain or allowable loss.

Section 225 extends the scope of private residence relief to gains or losses accruing to trustees on the disposal of settled property. The property must be a dwelling house, and/or its garden or grounds if it has any, which has been occupied as the only or main residence of a person entitled to occupy it under the terms of the settlement during the period of ownership of the trustees.

If these conditions are fulfilled, private residence relief is applied in the same way as it would be applied on a gain accruing to an individual. Further relief may also be available to the trustees under *s 223(4)* if that dwelling house has been let, in the same way as it would be available to an individual.

If a life tenant or other beneficiary, who has satisfied those conditions from the time of acquisition of the house by the trustees, or 31 March 1982 if later, subsequently becomes the absolute owner of the residence, no chargeable gain or allowable loss will arise on that event under *s 71(1)*.

If the asset to which the beneficiary becomes absolutely entitled was previously occupied as an only or main residence by another beneficiary under the terms of the settlement, then *s 225* also may apply.

CGT small disposal rule

8.37 As explained in **4.25** in relation to individuals, a gain is not chargeable if it arises on the disposal of an asset which is tangible moveable property (a chattel) and the consideration does not exceed £6,000.

For the application of marginal relief, where the consideration exceeds £6,000, see **4.25**.

The same rules apply to disposals made by trustees.

SETTLOR-INTERESTED SETTLEMENTS

General considerations

Disposals after 5 April 2008

8.38 The *Finance Act 2008* abolished the settlor-interested provisions in *ss 77–78* for disposals made after 5 April 2008, as the new single rate of CGT of 18% removed any tax advantages to higher rate tax-paying settlors.

Any gains therefore are now returned by the trustees on the trust tax return rather than by the settlor. Settlor-interested trusts are now entitled to an annual capital gains tax amount of half the normal amount (£5,050 for 2010/11).

Disposals between 5 April 1988 and 5 April 2008

8.39 For disposals prior between 6 April 1988 but before or on 5 April 2008 special capital gains tax rules deal with the case where the person who made the settlement (the 'settlor'), the settlor's spouse or the settlor's minor unmarried children who are not in a civil partnership retain an interest in the settlement (see *ss 77–78*). Therefore, where:

- both the settlor and the trustees are resident in the UK during any part of the year (or ordinarily resident in the UK during the year); and
- the settlor, the settlor's spouse or the settlor's unmarried minor children who are not in a civil partnership, at any time during the tax year have an interest in the settlement, or enjoy a benefit deriving from the settlement income or property (see *ITTOIA 2005, s 265*).

A settlor has an interest in the settlement if the settlor, his spouse or minor children have a present or future interest in income or capital under the settlement, whether vested or contingent, even if they never have or will actually receive any income or capital from the trust.

8.40 'Benefit' is a rather vague concept, but it will include the use of trust income or property on non-commercial terms, which may include a low or nil interest loan, rent-free occupation of trust property, or appointments of trust income or capital (including the writing off of a loan to the settlor).

It is accepted that a small *de minimis* benefit will not bring the settlement within *s 77*.

Following *s 77(3)*, a 'spouse of the settlor' does not include the following:

- a person to whom the settlor is not presently married but might marry later;
- a person of whom the settlor is not for the time being a civil partner but of whom he may later be a civil partner;
- a spouse from whom the settlor is separated under a court order, under a separation agreement or in other circumstances such that the separation is likely to be permanent;
- a widow or widower of the settlor. (In other words, if the person who is presently the spouse of the settlor can only benefit after the settlor is dead, he or she is disregarded.)

Following *s 77(4)* certain interests are to be disregarded when determining whether someone has an interest in the settlement if the settlor can only benefit on:

- the bankruptcy of a beneficiary;
- any assignment of, or charge on, the beneficiary's interest in the property or income;

- the failure of a marriage settlement or civil partnership settlement by reason of both parties to the marriage or civil partnership and all or any of the children of the marriage or civil partnership;
- the death of a child of the settlor who had become beneficially entitled to the property or the income at an age not more than 25; or
- so long as a person is alive and under 25, during whose lifetime none of the property or income may become payable to the settlor unless that person becomes bankrupt or assigns, etc his interest.

Computation of trust gains

8.41 The chargeable gains of the settlement are computed in the normal way subject to allowable reliefs and exemptions, but any charge to capital gains tax accrues to the settlor. The trustees' own annual exempt amount is not taken into account in these computations.

Any tax paid by the settlor as a result of these provisions can be recovered from the trustees of the settlement.

OFFSHORE SETTLEMENTS

General considerations

8.42 The capital gains tax rules applying to offshore settlements are complex and are beyond the scope of this book.

Offshore settlements are used to offer substantial capital gains tax advantages, as they are not liable to capital gains tax on gains accruing to them on disposals of the trust property. Therefore, they were much reviled by the Inland Revenue which tightened the rules and closed many tax-planning loopholes. Consequently, there are special provisions to charge the gains accruing to such trustees to capital gains tax in so far as they are reflected in payments made to beneficiaries resident and/or domiciled within the UK.

While it will be necessary to consult a tax practitioner or a specialist text on offshore tax planning, an inadvertent export of the trust may catch the unwary and trigger a charge to capital gains tax. Practitioners will therefore have to have an understanding of the residence rules of trusts and the ensuing consequences of the inadvertent export of a trust. The area is strictly policed by HMRC: see for example the decision of the High Court in favour of HMRC on the unsuccessful appeal from the Special Commissioner in *Snell v HMRC* [2006] EWHC 3350, where the taxpayer emigrated to the Isle of Man but was still caught. There an exchange of securities was held not to be for *bona fide* commercial purposes.

Residence of trust

8.43 Prior to *FA 2006* the rules for residence of trustees were different depending upon whether it was income tax or capital gains tax that was under consideration. For capital gains tax a trust was considered as non-resident if its administration was ordinarily carried on outside the UK and the trustees for the time being, or a majority of them, were neither resident nor ordinarily resident in the UK. A resident professional trustee may be treated for this purpose as not resident in the UK if the settled property was provided by a settlor who was not domiciled, resident, or ordinarily resident when he settled the property.

FA 2006 introduced new rules effective as from 5 April 2007, ie only for 2007/08 and later years, which in theory allowed trustees to alter their arrangements if required. The new rules are modelled on the old income tax test based initially on the residence status of the trustees and using the residence and domicile status of the settlor as a tiebreaker where the body of trustees contains a mixture of UK resident and non-UK resident trustees. Therefore:

- If all the persons who are the trustees of the settlement are UK resident, the trust is both UK resident and ordinarily UK resident (new *s 69(2A)*).
- If all the persons who are the trustees of the settlement are non-UK resident, the trust is both non-UK resident and not ordinarily UK resident.
- If at least one trustee is UK resident and at least one is non-UK resident, then the residence and ordinary residence of the trust is treated as UK resident if a settlor in relation to the settlement meets the conditions specified below (new *s 69(2B)*):
  - a settlor in relation to a settlement was UK resident, ordinarily UK resident or domiciled in the UK when the settlement was established;
  - if the settlement arises on the death of the settlor (whether by will, intestacy or otherwise), the settlor was UK resident, ordinarily UK resident or domiciled immediately before his death;
  - in any other case the settlor was UK resident, ordinarily UK resident or domiciled when the settlor makes, or is treated as making, the settlement.

Thus, if a settlement has both resident and non-resident trustees, irrespective of whether the majority are either resident or non-resident, then if the settlor is UK resident, etc at the relevant time then the settlement is UK resident.

Example 8.13—Residence of trustees

A trust has three trustees. All three are resident in the UK; two of them are partners in a firm of solicitors in London. The settlor is resident and domiciled in Switzerland. The administration of the trust was carried out in Guernsey.

Under the old rules, the trustees are resident in the UK because a majority are so resident; however, as two of the trustees are professional trustees, they are treated as non-resident, which means that a majority of the trustees are non-resident. In addition, the administration of the trust was carried on in Guernsey, which makes the trust non-resident under *s 69(1)*. If the administration of the trust had been carried out in London, the trust would have been treated as a resident trust.

Under the new rules, however, all the trustees are treated as resident in the UK: as the professional trustee exemption under *s 69(2)* no longer exists, the trust will be treated as a UK trust for capital gains tax purposes.

The trustees had until 5 April 2007 to introduce a non-UK resident trustee, to ensure that the trust remained offshore.

There were strong representations to HMRC that these new rules seriously damaged the trust provider sector, especially for smaller firms that did not have an international network of offices to which trusts could be redirected. HMRC confirmed the position and advised that there is no alleviating treatment. The point is more likely to have caught non-professional trustees unawares. Presumably HMRC's position would be that there was a year or so between announcement and the effective date of the new rule during which action could have been taken, in this case for all the non-UK resident trustees to retire in favour of UK residents.

Charge to tax on emigration of trust under s 80

8.44 If the trustees cease to be resident in the UK, even if this happens inadvertently, a charge to capital gains tax may arise on the deemed disposal and reacquisition of the settled property at its market value on the date of emigration (*TCGA 1992, s 80*).

TRUSTS AND VULNERABLE BENEFICIARIES

General considerations

8.45 *Finance Act 2005, ss 23–45* created a new trust tax regime for a 'vulnerable person' which was backdated to 6 April 2004.

A 'vulnerable person' is a 'disabled person' or a 'relevant minor'. A 'vulnerable persons' election' has to be made to HMRC in writing on the requisite form for the beneficial tax treatment to apply (*FA 2005, s 37*).

'Disabled person'

8.46 A 'disabled person' is defined in the *Finance Act 2005, s 38* as a person who:

- by reason of mental disorder within the meaning of the *Mental Health Act 1983* is incapable of administering his property or managing his affairs;
- is in receipt of attendance allowance;
- is in receipt of a disability living allowance by virtue of entitlement to the care component at the highest or middle rate; or
- satisfies HMRC that, if he were to satisfy the residence allowances, he would be entitled either to the attendance allowance or disability allowance.

Where property is held on trust for the benefit of a disabled person, those trusts are 'qualifying trusts' if any property is applied for the benefit of the disabled person and either the disabled person is entitled to all the income arising from the property or no such income may be applied for the benefit of any other person (*FA 2005, s 34*).

'Relevant minor'

8.47 A person under the age of 18 is a 'relevant minor' if at least one parent has died (*FA 2005, 39*).

Where property is held on trust for the benefit of a relevant minor, those trusts are 'qualifying trusts', if they are statutory trusts for the relevant minor under the *Administration of Estates Act 1925*, or they are established under the will of a deceased parent of the relevant minor, or trusts established by the Criminal Injuries Compensation Scheme (*FA 2005, s 35*).

Capital gains tax treatment

8.48 Following *FA 2005, s 30* special capital gains tax treatment applies for a tax year if:

- chargeable gains accrue in that tax year to the trustees of a settlement from the disposal of settled property which is held on qualifying trusts for the benefit of a vulnerable person;
- the trustees would be chargeable to capital gains tax in respect of those gains;
- the trustees are UK resident; and
- a claim for special tax treatment has been made by the trustees for this tax year.

For disposals prior to 6 April 2008, the special tax treatment determines that a UK-resident vulnerable person will be treated as the settlor of the settlement in that tax year. He is therefore able to use his full annual exemption and will be taxed at his marginal tax rate. The vulnerable person is then able to reclaim any tax paid back from the trustees.

The *Finance Act 2008* replaced the previous rule, which used the settlor-interested provisions in *s 77*, and which charged the vulnerable person to CGT as though the trust gains arose directly to him. Therefore, where a vulnerable person is resident in the UK, the trustees' liability to CGT for gains realised after 5 April 2008, is reduced to the amount, which would have been payable by the vulnerable person, if the gains arose directly to him.

If the vulnerable person is not resident in the UK during the tax year, the vulnerable persons' liability has to be calculated according to the formulae described in *FA 2005, ss 32* and *33*, which are complex and beyond the scope of this book.

COMPLIANCE

8.49 One change introduced by *FA 2007, s 89* is to accelerate the filing date for trust and estate tax returns. Paper returns must be filed by 31 October, unless notice to file was given after 31 July, in which case the return must be filed within three months. If notice is given after 31 October, the old filing date of 31 January still applies. For electronic returns, the filing date remains at 31 January, unless the notice to file was made after 31 October, in which case the filing date is three months from the notice.

This is all very well. It may save HMRC manpower and other resources. It may eventually encourage trustees to file electronically. However, for a certain age group of trustee and, it must be said, their advisers, it will be seen as victimisation and the infliction of further expense for which the taxpayer sees absolutely no benefit. This is because many trust and estate returns are done by lawyers manually, if at all. Lawyers with trust practices of moderate size may be slower than their accountant colleagues to espouse the electronic revolution and to buy the specialised software that is, frankly, indispensable to the preparation of the trust and estate return. For as long as HMRC still print out the returns, which are filed online, and re-enter the information on their system, there seems to be little advantage of filing online, especially in relation to smaller less complex trusts.

Chapter 9

Companies

INTRODUCTION

9.1 Companies are chargeable to corporation tax in respect of chargeable gains accruing to them. The relevant legislation is contained in *Corporation Tax Act 2009* (*CTA 2009*), *s 2* and elsewhere in the *Taxes Acts* (*TCGA 1992, s 1(2)*).

For further information on the general scheme of corporation tax, including how taxable profits are computed and the rates of tax, see *Corporation Tax 2010/11* (Bloomsbury Professional).

BASIS OF CHARGE

9.2 Generally, the amount included in a company's profits for an accounting period in respect of chargeable gains is the total amount of chargeable gains accruing to the company in that accounting period, less:

- any allowable losses accruing to the company in the period; and
- any allowable losses that (i) accrued to the company in earlier periods when it was within the charge to corporation tax, and (ii) have not already been allowed as a deduction from chargeable gains (*TCGA 1992, s 8(1)*).

A loss is not an allowable loss if the disposal that generated a loss would be exempt from corporation tax, should that disposal have created a gain. A loss accruing on a disposal made on or after 5 December 2005 is not an allowable loss if it is disqualified by the anti-avoidance rules (*TCGA 1992, s 16A*) (see **9.22**).

The rate of corporation tax payable on chargeable gains is the rate appropriate to the accounting period in which the gains accrued. Companies are not entitled to the annual CGT exemption generally available to individuals, trustees and personal representatives (see **1.17**).

The total amount of the chargeable gains is computed in accordance with CGT principles, and the CGT provisions are used to determine questions as to:

- the amounts taken into account as chargeable gains or as allowable losses, or in computing gains or losses, or charged to tax as a person's gain; and
- the time when any such amount is treated as accruing.

These questions are determined as if accounting periods were tax years (*TCGA 1992, s 8(3)*).

As a general rule, references in CGT legislation to income tax or the income tax acts (except those restricted, for example, to individuals) are to be read, in relation to a company, as references to corporation tax or to the corporation tax acts. The income tax acts are the enactments relating to income tax, including any provisions of the corporation tax acts which relate to income tax (*TCGA 1992, s 8(4), (5)); ICTA 1988, s 831(1)*).

The acts of a liquidator in whom the assets of a company have been vested are treated as if they were the acts of the company, and the assets are treated as remaining vested in the company. Transfers of assets between the liquidator and the company are ignored (*TCGA 1992, s 8(6)*).

Corporation Tax 2010/11 (Bloomsbury Professional) has detailed coverage of corporation tax on chargeable gains. Various matters relevant to disposals by companies are discussed in this chapter or elsewhere in this book, as shown in **Table 9.1**.

Table 9.1

Chapter 2	**Disposal**
2.7	No gain, no loss disposals
2.10	Assets lost, destroyed or becoming of negligible value
2.21	Deemed disposal by non-resident
Chapter 3	**Computation**
3.11	Disposals to connected persons
3.12	Assets disposed of in a series of transactions
3.20	Companies as connected persons
3.22	Delayed or irrecoverable consideration
3.29	Election to carry back loss on disposal of a right
Chapter 4	**Particular assets**
4.22	Furnished holiday lettings

4.35	Debts
Chapter 5	**Residence**
5.16	Non-residents doing business in the UK
5.36	Apportionment of non-resident company's gains
Chapter 6	**Partnerships**
6.23	When transparency ends for an LLP
Chapter 14	**Roll-over relief for replacement of business assets**
14.6	Non-residents with UK presence
14.23	Intangible assets
14.36	Transfer to a European Company or Societas Europaea (SE)
14.39	Claims for roll-over relief
Chapter 17	**Other reliefs**
17.11	Relief for loans to traders
17.20	Losses on shares in unlisted trading companies

COMPUTATION

9.3 The gain accruing on the disposal of a company's chargeable asset is computed according to normal capital gains tax principles (see **Chapter 3**).

The rules setting out the consideration for the disposal (see **3.4**) and the expenditure allowable as a deduction (see **3.36**) in the computation apply to companies except where otherwise stated.

Assets held by companies at 31 March 1982 are not automatically rebased to that date, as they are for individuals and trustees who make disposals after 5 April 2008 (see **9.4**). Corporate disposals are also eligible for indexation allowance, calculated from the date the asset was acquired or 31 March 1982 if later, to the month in which the asset was disposed of (see **9.11**).

Rebasing to 31 March 1982

9.4 The discussion in **9.4–9.10** relates to disposals made after 5 April 2008, and as such is restricted to taxpayers that are subject to corporation tax. For the application of rebasing to disposals made by other taxpayers please see *Capital Gains Tax 2007/08* (Tottel Publishing) or an earlier edition.

The general rule is that where a company held an asset at 31 March 1982 and makes a disposal of it after 5 April 1988, the gain or loss accruing is calculated on the assumption that the company sold the asset on 31 March 1982, and immediately reacquired it at its market value on that date. The effect is to substitute the 31 March 1982 value for the actual cost of the asset and any enhancement expenditure incurred prior to that date. If the value of the asset being disposed of is derived from another asset held on 31 March 1982 rebasing may apply by reference to the original asset's value on that date (*TCGA 1992, s 35(1), (2), Sch 3, para 5*).

Exceptions to the rebasing rule

9.5 These exceptions do not apply in any case where a rebasing election has been made (see **9.6**). The exceptions to the general rebasing rule are (*TCGA 1992, s 35(3)*):

(a) where the effect of rebasing is to increase a gain arising under the normal rules, or to turn a loss arising under the normal rules into a gain;

(b) where the effect of rebasing is to increase a loss arising under the normal rules, or to turn a gain arising under the normal rules into a loss;

(c) where neither a gain nor a loss would accrue in the absence of rebasing, either on the facts or because of the rules for assets held on 6 April 1965 (*TCGA 1992, Sch 2*) (see **9.18**);

(d) where neither a gain nor a loss would accrue on the disposal by virtue of any of the provisions listed in *TCGA 1992, s 35(3)(d)*. Many of those provisions are not relevant for disposals made after 6 April 2008. The ones that remain relevant relate to the following disposals (statutory references being to *TCGA 1992* unless otherwise stated):

- transfers of assets on company reconstructions – *s 139*;
- transfers of UK trades by non-resident companies in exchange for securities – *s 140A*;
- transfers of assets as part of a merger forming a European Company or SE – *s 140E*;
- transfers within a group of companies – *s 171*;
- disposals on amalgamations of building societies – *s 215*;
- transfers of assets from a building society to a company – *s 216*;
- transfers of assets on incorporation of a registered friendly society – *s 217A*;
- certain disposals by housing associations – *ss 218–220*;
- certain transfers of assets to a harbour authority – *s 221*;
- deemed disposals where a charity becomes absolutely entitled to settled property – *s 257(3)*;

- gifts of heritage property – *s 258(4)*;
- transfers of land between local constituency associations of political parties on reorganisation of constituencies – *s 264*;
- disposals relating to the sharing of transmission facilities between national broadcasting companies – *s 267(2)*;
- transfers on the amalgamation of industrial and provident societies – *s 217D*.

A disposal is treated as giving rise to neither a gain nor a loss in a case where:

- the effect of the rebasing rule would be to turn a gain into a loss, or to turn a loss into a gain; but
- that rule has been disapplied by one of the exceptions listed above (*TCGA 1992, s 35(4)*).

Rebasing election

9.6 The company may elect that the rebasing rule will apply to any disposal that company makes of assets that it held at both 31 March 1982 and 5 April 1988, whether or not the disposal is within the list of exceptions at **9.5**. The election, once made, is irrevocable and applies to all such disposals, including those made before the time of the election.

The election is to be made at any time before 6 April 1990 or during the period beginning on the day of the 'first relevant disposal' (see below) and ending two years after the end of the accounting period in which that disposal takes place; and at such later time as HMRC may allow (*TCGA 1992, s 35(6)*).

The 'first relevant disposal' is the first disposal to which the 31 March 1982 rebasing rules apply. HMRC take the view that, strictly, the disposal of any asset, whether chargeable or not, can be the first relevant disposal, but in exercising their discretion to extend the time limit they will disregard certain disposals. These are set out in HMRC Statement of Practice 4/92 and include:

- disposals on which a gain would not be a chargeable gain by virtue of a particular statutory provision, eg the exemption for gilt-edged securities;
- disposals that do not give rise to a chargeable gain in practice, eg a gift of eligible property for the benefit of the public or to a charity; and
- certain disposals that could not be covered by a rebasing election (see 'excluded disposals' in **9.7**).

Excluded disposals

9.7 From 6 April 2008 only companies can make a rebasing election, and that election will exclude disposals of (or disposals of an interest in) plant or machinery, or an asset used in a trade of working mineral deposits, where in either case capital allowances were available. These disposals are also excluded if (i) the person making the disposal acquired the asset on a no gain, no loss transfer, and (ii) capital allowances were available to either the last person to acquire the asset other than on such a transfer or to any person who subsequently acquired the asset on such a transfer (*TCGA 1992, Sch 3, para 7*).

As a general rule, a rebasing election to cover assets held by a group of companies on 31 March 1982 may be made only by the group's principal member (*TCGA 1992, Sch 3, paras 8, 9*).

Assets acquired on a no gain, no loss transfer

9.8 Where the company makes a disposal after 5 April 1988 of an asset it acquired after 31 March 1982 by virtue of a no gain, no loss transfer (ie a disposal to which any of the provisions listed in *TCGA 1992, s 35(3)(d)* applies – see (d) in **9.5**), that company is treated as having held the asset on 31 March 1982 (*TCGA 1992, Sch 3, para 1*).

If the company ('the transferee') acquired the asset after 5 April 1988 and the no gain, no loss transfers principles applied to the acquisition (*TCGA 1992, s 171* between group companies), then:

(a) any rebasing election made by the transferee does not cover the disposal by the transferee of that asset;

(b) any rebasing election made by the transferor causes the disposal to fall outside the exceptions listed above, so that rebasing applies on the transferee's disposal whether or not the transferee makes a rebasing election.

If the transferor in this situation acquired the asset after 5 April 1988, and *TCGA 1992, s 171* applied to his acquisition, a rebasing election made by the transferor will not have the effect noted in (b) above. However, an election made by either of the following taxpayers will have that effect:

- the last company to acquire the asset after 5 April 1988 on a transfer outside *TCGA 1992, s 171*; or
- if there is no such taxpayer, the person who held the asset on 5 April 1988 (*TCGA 1992, Sch 3, para 2*).

Assets held on 6 April 1965 and 31 March 1982

9.9 Special rules (set out in *TCGA 1992, Sch 2*, see **9.18**), apply to a disposal of an asset held on 6 April 1965 in a case where:

- the rebasing rule in **9.5** does not apply; and
- the no gain, no loss rule in **9.8** does not apply.

Halving relief

9.10 Halving relief applies to reduce by half a deferred gain when it crystallises after 5 April 1988 (*TCGA 1992, s 36, Sch 4*). The gain must have been deferred between 31 March 1982 and 6 April 1988, in respect of an asset held on 31 March 1982 when the rebasing rules came into effect.

INDEXATION ALLOWANCE

9.11 The discussion in **9.11–9.21** relates to disposals made after 5 April 2008, and as such is restricted to taxpayers that are subject to corporation tax. For the application of the indexation allowance to disposals made by other taxpayers in earlier periods please see *Capital Gains Tax 2008/09* (Tottel Publishing) or an earlier edition.

The indexation allowance was introduced in 1982 in order to eliminate 'paper gains' attributable to inflation. Combined with the rebasing of assets by reference to 31 March 1982 values (see **9.4**) with effect from April 1988, indexation provided 'inflation-proofing' of all gains accruing since 31 March 1982. The indexation allowance can only be claimed by organisation subject to corporation tax for disposals made after 5 April 2008 (*TCGA 1992, s 52A*).

Calculation of indexation allowance

9.12 If an 'unindexed gain' accrues on a disposal of an asset, an indexation allowance is allowed against it. No allowance is available where a loss has accrued. The allowance is set against the unindexed gain and the result is the 'gain' for the purpose of *TCGA 1992* (also known as the 'indexed gain').

Where the indexation allowance is equal to or greater than the unindexed gain, the result is that neither a gain nor a loss accrues. The 'unindexed gain' is the gain computed as required by *TCGA 1992, Pt II* (see **Chapter 3**) (*TCGA 1992, s 53(1)*).

The indexation allowance is the aggregate of the 'indexed rise' in each item of 'relevant allowable expenditure'. The 'indexed rise' for each item of expenditure is found by multiplying the amount of the expenditure by the figure (the 'indexation factor') given by the formula:

$$\frac{(RD - RI)}{RI}$$

where:

- RD is the retail prices index for the month in which the disposal occurs; and
- RI is the retail prices index for the later of March 1982 or the month in which the expenditure was incurred.

There is no indexed rise if RD is equal to or less than RI. The indexation factor is expressed as a decimal and rounded to the nearest third decimal place, but HMRC may accept computations prepared using computer software where this rounding adjustment is not made, so long as computations are prepared on a consistent basis that favours neither HMRC nor the taxpayer (CG17274). HMRC publish indexation factors at www.hmrc.gov.uk/rates/c_gains_subject_c_tax.htm and announces the retail prices index on a monthly basis together with indexation factors for disposals in each month.

There is no indexed rise where expenditure concerned relates to acquisition of 'relevant securities', as defined in *TCGA 1992, s 108*, and the securities are disposed of within ten days of the expenditure being incurred (*TCGA 1992, 54(2)*). Other aspects of indexation allowance are also modified in relation to disposals of shares, securities and options (see **9.24**).

Relevant allowable expenditure

9.13 'Relevant allowable expenditure' above means any sum allowed as a deduction by *TCGA 1992, s 38* in computing the unindexed gain, adjusted as necessary for any provision increasing, reducing, writing down or excluding such expenditure. It includes, therefore, incidental costs of disposal as well as incidental costs of acquisition and enhancement expenditure. Any foreign tax charged on a gain is not regarded as relevant allowable expenditure. Costs of acquisition are taken to have been incurred when the asset was acquired or provided, and costs of enhancement are taken to have been incurred when the expenditure became due and payable (*TCGA 1992, s 54(4)*).

Part disposals

9.14 The apportionment of allowable expenditure on the part disposal of an asset (see **3.45**) takes place before the calculation of indexation allowance. This means there is no indexed rise to be computed for the part of the relevant allowable expenditure that is apportioned to the part retained (*TCGA 1992, s 56(1)*).

Assets held on 31 March 1982

9.15 Where the asset has been rebased to 31 March 1982 the indexation allowance is based on the market value at that date.

The rebased value can only apply where the company has made a rebasing election (see **9.6**). Where the rebasing election has not been made, the indexation will normally be based on the greater of the actual expenditure (or possibly market value at 6 April 1965) or the market value at 31 March 1982.

Assets acquired on a no gain, no loss transfer

9.16 Where the asset has been acquired on a no gain, no loss transfer (see **9.8**), then:

- in computing the indexation allowance on the disposal the taxpayer is treated as having held the asset on 31 March 1982 so that the allowance may be based on the market value at that date; but
- in computing the gain or loss accruing on the disposal, any indexation allowance taken into account in fixing the consideration that the taxpayer has deemed to have given for the asset is deducted from that consideration (*TCGA 1992, s 55(5), (6)*).

For this purpose, a no gain, no loss disposal is one on which neither a gain nor a loss accrues by virtue of:

- any of the provisions listed in the *TCGA 1992, s 35(3)(d)* (rebasing, see **9.5**); or
- the rules relating to gifts to charities, registered clubs and relevant housing providers in *TCGA 1992, s 257(2)* and *259(2)* respectively (*TCGA 1992, s 55(5)*).

Acquisition on a no gain, no loss transfer before 30 November 1993

9.17 As indicated in **9.12**, the indexation allowance can neither create nor increase a loss – it can only reduce the unindexed gain to nil. This was not the case before 30 November 1993. Special rules apply where the person making a disposal on or after that date acquired the asset on a no gain, no loss transfer before that date. Broadly, the effect is that a measure of indexation allowance that accrued on the no gain, no loss transfer – called the 'rolled-up indexation' – may create or increase a loss on the subsequent disposal.

For this purpose, it is necessary to compute the gain under the normal rules and compute the amount of the rolled-up indexation. No adjustment is required if indexation allowance included in the computation exceeds the rolled-up indexation. If it is less than the rolled-up indexation, the full amount of the rolled-up indexation is allowed in computing the chargeable gain or allowable loss (*TCGA 1992, s 55(7)–(11)*; CG17766).

Assets held on 6 April 1965

9.18 The rules for assets held on 6 April 1965 described in **9.19–9.21** only apply to companies where a universal rebasing election has not been made, so in practice will be very rarely encountered.

Quoted shares and securities

9.19 A gain or loss on disposal of quoted shares or securities is computed by reference to both the original cost and the market value of the asset as at 6 April 1965. The lower gain (or loss) arising is taken. If one computation produces a gain and the other produces a loss, the disposal is treated as giving rise to no gain and no loss. An irrevocable election (similar to the 31 March 1982 rebasing election, see **9.6**) can be made to use the 6 April 1965 market value of quoted shares and securities instead of their original cost (*TCGA 1992, Sch 2, Pt I*).

Land reflecting development value

9.20 The gain or loss on the disposal of land reflecting development value that was held at 6 April 1965 is computed as described for quoted shares and securities in **9.19** if special provisions relating to development land apply (*TCGA 1992, Sch 2, Pt II*).

Other assets held on 6 April 1965

9.21 Where an asset, other than quoted shares or land with development value, was acquired before 6 April 1965, the general rule is that gains are calculated on the basis of original cost but those gains are then time-apportioned.

Only that part of the gain relating to the period falling after 6 April 1965 is chargeable. Any period of ownership before 6 April 1945 is ignored for time-apportionment purposes. The gain is reduced by any indexation allowance before being time-apportioned. However, the calculation using the 31 March 1982 value (see rebasing, **9.6**) should normally give rise to a lower gain and this time-apportionment method is now likely to be used only rarely.

The taxpayer may make an irrevocable election to ignore the original cost and compute the gain by reference to the asset's market value on 6 April 1965. Alternatively, where a rebasing election has been made, the asset's market value at 31 March 1982 replaces the original cost and no time-apportionment of the gain is necessary (*TCGA 1992, Sch 2, Pt III*).

Example 9.1

The West End Trading Co Ltd prepares accounts to 31 March each year. The company disposes of an office block on 3 February 2010 for £40 million. The incidental costs of sale are £1 million. The block was purchased in January 2002 for £15.5 million. Costs of acquisition amounted to £0.5 million. In January 2003 a new frontage at a cost of £2 million was added to the building that was deemed to be capital expenditure. The chargeable gain to be included within the corporation tax computation for the year ended 31 March 2010 is calculated as follows:

		£000	£000
Feb 2010	Gross sale proceeds		40,000
	Less: Incidental costs of sale		(1,000)
	Net sale proceeds		39,000
	Less: Relevant allowable expenditure:		
January 2002	Acquisition cost	15,500	
January 2002	Incidental costs of acquisition	500	
January 2003	Enhancement expenditure	2,000	
			(18,000)
	Unindexed gain		21,000
	Less: Indexation allowance		
	Cost 16,000 × 0.265	4,240	
	Enhancement 2,000 × 0.229	458	
			(4,698)
	Chargeable gain		16,302

Workings: calculation of indexation factor

RPI	February 2010	219.2
RPI	January 2002	173.3
RPI	January 2003	178.4
Factor:	Rounded to three decimal places	
Cost	(RPI Feb 2010 – RPI January 2002) ÷ RPI January 2002	0.265
Enhancement	(RPI Feb 2010 – RPI January 2003) ÷ RPI January 2003	0.229

CAPITAL LOSSES

9.22 As a general rule, capital losses may only be set against capital gains of the current accounting period or carried forward to be set against future capital gains. There are no provisions that permit corporate taxpayers to carry back capital losses (see **7.3** for individuals). However, a capital loss on the disposal by an investment company of shares, for which it subscribed, in an unlisted trading company may be set against income for corporation tax purposes (see **17.20**). A loss made on shares acquired under the Corporate Venturing Scheme (CVS) before 31 March 2010 may also be set against income under certain circumstances (see **9.48**).

Where losses are made by a company within a group of companies, elections can be made effectively to transfer the loss to another group company (see **9.28** and **9.29**).

The effect of a claim to relief for trading losses under *CTA 2010, s 37* may be to set such losses against chargeable gains, because the losses are set against total profits including chargeable gains.

A targeted anti-avoidance rule (TAAR) in *TCGA 1992, s 16A* applies to any company that is seeking to make use of a capital loss that is not a genuine commercial loss, which arose from a genuine commercial disposal. A capital loss is not an allowable loss if it accrues directly or indirectly in consequence or in connection with any arrangements of which the main purpose is to secure a tax advantage (*TCGA 1992, s 16A, (1)*). This is a very wide-ranging provision, but in practice its scope is limited by the HMRC guidance contained in Appendix 9 to the HMRC Capital Gains Manual, see also **10.2**. There are also three targeted anti-avoidance rules that apply to companies with effect from 5 December 2005 that seek to target:

- the buying of capital losses and gains (*TCGA 1992, ss 184A, 184B*);

- the conversion of an income stream into capital and the use of capital losses to create a deduction against it (*TCGA 1992, s 184G*); and
- the artificial generation of capital losses (*TCGA 1992, s 184H*).

The detailed rules for these provisions are discussed in Chapter 22 of *Corporation Tax 2010/11* (Bloomsbury Professional).

IDENTIFICATION OF SHARES

9.23 The changes made from 6 April 2008 to simplify the calculation of gains on the disposal of shares and securities (see **4.2**) do not apply for corporation tax. This means that the various pools used to identify shares acquired at different times continue for corporation tax.

All shares of the same class in the same company that are acquired after 31 March 1982 are 'pooled', ie treated as a single asset with a single average indexed cost per share. Each disposal of shares out of the pool represents a part disposal of a single asset and the chargeable gain or allowable loss is computed by reference to the averaged indexed cost of the shares sold.

Shares disposed of are identified with acquisitions in the following order:

(a) acquisitions on the same day as the disposal;

(b) securities treated as part of the *section 104* holding where acquisitions were made during the nine days before the disposal date (earlier acquisitions first);

(c) shares acquired after 31 March 1982 and comprised in the '*section 104* holding' (see **9.24**);

(d) shares acquired before 1 April 1982 (the '1982 holding', see **9.25**);

(e) shares acquired before 6 April 1965 (taking later acquisitions first); and

(f) acquisitions after the disposal (taking earlier acquisitions first) (*TCGA 1992, ss 105–107*; CG50562).

Special rules apply to 'relevant securities', ie qualifying corporate bonds, securities within the accrued income provisions, deep discount securities and material interests in non-qualifying offshore funds (*TCGA 1992, s 108*).

Section 104 holding

9.24 The *section 104* holding comprises shares of the same class that were acquired after 31 March 1982. For non-corporate shareholders this pool was restricted to shares acquired after 5 April 1982 and before 6 April 1998 by the same person in the same capacity. See Chapter 4 of *Capital Gains Tax 2007/08* (Tottel Publishing) for a full description of the share identification rules that applied for 2007/08 and earlier tax years for individuals, trustees and personal representatives.

Shares in the *section 104* holding are treated as indistinguishable parts of a single asset. A disposal of some of the shares in a *section 104* holding is treated as a part disposal of an asset (*TCGA 1992, s 104(1), (3), (6)*).

There are special rules for calculating indexation allowance for shares in this pool (*TCGA 1992, ss 110*). The gain is computed by reference to the averaged indexed cost of each share disposed of. The shares in the *section 104* holding are referred to as the 'new holding' by HMRC and detailed guidance is given at CG50590–CG50801.

Example 9.2

Imperious Capital Ltd holds 1,500 shares in Destroying Angel Ltd, which represents 1.5% of ordinary share capital of that company, so the substantial shareholding exemption does not apply (see **9.42**). The Destroying Angel shares were acquired as follows:

Date	Number of shares	Cost £	Indexed cost £
1 June 2000	1,000	80,000	7,360
Indexed to April 2004, factor: 0.092			87,360
3 April 2004	300	9,000	96,360
Indexed to Dec 2007, factor: 0.136			13,104
7 December 2007	200	1,000	110,464
Indexed to March 2010, factor: 0.046			5,081
	1,500	90,000	115,545
Disposal in March 2010	(500)		(38,515)
Remaining pool:	1,000		77,030

Imperious Capital Ltd disposed of 500 of the Destroying Angel shares on 18 March 2010, and the cost of that part disposal is calculated as: 500/1,500 × £115,545 = £38,515.

The 1982 holding

9.25 This comprises all shares of the same class in the same company that were acquired between 6 April 1965 and 31 March 1982. The holding is treated as acquired on 31 March 1982 (*TCGA 1992, s 109*).

ROLL-OVER RELIEF FOR REPLACEMENT OF BUSINESS ASSETS

9.26 The effect of roll-over relief is to defer a chargeable gain where the proceeds of disposal of business assets (the 'old assets') are used to invest in new business assets. The old and the new assets must be used in the business. The detailed rules are discussed in **Chapter 14** (and see **Table 9.1** at **9.2**, listing matters contained in that chapter that are of particular relevance to companies). See also **9.36** regarding groups of companies (*TCGA 1992, ss 152–158).*

GROUPS OF COMPANIES

Definitions

9.27 Tax charges and reliefs relating to chargeable gains can depend on whether a company is part of a group. For these purposes a group broadly consists of a company (known as the principal company) and all of its 75% subsidiaries. If any of those subsidiaries have 75% subsidiaries of their own, the group includes them and their 75% subsidiaries. Any subsidiary that is not an effective 51% subsidiary of the principal company of the group is excluded.

A company that is a 75% subsidiary of another company cannot be the principal company of a group. The principal company can be UK or overseas resident and the inclusion of a non-resident subsidiary does not disturb the group relationship.

Example 9.3

A Ltd owns 75% of the ordinary share capital of B Ltd.

B Ltd owns 80% of the ordinary share capital of C Ltd.

A Ltd and B Ltd are a group, as A Ltd owns 75% of B Ltd.

A Ltd and C Ltd are a group because A Ltd effectively owns 60% (75% × 80%) of C Ltd.

A company cannot be a member of more than one group. Where a company would be a member of two or more groups but for this rule, the group to which it is treated as belonging is determined by reference to its links to the principal company. If the group conditions are not met the links should then be established with the next group – see **Example 9.4** (*TCGA 1992, s 170*).

Example 9.4

A Ltd owns 75% of the ordinary share capital of B Ltd.

B Ltd owns 80% of the ordinary share capital of C Ltd.

C Ltd owns 75% of the ordinary share capital of D Ltd.

D Ltd owns 75% of the ordinary share capital of E Ltd.

A Ltd and B Ltd are a group.

A Ltd and C Ltd are a group.

A Ltd and D Ltd are not a group because A Ltd effectively owns 45% (75% × 80% × 75%) of D Ltd.

D Ltd and E Ltd are a group.

Transfers within a group of companies

9.28 For chargeable gains purposes, intra-group transfers of assets are deemed to be made at a price that results in neither a gain nor a loss accruing to the transferee company (*TCGA 1992, s 171*) (*Innocent v Whaddon Estates Ltd* (1981) 55 TC 476, [1982] STC 115).

This no gain, no loss rule is applied automatically – no claim is required, but it does not apply to a disposal:

- arising on the satisfaction of a debt due from the transferee company;
- arising on the redemption of redeemable shares in a company;
- by or to an investment trust, a Venture Capital Trust (VCT), a qualifying friendly society, or a dual-resident investing company; or
- by or to a real estate investment trust (*TCGA 1992, s 171(2)*).

The effect of this no gain, no loss rule is that when the transferee company eventually disposes of the asset to a third party, its allowable acquisition expenditure in the chargeable gains computation will comprise the original base cost of the asset to the group, plus indexation allowance for the period to the date of the transfer. The transferee company will be eligible for indexation on this deemed acquisition expenditure as well as any allowable enhancement expenditure that it incurs.

Although a non-UK resident company can be a member of the group, it cannot take part in a no gain, no loss transfer unless it trades in the UK through a permanent establishment in the UK. The asset must be in the UK and be used for the purposes of that trade (*TCGA 1992, s 171(1A)*).

On a company reconstruction involving an exchange of shares or debentures under the conditions set out in *TCGA 1992, s 135,* the no gain, no loss rule in *s 171* does not apply as the alternative no gain, no loss treatment in *TCGA 1992, ss 127–131* takes preference (*TCGA 1992, s 171(3)*). For further discussion of company reconstructions please refer to Chapter 18 of *Corporation Tax 2010/11* (Bloomsbury Professional).

Election to transfer gains and losses within a group

9.29 With effect for gains or losses accruing from 21 July 2009 group companies can transfer any capital gain or loss between each other to allow full matching of losses and gains that arise within the group. There is no need actually to transfer the ownership of assets within a group. Losses arising as a result of a negligible value claim (see **2.10**) can be transferred as well as realised losses (*TCGA 1992, ss 171A–171C*).

The gain or loss is transferred by way of a joint election by the two group companies made within two years of the end of the accounting period for the company where the gain or loss is accrued (*TCGA 1992, s 171A*). The companies concerned must both be members of the same group at the time the gain or loss accrues, and the no gain, no loss conditions under s *171* must apply (see **9.28**).

Gains or losses made before 21 July 2009 could only be transferred between group companies where the asset concerned was transferred outside the group. The transfer of the loss or gain was achieved in the same fashion by joint election between the two group companies.

Company leaving the group

9.30 If a company leaves a group within six years of an intra-group transfer of an asset that was treated as a no gain, no loss disposal (see **9.28**) and the company still owns that asset when it leaves the group, a chargeable gain arises on that occasion (*TCGA 1992, s 179*). The gain is calculated on the basis that the company leaving the group sold and repurchased the asset at its market value at the time of the no gain, no loss transfer, but the gain is charged in the accounting period in which the company leaves the group (*TCGA 1992, s 179(3)*).

The transferee company and another group company may elect jointly that this 'degrouping charge' (gain or loss) be treated as accruing to the other company (*TCGA 1992, s 179A*). Roll-over relief (see **Chapter 14**) may be available if the relevant conditions are met (*TCGA 1992, s 179B*).

Example 9.5

In 1988 Nereus Ltd acquired a freehold property for £280,000. On 30 December 2003 when the market value was £500,000, and the indexation to date was £20,000, Nereus Ltd transferred the freehold property to Pontus Ltd (a fellow group member). Pontus Ltd leaves the group on 1 January 2010. Both companies prepare accounts to 30 June each year.

The *TCGA 1992, s 179* gain for the year ended 30 June 2010 is calculated as follows:

Pontus Ltd	£	£
Market value at date of transfer:		500,000
Original cost	280,000	
Indexation:	20,000	
Indexed cost:		(300,000)
Capital gain		200,000

If Pontus Ltd purchases another qualifying asset, Pontus Ltd will be able to make a roll-over relief claim under *TCGA 1992, s 152*.

If Nereus Ltd and Pontus Ltd jointly elect for the *s 179* deemed gain to be treated as accruing to Nereus Ltd, then Nereus Ltd may be able to make a roll-over relief claim against its acquisition of a qualifying asset.

9.31 HMRC confirmed that a degrouping charge will not be imposed on assets transferred to the parent of a two company group which disposes of its single subsidiary (CG45450). However the degrouping charge under *s 179* does create problems for larger groups. For example a new subsidiary may be formed to contain the trade and assets of a particular activity, which the parent group wants to dispose of. The deemed *s 179* gain arises in the new subsidiary rather than in the vendor company.

The law relating to capital gains in groups of companies is under review (see www.hm-treasury.gov.uk/d/consult_simplification_capitalgains.pdf) and changes may be made with effect from 1 April 2011. For a detailed discussion of the tax effects of company mergers and demergers please refer to *Taxation of Company Reorganisations* (3rd edition) (Bloomsbury Professional).

Series of transactions

9.32 A transfer of assets between members of a group of companies is not a material transaction if it is a 'no gain, no loss' transfer by virtue of *TCGA 1992, s 171* (*TCGA 1992, s 19(5)*) (see **9.29**).

An anti-avoidance rule applies to prevent a group circumventing the rule concerning the valuation of assets as part of a series of transactions (see **3.12**) by having one company transfer assets to other group companies under the no gain, no loss rule in *TCGA 1992, s 171* and then arranging for the assets to be transferred to connected persons outside the group (*TCGA 1992, s 19(6)*; CG14702).

Transfers of assets to trading stock

9.33 Where one group member acquires a capital asset from another member and appropriates that asset to trading stock, the intra-group asset transfer will be treated as a no gain, no loss disposal (see **9.28**) but as soon as the asset is transferred to stock a chargeable gain will arise in the hands of the transferee. The transferee adopts the transferor's asset base cost and indexation to the date of the transfer (*TCGA 1992, ss 171, 173*).

Alternatively, the transferee can elect under *TCGA 1992, s 161(3)* to treat the asset as acquired at market value less the capital gain arising. The gain will therefore be taken as part of the trading profit on the asset.

Example 9.6

Odin Ltd transfers a fixed asset to its holding company Thor Ltd which has a market value of £20,000, and a cost plus indexation allowance (the indexed cost) of £12,500. Thor Ltd immediately appropriates the asset to its trading stock, and eventually sells the asset to a third party for £30,000.

Without a *TCGA 1992, s 161(3)* election the position is as follows:

Thor Ltd	£
Market value at time of transfer to stock	20,000
Indexed cost from no gain, no loss acquisition	(12,500)
Capital gain	7,500
Thor Ltd	
Sale proceeds	30,000
Deemed cost (market value)	(20,000)
Trading profit	10,000

With a *TCGA 1992, s 161(3)* election the position is as follows:

Thor Ltd	£
Sales proceeds	30,000
Indexed cost	(12,500)
Trading profit	17,500

9.34 There is the potential here to turn a capital loss into a trading loss. The loss will only be allowed if there is a true trading intention (*Coates v Arndale Properties Ltd* (1984) 59 TC 516, [1984] STC 637, [1984] 1 WLR 1328, [1985] 1 All ER 15).

Transfers of assets from trading stock

9.35 Where a group company transfers an asset that it holds as trading stock to another group company, and the transferee holds it as a capital asset, the asset is deemed to be transferred at market value giving rise to a trading profit in the hands of the transferor (*CTA 2009, s 157*). When the transferee company sells the asset outside the group it adopts as its base cost the market value of the asset at the time of the transfer, plus indexation allowance.

Example 9.7

Thor Ltd transfers a chargeable asset from its trading stock to its subsidiary company Odin Ltd. Odin Ltd holds the asset as an investment. The cost of the asset was £10,000 and the market value on transfer is £30,000. Odin Ltd then sells the asset to a third party for £40,000. The indexation from the time of transfer is £500.

Thor Ltd	£	£
Market value		30,000
Cost		(10,000)
Trading profit		20,000
Odin Ltd		
Sale proceeds		40,000
Deemed cost (market value)	30,000	
Indexation	500	
		(30,500)
Capital gain		9,500

Roll-over relief and groups

9.36 Roll-over relief (see **9.26**) is extended to group situations. For this purpose all trades carried on by the members of a group are treated as a single trade. The new assets must be purchased from outside the group (*TCGA 1992, s 175*).

Losses attributable to depreciatory transactions

9.37 A transfer of assets between group companies for a consideration other than market value may have the effect of deflating the value of a group company. Any capital loss accruing on the sale of the shares in that company may not be an allowable loss to the extent that it is attributable to the 'depreciatory transaction'. The detailed rules are set out in *TCGA 1992, s 176*, and are discussed in greater depth in Chapter 22 of *Corporation Tax 2010/11* (Bloomsbury Professional). HMRC guidance is given at CG46500–CG46680.

Dividend stripping

9.38 The rule in **9.37** may also apply in a non-group situation. Where a company (A) owns 10% or more of all holdings of the same class of shares of another company (B), but company A is not part of the same group as company B and does not hold the company B shares as trading stock. A distribution is made by company B which materially reduces the value of the shares held by company A. Company A then sells its shares in company B, but an adjustment is made for that distribution in calculating the chargeable gain or loss accruing on a disposal of the company B shares (*TCGA 1992, s 177*).

Pre-entry losses and gains

9.39 A pre-entry asset is an asset owned by a company before it joins a group. A loss or gain accruing on the disposal of that asset, either before or after the company joins the group, is a pre-entry loss or gain. Where a company joined a group before 5 December 2005, it is prevented from setting its pre-entry losses or gains against gains or losses transferred from another group member (*TCGA 1992, Sch 7AA,* repealed by *FA 2006, s 70(4)*).

The pre-entry loss rules are largely replaced from 5 December 2005 by the anti-avoidance rule in *TCGA 1992, s 184A,* which only applies if there is an arrangement to avoid tax. The ability of a group company to set its capital losses against capital gains accruing in another group company (see **9.29**) is denied in the following circumstances:

(a) where there is a direct or indirect change in ownership of a company;

(b) where a loss accrues to the company or another company on a pre-entry asset;

(c) where the main purpose of the change in ownership is to secure a tax advantage; and

(d) the tax advantage involves the deduction of losses from chargeable gains.

The operation of the anti-avoidance rules in *TCGA 1992, ss 184A–184H* are discussed in greater detail in Chapter 22 of *Corporation Tax 2010/11* (Bloomsbury Professional).

The rules regarding pre-entry losses or gains, and depreciatory transactions are under review (see www.hm-treasury.gov.uk/d/consult_simplification_capitalgains.pdf). Any changes in the law are likely to be introduced from 1 April 2011 or a later date.

RELIEF ON DISPOSAL OF SHARES

9.40 Three important reliefs are available in relation to a company's disposal of shares. These relate to:

- losses on shares in unlisted trading companies (see **9.41**);
- substantial shareholdings (see **9.42**); and
- the corporate venturing scheme (see **9.46**).

Losses on shares in unlisted trading companies

9.41 Relief against income is available to an investment company incurring an allowable loss for corporation tax purposes on the disposal of shares, for which it subscribed, in a qualifying trading company (see **17.20**).

Substantial shareholdings exemption

9.42 Where a trading company (the investing company) holds at least 10% of the share capital of another trading company (the investee company), and the other conditions of the substantial shareholdings exemption (SSE) are met, a gain made on the disposal of any investee company shares is not a chargeable gain. Also a loss accruing on the disposal of any of the investee company shares by the investing company is not an allowable loss (*TCGA 1992, s 192A, Sch 7AC*).

SSE relief applies automatically if the conditions are met; there is no requirement to make an election. The requirements for SSE relief for the investing company are:

(a) it must hold at least 10% of the investee company's ordinary share capital and be entitled to at least 10% of the profits and assets available for distribution to equity holders.

(b) it must have held the shares for a continuous period of at least 12 months beginning not more than two years before the disposal (*TCGA 1992, Sch 7AC, para 7*).

Group member holdings can be aggregated in order to calculate whether the 10% holding condition is met (*TCGA 1992, Sch 7AC, para 9*). The capital gains tax group definition is used (see **9.27**) but a 51% relationship is required rather than a 75% relationship.

The period of ownership may be extended to take account of earlier no gain, no loss transfers and share reorganisations. There are provisions dealing with deemed disposals and reacquisitions, repurchase agreements, stock-lending arrangements, demergers and liquidations (*TCGA 1992, Sch 7AC, paras 10–16*).

The SSE relief applies to gains or losses made on all disposals of all types of shares in the investee company, not just the ordinary shares which are held to meet the 10% test. SSE relief does not apply where the disposal is deemed to be a no gain, no loss transfer for capital gains under *TCGA 1992, s 171* (see **9.28**).

Conditions affecting the investing company

9.43 The investing company must have been a sole trading company or a member of a trading group throughout the 12-month period (see **9.42**) and immediately after the disposal. The relief also applies in a group situation where the company holding the shares does not qualify but, assuming an intra-group transfer under *TCGA 1992, s 171*, another company would qualify. Where completion takes place after the time of disposal (as provided by *TCGA 1992, s 28*) the investing company must qualify at the time of completion (*TCGA 1992, Sch 7AC, para 18*).

Conditions affecting the investee company

9.44 The investee company must have been a trading company or the holding company of a trading group during the 12-month period (see **9.42**), and it must also be a qualifying company immediately after the disposal of the shares. The responsibility for determining whether a company in which shares (or an interest in shares or assets related to shares) were held and since disposed of was a qualifying company lies with the investor company concerned (see CG53120). Where there is uncertainty over the trading status of the investee company the investing company can ask HMRC for an opinion on this point under their non-statutory business clearance service (see www.hmrc.gov.uk/manuals/nbcgmanual/index.htm).

Where completion takes place after the time of disposal (as provided by *TCGA 1992, s 28*) the investee company must qualify at the time of completion (*TCGA 1992, Sch 7AC, para 19*).

Trading company

9.45 The meanings of 'trading company', 'trading group' and 'holding company' are now common to all capital gains reliefs and are defined in *TCGA 1992, s 165A*. See **11.11–11.18** for a detailed discussion of these terms.

Example 9.8

Atlantic Ltd is a trading company, with two wholly-owned subsidiary companies, India Ltd and China Ltd.

On 1 July 2008, Atlantic Ltd acquired 25% of the ordinary share capital of Pacific Ltd.

On 1 September 2008 Pacific Ltd is taken over by Adriatic Ltd.

Atlantic Ltd received an exchange of shares under the no gain, no loss treatment (*TCGA s 127*). As a result Atlantic Ltd now owns 20% of Adriatic Ltd.

On 1 March 2009 Atlantic Ltd transfers its holding in Adriatic Ltd on a no gain, no loss basis so that *TCGA 1992, s 171* applies, to its 100% subsidiary India Ltd.

On 1 June 2010 India Ltd sells the holding to a third party.

The holding was bought on 1 July 2008 and sold on 1 June 2010. It is necessary to look back through the period of ownership to ascertain whether the substantial shareholdings exemption applies (*TCGA 1992, Sch 7AC, para 10*). The holding throughout has remained within the group. India Ltd is treated as owning the shares for 12 months prior to disposal and so the exemption applies.

Corporate venturing scheme

9.46 Relief under the corporate venturing scheme is available for investments in qualifying shares issued during the period from 1 April 2000 to 31 March 2010. The scheme is discussed in detail in Chapter 12 of *Corporation Tax 2009/10* (Bloomsbury Professional), and the legislation is found in *FA 2000, s 63* and *Sch 15*. HMRC guidance is available in the venture capital schemes manual at VCM50010–VCM50160.

Tax reliefs

9.47 Three types of relief are available:

- investment relief – relief against corporation tax of up 20% of the amount subscribed for the full-risk ordinary shares (CVS shares) held for at least three years;
- deferral relief – any gain on the sale of CVS shares can be rolled into the cost of new shares acquired under the scheme; and
- loss relief – any loss on the sale of the CVS shares can be relieved against income or chargeable gains.

The conditions for the reliefs to apply are not discussed here, as the scheme has closed for new investments. Only loss relief may be relevant to companies who hold CVS shares on 1 April 2010. However, if the qualifying conditions for the SSE apply, in particular where 10% or more of the ordinary shares of the investee company are held, any gain arising on the disposal of the CVS shares is ignored for corporation tax purposes. Thus, the deferral relief is unnecessary and the loss relief (see **9.48**) is overridden.

Relief for losses

9.48 A loss accruing on a disposal of shares that have attracted CVS investment relief may be set against a chargeable gain, or carried forward to set against future chargeable gains, in the normal way, provided the loss is not overridden by SSE relief (see **9.47**). Alternatively, the investing company may claim that the loss be set against its income for the accounting period in which the disposal was made, with any excess carried back to periods ending in the 12 months before that period. Several conditions are set out in *FA 2000, Sch 15, paras 67–72*.

Example 9.9

An investing company subscribes £100,000 for 100,000 shares (obtaining investment relief of £20,000).

It retains the shares for four years before disposing of them all for £55,000.

The allowable loss is calculated as follows:

Disposal proceeds: £55,000 – £80,000 (consideration given for shares less investment relief given and not withdrawn) giving an allowable loss of £25,000.

Any unutilised loss cannot be carried forward as a trading loss but may be carried forward as a capital loss.

Chapter 10

Capital gains tax planning

10.1 This chapter provides an overview of some of the matters that should be considered by taxpayers seeking to ensure that they do not pay more CGT than the law requires. It does not examine every possible legal step that could be taken to reduce or eliminate a potential tax liability and, taxpayers and their advisers need to bear in mind the implications of recent developments in relation to tax avoidance. These are discussed briefly below.

TARGETED ANTI-AVOIDANCE RULES

10.2 The system for disclosure of tax avoidance schemes (DOTAS), introduced in the *Finance Act 2004* and modified in successive Finance Acts (see **10.5**), has led to the disclosure of a large number of tax schemes to HMRC and an increase in targeted anti-avoidance legislation.

Three targeted anti-avoidance rules (TAARs) were introduced with effect from 5 December 2005, which apply to the use of capital losses by companies (see **9.22**). From 6 December 2006 those anti-avoidance provisions are effectively replaced, but not removed, by *TCGA 1992, s 16A,* which also covers the use of capital losses by individuals, trustees and personal representatives of deceased persons.

Where *TCGA 1992, s 16A* applies to a capital loss, that loss is not an 'allowable loss' for the purposes of CGT and cannot be set off against chargeable gains, or against income, to reduce income tax or corporation tax. It is irrelevant that there are no chargeable gains available at the time the loss arises, from which it may have been deductible.

Scope of the TAAR

10.3 *TCGA 1992, s 16A* (the TAAR) is effective for individuals, trustees and personal representatives from 6 December 2006, so it potentially catches transactions in the 2006/07 tax year, as well as subsequent periods. It is intended to apply where a person (which can be a company or an individual) deliberately and knowingly enters into an arrangement to gain a tax advantage.

The terms 'arrangement' and 'tax advantage' are very widely drawn. As a result the TAAR potentially catches a wide range of transactions including those that have been previously ignored for CGT purposes, such as transfers between spouses.

In practice the scope of this legislation is limited by the HMRC guidance set out in Appendix 9 to their Capital Gains Manual. Specifically, the HMRC guidance seeks to limit the extent of the TAAR to artificially created losses. It states:

> 'This legislation will not apply where there is a genuine economic transaction that gives rise to a real economic loss as a result of a real disposal. In these circumstances there will be no arrangements with a main purpose of securing a tax advantage. Conversely, where there is either no real disposal, or no real economic loss, or any combination of the foregoing, then there are likely to be arrangements in place with a main purpose of securing a tax advantage so the legislation will apply.'

In addition the guidance appears to further limit the scope of the TAAR at para 3 of the introduction to Appendix 9:

> 'In particular it is unlikely that individuals with a normal portfolio of investments who make disposals in the ordinary course of managing their portfolio would be affected by these new rules because there is currently little evidence to suggest that such individuals undertake the type of arrangements that are targeted by this legislation.'

In spite of this comforting statement many active investors do use capital losses arising on their investments to reduce the taxable gains from other holdings.

It should be noted that:

- The HMRC guidance does not have the force of law; it can be amended at any time, with retrospective effect, and cannot be the subject of an appeal in the courts.
- There is no HMRC guidance on the records a taxpayer must keep in order to prove the capital losses achieved are not blocked by the TAAR.
- There is no guidance on the level of disclosure a taxpayer should make on their tax return to provide HMRC with enough evidence to show the TAAR does not apply.

Clearance procedure

10.4 There is no specific clearance procedure attached to the TAAR to provide taxpayers with certainty that a particular transaction will not fall within the rules. However, HMRC have said that they will give guidance under the Code of Practice 10 procedure about the interpretation of the wording of the legislation where there is genuine uncertainty. Code of Practice 10 generally only applies to the interpretation of legislation passed in the last four Finance Acts. HMRC interpret this as meaning within the last four years, so although 2010 may see three Finance Acts passed, questions regarding the operation of *TCGA 1992, s 16A* may be raised until mid-2011.

DISCLOSURE OF TAX AVOIDANCE SCHEMES

10.5 The regime requiring disclosure of tax avoidance schemes (DOTAS) is designed to alert HMRC to certain schemes or arrangements that are intended to provide a tax advantage when compared to a different course of action. It is not intended to catch mainstream or 'legitimate' tax planning.

The DOTAS regime now applies generally to income tax, national insurance contributions, corporation tax, CGT, VAT and stamp duty land tax. A tax arrangement must be disclosed when:

- it will, or might be expected to, enable any person to obtain a tax advantage;
- that tax advantage is, or might be expected to be, the main benefit or one of the main benefits of the arrangement; and
- it is a tax arrangement that falls within any prescribed hallmarks.

The current hallmarks for income tax, CGT and corporation tax are:

(a) wishing to keep the arrangements confidential from a competitor;

(b) wishing to keep the arrangements confidential from HMRC;

(c) arrangements for which a premium fee could reasonably be obtained;

(d) arrangements that include off-market terms;

(e) arrangements that are standardised tax products;

(f) arrangements that are loss schemes;

(g) arrangements that are certain leasing arrangements;

(h) arrangements for certain pension benefits.

The March 2010 Budget suggested that hallmark (d) above should be removed and hallmarks (a), (b), (c) and (f) be strengthened. In addition the following new hallmarks have been proposed:

- arrangements that convert income into an asset, which would be subject to CGT on disposal;
- employment remuneration strategies; and
- off-shore planning involving a territory in the OECD list of uncooperative tax havens.

The new hallmarks are likely to be introduced by regulations late in 2010. The disclosure requirements for schemes involving the avoidance of national insurance, VAT or stamp duty land tax are based on different hallmarks and have varying *de minimis* levels below which a disclosure is not required.

In most situations where a disclosure is required it must be made by the scheme 'promoter' within five days of it being made available. However, the scheme user may need to make the disclosure where:

- the promoter is based outside the UK;
- the promoter is a lawyer and legal privilege applies; or
- there is no promoter.

Upon disclosure of the scheme, HMRC issue the promoter with an eight-digit scheme reference number, which each client who uses the scheme must include on their tax return or form AAG4. A person who designs and implements their own scheme must disclose it within 30 days of it being implemented.

Detailed guidance of the operation of DOTAS is available on the HMRC website: www.hmrc.gov.uk/aiu/index.htm. These pages are also used by HMRC to announce 'spotlights', which are arrangements or schemes that HMRC have become aware of and are likely to challenge.

'*RAMSAY*' AND ANTI-AVOIDANCE LEGISLATION

10.6 A series of appeals heard by the courts during the 1980s established the principle that one or more steps in a pre-ordained tax avoidance scheme could be ignored, with the result that the scheme did not have the intended tax consequences. See, in particular, *W T Ramsay Ltd v CIR* [1981) 54 TC 101, HL and *Furniss v Dawson* (1984) 55 TC 324, HL. Subsequent cases have scaled back the impact of the *Ramsay* (or *Furniss v Dawson*) principle, but the possibility of an HMRC challenge on these grounds should always be borne in mind.

The ever-increasing length and complexity of recent Finance Acts is largely due to the addition of detailed legislation to counter artificial or contrived arrangements designed to obtain a tax advantage, and to close loopholes (ie flaws in the legislation which mean that it did not work as intended). They include:

	TCGA 1992
Temporary non-residents	*s 10A*
Attribution of gains to members of non-resident companies	*s 13*
Transactions between connected persons	*s 18*
Assets disposed of in a series of transactions	*ss 19–20*
Value shifting	*ss 29–34*
Shares in close company transferring assets at an undervalue	*s 125*
Company reconstructions	*s 137*
Emigration of donee	*s 168*
Concessions that defer a charge	*s 284A*
For companies:	*CTA 2010*
Transactions in securities	*Pt 15*
Transactions in land	*Pt 18*
For individuals and trustees:	*ITA 2007*
Transactions in securities	*Pt 13 ch 1*
Transfer of assets abroad	*Pt 13 ch 2*
Transactions in land	*Pt 13 ch 3*

Other anti-avoidance measures specific to particular situations or tax reliefs are discussed where appropriate in the relevant chapter of this book.

TAX PLANNING

10.7 It is important to distinguish between mainstream tax planning from the use of artificial or contrived schemes to avoid tax. HMRC regard the former as legitimate but appear determined to eliminate the latter. This section focuses on some of the matters to be considered by, or on behalf of, taxpayers wishing to make the most of exemptions or reliefs provided by the legislation.

This is only a brief summary of the basic planning issues to be considered when dealing with capital gains. For a more detailed discussion of tax planning in general and in relation to some specific common transactions see *Tax Planning 2010/11* (Bloomsbury Professional).

Residence and domicile

10.8 In most cases it is the residence and domicile status of the taxpayer, rather than the location of the assets, that determines liability to CGT. Non-residents are generally not chargeable except in relation to gains on assets used in connection with a UK business.

Certain UK-resident individuals who retain a non-UK domicile can use the remittance basis to shelter from UK tax gains accruing outside the UK, and in this respect they have a distinct advantage over UK-domiciled taxpayers. However, the use of the remittance basis for any tax year from 2008/09 onwards means that the annual exemption is lost for that particular tax year (see **Chapter 5**).

The scope for avoiding CGT by attaining non-resident status for a relatively short period and making disposals during the period of absence from the UK was significantly reduced by the special rules for temporary non-residents (see **5.27**).

Exemptions

10.9 The next question to consider is whether a gain is going to be exempt as a result of a specific provision or because it falls within the annual CGT exemption. Exemptions for specific persons, assets or gains are listed at **1.9**. An outright exemption is clearly better than a deferral of CGT.

Annual exemption

10.10 The annual CGT exemption is discussed at **1.17**. It is currently worth £10,100 to an individual and, in effect, £20,200 for a couple. However, the Liberal Democrat policy announced before the election on 6 May 2010 was to decrease this exemption to around £2,000. The coalition government has not indicated that a major change will be made to the level of the exemption, but future policy is difficult to predict.

Planning regarding the use of the exemption became more complicated in 2010/11, as for that tax year and later years the taxpayer has the freedom to deduct the annual exemption in the way that produces the lowest possible tax charge (*TCGA 1992, s 4B*). This flexibility is necessary due to the different rates of CGT that may apply to gains realised before and after 23 June 2010 (see **1.23**). In spite of this change the annual exemption cannot be carried forward from one tax year to the next. Any part of it that is unused in the current year is lost for good.

The benefit of the annual exemption may be maximised by careful timing of the disposal of assets, but as ever it is important to remember that personal and commercial considerations will often be more important than saving tax. The taxpayer should also bear in mind that HMRC may wish to examine the timing of disposals stated to fall shortly before or after the end of a tax year, or the change in the rate of CGT on 23 June 2010 (see **2.8**). The practice of 'bed and breakfasting' shares was made ineffective by a change in the identification rules, but variations on the theme remain possible (see **10.20**).

A member of a married couple or civil partnership who has already used their annual exemption might consider transferring an asset to the other spouse or partner, leaving the transferee free to sell the asset and utilise their own annual exemption. Care is needed to safeguard against a possible HMRC challenge here. They may seek to establish that the transferor has made a transfer of sale proceeds rather than the asset itself.

A deferral relief claim, made on the basis that a gain has been reinvested in enterprise investment scheme shares (see **Chapter 16**) operates by reducing the allowable expenditure on the shares. The claim may be limited in order to set the annual exemption against a part of the gain that would otherwise be deferred and subject to a potential CGT charge in the future.

The structure of hold-over relief for gifts, roll-over relief for replacement of business assets and incorporation relief (see **Chapters 13, 14** and **15**) is such that some gains may be left in charge to be covered by the annual exemption. These reliefs may also be combined in some cases with entrepreneurs' relief (see **Chapter 11**). However, the conditions required for entrepreneurs' relief to apply are in most circumstances more restrictive than other CGT reliefs.

Exemption on death

10.11 The general CGT exemption that applies to deemed disposals on a taxpayer's death should not be overlooked in any tax planning exercise. Assets that the taxpayer was competent to dispose of are deemed to be acquired by the personal representatives or legatees at their market value (see **Chapter 7**). The absence of a CGT charge, on what may well be significant capital appreciation in many cases, means it may be worthwhile retaining an asset until death rather than, for example, making a lifetime gift.

Hold-over reliefs

10.12 Hold-over relief for gifts effectively transfers the potential CGT liability to the transferee (see **Chapter 13**). It is worth noting that this liability is based on the market value of the asset gifted at the time of the transfer – regardless of any later reduction in value.

As the time period for making a hold-over claim is now four years from the end of tax year of disposal, taxpayers have an opportunity to review transactions undertaken in the years since 6 April 2006 to see if a hold-over claim is still worthwhile, or should be made before 6 April 2011. If an asset previously gifted has been sold since 6 April 2008 with CGT paid at 18%, there may be an overall tax saving if the gain could be held-over completely on the gift, rather than being subject to CGT at 40% after deduction of taper relief. However, the climate of changing CGT rates introduced from 22 June 2010, means that caution must be exercised with hold-over claims for gains made since that date. The CGT rate applicable for the gain will not be certain until the taxpayer's net taxable income for the year of disposal can be estimated with some accuracy.

There is no substitute for calculating the net assessable gain with and without the hold-over relief as may apply in the earlier tax year as opposed to the later year in which the gain falls back into charge to CGT.

The inheritance tax position may point towards lifetime giving, but in many cases the potential IHT bill can be substantially reduced or eliminated by business property relief or agricultural property relief. For further discussion of those reliefs refer to *Inheritance Tax 2010/11 (Bloomsbury Professional).*

The computation

10.13 In the absence of any exemption it is useful to estimate a potential CGT liability in order to establish whether any claim or other action to reduce or defer the liability is appropriate or desirable. The reduction in the CGT rate to 18% for all non-corporate taxpayers from 6 April 2008 to 22 June 2010 means that for gains made in this period the taxpayer may regard the CGT liability as acceptable. The increase in the rate of CGT to 28% for trustees, personal representatives, and those paying higher rate tax, from 23 June 2010 may stimulate further tax planning both before and after the gain is realised.

The disposal of businesses and business assets often generate very large gains, which may be subject to CGT at 10% if entrepreneurs' relief can be claimed in respect of the disposal (see **Chapter 11**).

It is important to check for any reduction in allowable expenditure that may be required as a result of a claim to roll-over or hold-over relief, increasing the chargeable gain on the disposal being considered.

From 6 April 2008, all assets held by non-corporate taxpayers on 31 March 1982 need to have the value at 31 March 1982 substituted for the actual cost of an asset (see **3.59**). The benefits of obtaining a professional valuation and ensuring that all items of allowable enhancement expenditure are identified can be substantial. The value at that date will determine the amount of the gain before any other CGT reliefs.

Where the disposal has already taken place and a valuation is required, it may well be useful to take advantage of HMRC's post-valuation service using form CG34 (see **1.35**) before the end of the tax year to allow time for consideration of any other possible action as part of a pre-year end tax planning review.

Entrepreneurs' relief

10.14 As indicated in **Chapter 11**, the conditions for entrepreneurs' relief to apply are complex as different conditions attach to both the owner of the asset and the use to which it was put before disposal. In the case of shares there may be uncertainty surrounding the company's status as a trading company, if it has significant non-trading activities. It is important to monitor the company's activities and examine the possible impact of non-trading activities such as, the letting of surplus property.

Shares must be held in the individual's own personal company, the definition of which depends on the individual holding at least 5% of ordinary shares and voting rights in their own name, not jointly with another person or trust. Any adjustment in the number of ordinary shares issued by the company should be monitored closely to ensure the 5% holding is not diluted. Shareholders who hold less than 5% of the ordinary shares, but possibly hold some other form of investment such as preference shares or debentures, may wish to rearrange their holdings to achieve entrepreneurs' relief.

It should be noted that shareholders also need to be an officer-holder (director or company secretary), or an employee of their personal company, or a company in the same group, for at least a 12-month period ending with the date of disposal of shares in the personal company. Directors who resign their post, or employees who leave before selling their shares may miss out on entrepreneurs' relief due to the timing of their departure from the company. Non-working shareholders could be appointed as non-executive directors to achieve the office-holder status required.

The interaction of entrepreneurs' relief and the deferral of gains using EIS, VCT or qualifying corporate bonds, can produce some unexpected results (see **11.39–11.44**).

Losses

10.15 Allowable losses must be set against chargeable gains arising in the same tax year. There is no facility to restrict the set off of losses against such gains (see **1.20**). However, in 2010/11 and in subsequent years where the taxpayer has gains that are chargeable to CGT at more than one rate, the taxpayer can choose which gains their losses are set against, such that the CGT liability for the year is reduced to the lowest possible charge (*TCGA 1992, s 4B*) (see **1.23**).

A taxpayer who is contemplating a disposal on which a loss will accrue might consider deferring the disposal until after 5 April if the gains would be covered in any event by the annual exemption. The delay would avoid wasting the exemption, and having the loss accruing in the following tax year might have the effect of reducing a potential CGT liability on other gains. Relief for allowable losses carried forward is more flexible. It may be restricted in order to preserve the benefit of the annual exemption.

Spouses or civil partners may consider a transfer of assets under the no gain, no loss rule (see **3.62**) where one spouse or partner has an unrealised loss that he or she is unlikely to use. The transferee may be able to realise the loss on a later disposal to an unconnected third party and set it against chargeable gains in excess of the annual exemption. Care is needed to safeguard against a possible HMRC challenge under *TCGA 1992, s 16A* as discussed in **10.3**.

Monitoring unrealised gains and losses, and planning to make the best use of the annual exemption, are key features of basic CGT planning. It is also important to identify any allowable losses that might be generated by means of, for example:

- realising a loss on quoted shares;
- making a negligible value claim (see **2.10**); or
- claiming relief on a loan to a trader, where the loan has become irrecoverable (see **17.11**).

The possibility of setting any unused trading losses against capital gains (see **3.52**) might also be considered, although care is needed in assessing the interaction of this relief with the annual exemption. A capital loss arising on shares subscribed for in an unlisted trading company may be relieved against income tax where certain conditions are met (see **17.16**).

Spouses and civil partners

10.16 Each member of a married couple or registered civil partnership is taxed independently of the other and is required to make a separate return of his or her own chargeable gains. There is no joint assessment and losses borne by one spouse cannot be set against gains accruing to the other. However, chargeable assets transferred from one spouse or civil partner, to the other are treated as taking place on a no gain, no loss basis (see **3.62**).

Main residence relief

10.17 The CGT exemption for an individual's only or main residence can be very valuable. The relief is extended to cover certain periods of absence and periods during which a house is let. It is examined in detail in **Chapter 12**.

Connected persons

10.18 The possible impact of the market value rule outlined in **3.6** should be considered where, for example, there are transactions within a family and the no gain, no loss rule mentioned in **10.16** does not apply.

Losses accruing on a disposal to a connected person cannot be set against gains other than those accruing on a disposal to the same connected person (see **3.21**). On the other hand, the gift of a chargeable asset showing a gain may be eligible for hold-over relief (see **Chapter 13**) so in some cases care in choosing which asset to give away can be worthwhile. Other provisions that may be relevant to transactions between connected persons include those applying to:

- assets disposed of in a series of transactions (see **3.12**);
- the disposal of chattels forming part of a 'set of articles' in order to secure the chattels exemption (**4.25**); and
- the value shifting provisions (*TCGA 1992, s 29*).

Ownership of assets

10.19 There may be some flexibility as to who should be the beneficial owner of an asset, for example, where a family company is involved. Factors that might be considered, preferably before an asset is acquired, include:

- whether the value of the asset is likely to increase significantly in the future;
- the effect of any deferral relief on the new owner's allowable expenditure for CGT purposes;
- the potential 'double charge' to tax on gains accruing on a disposal of assets owned by a company, and then realised by the shareholder in the form of increased gains on sale of the shares or on a liquidation;
- the availability of main residence relief (this is not available to companies);
- whether the conditions for entrepreneurs' relief are going to be met;
- the potential tax and other benefits of having business property owned by a pension scheme; and

- the merits of any trust arrangements (bearing in mind that the inheritance tax advantages previously available to accumulation and maintenance trusts and interest in possession trusts have been reduced substantially following *FA 2006*).

Bed and breakfast transactions

10.20 'Bed and breakfasting' is the practice of selling shares and repurchasing them the following day. This used to be a common year-end tax planning technique, undertaken for many years by taxpayers wishing to:

- utilise their annual CGT exemption;
- realise gains that could be covered by unused capital losses; or
- realise losses and set them against gains that would otherwise give rise to a tax liability.

The cost of the new acquisition would represent the allowable expenditure on its future disposal. The exercise would, therefore, achieve an uplift in the CGT base cost of the investment.

However, the effect of the 30-day rule introduced in April 1998 (see **4.3**) was to negate the effect of such transactions. The disposal on day 1 would now be matched with the acquisition on day 2, leaving a small loss in most cases where there was little movement in the share price.

'Bed and spousing' is the rather undignified term for a technique that is sometimes suggested as an alternative to a bed and breakfast arrangement. One spouse or civil partner sells the shares and the other spouse or partner buys a similar holding shortly afterwards. This technique can now be attacked under *TCGA 1992, s 16A* where the sale of the original shares has generated a loss (see **10.3**). Alternatively, the taxpayer might:

- identify shares in the same industry sector that would make a suitable replacement for the initial investment; or
- sell the shares in one capacity and buy the new holding in another capacity – shares bought within an individual savings account are free of CGT in the hands of the investor (see **1.9**).

Chapter 11

Entrepreneurs' relief

INTRODUCTION

11.1 Entrepreneurs' relief (ER) was introduced by *FA 2008, Sch 3* and it has effect for qualifying disposals made on and after 6 April 2008. The relief can be claimed in respect of gains made by individuals, by trustees of interest in possession trusts where there is a qualifying beneficiary (see **8.34**), but not for gains made by companies, or by personal representatives.

The relief was introduced in response to the abolition of business asset taper relief from 6 April 2008, which reduced the effective rate of CGT from 40% to 10% on the disposal of qualifying business assets held for two years or more (see **17.22–17.41**). Entrepreneurs' relief also reduces the effective rate of CGT to 10% on gains arising from qualifying disposals of businesses and certain business assets. However, the mechanism that achieves the 10% rate changed with effect for disposals made on and after 23 June 2010 (see **11.4**).

The range of assets that qualify as business assets under entrepreneurs' relief is much more restrictive than those which qualified as business assets for taper relief (see **11.9, 11.21**). The other restriction with entrepreneurs' relief is that the maximum amount of gains that can be included in claims for the relief made by a particular taxpayer is capped for that taxpayer's lifetime. This lifetime cap was set at £1 million for gains made before 6 April 2010, it was increased to £2 million for gains accruing from 6 April 2010 to 22 June 2010, and was increased once more to £5 million for gains accruing on and after 23 June 2010 (*TCGA 1992, s 169N(3)*).

It is the taxpayer's responsibility to keep a record of how much relief has been claimed, but HMRC should also keep a record on the taxpayer's self-assessment permanent notes (CG63960).

Entrepreneurs' relief must be claimed (see **11.8**); it does not apply automatically like taper relief where the conditions are met. The taxpayer can choose not to claim the relief to preserve the lifetime cap so it can be used for another disposal, or to claim an alternative CGT relief.

Legislation and guidance

11.2 The legislation that governs entrepreneurs' relief is crammed into *TCGA 1992, ss 169H–169S* in such a fashion to make its comprehension even more difficult than it has to be. There are transitional reliefs for gains that arose before 6 April 2008, which have been deferred using VCTs or EIS (*FA 2008, Sch 3, para 7*), (see **11.44**). Also where gains from the disposal of shares or securities have rolled into qualifying corporate bonds on a company reorganisation before 6 April 2008, those gains can be subject to entrepreneurs' relief if they crystallise on or after 6 April 2008 (*FA 2008, Sch 3, para 6*) (see **11.40**).

The HMRC guidance on the operation of entrepreneurs' relief is found in its capital gains manual at paras CG63950–CG64170. This chapter refers to that guidance where necessary, but be aware that the HMRC guidance does not have legal effect and there may be other valid interpretations of the law. In particular, there are different views on the interaction of entrepreneurs' relief with other CGT reliefs (see **11.45**).

OPERATION OF THE RELIEF

What disposals qualify

11.3 Entrepreneurs' relief is available on gains made by individuals arising from qualifying business disposals, which consist of:

(a) all or part of a sole trader business (see **11.20**);

(b) all or part of an interest in a partnership, including an interest in an LLP (see **11.23**);

(c) shares or securities held in the shareholder's personal company (see **11.9**);

(d) certain post-cessation disposals of former business assets (see **11.27**); and

(e) associated disposals (see **11.33**) which are disposals of assets owned by the individual but used in the business of either:

- a partnership of which he was a member; or
- his personal company.

In addition, disposals of certain business assets by trustees can qualify for entrepreneurs' relief, but only where there is a qualifying beneficiary who also holds enough shares in their own right for the company to qualify as his personal company, or operates or has operated the business that used the assets (see **8.34**).

A disposal for entrepreneurs' relief can be:

- a sale;
- a gift or transfer at undervalue;
- where a capital distribution is received in respect of shares held in a company, for example on the liquidation of that company; or
- a capital sum derived from an asset (see **2.12**).

How the relief is calculated

11.4 For gains made up to and including 22 June 2010, entrepreneurs' relief is given by reducing the amount of the capital gain by 4/9ths leaving the residue of 5/9ths to be charged to CGT at 18%, before deduction of unrelated losses and the annual exemption. As the rate of CGT increased to 28% for higher rate taxpayers on 23 June 2010 (see **1.23**), this fractional reduction would no longer produce a 10% rate for taxpayers subject to the higher rate. Gains that accrue on and after 23 June 2010 and which are subject to entrepreneurs' relief, are taxed at 10% irrespective of the level of the taxpayers' other income for the year, see **Example 11.1.**

However, when calculating the taxpayer's level of income and gains to determine the rate of CGT that applies to any post-22 June 2010 gains (18% or 28%), those post-22 June gains that are subject to entrepreneurs' relief are taken into account, see **Example 11.2.**

The taxpayer can choose which gains should absorb the annual exemption or losses in 2010/11 to achieve the lowest possible charge to CGT (*TCGA 1992, s 4B*).

Example 11.1

Milo gave 25% of the shares in his company M Ltd to his son on 10 May 2010, and sold the remaining shares in M Ltd on 12 July 2010 for £3 million. Milo formed M Ltd in 1980 and was a director until the sale in July 2010. The 31 March 1982 value of M Ltd was £400,000. The market value of the gift in May 2010 is judged to be £1 million. Milo claims entrepreneurs' relief on both disposals, but has set his annual exemption against an unrelated gain in 2010/11. His CGT liability on the gains made on the disposal of M Ltd is calculated as follows:

2010/11		May 2010	July 2010
Lifetime cap:		£2 million	£5 million
		£	£
Market value/proceeds		1,000,000	3,000,000
31 March 1982 value		(100,000)	(300,000)
Gain		900,000	2,700,000
Entrepreneurs' relief reduction	4/9 × £900,000	(400,000)	–
Taxable gain:		500,000	2,700,000
Tax due at 18%/10%		90,000	270,000

The effective or actual rate of CGT on both gains is 10%.

Operation of the lifetime cap

11.5 The lifetime cap for entrepreneurs' relief was increased twice in 2010/11: on 6 April 2010 from £1 million to £2 million, then on 23 June 2010 to £5 million. All gains that the taxpayer includes in a claim for entrepreneurs' relief are deducted from the available lifetime cap. Any amount of gain that is not covered by the lifetime cap that existed at the time the gain arose, is taxed at the relevant rate of CGT that applies in that period. The taxpayer can only take advantage of the increased lifetime cap where gains are made on or after the dates of increase in the cap limit, see **Example 11.2.**

Example 11.2

Fred is the director and sole shareholder of F Ltd, which is a trading company. He sells his shares in F Ltd on 5 May 2010 making a gain of £2.5 million. This gain qualifies for entrepreneurs' relief because F Ltd was Fred's personal company and the employment condition applied (see **11.11**). Fred sells the buildings that were occupied by F Ltd on 1 July 2010 making a gain of £4 million. This disposal is associated with Fred's disposal of the F Ltd shares and his withdrawal from that business, so that gain also qualifies for entrepreneurs' relief (see **11.33**). In 2010/11 Fred has net taxable income of £20,400, and he has not previously used any of his life-time cap. Fred's CGT liability for 2010/11 is calculated as follows:

	May 2010 gain	*CGT payable*	*July 2010 gain*	*CGT payable*
	£	£	£	£
Taxable income	N/A		20,400	
Basic rate threshold	N/A		37,400	
Available basic rate band			17,000	
Gross gains	2.5 million		4 million	
ER cap available	2 million		3 million	
Gain not subject to ER	500,000		1,000,000	
Less annual exemption	–		10,100	
Taxable at 28%			989,900	277,172
Taxable at 18%	500,000	90,000		
Gains subject to ER	2,000,000		3,000,000	
ER reduction 4/9th	888,888		–	
Gain taxed at 18%	1,111,111	200,000	–	
Gain tax at 10%			3,000,000	300,000
Total CGT payable		290,000		577,127

Fred has chosen to set his annual exemption of £10,100 against his later gain as that gives him tax relief at 28%. Although Fred has £17,000 of basic rate band available in 2010/11, the full July gain is taken into account when considering his total income and gains for 2010/11, even though part of that gain is automatically subject to CGT at 10% as it qualifies for entrepreneurs' relief. Thus no part of the July gain is actually taxed at 18%. Fred's total CGT liability for 2010/11 is £867,127 (£290,000 + £577,127) which is payable by 31 January 2012.

Aggregation of gains and losses

11.6 When a business is sold some assets may crystallise gains and other disposals may create losses. Before calculating entrepreneurs' relief the gains and losses arising on the same business disposal must be aggregated (*TCGA 1992, s 169N(1)*). Note that separate disposals of shares and securities from one company should never be aggregated before the relief is applied (see **11.9**)

There is no requirement for the disposal of the business to be made in one contract to one purchaser to qualify for the relief. In practice the business assets may be sold to a number of different purchasers over a period of time. The disposal of a single business could conceivably be spread over two tax years.

However, a distinction must be drawn between assets that are disposed of as part of the business, and assets that are disposed of after cessation of the business (see **11.27**). The taxpayer may claim entrepreneurs' relief on several qualifying disposals, as long as the lifetime cap is not breached. The difficulty in practice will be distinguishing between the disposal of parts of the business which each separately qualify for entrepreneurs' relief, and the disposal of qualifying assets after the business has ceased trading. The gains and losses realised by disposing of separate parts of the business should not be aggregated before the relief is applied, but where assets comprising of a single business disposal accrue both gains and losses those should be aggregated before the relief is applied. This is illustrated in **Example 11.3**.

Example 11.3

Nelson owned a grocery business for which he had two outlets: a freehold shop and a leasehold shop. He retired in April 2010 and sold the freehold premises and business on 1 April 2010 and the leasehold shop and business on 17 May 2010, each as a going concern. He made the following gains and losses on the property and goodwill in each case. After claiming entrepreneurs' relief Nelson's assessable gains are calculated as follows:

2009/10	£	£
Freehold shop – sold 1 April 2010		
Freehold		520,000
Goodwill		200,000
Net gain		720,000
Entrepreneurs' relief 4/9 × 720,000		(320,000)
Taxable gain:		400,000

2010/11	£	£
Leasehold shop – sold 17 May 2010		
Leasehold		(40,000)
Goodwill		400,000
Net gain		360,000
Lifetime cap for entrepreneurs' relief	2,000,000	
Gains used in an ER claim previously	(720,000)	
Available to use against 2010/11 gain	1,280,000	
Entrepreneurs' relief 4/9 × 360,000		(160,000)
Taxable gain:		200,000

The two grocery shops are parts of Nelson's whole business which make a significant difference to the whole business when disposed of, so they are qualifying disposals in their own right (see **11.22**). The gains from the two shops are thus not aggregated before applying the relief. Nelson's claim for entrepreneurs' relief in 2010/11 is not restricted as his total qualifying gains do not exceed the lifetime cap of £2 million that applies in that period.

Interaction with losses

11.7 Once the losses arising on the disposal of the assets of a single business have been aggregated with gains from that business (see **11.6**), any other allowable capital losses brought forward or arising in the same tax year may be set off against the gains in the year as the taxpayer chooses (*TCGA 1992, s 4B*).

If entrepreneurs' relief is claimed for a pre-23 June 2010 gain, any loss is deducted after the reduction of 4/9ths is applied to the gain, and thus achieves relief at 18%. For gains made on and after 23 June 2010 there is no reduction to achieve entrepreneurs' relief as the full gain is taxable at 10% where the relief applies. Any loss is deducted from the full gain and receives relief at only 10%. To achieve the lowest possible charge to CGT the taxpayer should offset the loss against the gains which bear the highest rate of CGT.

Example 11.4

Oliver sold 25% of the shares in his personal company in September 2010 making a gain of £200,000. This gain qualifies for entrepreneurs' relief. Oliver also gave a property to his grand-daughter in December 2010, which realised a gain of £270,000. This gain did not qualify for entrepreneurs' relief. Oliver has a capital loss brought forward of £100,000 and other taxable income after allowances of £150,000 in 2010/11. He needs to decide how to set off the loss and his annual exemption for 2010/11.

2010/11	*Gain subject to ER*	*Gain not subject to ER.*
	£	£
Gain on sale/gift	200,000	270,000
Loss brought forward		(100,000)
Annual exemption		(10,100)
Taxable gain	200,000	159,900
Taxable at 10%/28%	20,000	44,772

The losses have been relieved at the higher rate of CGT of 28%.

CLAIMING THE RELIEF

11.8 Entrepreneurs' relief must be claimed by the individual who makes the gain, although in the case of gains made by trustees the claim must be signed by both the trustee and the qualifying beneficiary (*TCGA 1992, s 169M*) (see **8.34**). The claim will normally be attached to the tax return for the tax year in which the gain arose, and there is a template for the claim in HMRC helpsheet HS275 to assist with this. Where no tax return is issued, or the return has already been submitted, the claim may be made by letter to HMRC.

The claim must be made by the first anniversary of 31 January following the tax year in which the gain arose. The claim may be amended or withdrawn within the same period. If an assessment is made under *TMA 1970, s 36* to make good a loss of tax, the time limit for the claim may be extended (CG63970).

SHAREHOLDERS

11.9 In order for a shareholder to claim entrepreneurs' relief on the disposal of shares or securities (referred to as shares from here on) all of the following conditions must be met:

(a) the company in which those shares are held must be the individual's personal company (see **11.10**)

(b) the shareholder must be an employee or officer of the company, or of a company in the same trading group (see **11.11**); and

(c) the company must be a trading company or a holding company of a trading group (see **11.12**).

All of these three conditions must be met for the whole of a 12-month period that ends either with the disposal of the shares, or the cessation of the trade, or the company leaving the trading group.

The relief may also be claimed if the business has ceased trading when the shares are disposed of, if the disposal date falls up to three years after the date the company ceased to be a trading company or to be a member of a trading group (see **11.18**). The relief can thus apply where the company has been liquidated or wound up, either formally, or using the ESC C16 procedure (see **11.32**).

Personal company

11.10 A company is the personal company of the individual at any time when both (a), and (b) below apply (*TCGA 1992, s 169S(3)*):

(a) the individual holds at least 5% of the ordinary shares of the company;

(b) the individual controls at least 5% of the voting rights of the company which are associated with those ordinary shares.

The shareholding must meet the 5% threshold without including shares held by associates or shares held in another capacity, for instance as a trustee of a settlement. Where shares are held in the joint names of a married couple or civil partners, each spouse is deemed to have a 50% beneficial interest in the whole shareholding.

Example 11.5

Terry and June are married and jointly own 9.4% of the ordinary shares of Sweet Home Ltd. They are each treated as owning 4.7% of Sweet Home Ltd, so the company will not qualify as their personal company. If they each acquire a further 0.3% of the ordinary shares in their sole names Sweet Home Ltd will qualify as their personal company, but they both need to meet the employment requirement for their disposals of shares in Sweet Home Ltd to qualify for entrepreneurs' relief (see **11.11**).

The shares disposed of by the individual do not have to be ordinary shares, for the gain to qualify for entrepreneurs' relief. As long as ordinary shares in the company are held at or above the minimum threshold level of 5%, any other disposals of shares or securities in the company can qualify for the relief. The shareholder may make several disposals of shares in the same company and claim entrepreneurs' relief on all gains made as long as the employment requirement is met for the required one-year period in respect of each disposal.

Employment requirement

11.11 The shareholder must be either an officer or employee of the company in which he disposed of shares (*TCGA 1992, s 169I(6)(b)*). However, if the company was a member of a trading group (see **11.18**), the employment requirement is satisfied where the shareholder was employed by another member company of that trading group.

Example 11.6

Pauline has worked for Laundrette Ltd for 20 years and owns 7% of the ordinary shares and voting rights. She also owns 5% of the ordinary shares in Handwash Ltd, but she does not work for Handwash Ltd. The remaining shares in Laundrette and Handwash are held by the holding company East Ltd. When Laundrette and Handwash are sold, Pauline will qualify for entrepreneurs' relief in respect of her shareholdings in both companies, as she has satisfied the employment requirement by working for either the actual trading company or another trading company in the same trading group.

Whether an individual was an officer of the company (director or company secretary), should easily be confirmed by records held at Companies House. The position of company secretary became optional for private companies from 6 April 2008. Small family companies may consider retaining this post so a member of the family can hold the office of company secretary and qualify for entrepreneurs' relief. Non-executive directors count as officers, but shadow directors do not (*ITEPA 2003, s 5(3)*).

An employee is defined in *ITEPA 2003, s 4*, but for the purposes of entrepreneurs' relief the employment does not need to be full time, or cover any minimum hours. There is also no requirement for the shareholder/employee to be paid, although without a contract of employment it may be difficult to show that an individual who received no pay was actually employed. The requirements of the national minimum wage will normally require the company to make some payment to all of its employees.

Trading company

11.12 The definitions of trading company, trading group and holding company are now brought together in *TCGA 1992, s 165A*. These are the same definitions that applied for taper relief. Unfortunately, there is no decided tax case that examined the question of whether a company is a trading company for taper relief purposes, but it may be possible to obtain a ruling from HMRC on this point (see **11.19**).

Trading company means a company carrying on 'trading activities' whose activities do not include to a substantial extent (see **11.16**), activities other than trading activities.

Trading activities

11.13 HMRC interpret 'activities' as meaning 'what a company does'. Activities would include 'engaging in trading operations, making and holding investments, planning, holding meetings and so forth'.

Trading activities are those carried on by the company in the course of, or for the purposes of, a trade that it is carrying on or is preparing to carry on. HMRC regard such activities as including certain activities that a company has to carry out before it can start trading, such as developing a business plan, acquiring premises, hiring staff, ordering materials and incurring pre-trading expenditure (CG64065).

Trading activities also include activities undertaken with a view to the company acquiring or starting to carry on a trade, or with a view to its acquiring a 'significant interest' (see **11.14**) in the share capital of another company that is a trading company or the holding company (see **11.17**) of a trading group (so long as, where the acquiring company is a member of a group of companies, it is not a member of the target company's group). These activities qualify as trading activities only if the acquisition is made, or (as the case may be) the company starts to carry on the trade, as soon as is reasonably practicable. HMRC accept that a company that has disposed of its trade and invested the proceeds and is 'actively seeking' to acquire a new trade or trading subsidiary might still be a trading company if it does not have substantial non-trading activities. What is 'reasonably practicable in the circumstances' will depend on the particular facts of the case (CG64075).

Where a company holds a significant cash balance generated from trading activities, it may not be clear whether the company has become an investment company, due to the ratio of investment activities to trading activities. The HMRC guidance is that short-term lodgement of surplus funds in a deposit account could count as a trading activity rather than an investment activity. Also funds retained to distribute as dividends would not be an investment activity. However, the long-term retention of surplus earnings would be considered an investment activity unless those funds had been preserved for a particular trading purpose (CG64060).

See **11.16** regarding the letting of surplus business property.

Significant interest

11.14 An acquisition by a company (A) of a 'significant interest' in the share capital of another company (B) is defined as an acquisition of ordinary share capital in company B that would make company B a 51% subsidiary of company A, or would give company A a 'qualifying shareholding in a joint venture company' without making the two companies members of the same group of companies (*TCGA 1992, s 165A(6)*). Ordinary share capital takes the meaning given by *ITA 2007, s 989*. See **11.17** for the definition of a subsidiary.

Trade

11.15 Trade means anything which:

- is a trade profession or vocation within the meaning of the *Income Tax Acts*; and
- is conducted on a commercial basis with a view to the realisation of profits (*ITA 2007, s 989*).

For entrepreneurs' relief a trade also includes the commercial letting of furnished holiday accommodation (*TCGA 1992, s 241(3A)*). For the purposes of this relief the persons who carry on the furnished holiday lettings are treated as sole traders (see **11.20**). The conditions that must be met for commercial letting of furnished holiday accommodation are discussed in detail in chapter 7 of *Income Tax 2010/11* (Bloomsbury Professional).

Substantial extent

11.16 Where a company carries on activities other than trading activities, the existence of those non-trading activities will not disturb the trading status of the company if they are not carried on to a substantial extent. HMRC regard 'substantial extent' in this context as meaning more than 20% (CG64090). There is no hard and fast rule about what must be considered in ascertaining a company's trading status, but HMRC indicate the following may be indicators:

- income from non-trading activities;

- the company's asset base;
- expenses incurred, or time spent, by officers and employees of the company in undertaking its activities; and
- the company's history.

These measures should not be regarded as individual tests which all need to be passed; they are just factors which may point one way or the other. The HMRC officer is instructed to weigh up the relevance of each measure in the context of the individual case and judge the matter 'in the round' as demonstrated by the approach of the Special Commissioner in *Farmer (Farmer's Executors) v IRC* [1999] STC (SCD) 321.

Where a company lets property surplus to its current requirements HMRC do not consider that the following necessarily consist of non-trading activities (CG64085):

- letting part of the trading premises;
- letting properties that are no longer required for the purpose of the trade, where the company's or group's objective is to sell them;
- subletting property where it would be impractical or uneconomic in terms of the trade to assign or surrender the lease;
- the acquisition of property (whether vacant or already let) where it can be shown that the intention is that it will be brought into use for trading activities.

Holding company

11.17 A holding company is a company that has one or more 51% subsidiaries (*TCGA 1992, s 165A(2)*).

A 51% subsidiary takes its meaning from *CTA 2010, s 1154*, so that for entrepreneurs' relief purposes a company (B) is a 51% subsidiary of another company (A) if company A owns directly or indirectly more than 50% of company B's ordinary share capital. Thus a company where 50.1% of its ordinary shares were held by another company would count as a 51% subsidiary.

Trading group

11.18 A group of companies means a company that has one or more 51% subsidiaries. It is important to determine that the companies where the shareholder is employed are members of the same group based on the 51% subsidiary definition, and are not just associated companies.

When looking at whether the group is trading all the activities of the members of the group are taken together as one business (*TCGA 1992, s 165A (11)*). This allows the group to contain one or more companies that are not trading and still qualify as a trading group. The intra-group transactions are ignored.

However, where shares in a subsidiary company are disposed of, that particular company must be a trading company in order to qualify for entrepreneurs' relief. The only circumstances in which shares in a non-trading company will qualify for the relief is if the company is a holding company of a trading group or the shares are disposed of within three years after the company has ceased to be a trading company and left the trading group (see **11.32**).

HMRC ruling

11.19 Where a taxpayer has disposed of, or plans to dispose of shares, and is unsure as to whether the company would qualify as a trading company during the relevant period, he should in the first instance apply to the company for confirmation. HMRC suggest that where the company cannot confirm its trading status the taxpayer should record this fact on the additional information area of their tax return, and take a view themselves on the trading status in order to complete their claim for relief (CG64100).

This seems a particularly unsatisfactory solution for the taxpayer as it provides him with no certainty that his claim for entrepreneurs' relief is valid, and hence whether he has self-assessed the right amount of CGT. An alternative approach is for the individual to apply to HMRC for a post-transaction ruling under the procedures set out in HMRC code of practice COP10 (see www.hmrc.gov.uk/pdfs/cop10.htm#giving_'post-transaction_rulings'). However, HMRC will only give a ruling where the issue involves an interpretation of the tax law or its application to a particular circumstance. The HMRC guidance is not clear as to whether a question of trading status falls within these criteria. The operation of the COP10 procedure for non-business taxpayers is currently under review.

A company that wants to clarify its trading status so that it can inform non-corporate shareholders may ask HMRC for an opinion in accordance with the non-statutory clearance service, as described in the HMRC manual: Non-Statutory Business Clearance Guidance. However, unless the issue has a real commercial impact on the company concerned, HMRC may decline to give a clearance. HMRC will not give a clearance where the transaction falls within the area of personal taxation of individuals (NBCG2200).

SOLE TRADERS

11.20 A sole trader may qualify for entrepreneurs' relief on gains arising in three specific circumstances:

- on the disposal of his whole business;
- on the disposal of part of his business;
- on the disposal of qualifying business assets up to three years after the cessation of his business (see **11.28**).

Disposal of a business

11.21 The disposal of a business will qualify for entrepreneurs' relief if the following conditions are met at the date of disposal:

(a) the business has been owned by the individual who is making the claim for relief for at least 12 months; and

(b) the disposal includes at least one relevant business asset (see **11.29**).

The disposal of the business does not need to be made as a going concern, and all of the assets do not have to be sold to the same purchaser. Where several purchasers are involved careful timing of the disposals of the main assets will be required. If some minor assets are sold well before the main part of the business and the trade continues, the gains made on those minor assets may not qualify for entrepreneurs' relief, if those minor assets do not comprise 'part of a business' (see **11.22**) and they are not in use at the time the business ceases (see **11.27**).

However, HMRC are prepared to accept that the disposal of a business may be spread over several weeks, in which case the delay between disposals should not prevent the relief from applying to all the assets, see **Example 11.7**

Example 11.7

Ross ran a retail shop for many years from his freehold property, but wished to retire. He found a company willing to buy the freehold property, but that company did not want to take on the retail business. Ross exchanged contracts to sell the property on 16 June 2010, but did not complete the contract until 31 July 2010 when he sold the retail business including the goodwill to a different purchaser. Ross ceased trading on 31 July 2010.

The disposal of the retail business on 31 July 2010 will qualify for entrepreneurs' relief as Ross has disposed of the whole of his business. Although the disposal date of the property for CGT purposes is 16 June 2010 (see **2.8**), that disposal is treated as being part of the disposal of the whole business on 31 July 2010, so will also qualify for entrepreneurs' relief.

Disposal of part of a business

11.22 It is often difficult to distinguish between the disposal of a collection of business assets and the disposal of 'part of a business'. The disposal of one or more business assets will not attract the relief if those assets were either not in use when business ceased, or the business has not ceased (see **11.28** for post-cessation disposals), whilst the disposal of 'part of a business' will attract entrepreneurs' relief. There is no clear definition of 'part of a business', and as this term has been imported from the retirement relief provisions the tax cases on this issue heard for that relief are now considered to be relevant to entrepreneurs' relief (see CG64035).

In particular, the case of *McGregor (HMIT) v Adcock* (1977) 51 TC 692 established the 'interference test', where the HMRC officer would look at the impact of the sale on the business and establish what had changed. If the sale made a significant difference to the way the business operated then there had been a sale of part of the business, if not then the sale was probably one of assets out of the business, which would not qualify for relief.

There were many cases of farmland disposals under retirement relief and an unofficial practice emerged of treating disposals of 50% or more of the farmland occupied by the farm as a disposal of part of the business, although the facts would have to be established in each case.

HMRC acknowledge that the existing case law established under retirement relief will not always provide certainty for the taxpayer, so difficult cases may have to be agreed by informal agreement between the taxpayer and the HMRC Capital Gains Technical team, or determined by the First-tier Tax Tribunal (CG64015).

PARTNERS

11.23 The taxation of gains made by partners and members of LLPs are dealt with in **Chapter 6**. Disposals by the partnership of the whole or part of the business attracts entrepreneurs' relief as if the whole partnership was one sole trader (see **11.20**). However, there are three special rules in *TCGA 1992, s 169I(8),* which are there to ensure that certain disposals made by an individual partner attract relief as if he had been a sole trader.

Special rules for partnerships

11.24 The three circumstances that attract relief for established or new partners are as follows:

(a) where an individual transfers assets to a partnership, on the occasion of him joining that partnership and the partnership takes over his business (*TCGA 1992, s 169I(8)(a)*);

(b) where a partner disposes of the whole of part of his interest in the assets of the partnership (*TCGA 1992, s 169I(8)(b)*);

(c) where any partner disposes of a business asset he is treated as if he had owned the whole of the partnership business (*TCGA 1992, s 169I(8)(c)*).

The situation in (a) would provide relief for the capital gains that arise when a new partner introduces an asset to the partnership as the whole or part of his capital contribution (see **6.16**). Prior to 21 January 2008 it was thought that a gain would not arise in this situation using the well-established practice in Statement of Practice D12 (SP D12). However, Revenue & Customs Brief 03/08 announced a new practice in this area, which has yet to be challenged in the courts (see **6.17**).

Where a sole trader merges his business with an established partnership the relief in (a) and (b) above, will ensure that any gains arising on the transfer of assets between those partners, either the new partner transferring his assets into the partnership, or the existing partners transferring an interest in the partnership assets (such as goodwill) to the new partner, will be covered by entrepreneurs' relief.

Example 11.8

Brian and Tony have been trading in partnership for some years sharing profits 60:40 (Brian: Tony). Charles joins the partnership and the profits are to be shared from that point on as 40:30:30 (Brian: Tony: Charles). Under SP D12 Brian has disposed of one-third of his interest in the partnership and Tony has disposed of one-quarter of his interest in the partnership to Charles. The gains arising to Brian and Tony may be reduced by entrepreneurs' relief.

The rule described in (c) above is required to ensure that every partner in the partnership qualifies for the relief where there is a disposal of all or part of the partnership business, but the following conditions must also apply:

(a) the partnership business has been carried on for at least a year at the date of disposal; and

(b) the disposal consists of one or more relevant assets (see **11.29**).

Example 11.9

Rachel and Martyn established a nursery business as a partnership on 1 October 2009. Helen joins the partnership on 1 May 2010, paying £30,000 for her share of the goodwill of the business. Entrepreneurs' relief is not available on the gains realised by Rachel and Martyn as the business has not been established for at least one year. If Rachel had run the nursery business as a sole trader for some years before Martyn joined as a partner on 1 October 2009, the gain realised by Rachel on 1 May 2010 would qualify for entrepreneurs' relief, but the gain made by Martyn on that date would not qualify.

Post-cessation disposals

11.25 Where a partnership business ceases and within three years after that cessation, the partnership disposes of some assets which were in use at the time the business ceased, entrepreneurs' relief should be available to the gains realised by all the partners. The rules follow those that apply for sole traders (see **11.27**).

TRUSTEES

11.26 This chapter discusses entrepreneurs' relief as it applies to disposals made by individuals disposing of assets as a sole trader, a partner or a shareholder. It does not deal with individuals' disposals of assets as a beneficiary of a trust, or as a trustee. These aspects of entrepreneurs' relief are discussed in **8.34**.

POST-CESSATION DISPOSALS

Business assets

11.27 Where the owners of an unincorporated business cease trading they may retain certain business assets to be disposed of at a later date. Entrepreneurs' relief can still apply to these later disposals if they occur within three years after the date the business ceased (*TCGA 1992, s 169I(4)*), and the other conditions listed in **11.28** apply. HMRC have no discretion to extend the three-year period, so it is vital to pin down the business cessation date. Any disposals outside of the three-year period will not qualify for the relief even if the asset can be clearly linked to the disposal of the main business. The date the business ceased is a question of fact, according to HMRC (CG64105), but there will be cases where the cessation date is not clear cut. Further guidance on this issue is given in the HMRC business income manual at BIM 70565–70585. The cessation of the business does not have to fall after the commencement of entrepreneurs' relief, as long as the disposal of the asset does.

Example 11.10

Stephen ran a hairdressing salon from his freehold property until 20 May 2007 when he stopped trading due to ill health. He managed to sub-let the property from 1 September 2007 to the date of disposal on 1 May 2010. Stephen's gain on the sale of the property should qualify for entrepreneurs' relief as it was used in Stephen's business at the date the trade ceased on 20 May 2007, which is less than three years before the date of disposal.

11.28 The other conditions that must apply for the gain on the disposal of the asset to qualify for entrepreneurs' relief are:

(a) the asset must have been a relevant business asset for the business;

(b) the asset must have been in use at the time the business ceased; and

(c) the owner of the asset must have owned the business for at least 12 months ending with the date the business ceased.

Relevant business asset

11.29 Relevant business assets are any assets including goodwill used for the purposes of the business carried on by the sole trader or partnership, but not 'excluded assets' which are:

- shares and securities; and
- other assets held as investments (*TCGA 1992, s 169L(4)*).

Shares and securities held by a sole trader or partnership will never be relevant business assets even if there is some business-related reason for holding the shares. For example, a farmer may hold shares in a milk marketing co-operative.

Used in the business

11.30 For the asset to qualify under (b) in **11.28** it does not have to be used for any particular length of time before the business ceased, it just needs to be in use at the date the business ceased (*TCGA 1992, s 169I(2)(b)*).

Assets that have a mixed business and non-business use can qualify as relevant business assets. There is no requirement for the asset to be used *wholly* for the purposes of the business at the date of cessation.

Use after the business ceased

11.31 There is no restriction on the use of the asset between the date the business ceased and the disposal of that asset. This period can be up to three years, so the owner is free to let the asset at a commercial rent for that three-year period and still claim entrepreneurs' relief on the disposal of the asset. The asset could even be used in a different business operated and owned by the asset owner, and then when it is sold relief is claimed in respect of the use of the asset in the ceased business. This contrasts with the restrictions on the use of assets sold as an associated disposal, where the gain that qualifies for the relief may be reduced (see **11.38**).

Shares

11.32 Shares or securities in a company may be disposed of after the company has ceased trading on the occasion of the liquidation or winding-up of the company. The shareholder is treated as if he had disposed of his interest in the shares when he receives a capital distribution (*TCGA 1992, s 122*). HMRC have indicated that the informal procedure used to wind up small companies under ESC C16 will also allow the distribution of capital to shareholders to qualify for entrepreneurs' relief, as long as the clearance is given for a capital distribution (CG64115). Such a disposal can qualify for entrepreneurs' relief under *TCGA 1992, s 169S(2)* if the conditions listed below apply:

(a) the company must have been the individual's personal company (see **11.10**);

(b) the shareholder must have been an employee or officer of the company, or of a company in the same group (see **11.11**); and

(c) the company must have been a trading company or a holding company of a trading group (see **11.12**).

All of these three conditions must apply for the whole of a 12-month period that ends with either the cessation of the trade of the company, or the date the company left the trading group and did not continue to trade outside of that group. This date must also fall not more than three years before the date the shares are treated as being of disposed of, which will normally be the date the shareholder receives the capital distribution.

ASSOCIATED DISPOSALS

11.33 This is a tricky concept to grasp. It is not well explained in the legislation, so it may catch people out. The concept of an associated disposal has been imported from the retirement relief legislation, so cases concerning the determination of an associated disposal under those provisions are considered to be relevant to entrepreneurs' relief.

An associated disposal of business assets can only occur in connection with:

- the disposal of shares or securities in a company (see **11.9**); or
- the disposal of a partnership interest (see **11.23**).

The relief cannot apply on the disposal of assets following the disposal of a sole-trader business, as such a disposal would fall into the more flexible post-cessation rules (see **11.27**).

Disposal of shares

11.34 If a shareholder who is also an employee or officer of his personal company disposes of shares or securities in that company, the gain arising will be eligible for entrepreneurs' relief if the other conditions apply (see **11.9**). Where that individual disposes of an asset which was used by the company, at around the same time as the share disposal (see **11.36**), the gain on that asset will qualify for the relief as an associated disposal, if both of the following conditions also apply:

(a) the asset is disposed of as part of the shareholder's withdrawal from participation in the business carried on by his personal company or the business carried on by the trading group (*TCGA 1992, s 169K(3), (5)*);

(b) the asset was used for the purpose of the business for at least one year to the date of disposal of the shares, or to the date of cessation of the company's business if earlier (*TCGA 1992, s 169K(4)*).

To summarise:

- the first disposal of shares must qualify for entrepreneurs' relief, or would qualify if a gain had been made on that disposal but a claim for entrepreneurs' relief does not have to be made for this gain; and
- the second disposal of the asset must meet conditions (a) and (b) above.

Withdrawal from participation in the business

11.35 This condition is imposed to prevent a shareholder from disposing of a single asset and claiming it was an associated disposal because he also disposed of a small number of shares at the same time. The two disposals must be clearly linked and in total comprise a withdrawal from participation in the business. This was established in *Clarke v Mayo* [1994] 66 TC 728.

However, this withdrawal need not be a complete divorce from the business, and there is no *de minimis* amount of shares which must be disposed of for the two disposals to constitute a withdrawal from the business. The HMRC guidance (CG63995) says it is not necessary for the individual actually to reduce the amount of work they do for the business for this condition to be met.

Example 11.11

Lewpyn owns the intellectual property used by his internet games company Level 6 Ltd, which is his personal company. Level 6 Ltd was sold on 6 August 2010, and on the same date he also sold the intellectual property used by the company. Lewpyn remains the technical director for the company under the terms of the sale. Lewpyn has withdrawn from the business of the company because he has disposed of all his shares and in connection with that disposal also sold his interest in the intellectual property used by the company. The disposal of the intellectual property therefore qualifies as an associated disposal.

Time limit

11.36 The legislation does not specify a time period during which the associated disposal must be made, but the HMRC guidance (CG63995), stipulates that both the disposal of the shares and the associated disposal of the asset must be caused by the same event and there should be no significant time interval between the disposals. It is also implied in the HMRC guidance that the event causing both disposals should be the withdrawal from participation in the business, although the legislation only says the asset disposal must be connected with the withdrawal from the business.

HMRC realise that there will often be a delay between the disposal of the shares, perhaps on the cessation of the business, and the disposal of the asset which potentially qualifies as the associated disposal. They have therefore laid down some guidelines as to when a later disposal of an asset can be accepted as an associated disposal.

The disposal may be an associated disposal if the disposal occurs:

- within one year of the cessation of business; or
- within three years of the cessation of business and the asset has not been leased or used for any other purpose at any time after business ceased;
- where the business has not ceased, within three years of the material disposal provided the asset has not been used for any purpose other than that of the business.

These extra-statutory conditions are not as flexible as the legally imposed conditions relating to the post-cessation disposals for a sole trader business (see **11.28**). HMRC guidance (CG63995) indicates that any significant use of the asset, other than for the business of the company, between the first disposal of shares and the disposal of the asset, will disqualify that asset from being an associated disposal. This is in addition to the statutory restrictions imposed by *TCGA 1992, s 169P* (see **11.38**).

Disposal of partnership interest

11.37 Where a partner disposes of his interest in the partnership or part of that interest so the disposal would qualify for entrepreneurs' relief where a gain arises (see **11.23**), a disposal of an asset held personally may qualify as an associated disposal for the relief if the following conditions apply:

(a) the asset is disposed of as part of the partner's withdrawal from participation in the business carried on by the partnership (*TCGA 1992, s 169K(3), (5)*);

(b) the asset was used for the purpose of the partnership business for at least one year to the date of disposal of the partnership interest, or to the date or cessation of the partnership business if earlier (*TCGA 1992, s 169K(4)*).

The definition of withdrawal from the business of the partnership is similar to that discussed with reference to a company (see **11.35**). The HMRC guidance (CG63995) indicates that the partner does not have to step down as a partner completely. There is no *de minimis* amount that the withdrawing partner must reduce his interest in the partnership by, for the combined disposals to constitute a withdrawal from the business.

Example 11.12

Graham is in partnership with his son Tristan, sharing all profits: 7/8ths to Graham, 1/8th to Tristan. Graham owns the office that the partnership trades from. On his sixtieth birthday Graham gifts the office to his son and the profit-sharing ratios are changed to 1/4 to Graham and 3/4 to Tristan, but Graham continues to work full time for the partnership. The disposal of the office to Tristan qualifies as an associated disposal as Graham has also reduced his share in the assets of the partnership.

The time period in which the associated disposal by the partner must take place is subject to the same restrictions as apply to disposals associated with the withdrawal from the business of a trading company (see **11.36**).

Restrictions

11.38 Where there is a material disposal of shares or of a partnership interest, there are four additional restrictions on the use of any asset that is the subject of the associated disposal (*TCGA 1992, s 169P(4)*). If any of the following apply, the amount of the gain arising on the associated disposal of the asset, which would be subject to entrepreneurs' relief, is reduced on a just and reasonable basis.

(a) The asset has only been used by the business for part of the period of ownership by the individual, in which case the gain taken into account will reflect the period of business use.

(b) Only part of the asset has been used for the purposes of the business, so the gain taken into account will reflect the proportion of the asset used for business purposes.

(c) The individual concerned has only been involved in the business as a partner of the partnership or employee/officer of the company for part of the time during which the asset was used by the business. This is less likely than situations (a) or (b), but is possible where an individual was a salaried partner before becoming a full partner.

(d) Any payment of rent was made for the use of the asset by the personal company or partnership for a period after 5 April 2008.

The payment of 'rent' in restriction (d) means any form of consideration paid for the use of the asset, including licence fees for the use of intellectual property, see **Example 11.13.** Where the rent paid is less than a full market rent for the use of the asset, the gain is restricted proportionately.

The restriction in (d) is likely to cause the most aggravation, as it was good tax planning practice under taper relief to hold business property outside of the company, and to charge the company a commercial rent for its use. Full business asset taper relief would apply on any gain made on the disposal of the let property and the rent paid was a useful way to extract funds free of NIC from the company. Now that situation is turned on its head, so property owners must calculate whether the long-term possibility of entrepreneurs' relief is worth more than the short-term benefit of NIC-free rent. There may be strong commercial reasons for keeping the property in personal hands. Even if it is desirable to hold the property within the company, the transfer into the company may well involve high transactional costs such as stamp duty land tax, mortgage and valuation fees. The transfer may also create a personal capital gain that will not qualify for entrepreneurs' relief.

Example 11.13

In **Example 11.11** Lewpyn sold the intellectual property used by Level 6 Ltd on 6 August 2010 making a gain of £280,000. However, Level 6 Ltd had paid Lewpyn a commercial rate licence fee for the use of that intellectual property until 6 July 2008, when his tax advisers realised such a payment could cause a problem on a future sale. The gain to be brought into account for entrepreneurs' relief must be reduced by 3/28 months. The assessable gain on the associated disposal is calculated as:

2010/11	£
Total gain	280,000
Reduction for rent received: £280,000 × 3/28	(30,000)
Net gain	250,000
Annual exemption	(10,100)
Gain subject to entrepreneurs' relief	239,900
CGT payable at 10%	23,990

DEFERRED GAINS

11.39 Where a gain is rolled over or deferred on the acquisition of new shares or corporate bonds, that deferred gain will fall into charge for CGT on the disposal of the new security, which may not meet all the qualifying conditions for entrepreneurs' relief. In these cases special provisions may apply to grant entrepreneurs' relief in respect of gains deferred by acquiring the following shares or securities:

- qualifying corporate bonds (QCBs) (see **11.40**);
- share for share exchanges (see **11.43**); and
- Enterprise Investment Scheme (EIS) or Venture Capital Trust (VCT) shares (see **11.44**).

Qualifying corporate bonds

11.40 When a shareholder sells his personal company he may receive qualifying corporate bonds (QCBs) in exchange for some or all of his shares. The gain that arises on the disposal of the personal company shares is rolled into the QCBs and becomes taxable at the point the QCBs are exchanged for cash, normally on the maturity of the bonds. Under the taper relief rules, the gain on the disposal of the shares was frozen and taper relief would apply when the gain became chargeable, but only in relation to the period the original shares were held, not the period the QCBs were held. QCBs exchanged for shares prior to 6 April 2008 thus present a problem, as the gain is frozen, but taper relief no longer applies.

This problem is eased by a special relief for QCBs that were exchanged for shares before 6 April 2008 (*FA 2008, Sch 3, para 7*) (see **11.41**). There is also a separate relief for QCBs exchanged for shares on or after 6 April 2008 (*TCGA 1992, s 169R*) (see **11.42**). These valuable reliefs could be lost if the taxpayer is unaware of the implications of his actions, or does not make the appropriate claim or election within the tight time limit.

Pre-6 April 2008 QCBs

11.41 Where an individual disposes of QCBs that were acquired in exchange for shares or securities in his personal company before 6 April 2008, any chargeable gain that was rolled into the QCB on the exchange for the shares, becomes chargeable to tax on disposal of the QCBs. However, the individual will not qualify for entrepreneurs' relief on the basis of the QCBs held in the acquiring company, if he does not hold 5% of the ordinary shares of the company that issued the QCBs, or meet the employment condition (see **11.11**).

In this situation the gain deferred by acquiring the QCBs can qualify for entrepreneurs' relief, if at the time the QCBs were acquired the gain would have qualified for that relief, assuming for this purpose that the relief had been in place at that date. The tests discussed in **11.9** must effectively be backdated to the point that the original gain arose. However, to benefit from the relief on the chargeable gain the taxpayer must make a claim under *FA 2008, Sch 3, para 7* no later than the first anniversary of 31 January following the end of the tax year in which the first disposal after 6 April 2008 of the QCBs occurs. The QCBs must be held by the same person who acquired them before 6 April 2008, in order for the gain that becomes chargeable after 5 April 2008 to qualify for the relief.

There is a quirk to watch out for with this transitional relief. The claim applies to the whole of the gain that has been deferred by acquiring QCBs, and has the effect of reducing the whole gain by 4/9ths. The reduced gain falls into charge when the QCBs are disposed of. If at that time the reduced gain is charged to CGT at 18%, there is an effective rate of CGT of 10% on the full deferred gain. However, where some of those QCBs are disposed of on or after 23 June 2010 the rate of CGT may be 28%, in which case the effective rate of CGT with entrepreneurs' relief is not 10% but 15.5% (see **Example 11.14**). Where the first disposal of the QCBs is made on or after 23 June 2010, the full deferred gain is chargeable to CGT at 10%.

Post-6 April 2008 QCBs

11.42 Where an individual acquires QCBs in exchange for shares in his personal company on or after 6 April 2008 the gain inherent in those personal company shares is rolled into the QCBs and falls into charge to CGT when the QCBs are disposed of (*TCGA 1992, s 116(10)*). On the disposal of those QCBs the tests for entrepreneurs' relief to apply to the deferred gain would normally look at the individual's shareholding and employment conditions in the company that issued the QCBs, not the original personal company. The individual will not meet the tests (see **11.9**), if he does not hold at least 5% of the ordinary shares of the company that issued the QCBs, even if he is an employee of that company, or another company in the same trading group.

The taxpayer can elect under *TCGA 1992, s 169R* for the gain that arose on the disposal of the personal company shares to qualify for entrepreneurs' relief, if that disposal would have qualified for entrepreneurs' relief using the tests outlined in **11.9**. However, the effect of that election is quite different where the exchange of the personal company shares for QCBs occurs before 23 June 2010, or after 22 June 2010.

Pre-23 June 2010 disposals

The gain on the disposal of the personal company shares is reduced by 4/9ths so when that gain comes into charge on the disposal of the QCBs the reduced amount is subject to CGT at 18%, giving an effective rate of 10% on the full gain. Although where the gain comes into charge on or after 23 June 2010 the rate of CGT applying may be 28%, giving an effective rate of CGT on the full gain of 15.5% (see **Example 11.14**).

Post-22 June 2010 disposals

If the taxpayer elects under the new *TCGA 1992, s 169R* the gain arising on the disposal of the personal company shares will not be deferred at all, but will have entrepreneurs' relief applied at that time and be subject to CGT at 10%, where the gain falls within the lifetime cap. This means the taxpayer has to pay CGT at 10% when they have received QCBs in return for their shares and may not have the cash to pay the tax. The alternative is not to elect under *s 169R*, and to accept the automatic deferral of the gain under *TCGA 1992, s 116(10)*. The deferred gain can then fall into charge as the QCBs are gradually cashed, but that gain will be subject to CGT at 18% or 28%, depending on the taxpayer's level of income and gains for the tax year of encashment.

In both cases the election under *TCGA 1992, s 169R* must be made by the first anniversary of 31 January following the end of the tax year in which the shares in the personal company were disposed of, which will normally be the acquisition date of the QCBs, not the disposal date of the QCBs. Tax advisers need to watch this election deadline as the deferred gain may not come into charge for some years, by which time it will be too late to elect under *TCGA 1992, s 169R* for entrepreneurs' relief to apply.

Example 11.14

On 20 June 2008 Alice exchanged all her shares in her personal company; Wonderland Ltd for QCBs issued by Red Queen Plc. Alice had formed Wonderland Ltd and had been its sole director and shareholder for ten years. The gain accruing on the disposal of her shares was £990,000, which was just within the lifetime cap at the time of the disposal. This gain was fully deferred by the acceptance of QCBs and Alice elected under *TCGA 1992, s 169R* for the gain to be subject to entrepreneurs' relief. This had the effect of reducing the deferred gain to £550,000 (5/9ths × £990,000).

On 20 July 2010 Alice received a cash payment for half of her QCBs, so half the reduced deferred gain came into charge; being £275,000. Alice's net taxable income for 2010/11 is £40,000, which exceeds the basic rate band, so the full gain of £275,000 is taxed at 28%. Alice's CGT liability on the encashment of the QCBs is £77,000 (£275,000 × 28%), when she may have expected a liability of £49,500 (10% × (£990,000/2)).

Share exchanges

11.43 Another situation where gains may be deferred is on a share-for-share exchange, which often occurs on the takeover of a company. A shareholder may exchange shares in his personal company (the old shares) for a small holding of shares (new shares) issued by the acquiring company. No capital gain arises at the time of the share exchange as the new shares are considered to stand in the shoes of the old shares (*TCGA 1992, s 127*). However, on disposal of the new shares entrepreneurs' relief may not apply if the minority shareholder does not hold 5% of the ordinary shares of the acquiring company (see **11.10**).

In this situation, the shareholder can choose whether to defer the gain using *s 127* or to disapply *s 127* (using the election under *TCGA 1992, s 169Q*) and claim entrepreneurs' relief on the gain as it arises on the disposal of the old shares. This will make the effective rate of CGT on that gain 10% whether the share exchange occurs before or after 23 June 2010.

The disadvantage for the shareholder is that if he disapplies the deferral in *s 127*, he will have to pay CGT on the residue of the gain (at 10%) where he has not received cash proceeds for those old shares. The election under *TCGA*

1992, s 169Q can only apply where the share exchange occurs on or after 6 April 2008.

The election under *TCGA 1992, s 169Q* must be made by the first anniversary of 31 January following the tax year in which the old shares were exchanged. Where the old shares were held by a trust, the election must be made jointly by the trustee and the qualifying beneficiary. As with the election under *TCGA 1992, s 169R*, the timing of this election is likely to trip up taxpayers and tax advisers alike. The gain on the old shares is rolled over into the new shares, and likely to be forgotten until the new shares are disposed of. However, by that date it may be too late to elect under *TCGA 1992, s 169Q*.

Another problem that can arise is when the new shares are disposed very shortly after acquisition. Where the taxpayer would qualify for entrepreneurs' relief on the basis of his holding of ordinary shares and employment in the acquiring company (see **11.10**), he still needs to satisfy those conditions for 12 months to the date of disposal of the new shares. HMRC have confirmed that where *s 127* applies, such that the new shares are treated as the same asset as the old shares, the exchange can be looked through to ascertain the 12-month holding period for the ordinary shares and the employment condition. This look-through can only apply if the election under *TCGA 1992, s 169Q* has not been made, and the old shares also qualified for entrepreneurs' relief (CG64155).

Enterprise investment scheme or venture capital trust shares

11.44 Deferral of gains by acquiring enterprise investment scheme (EIS) shares is discussed in **Chapter 16**, and the similar deferral of gains that applied on the acquisition of venture capital trust (VCT) shares before 6 April 2004 is discussed in **17.8**.

Where such gains were deferred before 6 April 2008 and fall into charge after that date, for any reason, the shareholder may claim entrepreneurs' relief in respect of that deferred gain if the conditions apply (*FA 2008, Sch 3, para 8*). Those conditions are broadly that the original gain, which was rolled into the EIS or VCT shares, would have qualified for entrepreneurs' relief if it had accrued on or after 6 April 2008. So a fiction is invented to apply the tests set out in **11.9** or **11.20** as appropriate, to the original gain looking at the ownership circumstances that related to the original asset which was disposed of.

This claim for entrepreneurs' relief must apply to the whole of the deferred gain that attaches to the EIS or VCT shares, which were acquired to defer the original gain, even if some of those shares continue to be held, such that part of the deferred gain has not yet fallen into charge to CGT (CG64170). If the first chargeable event for the shares occurs before 23 June 2010, but after 5 April 2008, and a claim for entrepreneurs' relief is made the whole of the deferred gain is reduced by 4/9ths at that time. This is not the point at which all the gain comes back into charge for CGT. This means same problem created by the change of the rate of CGT applies to this deferred gain as it does to gains deferred using QCBs, (see **11.41**).

Where the first chargeable event for the EIS or VCT shares occurs on or after 23 June 2010, and entrepreneurs' relief is claimed the deferred gain is charged at the entrepreneurs' relief rate of 10%

The taxpayer must claim this relief by the first anniversary of 31 January following the end of the tax year in which he first disposed of the EIS or VCT shares after 5 April 2008.

There may also be a separate gain that has arisen through the growth in value of the EIS shares themselves. This EIS company generated gain will be exempt from CGT if the EIS shares have been held for at least three years and income tax relief has been given and not been withdrawn (see **16.3**). Where these conditions are not met, the EIS company gain will be subject to CGT. Entrepreneurs' relief may be available on that EIS company gain where the conditions in **11.9** apply in respect to those EIS shares.

INTERACTION WITH OTHER RELIEFS

11.45 When the legislation for entrepreneurs' relief was drafted little thought was given to the interaction between this new relief and the existing CGT reliefs. HMRC do not consider that entrepreneurs' relief takes the same place in the order of reliefs as was previously defined by retirement relief (see CG60120). The HMRC view on the interaction of entrepreneurs' relief and certain other CGT reliefs is as follows:

- Roll-over relief (*TCGA 1992, s 152*) applies before entrepreneurs' relief (CG64136).
- EIS deferral relief (*TCGA 1992, Sch 5B*) applies after entrepreneurs' relief (CG64135).
- Incorporation relief (*TCGA 1992, s 162*) applies before entrepreneurs' relief (see **15.19**).
- Hold-over relief (*TCGA 1992, s 165*) applies before entrepreneurs' relief (CG64137).

An alternative view is that entrepreneurs' relief can be claimed on the whole qualifying gain with hold-over relief soaking up the residual gain.

Chapter 12

Main residence relief

WHAT CONSTITUTES RESIDENCE?

Quality of occupation

12.1 Relief is allowed under *TCGA 1992, s 222* in respect of a gain that accrues to an individual (or, see at **12.24**, to trustees and personal representatives) on the disposal of an interest in 'a dwelling house or part of a dwelling house which is, or has at any time in his period of ownership been, his only or main residence'. The legislation does not define 'residence' though there is guidance in the decided cases and, from the standpoint of HMRC, in CG64427–CG64456. Lord Widgery described it well in *Fox v Stirk, Ricketts v Registration Officer for the City of Cambridge* [1970] 3 All ER 7 as 'the place where he sleeps and shelters and has his house'.

The HMRC Manual is very full: this perhaps reflects the complexity of the subject and that it is of very wide application. There are many cases (see, for example, *Goodwin v Curtis (Inspector of Taxes)* [1996] STC 1146), which concerned the redevelopment of a farmhouse and its outbuildings. One of the two partners engaged in the development purchased the farmhouse for his own use. He took up occupation and had the services and telephone connected. After only a matter of days the property was offered for sale. A few weeks later contracts were exchanged at a very substantial profit. The taxpayer then moved to another property which was much smaller. The then Inland Revenue considered that his residence at the farmhouse lacked the necessary permanence for him to claim relief under *s 222* on the gain that he had realised. The taxpayer appealed.

At the hearing it was revealed that, at the time of his purchase, the taxpayer was separated from his wife and family and had no need of a house as large as the farmhouse. That was supported by the evidence of the size of property to which he later moved. It also appeared that the property had been placed on the market before the taxpayer even took up 'residence'. There was little evidence that he intended to make the property his permanent home. He was denied relief on the gain. However, that case is not decisive: there is actually no minimum period – what matters is the quality of the occupation: see *Moore v Thompson (Inspector of Taxes)* [1986] STC 170.

12.2 In *Jones v Wilcox (Inspector of Taxes)* [1996] STI 1349, the argument was all the other way. The taxpayer had made a gain unconnected with property and was hoping to set against that gain a loss which he had sustained on the sale of the house because the market had gone against him. The taxpayer therefore argued that main residence relief should not apply, because of the anti-avoidance provisions in *s 224(3)* which provide that relief is not available to shelter a gain where the acquisition of the dwelling house 'was made wholly or partly for the purpose of realising a gain from the disposal of it'.

Again, the taxpayer's case fell down on the evidence. He and his family had lived in the property for a number of years. Children had been born and brought up there. The taxpayer and his wife had considered a number of properties. The only reasonable inference was that this particular house had been chosen, not to make a profit, but because they wanted to live there. Whilst making a gain from the eventual disposal of the house might have been a hope or even an expectation, everyone has to live somewhere and the main purpose of the purchase had been as a residence. There was no evidence that profit was the main motive for the purchase. As a result, in the same way that a gain would not have been chargeable, the loss was not relievable.

Lynch v Edmondson (Inspector of Taxes) [1998] STI 968 also illustrates some of the principles. A bricklayer purchased two plots of land. He developed them into two flats. One of them was immediately let at a premium for a term of 99 years. The then Inland Revenue considered that, taken together, the transactions amounted to dealing in land. Evidence before the Special Commissioner of the way in which the property had been financed, and transactions between the bricklayer and the woman with whom he was living, all tended to support that interpretation.

Helpfully, the Special Commissioner summarised the various tests that led to the final decision. Thus:

- this was a single transaction that could nevertheless amount to trading;
- it was a transaction in land, which was certainly a commodity in which it was possible to trade;
- the way that the taxpayer went about developing the land pointed towards trading, in that he realised substantial money from one of the units by letting it as soon as it was built;
- the way that the project was financed was consistent with trading, in that much of the cost of the development was repaid from the premium that was taken on the grant of the lease of the first unit to be finished;

- the fact that the bricklayer himself carried out the work was consistent with trading;
- the fact that the original purchase of the land was divided up into units for sale was consistent with trading; and
- it was relevant to consider the motive of the taxpayer. He had told the bank that had lent him the money that he would sell one of the flats. That was consistent with trading.

On the other hand there were factors that tended to point the other way, such as the fact that one of the units was not immediately disposed of on a long lease but was instead let in a manner that was more consistent with investment than with trade. Also, the way that the asset was used in the overall circumstances was ambiguous. Nevertheless, on balance, the taxpayer was held to be trading.

12.3 Some general principles emerge from these cases. The average person who buys a property, takes up occupation and later sells it will fall within the decision in *Jones v Wilcox.* Subject to the many qualifications that are discussed in this chapter in relation to the extent of property and periods of absence, most transactions affecting property that has been occupied by the taxpayer will escape taxation. No entry is required on a tax return in such cases: see CG64206.

It is, however, different where a clear pattern of dealing can be discerned and a person buys properties, renovates them and resells them on a regular basis. As a rule of thumb, to renovate one run down property or perhaps two is no more than 'nest building' for a young couple; but by the time the taxpayer(s) embark on a third renovation project it becomes easier to infer that they are engaged in a trade. The speed with which a taxpayer moves from one property to another is relevant, as was clear from the decision in *Goodwin v Curtis*. The statute stipulates nothing. Residence in a property for a full year is probably long enough to establish relief.

Usually, a careful examination of the facts will show the truth of the position and never more so than where a taxpayer has more than one residence available to him, a situation that is discussed at **12.18**. If, perhaps because no notice has been filed under *s 222(5)(a)*, the taxpayer is forced to show where he is resident, the following will be relevant to where the taxpayer claims to live:

- voting;
- letters to friends;
- bank and building society accounts and investments;
- registration to vote; and
- tax returns.

Evidence will be examined including, see CG64550, the way that a property is furnished and where the family spend their time.

Homeworkers: the use of a residence partly for business purposes

12.4 Relief under *s 222* is available in respect of the entirety of a dwelling house or of part only. As will be seen at **12.6**, the main apportionment of a residence required, where it does not all qualify for relief, is between the part that is within the 'permitted area' and the part that is not. A separate apportionment is recognised by *s 224(1)* for dwelling houses or part of dwelling houses which are exclusively used for a trade, business, profession or vocation. This will increasingly be the case, where a person works from home and either has an annex or outbuilding designated as an office or a room within his property which is exclusively used for office work.

The distinction to be drawn is a fine one. If the taxpayer, wishing to pay as little income tax as possible, claims that a proportion of the expenses of the building in which the business is carried on should be deductible from profits, there is an inference that that part of the building is not also the residence of the taxpayer. The result is a matter of fact and degree. HMRC may be aware that a house is used as a business: see CG64660–CG64690.

Example 12.1—Soft furnishings business

Alice lives in a former council house in Thetford. Immediately adjoining the property is a small row of lock-up garages which have for a number of years been used by various tenants. Alice buys the garages for two reasons: she wants more privacy and in any case she runs a small business from home, making curtains. She needs extra space for her stock. Following the purchase of the garages, she uses one for her domestic car, one for her delivery van, one for the stock of finished goods and she lets the remainder. For convenience she continues to run the business itself from the house. Customers like to sit in her kitchen over a mug of tea to discuss their requirements and she has set up the living room so that she can make curtains, watch television and keep an eye on her young children all at the same time.

On disposal of the house and the garages at a gain, Alice must apportion the gain between the different parts of the property. The garages that were let are a simple investment and taxable as such. The garages used respectively for the storage of stock and to house the delivery van have been used exclusively for the business and not for any domestic purpose and are therefore outside the scope of *s 222*. The remainder of the property, however, does qualify for relief, see CG64663, even though Alice may have claimed costs of services, etc against her business. There is only one kitchen. It is not used exclusively for the business. There is only one living room and the family spend their spare time in there. The garage for the family car is not used for business. Any reasonable apportionment should be accepted by HMRC: see CG64670.

The extent of the 'curtilage' of the dwelling house

12.5 There is usually little difficulty, on the disposal of urban properties, in claiming that the whole of the gain realised on a residence should qualify for relief. The 'curtilage' is, in layman's terms, the property that obviously 'goes with' the house, the part that, if the layman had to describe the extent of the property, he would not treat such parts as extra or needing specific mention. The curtilage is the house, not the grounds.

We have a slight difficulty here: HMRC at CG64245 and CG64255 describes the test as being what would be included in a legal description of the property for conveyancing purposes. That was fine when most land was unregistered: each conveyance had to set out a description of the extent of the land conveyed, perhaps by reference to an earlier conveyance and plan. Now, however, most land is registered. Lawyers transfer it simply by reference to a Title Number at the Land Registry. As a result, it would be difficult now to apply the test in the Manual. However, the Manual applies some reasonable tests: thus an off-lying garage may be included: see CG64290.

The 'permitted area'

12.6 The rules in *s 222(1)(b)* and following often create difficulties in relation to suburban and country properties. Relief is allowed in respect of 'land which [the taxpayer] has for his own occupation and enjoyment with that residence as its garden or grounds up to the permitted area'. That area is defined as being an area, which includes the house, of up to 0.5 of a hectare (about 1.25 acres; see CG64815 for an explanation for this limit) being, in case of dispute, the part of the grounds that is 'the most suitable for occupation and enjoyment with the residence'.

Section 222(3) recognises that the size and character of a dwelling house may make some larger area than 0.5 of a hectare appropriate as 'required for the reasonable enjoyment of the dwelling house' or of the part of the dwelling house with which the transaction is concerned. There are many cases on the subject. It is possible that, over time, our perception of how much of this planet we should each occupy may have changed. Some of the earlier cases on 'permitted area' are redolent of a more leisured and spacious age. The phrase 'garden or grounds' in *s 222(1)(b)* carries its normal meaning: it is a question of fact.

Lewis v Lady Rook [1992] STC 171 is a fairly recent case and a good starting point, being of high authority. A woman had purchased an eight-bedroomed house. The land extended to over ten acres. There were two cottages, one of which she sold many years later. It had been occupied by a gardener and it stood 190 yards from the main house. When assessed on the gain she appealed, claiming main residence relief.

The Court of Appeal held that the true test was whether the cottage was within the 'curtilage' of, and appurtenant to, the main property. For relief to be allowed the cottage must be part of the entity which, together with the main house, constituted the dwelling house for the purposes of *s 222* as being occupied by the taxpayer as her main residence. The cottage was too far away from the main building. It was separated by a large garden. It was not part of the main residence.

Another recent example of the principle is *Longson v Baker* (2000) SpC 08.05 2000. The Longsons were keen on riding. He purchased a property amounting to just over 7.5 hectares which included a farmhouse, some stables and an outhouse. A building was added for use as a riding school. As part of settlement between husband and wife the interest in the property was transferred to her. It became necessary to decide the extent of the 'permitted area'. He argued that 'required' in *s 222(3)* meant 'called for', whereas the Inspector argued that it meant no more than 'necessary'. Thus, whilst it was certainly convenient for a family interested in riding to enjoy the whole of the land that was available that was not actually necessary for the enjoyment of the property. The Special Commissioner agreed with the Revenue, allowing relief only in respect of a much smaller area, observing that to hold otherwise might tend to encourage widespread interest in riding to shelter gains on properties with substantial amenities.

Land which is separated from a house may not be its garden or grounds, though the Manual, at CG64367, fairly recognises that cottage gardens may lie across the village street. See also CG64270 for a flowchart that may be helpful.

Surplus land

12.7 In practice there is a difficult argument for the taxpayer to resist where the disposal is of only part of the property. It is addressed in CG64832 and following.

Example 12.2—Stable block conversion

Belinda for many years occupied the Old Coach House, built in 1850 as part of a much more extensive property and still enjoying 1 hectare of garden with access, down an unmade track 20 feet wide at the rear, to a side road. Belinda owns the track and uses it occasionally because there are, at the end of the garden, old stables, formerly used by Belinda's children as a play area and later for car repairs. The character of the neighbourhood has changed in the last 150 years. Belinda secures planning permission to convert the stable block into a mews residence, which she sells with 0.25 of a hectare of land.

It is difficult for Belinda to resist the HMRC argument that, if she is now selling the stable block and a parcel of land, that land is not 'required for the reasonable enjoyment of the (retained) dwelling house'. Clearly, if Belinda goes on living at the Old Coach House, the land is not now so required. An argument may perhaps be advanced that times have changed. Originally the Coach House itself was part of a much larger property. For most of the time that Belinda has owned it properties in that area have enjoyed large gardens and she has actually with her family occupied the whole property as a single unit. It is only recently, with changes in the locality, that it has been possible for her to obtain planning permission and therefore, for most of her period of ownership of the stables, the requirements of *s 222* have been met.

Note that if the land is within the permitted area, relief automatically extends to all of it, whether sold as one or with a plot sold off separately. In such a case the issue of 'surplus' land does not apply: CG64815, but the rule in *Varty v Lynes* [1976] STC 508 (see below) is still relevant.

Care should be taken where land exceeding the permitted area is owned before a residence is built on it. In *Henke and another v HMRC* [2006] STC (SCD) 561, the taxpayers bought 2.66 acres of land in 1982. In 1993, they built their main residence on part of the land. They later sold some of the land, on which houses were built. The taxpayers appealed against HMRC's refusal to allow main residence relief on the whole gain arising from the disposal of the land. The Special Commissioner considered that the permitted area should extend to 2.03 acres, based on the circumstances at the time of disposal. It was also held that because the land was owned for a period before the house was built, main residence relief should be apportioned (under *s 223(2)*), as the 'throughout the period of ownership' requirement in *s 223(1)* was not satisfied.

The problem of the residual building plot

12.8 A common pitfall is illustrated by the case of *Varty v Lynes* [1976] STC 508. See the following example.

Example 12.3—Sale of land delayed

Charles owned and occupied a suburban property with an extensive (over five hectare) corner plot. Work forced him to relocate. He obtained planning permission for a single dwelling on the plot and, as a temporary measure, purchased a residence nearer his new work. In the end, the sale of his former house goes through before the sale of the adjoining plot. Any gain on the sale of the house itself, after apportionment, is covered by main residence relief.

Unfortunately for Charles, in general there can be no relief on the eventual sale of the plot. At the time of the sale it is neither a dwelling house nor part of a dwelling house. It was, but is no longer: the legislation is precise in distinguishing the house from its grounds on this point. It would have been better for Charles to have sold the house and the plot together but with the benefit of the planning permission. Note, however, some relaxation of the strict rule in CG64377 where all the land was formerly occupied as garden, which is only reasonable.

Other forms of accommodation

12.9 A mobile caravan does not qualify for relief, but a static one may do. A 'live aboard' yacht in a marina does not qualify even if on 'shore power' as many cruising yachts are, but a houseboat permanently located, and connected to all mains services, may do. It seems that the claim in such cases usually relates to the site, rather than the van or vessel.

PERIODS OF RESIDENCE

12.10 In a straightforward case this issue gives no difficulty. A person buys a house, moves in, lives there until some change of circumstances, finds a buyer and moves out. In such a situation no apportionment is necessary and, assuming no other complications, the entire gain qualifies for relief. Difficulties arise in more complicated situations.

Delay in taking up occupation

12.11 ESC D49 applies where an individual acquires land on which he has a house built which becomes his main residence or buys an existing property and before moving in:

- arranges for alterations or redecorations; or
- completes the necessary steps for disposing of his previous residence.

Provided that the delay is no more than one year, this period of non-residence is treated as if it were a period of residence. If a taxpayer needs more than one year, he may have a second year if there are good reasons for delay which are outside the control of the taxpayer. If, however, the individual fails to move into the property within the period of one year (or two if extended) no relief will be given at all for that period of non-occupation. There may be overlap between the period of deemed occupation under this concession and relief on another property in respect of the same period.

Example 12.4—Relocation plans undermined

David lives in Warwick. He buys a scruffy house in Markfield, Leicestershire, with a view to renovating it and living there because it will be near his work. In fact the property suffers from mining subsidence that was not revealed before the purchase and the renovation takes 18 months.

Meanwhile, David has been promoted by his employers, so Markfield will no longer be convenient for him. The house in Warwick has increased in value, as has that in Markfield. If David had moved into the renovated house, the delay would not prejudice relief because it was not his fault.

If he decides simply to sell the house in Markfield without taking up occupation, the whole of the gain will be taxable. It might have been better for him to consider the possibilities that are discussed below in connection with owning two or more residences. As will be seen below, an election in relation to residences need not be permanent. Even a short period residence at Markfield would serve to bring David within ESC D49.

'Overlap' relief

12.12 Homeowners may experience significant delays in finding purchasers whilst personal circumstances compel them to move and to acquire a new residence before disposing of the old. Recognising this, *s 223(2)(a)* has the affect that, provided the taxpayer has been resident in the dwelling house at some point in his period of ownership, the last 36 months of ownership will qualify to be treated as a period of ownership 'in any event'. Apart from that, the basic rule is that main residence relief is calculated on a time-apportionment basis and is allowed in respect of periods of ownership but not of periods of absence.

Example 12.5—Last 36 months

Evan bought a scruffy property on 1 January 2006. He renovated it himself, but did not live onsite. He was so slow that the work took until 31 March 2008, so Evan was outside the terms of ESC D49. He lived in the property from 1 April 2008 to 31 December 2009. He sold on 31 March 2010 at a good profit, even after the cost of the improvements.

Evan does not benefit from ESC D49 because the improvements took too long. He qualifies for main residence relief from 1 April 2008 to 31 March 2010 under general principles, giving him relief in respect of ownership of 24 months out of 51. However, by virtue of *s 223(2)(a)* main residence relief will be allowed in respect of 36 months out of 51.

'Sandwich' reliefs

12.13 *Section 223(3)* recognises individual circumstances where a person is unable to continue to live at a property throughout his period of ownership. For a period of absence to be treated as a period of occupation under *s 223(3)*, the dwelling house must have been the only or main residence of the taxpayer both before and after the period of absence, ie sandwiched between periods of genuine occupation. If that condition is satisfied, the following periods of absence will be treated as if they were periods of occupation:

- A period during all of which the taxpayer worked outside the UK (without limit as to duration).
- A period, up to four years, or periods together not exceeding four years, during which the taxpayer could not live at the residence because of where he was working or as a result of any condition imposed by his employer that required him to live elsewhere. The condition must have been reasonable to secure the effective performance of his duties by the employee.
- Any other period of absence up to three years or periods together not exceeding three years.

Example 12.6—No place like home

Frances worked in the gas industry and on 1 January 2003 purchased a property in Bacton, Norfolk where she lived until 31 December 2003. She was then seconded to Aberdeen, working there until 31 December 2006; then to Norway, where she remained until 31 December 2007. Tiring of life on gas rigs, Frances then took an extended holiday from 1 January 2008 to 31 December 2009, returning to Bacton and living there from 1 January 2010 to 30 June in that year, when she sold the property at a profit.

The whole of the gain qualifies for relief. There are periods of residence to satisfy the 'sandwich' requirement. The period in Scotland is less than the maximum stipulated by *s 223(3)(c)*. During all of her time in Norway, Frances was working: the absence therefore complied with *s 223(3)(b)*. The extended holiday is less than the maximum stipulated by *s 223(3)(a)*.

Job-related accommodation

12.14 Apart from the provisions of *s 223* treating a period of absence as if it were a period of residence, there is a separate rule under *s 222(8)* which can help the taxpayer. If a property or part of it has been purchased with the intention that it should eventually be a residence, but the owner for the time being lives in job-related accommodation, the owner is deemed to occupy the property. It does not matter that the house is never, in fact, occupied, provided that the intention to occupy can be proved: CG64555.

Example 12.7—Getting away from work

Gemma is a prison officer on a low salary. She purchases at auction a terraced property in poor condition which is occupied by a tenant who is entitled to remain at the property for the rest of his life. Gemma meanwhile is required by the terms of her employment to live onsite, though not always at the same secure establishment.

The tenant dies. Gemma is still employed as a prison officer but uses her holidays to renovate the property. That takes time and it is seven years from the date of the purchase before Gemma is actually able to start to use the property as her home when she is on leave. Although she has always intended to use the property as her home a change in her circumstances involves a move to a completely different part of the country and she sells the property.

She can show that she always intended, once the property was available and fit for her use, to occupy it as her only or main residence. She can also show, in compliance with *s 222(8A)* and following, that her accommodation with the prison service is job related (see below).

12.15 Accommodation is job related where a person or his spouse or civil partner has some kind of work, whether employed or self-employed, that meets the following conditions.

Employment

If the taxpayer or spouse or civil partner is employed, there are three circumstances in which accommodation is job related:

- it is necessary for the proper performance of the work to live in specific accommodation;
- accommodation is provided by the employer for the better performance by the employee of his duties and it is customary in that trade or employment to provide living accommodation for employees; or

- there is a special threat to the security of the employee and to meet it special security arrangements are enforced as part of which the employee lives in particular accommodation.

Freelance

The contract must be at arm's length. Two conditions must be satisfied:

- the taxpayer is required as part of the contract to carry on the work on premises that are provided by another person (who may, but need not, be the other party to the contract); and
- it is a term of the contract that the contractor should live on those premises or on some other premises provided by the other party to the contract.

Link to a company: anti-avoidance

Special rules apply where a company provides the accommodation to an employee who is a director. To avoid the situation where a person might artificially create job-related accommodation for his own benefit, the provisions as to job-related accommodation for employees described at **12.14** will not apply, see *s 222(8B)*, unless two further conditions are satisfied.

The first is that the employee/director must have no material interest in the company. The second condition is that one of three sub-conditions is satisfied namely:

- the taxpayer is a full-time working director;
- the company is non-profit making; or
- the company is established for charitable purposes only.

Again, see *s 222(8C)*, to avoid abuse, relief in respect of job-related accommodation for a self-employed person under *s 222(8A)(b)* described at **12.14** is not available where the living accommodation is wholly or partly provided by certain entities that have a link to the taxpayer. In this subsection the person who would otherwise claim relief is described as 'the borrower'. The relief will not apply where the accommodation has been provided either by a company in which the borrower or his spouse or civil partner has a material interest; or by anyone who, together with the borrower or his spouse or civil partner, carries on any trade or business in partnership.

These provisions as to job-related accommodation were tightened up by *FA 1999*. The references to matters such as 'employment', 'director', 'full-time working director' and 'material interest' are taken from *ITEPA 2003*. The changes relate to residence on or after 6 April 1983.

Residence in the context of trusts and estates

12.16 Situations are often encountered where main residence relief may be in point on the disposal of a property by trustees or in the administration of an estate. This is discussed more fully at **12.26** and will particularly apply where the 'debt or charge' scheme has been used. Changes in inheritance tax in *FA 2008, s 10* and *Sch 4* have rendered the 'debt or charge' scheme obsolete, but there must be many still in operation. For a description of that scheme see *Inheritance Tax 2010/11* (Bloomsbury Professional), Chapter 14, relating to the family home generally; and more specifically Chapter 13, *Wills and Estate Planning*, at 13.2–13.11.

LETTINGS RELIEF

12.17 'Buy to let' properties do not qualify for main residence relief. There is, however, a specific relief which was no doubt designed to increase the availability of accommodation at moderate cost. It is in *s 223(4)* and can apply where a person lets all or part of his own home. For the relief to apply, the dwelling house, or the part on which the gain arises, must at some time in the ownership of the taxpayer have been a residence within the general terms of *s 222*, ie his only or main residence or a property that he owned whilst in job-related employment. The part in question must be let as residential accommodation. Up to a limit of £40,000 of the gain that would otherwise have been taxable is relieved.

Example 12.8—Money in the cellar

Henry buys as a single unit an urban terraced property for £480,000 of which 25% is represented by the value of accommodation in the basement that could be occupied separately; the remainder relates to the ground floor and upper floor. He lives there, allowing a lodger to occupy the basement, and later sells the entire property for £660,000. There is valuation evidence that the basement flat is still worth 25% of the whole. The gain on the ground floor and upper floor is exempt under general principles. The gain on the basement is £45,000 of which £40,000 is exempt under *s 223(4)(b)*. Note that if the basement had always been self-contained, it might have been regarded as a separate dwelling house and thus not part of Henry's property.

Separate relief, up to £40,000, may be allowed where part of the gain relates to the letting, for example by time-apportionment. This is illustrated in CG64723–CG64737.

TWO OR MORE RESIDENCES

12.18 It is arguable that, with the introduction of self-assessment, the law in this area may have changed slightly from what was established by the case of *Griffin v Craig-Harvey* [1994] STC 54 discussed below. This is probably the area of main residence relief that gives the most difficulties and perhaps spawns more claims in negligence against advisers than the rest of the main residence relief code. HMRC may be aware that the taxpayer has more than one residence: see CG64208 and CG64485.

Section 222(6) provides that an individual living with his spouse or civil partner can have only one main residence for both of them as long as they are living together. *Section 222(5)* applies where the taxpayer has two or more residences. If no action is taken by the taxpayer under the legislation, the question of which property is the main residence is one of fact.

Example 12.9—Home for the weekend

Ian, a VAT consultant, has a home at Empingham, overlooking Rutland Water, but the main demand for his services is from construction companies based in North London. He buys a studio flat in Hendon for use during the week. He and his family are keen on fishing and sailing. He spends as much time as possible in Empingham and the minimum in Hendon. On the balance of the facts, the property in Rutland is his main residence. Note that *Fox v Stirk, Ricketts v Registration Officer for the City of Cambridge* [1970] 3 All ER 7 contains the observation by Lord Denning MR that a man may have 'a flat in London and a house in the country. He is resident in both.'

Nomination of a property as the main residence

12.19 If a taxpayer has two properties that he could call home, *s 222(5)(a)* provides that, within two years of the date on which the second residence was available to him, he may give notice to HMRC identifying which property is his residence. If married or having a civil partner and living with that person, the notice binds them both. There is no precise form of notice, but see CG64520, but it must be signed by the resident, not by his agent: see CG64520.

Example 12.10—Timeous notice

Jessica, a social worker, buys her first home, a flat in a deprived area near where she works, on 1 January 2007 and lives there. On 1 July 2010 her aunt dies, leaving Jessica a bungalow which, following the death, is vacant and happens to be far more pleasant for Jessica to live in. Jessica has from 1 July 2010 to 30

June 2012 in which she may serve notice under *s 222(5)(a)*. If she does serve notice, the property notified may be treated as Jessica's main residence if it is a residence of hers, ie whether in fact she lives there for any appreciable time, or not. CG64485 suggests that a dwelling may not be nominated under *s 222(5)(a)* unless it is a 'residence' or deemed to be a residence since otherwise it is outside *s 222(1)*. The test will be as described at **12.1–12.3**, but bearing in mind Lord Denning's observations noted in **Example 12.9**.

Difficulties for the taxpayer arise because it is not always possible to predict which of two properties will appreciate in value the most and which the taxpayer will want to retain long term. Particular problems arise where in fact both properties will be sold.

Example 12.11—Overlap and sandwich reliefs

Returning to the example of Jessica, she gives notice to treat the bungalow as her main residence from 1 July 2010 onwards. She serves the notice within the two-year period. She does in fact move there but keeps the flat until 31 December 2012 when she sells it.

The flat has not been her residence for two and a half years but there is no reduction in relief because that period of absence falls within the 36 months discussed at **12.12**. It is difficult to argue that Jessica lives at the bungalow for the better performance of her work, except perhaps because of the respite it offers; that might help with relief but this is not a 'sandwich' period because Jessica never moves back to the flat. None of the 'sandwich' reliefs can therefore apply but fortunately they are not needed. In the event of a later sale of the bungalow at a profit all of that gain is relieved as well.

Varying the notice

12.20 The taxpayer may vary a notice given under *s 222(5)(a)* by giving further notice. The statute does not require any minimum period during which a person must reside at a property in order to claim relief. This is recognised by HMRC: see CG64510. A tightening of the rules for 'flipping properties' may well be introduced in the future.

Example 12.12—Well-sheltered gains

Kylie, rather like Jessica, bought a studio flat on 1 January 2001. Like Jessica, she inherited on 1 July 2004 a sum of money which she immediately laid out on buying a second property, which she let until 31 December 2004. Both properties were appreciating in value and Kylie gave notice to treat the second property as her main residence with effect from 1 January 2005 though in fact she continued to live at the original property. The second property was, as at 1 January 2005, available as a residence to Kylie. It was vacant.

Kylie later varied the notice so as to treat the original property as her residence again with effect from 31 March 2005. The second property was then let until its sale on 30 June 2008, realising a gain which is treated as accruing evenly over time (monthly in this example). The second property has, both in fact and by virtue of the notice, been (for a time) Kylie's main residence. She has owned it for 48 months in all. During the first six months the property was no more than an investment. For three months it was Kylie's main residence under the terms of notice. For 36 months the property is treated as her main residence under *s 223(1)*. The other three months, from 1 April to 30 June 2004, qualify for relief under *s 223(4)* because the property has been Kylie's main residence and is let as residential accommodation.

As a result, 6/48 of the gain does not qualify for main residence relief but the remainder, 42/48, of the gain is covered. On the eventual sale of the original property main residence relief is available from 1 January 2001 to 31 December 2004 and from 1 April 2005 until sale. The period of non-residence is sandwiched between two periods of residence and does not exceed three years. It therefore qualifies to be treated as a period of occupation under *s 223(3)(a)*, so the entire period of ownership under the original property qualifies as occupation and therefore for relief.

12.21 Social mobility adds complications which impinge on seemingly unrelated transactions.

Example 12.13—Filing the notices

Lucy and Greg are artists. They met whilst working in Cornwall. Lucy had bought a small studio on 5 January 2001 whilst Greg bought a cottage on 10 January 2002. Both their careers and their relationship flourished and on 1 January 2006 they jointly bought a flat in Highgate, London thereafter spending the summer months in Cornwall producing work which they sold in London during the winter months. They married on 31 March 2008. Hurriedly completing tax returns for 2007/08 they each included, when lodging them on 31 January 2009 – Lucy – and 31 December 2008 – Greg – a notice to treat Highgate as main residence from two years before. In April 2008 they wished to sell one of the Cornwall properties to reduce the mortgage of Highgate.

The notices were sent with the tax returns. Greg's notice is effective but that of Lucy is out of time. Highgate has been available to her since 1 January 2007 so strictly she should have lodged her notice at least one month earlier. On the face of it, the question whether Lucy's main residence is the studio in Cornwall or Highgate cannot be determined by the notice and must instead be decided according to the facts. Given the relationship between Lucy and Greg, it might at least be arguable that, at some time after Greg's purchase of his cottage in Cornwall, by virtue of the relationship, Lucy had available to her a second residence. *Section 222(5)* does not require the taxpayer to own both residences for notice to be appropriate. That is not the outcome, see at **12.22**. The facts bring into play two extra considerations, set out below, respectively ESC D21 and the HMRC interpretation.

Special considerations in dual-residence cases

12.22 The current thinking of HMRC is now contained in CG64530–CG64536 where a person has available more than one residence. It was originally thought that any residence, including one's club in London, could trigger the need for an election but, since October 1994, the new advice has been to interpret *s 222(5)* purposively, within the context of that section as a whole. Since the relief relates to gains on property in which the taxpayer has a legal or equitable interest it is not appropriate to consider notice of election where the second residence is merely occupied under licence and the taxpayer has neither a legal nor an equitable interest in it.

Thus, in the example of Lucy and Greg above, the fact that Lucy might spend time at Greg's cottage would not of itself be reason to serve notice because, absent any agreement to the contrary, Lucy would have neither a legal nor an equitable interest in the cottage. The Capital Gains Manual specifically confirms that no notice of election under *s 222(5)*, which relies on a residence occupied only under licence and which is made after 16 October 1994, will be regarded as valid. Clearly, therefore, Lucy in the above example cannot use Greg's cottage as a peg on which to hang a late election in respect of her studio.

ESC D21 addresses the issue of late claims in the very reasonable situation where a taxpayer becomes entitled to an interest in a second property without realising that by so doing time will begin to run against him or her under *s 222(5)(a)*. Where:

- the interest in the second property – or in each property if there is more than one – has a negligible capital value on the open market; and
- the individual is unaware that a nomination could be made,

there is an extension of the time limit. This will arise, for example, where the interest in the second property is no more than the tenancy of the flat or is accommodation provided by an employer. In each case the nomination to treat the other property, being the one in which the taxpayer does have a substantial interest, as the main residence may be made within a reasonable time of when the taxpayer first became aware of a possibility of making an election and it will be effectively backdated as far as is necessary.

Marriage or civil partnership

12.23 Where each party to a relationship has a residence, each may claim main residence relief unless and until they begin to be treated as living together within the context of marriage or a civil partnership. There can be only one residence for both parties to a marriage or a civil partnership by virtue of *s 222(6)(a)*. They must therefore do the sums and decide which property is to be home. If they give notice in time they can make the decision otherwise it will be based on the facts.

Returning to the example of Lucy and Greg, from 31 March 2008 they will have two years, see CG64525, in which to decide whether their home together is to be Highgate, Lucy's Cornwall studio or Greg's Cornwall cottage. Applying the rules relating to the last 36 months of ownership, they may decide to make sure that any property that is to be sold has been their main residence for a period so that, at the very least, the last 36 months of ownership qualify for relief.

RESIDENCES HELD BY TRUSTEES OR PERSONAL REPRESENTATIVES

12.24 The general rule is that, where trustees hold residential property and a beneficiary is 'entitled to occupy it under the terms of the settlement', main residence relief will be available. Specifically, *s 225* operates by substituting a reference to the trustees for a reference to the individual in *ss 222–224* and by providing that a notice under *s 222(5)(a)*, where there is more than one residence, is to be a joint notice by the trustees and the beneficiary.

The enactment of *FA 2006* will, over time, limit the number of life interest settlements. However, the amendments introduced in *FA 2006, Sch 20* do not specifically refer to main residence relief. As will be seen at **12.26**, this change may affect a situation, which has given difficulty in the past, where IHT and CGT interact. In a straightforward case the relief is valuable.

Example 12.14—Council house sold at a profit

Norma, widowed, was encouraged by her daughter Olive to buy the council house in which Norma had lived for many years. The open market value was £60,000 but Norma could buy it for £30,000. Olive agreed to help with the cost. Norma was advised that, if she entered into a deed of trust at the same time as buying the property, that would not contravene the restrictions on resale of council houses.

She therefore signed a declaration of trust, the first essential term of which was that she was entitled to live in the house and to any rents and profits of the house until sale or until her death, whichever should first occur. Subject to that prior interest, she declared herself trustee of the property for her only daughter Olive absolutely. The house sold, many years later, for £180,000.

The gain was entirely sheltered by relief under *s 225* because Norma was entitled to occupy the residence under the terms of the settlement. Had the property been retained until Norma's death, relief would have been available not only under the provisions of main residence relief but, this being a pre-2006 situation, by virtue of the tax-free uplift on death allowed by *s 73(1)(a)*.

Discretionary trusts

12.25 Where a trust instrument gives the trustees a complete discretion over what benefit may be enjoyed by any of the objects of the trust the effect is that, until the trustees take action, none of the beneficiaries actually has a right to any of the trust assets. This principle is seen in the rather specialist circumstances of *Judge and another (personal representatives of Walden, dec'd) v HMRC* (2005) SpC 506 which concerned the wording of a poorly drawn will where it was held, on the particular facts, that the widow of the testator did not have an interest in possession in the former matrimonial home. The result was that the house was not treated as part of her estate for IHT, which was the main point at issue, but the collateral consequence was that, if there had been any increase in the value of the property during her period of occupation since her husband's death, no relief was available under *s 225*, because she did not have a right to occupy as required by that section.

The correct treatment of gains arising to trustees of discretionary trusts on properties occupied as residences by beneficiaries was decided in *Sansom v Peay* [1976] STC 494. It had previously been thought, see CG65443, that no beneficiary was entitled to occupy a dwelling house under the terms of the settlement, so as to benefit from *s 225*, unless the trust instrument specifically gave a right of occupation to that beneficiary.

The trust in *Sansom v Peay* was a discretionary one, allowing the trustees 'to permit any beneficiary to reside in any dwelling house or occupy any property or building … for the time being subject to the trust hereof upon such conditions … as the trustees … think fit'. Beneficiaries occupied a trust property and it was held that the occupations resulted from the exercise by the trustees of their powers under the deed. When the beneficiaries moved into the house they were entitled to stay there unless and until permission was withdrawn by the trustees. As at the date of the disposal of the house the beneficiaries were still entitled to occupy it and were occupying it under the terms of the trust deed. The gain was therefore sheltered by main residence relief.

Nil rate band discretionary will trusts

12.26 The issue will commonly arise in the context of will trusts. For a full discussion of the IHT implications the reader is referred to *Inheritance Tax 2010/11* (Bloomsbury Professional). The issue has been relieved to a considerable extent by the introduction of the transferable nil rate band, but many situations still exist under the old rules that cannot be disturbed without significant IHT cost. In outline, there are many families whose main wealth is the family home, the value of which exceeds the nil rate band for IHT (£325,000 for 2010/11). Under the law as it was before *FA 2008, s 10* and *Sch 4* any transfer between husband and wife was exempt, which it still is, but on the death of the survivor of them, any value in excess of the nil rate band attracted a charge to IHT at 40%. That has now changed. With a view to using the nil rate band on the first death, wills used to be drawn which gave the nil rate band on discretionary trusts to beneficiaries including the surviving spouse, commonly with residue to that surviving spouse absolutely. The hope was that using the nil rate band on each death would combine to exempt the family property from IHT.

The argument ran that, where the house was occupied as tenants in common, each joint owner could occupy the entirety of it for the rest of their life, regardless of the fact that the other half of the property may have been given away. This argument was not always accepted by HMRC from the point of view of IHT. Circumstances might suggest that, even though the trustees were under no obligation to do so, they had actually so exercised their powers under the trust instrument that they had, in effect, created the situation that arose in *Sansom v Peay* and had therefore given the surviving spouse an interest in possession in the half of the property that that spouse did not own, with the result that, on the second death, the whole of the house becomes subject to IHT and the tax planning was thrown away.

Where the trustees could satisfy HMRC, from the standpoint of IHT, that in fact they had not exercised their powers in such a way as to grant the surviving spouse an interest in possession, the interest in the property that is held within the discretionary trust might escape IHT but, on any disposal of the property at a gain, CGT will become due because main residence relief is not available. Under the new rules, trustees will want to use their powers to create an immediate post-death interest in favour of the surviving spouse, but if more than two years have elapsed since the death that will be outside *IHTA 1984, s 144*, so the trustees must 'stick with' the original terms of the will.

Example 12.15—Hit for CGT but not for IHT

Percy was married to Prudence. Their house was worth £360,000 and held by them as tenants in common in equal shares. Percy died on 5 April 2001, having by his will left the nil rate band on discretionary trusts for the benefit of his children, further issue and Prudence. At the time of his death the nil rate band was £234,000. His estate comprised the house and cash of £50,000, all of which passed to the trustees. There was no residue and no IHT was payable.

The trustees then held the half of the house on discretionary trusts, but took no steps to grant Prudence any right of occupation of it. On 17 May 2010 the house was sold for £500,000. On her share of the property Prudence was able to take her gain tax free. The gain of £70,000 on half of the house within the discretionary trust is, however, subject to CGT (after allowance for the reduced annual exemption available to the trustees).

On the death of Prudence shortly after the sale, the matter is reopened for IHT purposes but it appears that the trustees have not handed over to her any part of the proceeds of sale that they received nor have they given Prudence benefit out of the trust fund. They insisted that she pay all outgoings, to save any burden on the small liquid trust fund. It also appears that they have met from time to time to consider their powers, so the trust has not just been 'in limbo'. The result for IHT purposes is that the estate of Prudence will be limited to her own share of the proceeds of sale of the house and to any other assets that she has and will not be deemed to include the half share in the house that sits within the discretionary trust.

Example 12.16—Hit the other way

Contrast the result in **Example 12.15** with the situation as it applied before 9 October 2007, see *FA 2008, s 10* and *Sch 4,* where the trustees have either taken no steps at all since Percy's death or can be seen positively to have exercised their powers in favour of Prudence with regard to the house as, for example, taking unequivocal steps to show that they are unwilling to sell the house whilst Prudence is still alive even though other beneficiaries are in urgent need of money.

In such a case the argument by HMRC that Prudence effectively has an interest in possession in the half of the house that sits within the trust is very likely to succeed. The tax consequence is that, on a sale as already described, there will be no CGT. However, the trust fund, here meaning the part that is represented by the share in the house rather than the cash, will be treated as agreeable with the estate of Prudence on her death. This is unlikely to be a problem under the new IHT rules, as Prudence is likely to have the benefit of Percy's transferable nil rate band.

Disregarding expenses and the like, in the event of the death of Prudence at any time in the seven years after the time when her interest ceased, which will probably be the date of sale, the value of the half of the house in the trust will be added to her free estate to establish the chargeable transfer on death.

The IHT charge, after taking account of the nil rate band (possibly enhanced under the transfer rules) is at 40% of the capital value. The CGT charge would have been at 40%, but only on the gain and would have been subject to reliefs. It used nearly always to be better to structure these transactions so that the tax paid was CGT rather than IHT. The downside is of course that CGT becomes payable as soon as there is a disposal of the property, which is likely to reduce the money then available for alternative accommodation. The transfer rules for IHT will remove much of the difficulty, though many lawyers advise retaining the nil rate trust for other reasons, including defence of the estate from care fees.

Estates in administration

12.27 Quite often there will be a substantial increase in the value of a dwelling house from the date of the death of its owner to the date on which the property can be sold. Delays can arise where there is a dispute about the terms of a will or where a claim is made under the *Inheritance (Provision for Family and Dependants) Act 1975* or where, quite simply, everything takes rather longer than it should.

Valuation issues

12.28 In the simple situation of a property that becomes vacant on death and is not thereafter occupied until sale, the normal rules will apply, as set out in **3.6**. However, so deep-rooted in the consciousness of the British public is the idea that a gain on a house is tax free that families will go to considerable lengths, on the disposal of a house, to avoid suffering any tax on it. It is often fondly imagined that the property can, for probate and IHT purposes, be valued at an artificially low level and that it can later be sold for much more and tax free.

That idea exhibits not only a cavalier attitude to the payment of tax, but some fundamental errors of tax law. First, there is no such thing as 'probate value', meaning some artificially low value approximating to the lowest price that anyone could accept in the open market further discounted by the costs of sale. The correct value for IHT purposes, as is explained in *Inheritance Tax 2009/10* (Bloomsbury Professional), is 'the price which the property might reasonably be expected to fetch if sold in the open market': see *ITA 1984, s 160*. That value is, as a general rule, imported into the CGT code by *s 274* which provides that, where the value at the date of death has been 'ascertained' for the purposes of IHT, that value is the market value of the asset at the date of death for CGT purposes, with the knock-on effect that under *s 62* it is the value at which the personal representatives are deemed to acquire the property as at the date of death of the deceased. *FA 2008, Sch 4 para 8* amends *s 274* so that it applies only for the purpose of the application of IHT to the chargeable estate, not to the estate which, by virtue of the transferable nil rate band, escapes IHT. This provision takes effect from 6 April 2008 rather than from 9 October 2007.

Quick sale

12.29 Naturally, if sale on the open market takes place quite soon after death, this is a strong guide as to market value at the earlier date. If, however, the value is established as at the date of death on a proper basis and with full disclosure and a substantial time elapses until sale it will not be necessary to substitute the eventual sale price for the probate value at date of death.

In this context, some 'hope' value should be included in the value at date of death if there is, say, a potential building plot. The case of *Prosser v IRC* (DET/1/2000) suggests that hope value is no more than 25% of the full development value.

Example 12.17—IHT followed by CGT

Quentin died on 4 April 2010. His estate comprised his home and other assets that were exactly matched by liabilities. The fair open market value of the house at date of death was £335,000. The nil rate band at that date was £325,000 so IHT was payable of £4,000, being 40% of the excess. Probate is obtained quickly and, despite the general market trend, the property is sold on 3 August 2010 for £362,000 less expenses (inclusive of VAT) of 3%.

CGT is calculated as follows:

	£
Net proceeds of sale	351,140
Less probate value	(335,000)
Less allowance available under SP 2/04	
(band C) at 1%	(3,350)
Gain after allowance	12,790

	£
Deduct annual allowance*	(10,100)
Taxable gain	2,690
Tax at 28%	753

* This being a disposal within the tax year in which death occurred or one of the two years following, the executors may claim the full allowance of £10,100.

Ongoing residence by major beneficiary

12.30 It sometimes happens that the main asset of an estate is a house that is given by its owner on death to someone who has been living with the owner prior to death. In the past a tax liability could arise on the disposal of such a property during the administration of the estate and only by concession was it possible to shelter any of the gain using main residence relief. The position has been made statutory by *s 225A*. For the relief to apply there are two conditions. The first may be called the 'permanent dwelling house' condition. It is that, both before and after the death of the deceased, the property in question 'was the only or main residence of one or more individuals'.

The second condition, which may be called 'main beneficiary' condition, is that the individual (or group of individuals) who was/were living in the property before and after the relevant death is/are entitled to at least 3/4 of the proceeds of sale of the property in question. The entitlement may thus be shared among several beneficiaries if they can all show that they were resident before and after the death and that they have a 'relevant entitlement', meaning an entitlement as a legatee of the person who has died or an entitlement to an interest in possession in the whole or some part of the net proceeds of the disposal of the house.

Section 225A(4) defines 'net proceeds of disposal' as the proceeds realised by the personal representatives less incidental costs as are allowable on computing the gain that would otherwise arise to the personal representatives, assuming, whether or not this be the case, that no part of the proceeds of sale is needed to meet liabilities of the estate (including liability to IHT). Relief is available only if the personal representatives claim it.

Example 12.18—Requirements not satisfied

Robert, a widower whose late wife had used her nil rate band in gifts to her children, had at the date of his death on 10 April 2010, a house worth £300,000 and net cash of £100,000 after all liabilities. His son (and daughter-in-law) moved in with Robert to look after him after his wife died. They continued to live there after his death. Robert's will leaves his estate equally between the son who was living with him and his daughter.

Relief under *s 225* is not available. The estate benefits from the nil rate band of £325,000 but the excess, £75,000, attracts IHT of £30,000. The net estate to divide between the son and the daughter is £370,000, £185,000 each. Even though the son and his wife might like to take the house, if necessary providing money by way of equalisation, they are outside the requirements of *s 225A(3)(b)* because their entitlement under the will is less than 75% of the proceeds of the disposal, if it were now to take place, of the house.

Example 12.19—A better solution

The facts are as in **Example 12.18** except that Robert, in recognition of the care provided by his daughter-in-law, had given her an equal share of residue with her husband and sister-in-law. The figures would work out differently. On his death the daughter would be entitled, net of IHT, to £123,333 whereas the son and daughter-in-law between them would be entitled to £246,667. That is more than 75% of the value of the house, unless (somewhat unusually in the present market) it has risen substantially in value since the death. Relief may therefore be available.

Property as asset of beneficiary

12.31 Relief under *s 225A* is not very common because in many circumstances there will be a simpler solution. If the value of the estate is sufficient, and liquidity available, for a property in the estate to be transferred to a beneficiary outright there will be no need for *s 225A* relief. The beneficiary will acquire the property as 'legatee' within the meaning of *s 64(3)* and will, on acquiring the property, step into the shoes of the personal representatives and be deemed to have acquired it at probate value. If that beneficiary then occupies the property, giving notice as appropriate if already the owner of another property, main residence relief will be available under general principles and there will be no need for *s 225A* relief.

There is, however, often a problem: IHT. For an asset to be dealt with, and any gain realised, by the beneficiary in this way the asset must first be placed unreservedly at the disposal of the beneficiary. Appropriation 'in book form', as sometimes suggested by exempt beneficiaries, is not in truth appropriation at all. The desire to avoid the trouble and fees involved in 'doing the job properly' can threaten the relief. In theory at least, the house could be assented to the beneficiary subject to a lien or charge in favour of the personal representatives for unpaid IHT but that situation is far from ideal, especially in the light of the principles seen on *Howarth's Executors v IRC* [1997] STC (SCD) 162 relating to accountability of executors for tax after parting with estate assets. A compromise might be to assent to the vesting in the beneficiary of a share only in the house equal to the proportion that can be released free of any lien for tax. The rest of the gain would then sit (and be taxed) in the estate, but that might be better than tax on the whole gain and in any case the total exemption would increase.

ANTI-AVOIDANCE

Washing the gain through a trust

12.32 The discussion of the relief in this chapter has touched on various minor anti-avoidance provisions. The main provision is *s 226A*, which applies to transactions on or after 9 December 2003 and which was introduced by *FA 2004*. The background to this legislation was the perceived abuse of 'washing the holiday cottage gain'.

Example 12.20—The 'mischief'

A family owns a main residence and a country property which had been acquired cheaply many years earlier. The children become too old to want to take holidays with their parents and consider the holiday cottage far too uncool to take holidays there with their friends. It is time for the cottage to be sold.

Commonly the arrangement was that mother and father would settle the cottage on discretionary trusts, holding over the accrued gain under *s 260*. There were then two ways to proceed. The tax planning required one of the children to be over the age of 18 (but preferably unemployed or otherwise free for a reasonable time to live in the country cottage).

Under one version of the scheme, the property would then be appointed out entirely to that child and the gain held over under *s 260*. The child would occupy the property as his or her main residence and soon afterwards sell it, claiming main residence relief on the gain that then arose, which would include the gain that had been held over on the transfer of the property into the trust and any further gain that had arisen and was likewise held over, with the previous held-over gain, on removal of the property from the trust. Thus, within the space of a few months, the gain arising on the holiday cottage could be washed. The only disadvantage with this plan was that the entire proceeds of sale ended legally, if not actually, in the hands of the child.

A variant of the scheme involved the appointment by the trustees of an interest in possession in the cottage to the beneficiary child. Some time later the trustees would sell the property and, because it had been the residence of a beneficiary entitled to occupy it under the terms of the settlement, part of the gain would be exempt under *s 225*. It did not matter too much that the trustees had not owned the property for very long; the period of ownership before the appointment of the life interest to the child would not qualify for main residence relief but, where the gain held over was substantial, the ability to shelter most of it by main residence relief made the exercise very worthwhile. Under this version, the money ended up in the 'right' place.

The statutory change

12.33 *Section 226A* nullified the scheme. The section is closely targeted. It applies where:

- main residence relief would otherwise apply to a gain or part gain accruing to an individual or trustees on the eventual disposal of a property;
- on the later disposal the amount of the gain would be reduced but for the effect of *s 223*; and
- the reduction would result, directly or indirectly, from a hold-over claim under *s 260* at an earlier stage in the arrangement.

Where a claim to hold over a gain under *s 260* was made on the earlier transaction (or any of them if more than one), main residence relief will not be available on the later disposal of the property. Where a hold-over claim is made under *s 260* after the later disposal of the property and provision just described does not apply, it is to be assumed for the purposes of CGT that main residence relief never was available in relation to the gain or part gain arising on the later disposal. The relief, if claimed, is withdrawn and adjustments are made that give effect to the anti-avoidance legislation.

It is possible for the taxpayer to be wise after the event. Where a gain was held over under *s 260* and it now appears that it would have been better to have relied on main residence relief and to have paid the tax on the earlier gain, the earlier claim for hold-over relief can be revoked and, if revoked, it is as if the claim had never been made.

There are exceptions from *s 226A* in connection with maintenance funds for heritage property. This is a complicated topic and readers are referred to specialist works on the subject.

Transitional relief

12.34 At the time of its introduction, *s 226A* was widely seen to be retrospective. The scheme described at **Example 12.20** had been in quite common use and it is fair to say that taxation advisers were taken by surprise. Their indignation, righteous or otherwise, was not really defused by the transitional provisions of *FA 2004, Sch 22, para 8*, inserting extra provisions into *s 226A*. The effect was to confer limited transitional relief where the held-over disposal occurred before 10 December 2003.

The residence in question was deemed not to have been the only or main residence of the individual from 10 December 2003 and any gain was apportioned between the time before that date and the time after. The gain that was time-apportioned included both the held-over gain and any later gain even though all the held-over gain had accrued before 10 December 2003. The effect was that, unless action was taken very quickly after 10 December 2003 to ameliorate the situation, a very large proportion of the gain fell into the tax net. The difficulty for advisers at the time was that they had no legislation to go on, only the scant details in the Pre-budget Report of the Chancellor in December 2003. This was unfair: effectively advisers did not know what the law was until about August 2004, and by then it was too late to bring structures within acceptable bounds.

Effect of the Finance Act 2006

Trusts of houses

12.35 The subject of the *Finance Act 2006* changes affecting settlements is discussed in **Chapter 8**. Few major changes of principle effecting main residence relief were introduced by *FA 2006, Sch 20*. The incidental changes have been those that arise from the way in which trusts are now treated. The fact that, with virtually no exceptions, the creation of a life-time trust will now be a chargeable transfer increases the number of occasions on which it will be possible to hold over gains under *s 260*; but in the light of the discussion of the effect of *s 226A* above, the ability to hold over a gain into a new trust is of limited value in a context of residences.

There are other changes introduced by *FA 2006* which may be relevant to trusts of houses, not because of main residence relief but because of those occasions where, on death, there is effectively a tax-free uplift. Thus, *s 72* is amended by *s 72(1A)–(1C)*, cutting down the availability of uplift on death so that it applies only to an immediate post-death interest (IPDI), a transitional serial interest (TSI) or a bereaved minor's trust (BMT) or disabled trusts.

DEPENDENT RELATIVE RELIEF

12.36 This relief has been left until last because, after 19 years, it is now seldom encountered in practice, though very valuable where it applies, especially with the loss of taper and indexation reliefs. The requirements are that, on or before 5 April 1988, an interest in a dwelling house or part of a dwelling house owned by the taxpayer was the sole residence of a dependent relative of that taxpayer and was provided rent free and without any other consideration. For this purpose 'dependent relative' means (see *s 226(6)*):

- any relative of the taxpayer or of his spouse or civil partner who is incapacitated by old age or infirmity from maintaining himself; or
- the mother of the taxpayer or spouse or civil partner who, whether or not incapacitated, is widowed or living apart from her husband, or who is a single woman in consequence of disillusion or annulment of marriage.

Relief is available only if claimed. If allowed, the 'dower house' that forms the subject matter of the claim is treated as if it had been the only or main residence of the taxpayer for as long as the dependent relative lived there and regardless of the fact that the taxpayer may have had another residence qualifying for relief. There is further apportionment so that a period of ownership after the 'dower house' ceases to be the sole residence of the dependent relative is disregarded and qualifies for no relief. The taxpayer may claim relief in respect of only one dower house at a time.

The chief difficulty in making a claim to this relief is likely to be one of proof. Arrangements between family members may have been informal. It may be difficult to show that the residence was 'provided' by the taxpayer, particularly where part of the funding of the residence arose on the sale of the relative's home and the whole scheme was intended to save the relative's estate from IHT or care fees.

BREAKDOWN AND SEPARATION

12.37 A common feature of the breakdown of marriage or of civil partnership is the disposal, by one party, of an interest in the residence that was formerly shared. Timing is everything, because a disposal between the parties that takes place within the tax year of separation is treated by *s 58* as if made on a no gain, no loss basis, whilst the more usual situation, where negotiations drag into the following or even a later year, triggers a disposal that may attract tax.

Example 12.21—Swift justice

Selena, the daughter of wealthy parents and successful in her own right, tires of Richard, the accountant of moderate means and abilities to whom she had been married for three years. They bought their London flat for £500,000 on marriage, 75% with Selena's money, Richard taking a mortgage for the balance. It had been worth much more, but thanks to the credit crunch is worth only £800,000 at Christmas 2010.

It is agreed that Richard will leave the flat. Selena pays him £200,000 to go, completing the arrangement on 13 March 2011. This is treated as the disposal by Richard of his share to Selena for £125,000 and his true gains of £75,000 are sheltered, not by main residence relief but by *s 58*. Selena is treated as acquiring Richard's share at an undervalue, but that does not worry her: even if she later sells that share of the flat for more than the deemed acquisition value of £125,000 that gain will be sheltered by main residence relief.

Example 12.22—The more usual situation on divorce

Jenny and Paul bought their house in East Anglia for £175,000 four years ago. Paul was made redundant and had to travel 90 miles per day to find work, staying away for part of each week. They drifted apart and finally separated in October 2009. Negotiations became bitter and finance for any settlement from any commercial lender became impossible by March 2010.

With help from her parents Jenny bought Paul's half share, after allowing for the mortgage, for £100,000. The transaction is at market value anyway, but would be treated as taking place at that value by *ss 17* and *18* because they are connected persons. Paul has made a gain of £12,500. However, after apportioning this over his period of ownership and claiming exemptions, Paul's gain escapes tax.

Section 225B (formerly Extra-statutory Concession D6) recognises that money may well be tight and that divorce may result in a *Mesher* order, so called from the case of that name, under which the house remains in the ownership of both parties and is not sold until the children are grown up. However, this will apply only to shelter a 'solo' gain, so if the 'dispossessed' party later acquires another residence the relief is curtailed.

Example 12.23—Life moves on

Ginny and Peter were in a similar situation to Jenny and Paul except that Ginny's parents could not help finance the arrangement and in any case there was a daughter, Emily, aged seven. They therefore agreed that the house would continue to be owned by them jointly as a home for Ginny and Emily until Emily turns 18.

At around the time Emily is 16, Ginny's friend Gordon finally moves in. Emily soon moves out and, after some difficulty, Gordon buys Peter's share of the house for much more than Peter paid for it. Peter has been in rented accommodation so has had no alternative residence. *Section 225B* gives Peter main residence relief on the whole of his gain, even though for several years he has not been living at the house.

The situation is more complicated where, in situations like the example above, the non-resident spouse has in fact acquired another residence and has elected to treat it as his main residence. Relief under *s 225B* does not, under its terms, then apply. *Section 225B* does not refer to any form of apportionment.

Strictly, HMRC regard the *Mesher* arrangement as creating a settlement of the entire house and therefore a disposal to the trustees which is an occasion of charge under *s 70*. Thus the interest of the trustees is exempt, not under *s 222* but under *s 225*. When the deemed trust expires, as at Emily's eighteenth birthday in the previous example, there is a deemed disposal by the trustees. The share of each spouse attracts a charge under *s 71* because each now becomes absolutely entitled to a share as against the (deemed) trustees but the entire gain qualifies for main residence relief under *s 225*. However, if there had, in a situation such as the example quoted above, been no Gordon but there had been a delay in selling after Emily was 18, any gain that might arise could attract tax.

For houses of moderate value the *Mesher* order often works well, but it is a settlement for IHT purposes so where the values are high the parties may seek other structures such as charges over the property in favour of the non-resident party.

Chapter 13

Hold-over relief for gifts

INTRODUCTION

13.1 The gift of a chargeable asset, or the sale of a chargeable asset 'otherwise than at arm's length' (see **13.2**), is treated for CGT purposes as a disposal at market value. See **3.6** regarding the market value rule (but note the special rules explained at **3.62** for transfers between spouses and civil partners). The person acquiring the asset is treated as acquiring it at its market value.

Two forms of hold-over relief are available to defer the CGT liability until there is a disposal by the transferee:

(a) hold-over relief for gifts of business assets, see **13.2** onwards (*TCGA 1992, s 165*); and

(b) hold-over relief for gifts on which inheritance tax is either immediately chargeable, or not chargeable because of a particular exemption, see **13.37** onwards (*TCGA 1992, s 260*).

The relief in (b) takes precedence over the relief in (a). A more detailed discussion of both of these reliefs can be found in *Capital Gains Tax Roll-over, Hold-over and Deferral Reliefs 2010/11* (Bloomsbury Professional).

Certain gifts are exempt from CGT (see **1.8**), so that hold-over relief is not necessary. Where neither an exemption nor any form of hold-over relief applies, it may be possible for the CGT due on the gift to be paid in instalments (see **3.34**). If the transferor does not pay the tax, it may be recovered from the transferee (*TCGA 1992, ss 281, 282*).

GIFTS OF BUSINESS ASSETS (SECTION 165)

13.2 Where an individual (or a trustee in some cases, see **13.24**) disposes of an asset otherwise than under a bargain at arm's length, any gain accruing may be deferred where the conditions in *TCGA 1992, s 165* are met. The amount held over reduces the transferee's acquisition (or base) cost used in calculating the gain on the subsequent disposal of the same asset. The capital gain is, in effect, transferred to the person who receives the asset.

'Otherwise than under a bargain at arm's length' encompasses outright gifts, and sales which include some gratuitous intention on behalf of one of the parties, so will generally be at less than market value. HMRC regard a bargain as made at arm's length if it is a normal commercial transaction and all the parties involved try to obtain the best deal for themselves in their particular circumstances (CG14541).

The date of an outright gift is the date on which it becomes effective. The date of a sale at a price below market value is, broadly, the date of the contract – see **2.8** regarding the time of a disposal.

Conditions

13.3 Hold-over relief is generally available where:

(a) an individual ('the transferor') makes a disposal otherwise than under a bargain at arm's length of an asset mentioned in **13.5**;

(b) both the transferor and the person acquiring the asset ('the transferee') make a claim to relief;

(c) the transferee is UK resident (see **13.17**).

There is no requirement for the transferee to make a claim if the transferee is the trustee (or a body of trustees) of settled property (*TCGA 1992, s 165(1)*).

Exceptions

13.4 Relief is not available:

- where relief would be available under *TCGA 1992, s 260* (see **13.37**);
- on a transfer of shares or securities to a company (*TCGA 1992, s 165(3)(ba)*);
- where the transfer is to a foreign-controlled company (see **13.21**);
- where the transfer is to a dual-resident trust (see **13.22**);
- where the transfer is into a settlor-interested trust (see **13.25**); or
- where a gain is deemed to accrue on the disposal of qualifying corporate bonds which were acquired in exchange for shares (*TCGA 1992, s 165(3)(c)*).

Qualifying assets

13.5 An asset may be the subject of a hold-over relief claim if it falls within one of (a) to (d) below:

(a) an asset (or an interest in an asset) used for the purposes of a trade, profession or vocation carried on by (i) the transferor (either alone or in partnership), or (ii) his personal company, or (iii) a member of a trading group whose holding company is his personal company (*TCGA 1992, s 165(2)*);

(b) shares or securities of a trading company, or of the holding company of a trading group, where either (i) the trading company or holding company is the transferor's personal company, or (ii) the shares or securities are not listed on a recognised stock exchange (shares listed on the alternative investment market (AIM) being regarded as not listed) (*TCGA 1992, s 165(2)*);

(c) farmland and buildings that would be eligible for inheritance tax agricultural property relief (*TCGA 1992, s 165(5), Sch 7, pt 1*); and

(d) certain settled property disposed of by the trustees of a settlement (see **13.24**) (*TCGA 1992, s 165(5), Sch 7*).

HMRC regard the condition in (a) as meaning that the asset has to have been in use for the trade, etc just before it was gifted (CG66950). See **13.8** regarding partial relief where an asset other than shares has not been used wholly for the purposes of the trade, etc during the entire period of ownership.

Operation of *TCGA 1992, s 165* relief

13.6 The effect of this relief, which must be claimed (see **13.32**), is that the 'held-over gain' (see below) is deducted from both:

- the chargeable gain (if any) that would otherwise accrue to the transferor; and
- the consideration which the transferee would otherwise be regarded as having given for the acquisition of the asset (or the shares or securities) (*TCGA 1992, s 165(4)*).

The 'held-over gain' on a disposal, where this relief is not restricted by reference to actual consideration received for the disposal, is the chargeable gain that would have accrued in the absence of hold-over relief (*TCGA 1992, s 165(6)*). The relief may be restricted where consideration is received (see **13.7**) or as described in **13.8**.

Example 13.1

Anthony has carried on a business as a sole trader since June 2001. His only chargeable asset is goodwill, which is now worth £150,000 although he paid only £10,000 for it.

He gives the business to his daughter Mary in August 2010, and they jointly claim hold-over relief under *TCGA 1992, s 165*. There is no actual consideration, so the whole of the gain accruing is held over. Anthony's gain of £140,000 is therefore reduced to nil, and Mary's allowable expenditure on any future disposal is reduced from £150,000 to £10,000. See **13.36** regarding the interaction between hold-over relief and other CGT reliefs including entrepreneurs' relief and taper relief.

Example 13.2

Barnaby purchased shares in Beach Plc, a company quoted on AIM, in May 1999 for £50,000. In September 2009, when they are worth £160,000, he settles the shares in a discretionary trust which is not settlor-interested (see **13.25**). Barnaby claims hold-over relief.

The held-over gain is £110,000 and the trustees' allowable expenditure is reduced from £160,000 to £50,000. The trustees sell the shares for £180,000 in April 2010. The gain accruing on their disposal is £180,000 – £50,000 = £130,000.

Consideration received

13.7 It may be difficult to ascertain whether consideration has been received where the transaction has involved an exchange of assets. Where land subject to a mortgage is transferred, and the transferee takes on responsibility for the mortgage, the amount of debt outstanding at the date of the transfer is treated as the actual consideration.

Where there is actual consideration for the disposal the calculation of the held-over gain becomes:

- the 'unrelieved gain' on the disposal (ie the chargeable gain that would have accrued in the absence of hold-over relief), *less*
- the excess of the actual consideration for the disposal over the allowable deductions (under *TCGA 1992, s 38*) in computing the gain (*TCGA 1992, s 165(7)*).

Where the value of the actual consideration does not exceed the allowable deductions no adjustment is necessary.

Example 13.3

The facts are as in **Example 13.1** but Mary pays £40,000 for the goodwill. The held-over gain becomes £110,000:

		Gain
	£	£
Unrelieved gain		140,000
less		
consideration received	40,000	
less allowable expenditure on the goodwill	(10,000)	(30,000)
Held-over gain		110,000

Therefore, Anthony's gain is reduced from £140,000 to £30,000 (being the consideration received less his allowable expenditure) and Mary's allowable expenditure on any future disposal is £150,000 – £110,000 = £40,000.

Partial relief

13.8 Hold-over relief is restricted if an asset, other than shares, has not been used wholly for the purposes of the trade, etc during the entire period of ownership, or if part of a building or structure was so used and part was not. In the case of shares, the gain eligible for hold-over relief may be restricted if the company's chargeable assets include non-business assets (see **13.11**).

Asset not used for trade throughout period of ownership

13.9 If the asset was not used for the purposes of the trade, etc throughout the transferor's period of ownership, the held-over gain is reduced by multiplying it by the fraction A/B, where:

- A is the number of days in that period of ownership during which the asset was so used; and
- B is the number of days in the entire period of ownership.

There is no restriction under this rule where the asset would qualify for inheritance tax agricultural property relief (*TCGA 1992, Sch 7, paras 4, 5*).

Partial use for the trade of a building or structure

13.10 If the asset disposed of is a building or structure, and during the transferor's period of ownership (or any 'substantial part' of that period) only a part of the building or structure was used for the purposes of the trade, etc, the gain is apportioned on a just and reasonable basis and only the fraction of the gain apportioned to the part of the building so used is held over. Again, there is no restriction where the asset would qualify for inheritance tax agricultural property relief.

Where both this restriction and the time restriction in **13.9** are appropriate, HMRC consider that the time restriction should be applied first (*TCGA 1992, Sch 7, paras 4, 6*; CG66952).

Example 13.4

Julian bought a shop, with a flat above, for £80,000. He gave the property to his son James five years later, having used the shop for the purpose of his trade throughout the last three years of ownership. Market values at the time of the gift are agreed at £180,000 for the whole property and £120,000 for the shop. The proportion of Julian's gain which is available for hold-over relief is calculated as follows:

		Gain
	£	£
Gain on whole property	180,000 – 80,000	100,000
Time restriction	3/5 years × 100,000	(60,000)
Partial business use restriction: value of shop to value of whole building:	120/180 × 60,000	40,000
Total held-over gain		40,000
Chargeable gain:	100,000 – 40,000	60,000

If the period of non-business use had occurred at the end of Julian's ownership period, HMRC would challenge Julian's right to make the hold-over claim, on the basis that the asset was not in use in the trade just before it was transferred (CG66950). This business use requirement is not interpreted so strictly for roll-over relief claims, where business use of the asset can cease before the transfer date (see **14.26**).

Shares: restriction for chargeable non-business assets

13.11 Where the disposal consists of shares in a company which was the transferor's personal company (see **13.12**), or he was able to exercise at least 25% of the voting rights of that company, both at any time within 12 months of the disposal date, the hold-over relief may be restricted (*TCGA 1992, Sch 7, para 7*).

The held-over gain is reduced by multiplying it by the fraction A/B, where:

- A is the market value of the company's (or group's) 'chargeable assets' that are 'business assets' (see definitions below); and
- B is the market value of all the company's (or group's) chargeable assets including non-business assets.

In both cases the market value is taken at the date of the disposal. For the purpose of this restriction, an asset is a business asset if it is used for the purposes of a trade, profession or vocation carried on by the company (or member of the group). An asset is a chargeable asset if, on a disposal of it, a gain accruing to the company (or member of the group) would be a chargeable gain.

In the case of a disposal of shares in the holding company of a trading group, a holding by one member of the group of the ordinary share capital of another member is not counted as a chargeable asset. If the holding company (X) does not own, directly or indirectly, all of the ordinary share capital of a 51% subsidiary (Y), the value of company Y's chargeable assets is reduced by multiplying it by the fraction A/B, where:

- A is the amount of company Y's ordinary share capital owned directly or indirectly by company X; and
- B is the whole of company Y's share capital.

Definitions

Personal company

13.12 A company is an individual's 'personal company' if he is able to exercise at least 5% of the voting rights in the company (*TCGA 1992, s 165(8)*). This is not the same definition of 'personal company' which is used for entrepreneurs' relief (*TCGA 1992, s 169S(3)*), (see **11.10**).

Trading company

13.13 Broadly, a company is a trading company if its business does not include non-trading activities 'to a substantial extent'. 'Holding company', 'trading company' and 'trading group' take the definitions given for entrepreneurs' relief purposes (see **11.12**). All three definitions are now brought together in *TCGA 1992, s 165A.*

Trade

13.14 'Trade', 'profession' and 'vocation' have the same meaning as in the Income Tax Acts. 'Trade' is taken to include the occupation of woodlands managed by the occupier on a commercial basis and with a view to the realisation of profits, both for the general purposes of hold-over relief and in determining whether a company is a trading company (*TCGA 1992, ss 165(8), (9)*). 'Trade' for this purpose also includes the commercial letting of furnished holiday accommodation (*TCGA 1992, s 241(3)*).

Relief for inheritance tax

13.15 Where the transfer of an asset is subject to both IHT and a claim to hold-over relief under *TCGA 1992, s 165,* the transferee may receive relief for the IHT paid when calculating the gain arising on latter disposal of the same asset. Although the deduction for the IHT paid cannot exceed the amount of the chargeable gain before the deduction.

The deduction is adjusted if the IHT liability is varied after it has been taken into account in this way, and in the event that a disposal which is a potentially exempt transfer for inheritance tax purposes becomes a chargeable transfer (*TCGA 1992, s 165(10), (11)*).

Example 13.5

In July 2010 Barbara sold a plot of land for £500,000. Her father gave her the land in March 1993 when it was valued at £150,000. He died shortly after the gift and inheritance tax of £60,000 was payable. He had purchased the land in May 1982 for £40,000. The held-over gain and Barbara's chargeable gain on the 2010/11 disposal are computed as follows:

Held-over gain on gift in March 1993:	£	£
Market value in March 1993		150,000
Cost in May 1982		(40,000)
Unindexed gain		110,000
Indexation to March 1993 £40,000 × 0.707		(28,280)
Held-over gain		81,720
2010/11		
Gain on Barbara's disposal:		
Sale proceeds, July 2009		500,000
Market value in March 1993	150,000	
Less gain held over	(81,720)	(68,280)
		431,720
Deduction for inheritance tax		(60,000)
Chargeable gain		371,720

Separation, divorce or dissolution of civil partnership

13.16 A transfer between spouses or civil partners is generally made at a no gain, no loss (see **3.62**), but not if it takes place after the end of the tax year in which the parties separate. Hold-over relief may be available to relieve the gain, in either of the following circumstances:

- a disposal from one spouse or civil partner to the other after the end of the tax year in which they separate but prior to the divorce decree absolute (or prior to the final dissolution order); or
- a transfer made under a court order, whether or not by consent, after divorce or dissolution.

HMRC consider that such a disposal or transfer is, where there is no recourse to the courts, usually made in exchange for a surrender by the transferee of rights to obtain alternative financial provision. The value of the rights surrendered would represent actual consideration, reducing the potential hold-over relief claim to nil. However, hold-over relief may be available if the parties can demonstrate a 'substantial gratuitous element' in the transfer.

The position where certain court orders are made is viewed differently. A court order may reflect 'the exercise by the court of its independent statutory jurisdiction' rather than being the consequence of a party to the proceedings surrendering alternative rights in return for assets. In such a case HMRC consider that the spouse or civil partner to whom the assets are transferred does not give actual consideration for the transfer (CG67190–CG67192).

Gifts to non-residents

13.17 Hold-over relief under *TCGA 1992, s 165* is denied where the transferee is:

(a) neither resident nor ordinarily resident in the UK (see **5.10**); or

(b) an individual who is resident or ordinarily resident in the UK, where double taxation relief arrangements have the effect that he is regarded as resident in another territory and he would not be liable in the UK to tax on a gain arising on a disposal of the asset (*TCGA 1992, s 166*).

Emigration of transferee

13.18 Where hold-over relief has been given under either *TCGA 1992, s 165* or *TCGA 1992, s 260* on a disposal of an asset to an individual, and that individual becomes neither resident nor ordinarily resident in the UK at a time when he has not disposed of the asset (see **13.19**), a chargeable gain equal to the held-over gain is deemed to accrue to the transferee immediately before he becomes non-resident.

The CGT annual exemption and any allowable losses available to the transferee at that time may be set against the deemed gain. However, the gain would not be eligible, for example, for roll-over relief on replacement of business assets (see **Chapter 14**) because it would not accrue on the actual disposal of an asset. Once the held-over gain has been clawed back in this way, the transferee's chargeable gain on a subsequent disposal is computed without any reduction in respect of the held-over gain.

No deemed gain arises where the transferee's change of residence status occurs more than six years after the end of the tax year in which the relevant disposal was made (*TCGA 1992, s 168(1), (4), (10)*).

Transferee's disposal of the asset

13.19 It may not be clear whether the transferee has disposed of all or only part of the asset he received, for which he has jointly claimed hold-over relief, before he emigrated. All disposals of similar assets made by the transferee before emigration should be reviewed to check whether all of the held-over gain has been taken into account in the computations of the gains/losses on those disposals. If only part of the held-over gain has been taken into account in gains/losses arising on pre-emigration disposals the balance of the held-over gain is deemed to accrue on the change of residence (*TCGA 1992, s 168(2)*).

The transferee's disposal of an asset to his spouse or civil partner under a no gain, no loss transfer (under *TCGA 1992, s 58*) does not count as a disposal for this purpose, but a subsequent disposal by the spouse or civil partner is taken into account as if the original transferee (not the spouse or civil partner) made that disposal (*TCGA 1992, s 168(3)*).

Example 13.6

Sidney gave a property to his brother Harry in May 1988, when they were both UK resident and they claimed hold-over relief. Harry gave the property to his wife Madeleine in 2000, and Harry and Madeleine emigrated in August 2002. A deemed gain does not arise at that time as the date of emigration is more than six years after the end of the tax year in which Harry acquired the property.

A temporary change of residence status will not trigger a deemed chargeable gain where the transferee:

- becomes neither resident nor ordinarily resident in the UK because he works in an employment or office and all the duties are performed outside the UK;
- becomes resident or ordinarily resident in the UK once again within three years of losing that status; and
- has not disposed of the asset in the meantime.

With regard to this last condition, the transferee is taken to have disposed of an asset only if he has made a disposal on which the allowable expenditure, deducted in computing his gain, would have been reduced by the held-over gain on the relevant disposal if he had been UK resident (*TCGA 1992, s 168(5), (6)*).

Payment of tax

13.20 The tax on the chargeable gain deemed to accrue to the transferee on emigration may be assessed and charged on the transferor, in the name of the transferee, if it has been assessed on the transferee but not paid within 12 months of the due date. The transferor is entitled to recover the tax from the transferee. No such assessment may be made more than six years after the end of the tax year in which the transferor made the relevant disposal (*TCGA 1992, 168(7), (8), (9)*).

Gifts to foreign-controlled companies

13.21 In the past the following trick has been used to avoid UK CGT. Assets were transferred to a UK company that was controlled by non-residents, and a claim for hold-over relief was submitted in respect of the gain. The non-resident owners would then sell the UK company, avoiding UK tax on the underlying assets. Hold-over relief under *TCGA 1992, s 165* is thus denied where the transferee is a company that is controlled by one or more persons who are neither resident nor ordinarily resident in the UK, and who are connected with the person making the disposal. The connection between the transferor and the company owners may be purely a commercial relationship, as shown in *Foulser and anor v MacDougall* [2007] STC 973.

A person who is resident or ordinarily resident in the UK is regarded as neither resident nor ordinarily resident in the UK for this purpose if:

- he controls a company – alone or with others – by virtue of holding assets relating to that company or another company; and
- double taxation relief arrangements have the effect that he is regarded as resident in another territory and would not be liable in the UK to tax on a gain arising on a disposal of the assets (*TCGA 1992, s 167*).

Gifts to dual-resident trusts

13.22 This is a similar anti-avoidance provision which denies hold-over relief available under either *TCGA 1992, s 165* or *TCGA 1992, s 260* where the held-over gain could slip out of the UK tax net, as the transfer is made into a dual-resident trust (*TCGA 1992, s 169(3)*). A dual-resident trust is one whose trustees are resident in the UK, but who are treated as being resident in another territory and therefore exempt from UK CGT under the terms of a double taxation agreement.

Agricultural property

13.23 Hold-over relief under *TCGA 1992, s 165* is available where the asset disposed of is, or is an interest in, agricultural property (as defined in *IHTA 1984, s 115*) if:

(a) the disposal does not qualify for hold-over relief under the normal rules only because the agricultural property is not used for the purposes of a trade carried on as set out in **13.5**; and

(b) agricultural property relief is obtained in respect of the transfer of value for inheritance tax purposes, or it would be obtained if the transfer was a chargeable transfer, or it would be obtained but for certain rules relating to transfers within seven years before the transferor's death (*TCGA 1992, s 165, Sch 7, para 1*).

FA 2009, s 122 amended the definition of agricultural property relief in *IHTA 1984, s 115* such that the relief is extended to all agricultural land situated in any EEA state, plus land in the Channel Islands and the Isle of Man, with retrospective effect. Hold-over relief claims under *s 165* may thus now be submitted for earlier years which are still in time. Claims for disposals made in the tax year 2006/07 need to be made by 5 April 2011, although where the taxpayer was not within self-assessment for the relevant tax year, claims for the years 2004/05 and 2005/06 may still be submitted (see **1.46**).

Agricultural property relief for inheritance tax purposes is available in respect of the agricultural value only, ie it is not available for any 'hope or development value' inherent in the property. However, HMRC consider that CGT hold-over relief can be allowed on the whole of the gain (not just the part reflecting agricultural value) because hold-over relief is given by reference to the nature of the asset transferred rather than its value (CG66962).

Trustees

13.24 Hold-over relief under *TCGA 1992, s 165* is available where the trustees of a settlement make a disposal of an asset mentioned in (a) or (b) below otherwise than under a bargain at arm's length:

(a) an asset, or an interest in an asset, used for the purposes of a trade, profession or vocation carried on by the trustees making the disposal, or by a beneficiary who had an interest in possession in the settled property immediately before the disposal;

(b) shares or securities of a trading company, or of the holding company of a trading group, where either the shares or securities are not listed on a recognised stock exchange, or the trustees are able to exercise at least 25% of the voting rights.

Such a disposal may occur where a person becomes absolutely entitled to the trust property as against the trustees and a deemed charge to CGT arises (see **Chapter 8**). Claims to hold-over relief in respect of disposals by trustees are made by trustees and the transferee (or by the trustees alone if the trustees of a settlement are also the transferee) (*TCGA 1992, Sch 7, para 2*).

The relief is extended to a disposal of agricultural property by trustees, as described in **13.23** in relation to non-settled property (*TCGA 1992, Sch 7, para 3*).

Hold-over relief under *TCGA 1992, s 260* is also available for transfers from certain trusts where an inheritance tax charge would arise but for their 'tax-favoured' status (see **13.38**).

Gifts to settlor-interested settlements

13.25 The anti-avoidance provisions in *TCGA 1992, ss 169B, 169D* were introduced from 9 December 2003 to block schemes designed to wash out gains through trusts (see **12.32**). This type of tax scheme was mostly used to eliminate a gain on a second home.

Hold-over relief under *TCGA 1992, s 165* or *TCGA 1992, s 260* is generally not available on a disposal to the trustees of a settlement in which the settlor has an interest. The settlor here can be someone other than the person making the disposal.

Relief may also be denied where there is an 'arrangement' for the settlor to acquire an interest in the settlement, and relief may be clawed back or blocked if the settlement becomes settlor-interested in the period ending six years following the tax year in which the disposal was made (see **13.26**).

Hold-over relief is excluded where the disposal (the 'relevant disposal') is made by a person ('the transferor') to the trustees of a settlement and either of the following two conditions is satisfied in relation to the disposal:

- Condition 1 is that immediately after the relevant disposal there is a 'settlor' who has an 'interest in the settlement', or an 'arrangement' exists under which the settlor will (or may) acquire such an interest. The various terms are defined in **13.27–13.31**.
- Condition 2 is that:
  - (a) a chargeable gain would (in the absence of hold-over relief under either *TCGA 1992, s 165* or *TCGA 1992, s 260*) accrue to the transferor on the disposal to the trustees;
  - (b) in computing the transferor's gain on that disposal, his allowable expenditure would be reduced directly or indirectly because of a hold-over relief claim made on an earlier disposal made by an individual; and
  - (c) immediately after the relevant disposal that individual has an interest in the settlement, or an arrangement exists under which that individual will or may acquire such an interest.

Relief is not available where either condition 1 or condition 2 is met. There are exceptions for maintenance funds for historic buildings and certain settlements for people with disabilities (*TCGA 1992, ss 169B, 169D*).

Clawback of relief: settlement becoming settlor-interested

13.26 Once obtained, hold-over relief may be clawed back where either condition 1 or condition 2 in **13.25** is met at any time during the 'clawback period'. This is the period beginning with the relevant disposal and ending six years after the end of the tax year in which the disposal took place.

Example 13.7

Mervyn transfers to trustees an asset used for the purposes of a trade carried on by his personal company. The transfer takes place on 10 May 2007 and he claims hold-over relief. He is the only settlor and does not have an interest in the settlement (see the definitions below). The relief may be clawed back if he acquires an interest in the settlement before 6 April 2014.

Where the clawback is triggered, a chargeable gain of an amount equal to the held-over gain is treated as accruing to the transferor at the 'material time', ie the time when either condition 1 or condition 2 is first met – not at the time of the relevant disposal. If no claim to hold-over relief is made before the material time, then the relief may not be claimed in relation to that disposal.

Once again, there are exceptions for maintenance funds for historic buildings and certain settlements for people with disabilities (*TCGA 1992, ss 169C, 169D*).

Definitions

13.27 The following definitions are provided for the purpose of the rules governing gifts to settlor-interested settlements.

Settlor

13.28 A person is a settlor in relation to a settlement if he is an individual and the settled property consists of, or includes, property originating from him. Property is deemed to originate from him if he has provided it directly or indirectly, or it represents such property (or any part of it, or accumulated income from it). Property provided directly or indirectly by another person under reciprocal arrangements with the settlor is treated as provided directly or indirectly by the settlor (*TCGA 1992, s 169E*).

Interest in a settlement

13.29 An individual is regarded as having an interest in a settlement if either (a) or (b) below applies:

(a) any property that is or may at any time be comprised in the settlement, or any 'derived property' (see **13.31**), is, or will or may become, in any circumstances, either payable to the individual or his spouse or civil partner, or a dependent child of the individual or applicable for their benefit; or

(b) the individual or his spouse or civil partner or dependent child enjoys a benefit deriving directly or indirectly from property comprised in the settlement, or from 'derived property'.

A separated spouse or civil partner, and a widow (or widower or surviving civil partner), are ignored in determining whether an individual has an interest in a settlement (*TCGA 1992, s 169F*). 'Dependent child' means a child who is under the age of 18, is unmarried, and does not have a civil partner. 'Child' includes a stepchild (*FA 2006, Sch 12, para 4*).

A future interest is ignored for this purpose if it could only arise:

- in the case of a marriage settlement or civil partnership settlement, on the death of both parties to the marriage or civil partnership and of all or any of their children; or
- on the death of a child of the individual where the child had become beneficially entitled to the property (or any derived property) by age 25 (*TCGA 1992, s 169F(5)*).

Arrangement

13.30 An arrangement includes any scheme, agreement or understanding, whether or not legally enforceable (*TCGA 1992, s 169G*).

Derived property

13.31 Property is 'derived property', in relation to any other property if it is:

(a) income from that other property;

(b) property directly or indirectly representing either proceeds of that other property or proceeds of income from that other property; or

(c) income from property that is derived property because it is within (b) above (*TCGA 1992, s 169F(6)*).

Claims

13.32 Hold-over relief must be claimed by both transferor and the transferee. However, if the gift is made into a trust, the relief claim is made by the transferor alone.

HMRC require claimants to use the form in the HMRC helpsheet HS295, or a copy of that form. Their guidance refers to 'serious problems' having arisen in some cases from a lack of information held by the transferee at the time of the eventual disposal of the asset. A claim must be made by the taxpayer personally, or by his personal representatives (CG66914).

The claim will usually be made when submitting the tax return, but otherwise it must be made within four years of the end of the tax year in which the disposal was made (*TMA 1970, s 43*). This time limit may effectively be extended where an assessment is made to recover tax lost through fraudulent or negligent conduct (under *TMA 1970, s 36*). Taxpayers who were not within self-assessment for the year of the claim, can use the longer claims period of five years from 31 January following the end of the tax year, provided the claim is submitted before 1 April 2012 (see **1.46**).

HMRC will accept claims to hold-over relief under *TCGA 1992, s 165* or *s 260*, in certain circumstances, without agreeing the market value of the asset transferred (see **13.46**).

Partial claims

13.33 It is not possible to limit the scope of a claim to hold-over relief in order, for example, to utilise the donor's annual exemption. However, where several assets are transferred the parties may choose to claim relief on some assets and not others.

Incorporation of a business

13.34 Hold-over relief under *TCGA 1992, s 165* may be available where a business carried on by an individual or a partnership is transferred to a company. Incorporation relief under *TCGA 1992, s 162* applies automatically where the business together with all of its assets (or all of its assets other than cash) is transferred to the company as a going concern in exchange for shares in the company, but the taxpayer can choose to disapply *TCGA 1992, s 162* by electing under *TCGA 1992, s 162A*. Incorporation relief is examined further in **Chapter 15**.

Where the taxpayer elects out of the automatic incorporation relief, or the conditions for that relief do not apply, hold-over relief under *TCGA 1992, s 165* may be used to defer gains on some or all of the assets transferred. Hold-over relief under *TCGA 1992, s 165* is a very flexible tool as it can be used where only some of the assets of the business are transferred to the company. The taxpayer must claim *s 165* relief on an asset-by-asset basis, and will thus choose which assets *s 165* is to apply to. However, hold-over relief can only apply where the disposal is made otherwise than by way of a bargain at arm's length. In most cases the transaction will be deemed to be made otherwise than by way of a bargain at arm's length because it will be made between connected persons (see **3.11**).

Where a claim to hold-over relief under *TCGA 1992, s 165* is made in relation to the incorporation of a business and there is actual consideration for the disposal, the held-over gain is reduced as explained at **13.7**. Care is needed where the consideration for goodwill, for example, takes the form of shares issued in exchange for assets because the amount of that consideration is determined by reference to the market value of the shares.

However, hold-over relief should be available without restriction on the transfer of goodwill if:

- the shares are subscribed for separately;
- goodwill is transferred to the company for a nominal cash sum;
- other assets are transferred at their book value; and
- the total consideration is credited to the transferor's loan account with the company.

HMRC guidance indicates that each asset will be considered separately providing there is no reason to suppose that the sale price of any of the assets is 'excessive'. HMRC may ask to see the sale agreement and compare it with the company's opening statement of affairs in order to determine precisely what consideration has been given for the various assets (CG66978, CG66979).

Example 13.8

Susan has carried on her antique dealing business for ten years. She let out the shop premises for one year before she commenced trading. In October 2010, Susan transferred the business as a going concern to a limited company that she formed with share capital of £1,000 held wholly by her, but elects not to use incorporation relief. The transfer consideration is £1.

The gain arising in respect of the freehold premises is £220,000 and on goodwill it is £30,000. Susan and the company must jointly elect to hold over the gain on the gift of business assets to the company. Susan's net taxable income for 2010/11 is £38,000, so the gain that is not held over is subject to CGT at 28%.

2010/11	Freehold	Goodwill	Total
	£	£	£
Total gains	220,000	30,000	250,000
Reduction for non-trade use 1/11 yrs	(20,000)		(20,000)
Held-over gains	200,000	30,000	230,000
Chargeable gain			20,000
Less annual exemption			(10,100)
Taxable gain			9,900
CGT due at 28%			2,772

Susan could claim entrepreneurs' relief instead of hold-over relief on the entire gain generated by the disposal of the business (see **13.36**).

Interaction with other reliefs

13.35 Where the conditions exist to allow hold-over relief for gifts of business assets to be claimed under *TCGA 1992, s 165*, those conditions may also permit certain other CGT reliefs to apply, either automatically or by way of a claim. Where several CGT reliefs potentially apply to the same disposal hold-over relief is given:

- after indexation allowance, for disposals made before 6 April 2008;
- before taper relief, for transfers made before 6 April 2008;
- before entrepreneurs' relief, for disposals made after 5 April 2008 (see **13.36**).

Where hold-over relief is obtained without restriction, any taper relief relating to the transferor's period of ownership is lost. Taper relief is discussed in **17.22** and the interaction of various CGT reliefs is examined further in **14.44–14.46**.

Entrepreneurs' relief

13.36 The HMRC view is that hold-over relief takes precedence over entrepreneurs' relief (see **11.45**) where hold-over relief covers the full gain accruing on the disposal of the business, or part of the business. However, where hold-over relief is only claimed in respect of certain assets leaving a chargeable gain accruing on other assets which form part of a business disposal, entrepreneurs' relief may be claimed to cover that residual gain that remains in charge (CG64137).

An alternative view is that entrepreneurs' relief can be claimed on the whole of the qualifying gain with hold-over relief soaking up the residual gain.

GIFTS SUBJECT TO IHT (SECTION 260)

13.37 Hold-over relief is available for gifts on which inheritance tax is immediately chargeable, or would be chargeable but for an exemption or the availability of the inheritance tax nil rate band. Such gifts include transfers to and from discretionary trusts (*TCGA 1992, s 260*).

Where such a hold-over claim is made (or could have been made) a deduction is available, in computing the gain on the subsequent disposal, for any IHT charged on the gift (see **13.42**).

Conditions

13.38 Both the transferor and the transferee must be either an individual or trustees of a settlement. Where the conditions set out below are met, the relief remains subject to various restrictions including:

- the restrictions set out in **13.8** in relation to *TCGA 1992, s 165* relief; and
- the exclusion mentioned at **13.43** for gifts to non-residents (*TCGA 1992, s 260(1)*).

The relief applies to a disposal that is made otherwise than under a bargain at arm's length, where the disposal meets any of the following conditions:

(a) it is a chargeable transfer for inheritance tax purposes (or would be a chargeable transfer but for the annual exemption for gifts) and is not a potentially exempt transfer (see *IHTA 1984, ss 2, 3A* and *19*);

(b) it is an exempt transfer to a political party, or an exempt transfer to a maintenance fund for historic buildings, etc, or a conditionally exempt transfer of designated property (*IHTA 1984, ss 24, 27, 30*);

(c) it is a disposition whereby property enters a maintenance fund meeting certain conditions and *IHTA 1984, s 57A* applies to the disposition;

(d) it is a transfer made by the trustees of an accumulation and maintenance trust, and inheritance tax is not chargeable by virtue of *IHTA 1984, s 71(4)*;

(e) it is a transfer made by trustees of a trust for a bereaved minor, and inheritance tax is not chargeable by virtue of *IHTA 1984, s 71B(2)*;

(f) it is a transfer made by trustees of an age 18-to-25 trust, and inheritance tax is not chargeable by virtue of *IHTA 1984, s 71E(2)*;

(g) it is a transfer of a work of art, etc qualifying for the conditional exemption in *IHTA 1984, s 78(1)*; or

(h) it is a disposal of an asset comprised in a settlement and the provisions of *IHTA 1984, Sch 4, paras 9, 16,* or *17* (dealing with transfers to maintenance funds for historic buildings, etc) apply to reduce or eliminate an inheritance tax charge where the asset becomes comprised in another settlement.

Conditions (e) and (f) were added with effect from 22 March 2006 (*TCGA 1992, s 260(2)*; *FA 2006, Sch 20, para 32*).

Operation of *TCGA 1992, s 260* relief

13.39 The effect of this relief, which must be claimed (see **13.45**), is that the 'held-over gain' (see below) is deducted from both:

- the chargeable gain (if any) that would otherwise accrue to the transferor; and
- the consideration which the transferee would otherwise be regarded as having given for the acquisition of the asset (*TCGA 1992, s 260(3)*).

The 'held-over gain' on a disposal, where this relief is not restricted by reference to actual consideration received for the disposal, is the chargeable gain that would have accrued in the absence of hold-over relief (*TCGA 1992, s 260(4)*).

The relief may be restricted where consideration is received (see **13.40**) or as described in **13.41**.

Consideration received

13.40 Where a claim to hold-over relief is made and there is actual consideration for the disposal, and that consideration exceeds the allowable expenditure deductible in computing the gain, the held-over gain is reduced by that excess. This restriction does not apply, however, to certain disposals deemed to occur in relation to accumulation and maintenance trusts, employee trusts or newspaper trusts (within *IHTA 1984, s 71(1)* or *s 72(1)*) (*TCGA 1992, s 260(5), (9)*).

Partial relief

13.41 If the disposal only partly meets the conditions in **13.38**, or the condition in **13.38**(h) is met and the inheritance tax charge is reduced but not eliminated, then hold-over relief applies only to an 'appropriate part' of the disposal (*TCGA 1992, s 260(10)*).

Relief for inheritance tax

13.42 Where there is a chargeable transfer for inheritance tax purposes as mentioned in **13.38**(a), CGT relief is available to the transferee as follows, whether or not hold-over relief is obtained under *TCGA 1992, s 260.*

The transferee is entitled to a deduction in computing for CGT purposes the chargeable gain accruing on his disposal of the asset. The deduction is equal to the inheritance tax attributable to the value of the asset, but it cannot exceed the amount of the chargeable gain before the deduction. The deduction is adjusted in the event that the inheritance tax is varied after it has been taken into account in this way (*TCGA 1992, s 260(7), (8)*).

Gifts to non-residents

13.43 Hold-over relief under *TCGA 1992, s 260* is denied where the transferee is:

(a) not resident or not ordinarily resident in the UK; or

(b) an individual who is resident or ordinarily resident in the UK, where double taxation relief arrangements have the effect that he is regarded as resident in another territory and he would not be liable in the UK to tax on a gain arising on a disposal of the asset (*TCGA 1992, s 261*).

Emigration of transferee

13.44 Where hold-over relief has been given under either *TCGA 1992, s 165* or *TCGA 1992, s 260* on a disposal ('the relevant disposal') to an individual, and the transferee becomes neither resident nor ordinarily resident in the UK at a time when he has not disposed of the asset (see **13.18**), a chargeable gain equal to the held-over gain is deemed to accrue to the transferee immediately before that time.

Claims

13.45 A claim for relief under *TCGA 1992, s 260* is made by the transferor and the transferee or, where the trustees of a settlement are the transferee, by the transferor alone. HMRC prefer that the standard hold-over relief claim form attached to HMRC helpsheet HS295 should be used (see **13.32**).

The claim will usually be made when submitting the tax return, but must otherwise be made within four years from the end of the tax year in which the disposal was made (*TCGA 1992, s 260(1)(c)*). Taxpayers who were not within self-assessment for the year of the claim, can use the longer claims period of five years from 31 January following the end of the tax year, provided the claim is submitted before 1 April 2012 (see **1.46**).

VALUATIONS

13.46 HMRC will accept claims to hold-over relief under either *TCGA 1992, s 165* or *TCGA 1992, s 260*, in certain circumstances, without formal agreement of the market value of the asset transferred. The conditions and procedures are set out in HMRC Statement of Practice 8/92 and are summarised below.

The market value rule (see **13.1**) requires the transferor to establish the market value of the asset at the date of the transfer in order to compute the chargeable gain accruing and the held-over gain where a claim is made. However, where hold-over relief is available without restriction, agreement of the asset's market value at the date of transfer has no bearing on the transferor's CGT liability.

HMRC will admit a claim to hold-over relief without requiring a computation of the held-over gain where both the transferor and transferee complete the 'request for valuations to be deferred', found on page ten of HMRC's helpsheet HS295 (and forming the second page of the hold-over relief claim). The form requires:

- a joint application by the transferor and the transferee;
- details of the asset, its history and an informal estimate of the asset's market value at the date of transfer – such an estimate is not binding on either the claimants or HMRC; and
- a statement that both parties are satisfied that the value of the asset at the date of transfer was such that there would be a chargeable gain but for the claim.

HMRC's guidance indicates that taxpayers will not be asked for a computation of the held-over gain so long as the asset is properly identified and the formalities of the hold-over relief claim are satisfied. The requirement for both parties to sign the application for deferral of the valuation applies where the transferee is a body of trustees, even though the trustees are not required to sign the actual hold-over claim. HMRC regard it as essential that anyone whose liability may be affected by the valuation has agreed to the postponement (CG67131, CG67132).

Once HMRC have accepted a hold-over relief claim made on this basis, the claim may not be withdrawn. The relevant statutory provisions will be applied, and assessments made as necessary, if it emerges that any information provided by either the transferor or transferee was incorrect or incomplete.

HMRC will not apply statement of practice 8/92 in a case where the held-over gain is restricted as shown in **13.8** (as provided in *TCGA 1992, Sch 7, paras 5, 6* and *7*) because the amount of chargeable gain accruing to the transferor depends in such a case on a valuation being made.

In some other cases it will be necessary to establish market value before a later disposal of the asset by the transferee. Statement of Practice 8/92 outlines some of those circumstances in relation to:

- assets held at 31 March 1982;
- retirement relief;
- relief in respect of deferred charges on gains before 31 March 1982; and
- time apportionment for assets held on 6 April 1965.

Chapter 14

Roll-over relief for business assets

INTRODUCTION

14.1 The effect of roll-over relief is to defer a chargeable gain where the proceeds of disposal of business assets (the 'old assets') are used to invest in new business assets. The old and the new assets must both be used in the business. Spouses and civil partners are separate persons for roll-over relief. The rules specific to groups of companies are examined at **9.27–9.36**. This chapter is of general application to corporates and non-corporates except where stated otherwise.

Roll-over relief is applied by deducting the gain from the acquisition cost of the new assets. The gain deferred – or rolled over – in this way may give rise to a CGT liability on a disposal of the replacement assets, but roll-over relief may be claimed on that subsequent disposal if the conditions are met. A chargeable gain may arise on the disposal of the old assets if the relief claimed on that disposal is restricted (see **14.29**) (*TCGA 1992, s 152*).

A rolled over gain escapes CGT in the event of the taxpayer's death. In some cases, however, the gain on the old asset is 'postponed' instead of being 'rolled over' or deducted from the cost of the new asset (see **14.33**).

There are separate time limits for reinvestment of the consideration for the disposal (see **14.7**) and claims (see **14.37**).

Where a provision of *TCGA 1992* fixes the consideration deemed to be given for the acquisition or disposal – for example, transactions between connected persons are treated as undertaken for a consideration equal to market value – the deemed consideration is treated as the actual consideration for the purpose of roll-over relief (*TCGA 1992, s 152(10)*).

CONDITIONS

Summary

14.2 Roll-over relief must be claimed by the person carrying on the business in which the asset is used. It is available if the taxpayer:

- carries on a trade or another qualifying activity (see **14.10**);
- disposes of assets (or his interest in assets) used only for the purposes of that trade throughout the period of ownership (the 'old assets') (see **14.27**);
- applies the consideration obtained for the disposal in acquiring other assets within the specified classes (see **14.18**) (the 'new assets');
- acquires those new assets within the permitted period (see **14.7**); and
- takes the new assets into use on acquisition, to be used solely for the purposes of the trade (see **14.25**).

The effect of the relief is that:

(a) the consideration for the disposal of the old assets is reduced to the amount that would give rise to neither a gain nor a loss accruing on the disposal; and

(b) the amount (or value) of the consideration that the taxpayer gives for the acquisition of the new assets is reduced by the amount of the reduction in (a).

Note it is the consideration (or deemed disposal) from the disposal of the old asset that must be reinvested, not the gain from the disposal as applies for EIS deferral relief (see **Chapter 16**).

The CGT treatment of the other parties to the transactions is not affected. Both the old assets and new assets must be within the classes of assets listed in *TCGA 1992, s 155*, although they do not need to be in the same class as each other (see **14.18**) (*TCGA 1992, s 152(1)*).

'Trade' has the same meaning for roll-over relief as it has in the Income Tax Acts, and *ICTA 1988, s 832* provides that 'trade' includes every trade, manufacture, adventure or concern in the nature of trade. However, relief is extended to other activities (see **14.12**) (*TCGA 1992, s 158(2)*).

Tracing the disposal proceeds

14.3 It is not normally necessary to trace the actual proceeds and match them to the funds invested in the new assets. The new assets can, for example, be funded by borrowings. HMRC recognise that seeking to trace the disposal proceeds through to the acquisition of the new assets would result in relief being denied in most cases. The permitted period for reinvestment starts one year before the old asset is disposed of (see **14.7**), so the new asset may be acquired with borrowed funds before the old one is disposed of (CG60770).

There is an exception, however, where the taxpayer is seeking an extension to the reinvestment period. In this case he may need to be able to demonstrate a continuing intention to reinvest the disposal consideration within the extended time limit (see **14.8**).

Example 14.1

Giles bought some farmland on 1 September 2009 for £140,000, which was immediately incorporated into his farming business. He sold a barn for £100,000 less expenses of £5,000 on 3 May 2010. Giles used a mortgage to fund the purchase of the land. For his roll-over relief claim Giles matches his sale of the barn with the purchase of the land eight months previously. The net disposal consideration of £95,000 is fully applied in acquiring the new asset comprising of the farmland so full roll-over relief is given.

Allocating the consideration

14.4 Where there is more than one acquisition HMRC will accept the taxpayer's allocation of the gain to be rolled over against the new assets. HMRC consider that there must be a specific allocation before the claim can be allowed (CG60775).

Residence

14.5 HMRC accept that relief may be claimed even if the replacement assets are outside the UK. Relief will not be denied where all the conditions are met and at the time the new assets are acquired, the taxpayer has ceased to be resident or ordinarily resident in the UK (CG60253).

However, there is a potential charge for 'temporary non-residents' (see **5.27**) where a gain has been the subject of a roll-over relief claim, either under the normal rules or under the special rules for new assets that are depreciating assets, see **14.33**, and there is a disposal of the new asset during a period of temporary non-residence. The gain may be treated as accruing to the temporary non-resident on his return to the UK (see **5.29**) (*TCGA 1992, s 10A(3), (4)*).

Non-residents with UK presence

14.6 If a gain arising on the old assets would be chargeable under *TCGA 1992, s 10(1)* (non-resident with a UK branch or agency) or *TCGA 1992, s 10B* (non-resident company with a UK permanent establishment) then roll-over relief is not available unless the new assets, immediately after they are acquired, would also fall within *s 10(1)* or *s 10B* on a disposal (*TCGA 1992, s 159(1)*).

This condition does not apply if:

(a) the relevant acquisition takes place after the disposal and the taxpayer is resident or ordinarily resident in the UK immediately after the acquisition; or

(b) immediately after the time the new assets are acquired:

- the taxpayer is a 'dual resident', ie a person who is both resident or ordinarily resident in the UK and regarded for double tax relief purposes as resident elsewhere, and
- the assets are 'prescribed assets', ie assets specified in a double tax agreement with the effect that the dual resident is regarded as not liable in the UK to tax on gains accruing to him on a disposal (*TCGA 1992, s 159(2), (3), (5)*).

PERIOD FOR REINVESTMENT

14.7 The general rule is that the new asset must be acquired in the period beginning one year before, and ending three years after, the disposal of the old asset, but this period may be extended either forwards or backwards (see **14.8**) as HMRC allow (*TCGA 1992, s 152(3)*).

An unconditional contract for the acquisition, made within the time limit, will be sufficient. The relief may be applied on a provisional basis where an unconditional contract for the acquisition is entered into, without waiting to see whether the contract is completed. Adjustments are to be made as necessary when the outcome is known. This rule is separate from the facility for the taxpayer to claim provisional relief before he has entered into any contract for acquisition of a replacement asset (see **14.41**) ((*TCGA 1992, s 152(4)*).

Where the replacement asset is newly constructed, or represented by improvement to an existing asset, HMRC consider that the date of acquisition may be taken as the date on which the asset or the works are completed and ready for use (CG60623).

Extension of time limits for reinvestment

14.8 HMRC guidance indicates that extension of the time limits is permitted where the claimant can demonstrate that he:

- firmly intended to acquire replacement assets within the time limit; but
- was prevented from doing so by some fact or circumstance beyond his control; and
- acted 'as soon as he reasonably could' after ceasing to be so prevented.

Each case is considered on its merits. Circumstances outside the claimant's control might include the death or serious illness of a vital party at a crucial time, unsettled disputes, difficulty in establishing good title or finding suitable replacement assets, or delay in receipt of disposal proceeds. They would not normally include a change of intention at a late stage, or a shortage of funds that arose because the taxpayer spent the proceeds on something other than new, qualifying assets.

The HMRC Band B Compliance Team Leader in the Area Office, or an Area Compliance Director can agree to extend the time limit for reinvestment to up to three years before, or six years after, the disposal of the old asset, if there are acceptable reasons for the delay (CG60640). However, the discretion to extend the time limit is vested solely in the HMRC officers. The taxpayer cannot appeal against a decision of an HMRC officer not to use this discretion (*R (on application of) Barnett) v IRC* [2004] STC 763).

Compulsory purchase

14.9 The Board of HMRC may allow an extension to the time limit in the case of the disposal of land:

- where there is a compulsory purchase order, or there is a threat of such an order, so long as the conditions set out in Statement of Practice D6 (see below) are satisfied; or
- where there is a significant delay between the disposal of the land and the agreement and receipt of compensation.

In the case of delayed compensation HMRC may allow the time limit to apply as if the date the first tranche of compensation was received was the date of disposal of the asset (CG60660).

Statement of Practice D6 covers situations where land is acquired by a local authority or New Town Corporation for development and leased back to the taxpayer for a period before it is developed, and reads:

> 'Where new town corporations and similar authorities acquire by compulsory purchase land for development and then immediately grant a previous owner a lease of the land until they are ready to commence building, [HMRC] will be prepared to extend the time limit for rollover relief under *TCGA 1992, ss 152* to *158* to 3 years after the land ceases to be used by the previous owner for his trade, provided that there is a clear continuing intention that the sale proceeds will be used to acquire qualifying assets; assurances will be given in appropriate cases subject to the need to raise a protective assessment if the lease extends beyond the statutory 6-year time limit for making assessments.'

It appears from the HMRC guidance that the land need not be purchased by compulsory purchase order to qualify for this concession.

In any application of Statement of Practice D6 HMRC will look for evidence of the taxpayer's continuing intention to reinvest the disposal proceeds within the extended time limit, including:

- an annual affirmation from the taxpayer or agent that such is the intention; and
- an assurance that the disposal proceeds remain available (though not necessarily in a completely liquid form) for the purchase. HMRC say that temporary investment of the funds even in equities or real property, 'should not of itself be taken as making the proceeds unavailable' (CG60660).

QUALIFYING ACTIVITIES

14.10 Roll-over relief is available where a person carrying on a trade reinvests the proceeds of disposal of assets used for the purposes of the trade in the acquisition of new assets to be used for the purposes of the same trade. If the business carried on does not amount to a trade the relief may be denied (CG60290). See **14.12** regarding qualifying activities other than trades.

No relief is due if the new assets are acquired wholly or partly for the purpose of realising a profit from their disposal (*TCGA 1992, s 152(5)*).

HMRC accept that this rule is not intended to deny relief merely because it is expected the asset will be sold at a profit at some stage. HMRC guidance says:

> 'The point turns on the claimant's intentions at the time of acquisition. If the intention is to keep the asset and to use it for trade purposes, relief may be allowed. If the intention is to dispose of the asset and its trade use is merely a temporary convenience, relief should be denied. An example is where a

farmer acquires more land than is required (perhaps because the vendor will not sell less than an entire estate) and intends to dispose of the surplus, often to finance the cost of the part retained' (CG60405).

Two or more trades

14.11 A person who carries on two or more trades, either at the same time or in succession, is regarded as carrying on a single trade (*TCGA 1992, s 152(8)*).

HMRC are prepared to regard trades as being carried on 'successively' if the interval does not exceed three years, but the time limits for reinvestment must still be met (see **14.7**). Relief will be available, but may be restricted by reference to non-trade use, if the old assets are disposed of during the interval. New assets acquired during the interval may qualify as replacement assets provided they are not used or leased for any purpose before the new trade begins, and are taken into use for the purpose of the trade on commencement (HMRC Statement of Practice 8/81; CG60500).

Activities other than trades

14.12 The main roll-over relief provisions in *TCGA 1992, ss 152–157* refer only to trades. The relief is extended to replacement of assets used for the purpose of a profession, vocation, office or employment (*TCGA 1992, s 158*).

Where relief is claimed in respect of assets used for the purposes of the claimant's office or employment, it will not be denied because the asset is also used by the employer for the purposes of the employer's trade. HMRC regard the 'sole use' condition as satisfied unless the asset is used for some purpose 'alien to' the office or employment (CG60540).

So far as land and buildings are concerned, the employee must occupy the asset as owner and not merely as a licensee of the employer. HMRC Statement of Practice 5/86 says:

> 'If land or buildings are owned by an employee etc, but made available to the employer for general use in his trade, the employee etc may nonetheless satisfy the occupation test of *TCGA 1992, s 155* provided the employer does not make any payment (or give other consideration) for his use of the property nor otherwise occupy it under a lease or tenancy. The qualifying use of assets by an employee etc for the purposes of *TCGA 1992, ss 152* and *153* will include any use or occupation of those assets by him, in the course of performing the duties of his employment or office, as directed by the employer.'

A taxpayer who is an officer or employee of his personal company (see **14.13**) may meet the conditions of *TCGA 1992, s 152* by reference to his office or employment and simultaneously meet the conditions of *TCGA 1992, s 157*. He can then choose to make a claim for roll-over relief under either section (CG60503).

The taxpayer may carry on two different activities, for example a trade and an employment, at the same time or successively. The fact that the two activities are different does not prevent relief applying so long as the various conditions including, where appropriate, the terms of HMRC Statement of Practice 8/81 (see **14.11**) are met.

'Trade', 'profession', 'vocation', 'office' and 'employment' have the same meaning for roll-over relief as they have in the Income Tax Acts, so that farming, and the commercial letting of furnished holiday accommodation that falls within *TCGA 1992, s 241*, may qualify (*TCGA 1992, ss 158(2), 241(3)(3A)*).

The relief also applies to the replacement of assets used for the purposes of the following activities, as it applies in relation to trades:

- the discharge of the functions of a public authority;
- the occupation of woodlands managed by the occupier on a commercial basis;
- the activities of a non-profit making body that are wholly or mainly directed to the protection or promotion of its members' trade or professional interests; and
- the activities of an unincorporated association or other body chargeable to corporation tax, but not established for profit, whose activities are wholly or mainly carried on otherwise than for profit.

The last category may include trade unions, sports clubs and local constituency associations of political parties. The body must use the assets for the purpose of its activities. In the case of land and buildings within Head A of Class 1 (see **14.18**), the body must both occupy and use them for those activities, rather than letting them (*TCGA 1992, s 158(1)(f)*).

TCGA 1992, s 158(1) is extended from 6 April 2009 to make it clear that the relief is available where the assets are held by a company in which at least 90% of the ordinary share capital is held by or on behalf of such a body or its members (*TCGA 1992, s 158(1A)*). Prior to this date the relief was given by concession (ESC D15).

Trade carried on by the taxpayer's personal company

14.13 Roll-over relief is extended to the situation where the owner of the asset is an individual but the trade is carried on by a company. The individual is deemed to be carrying on the trade(s), for the purpose of the conditions in *TCGA 1992, ss 152–156*, where:

(a) the person disposing of the old assets (or an interest in them) and acquiring the new assets (or an interest in them) is an individual; and

(b) the trade or trades in question are carried on by a company which is his 'personal company' (*TCGA 1992, s 157*).

The condition in (b) must be met both at the time of the disposal and at the time of the acquisition referred to in (a). A company is the taxpayer's 'personal company' if he can exercise at least 5% of the voting rights. Note this is not the same definition of 'personal company' as applies for entrepreneurs' relief (see **11.10**).

HMRC consider that both the old and new assets must be used for qualifying activities of the same personal company, on the basis that *TCGA 1992, s 157* directs that *TCGA 1992, s 152* should be read as if it said:

> 'If the consideration which an individual obtains for the disposal of … the old assets used and used only for the purposes of the trade carried on by his … personal company … is applied by him in acquiring … the new assets which on the acquisition are taken into use, and used only, for the purposes of the trade carried on by that … personal company …' (CG60503).

Trade carried on by a partnership

14.14 The CGT treatment of partnerships is examined in detail in **Chapter 6**. Roll-over relief extends to a business partner's interest in the chargeable assets of a partnership (*TCGA 1992, s 157*).

Where the partnership disposes of an asset qualifying for roll-over relief, or there is a reduction in the partner's share of the partnership's capital assets following a change in the asset-sharing ratio, the partner may obtain roll-over relief by means of either:

- the partnership's acquisition of qualifying assets in which the partner has an interest; or
- the partner's acquisition in qualifying assets, either used by the partnership (see below) or unrelated to the partnership's business.

Relief is also available for assets used in the partnership's trade but owned by an individual partner rather than the partnership. This applies even if the partner receives rent for the use of the asset (HMRC Statement of Practice D11).

Where land used for the purposes of a partnership's trade is 'partitioned' by the partners on a dissolution of the partnership, strictly speaking no roll-over relief is due because an exchange of interests in a single asset does not involve the acquisition of 'other assets'. By concession, HMRC will treat the land acquired as a new asset providing that:

- the partnership is dissolved immediately after the exchange; and
- the former partners retain an interest only in land used by them in a new trading enterprise and do not retain any interest in that part of the land no longer used by them for trade purposes (ESC D23, CG61170).

Example 14.2

A family partnership made up of Peggy, Philip and David jointly and equally own land which they farm as one business. David wishes to leave the partnership and farm one-third of the land on his own. David's interest in two-thirds of the land is exchanged for Peggy and Philip's interest in one-third of the land. David leaves the partnership and Peggy and Philip continue to farm the remaining two-thirds of the land now jointly owned by them. Roll-over relief is available to David, Peggy and Philip, based on the value of the land at the date the interests were exchanged.

Spouse and civil partners

14.15 In *Tod v Mudd* (1986) 60 TC 237, Ch D, it was established that spouses are separate persons for the purpose of roll-over relief so that the conditions for relief apply separately to each person's interest in an asset used by a husband and wife partnership. Mr Mudd and his wife acquired as tenants in common a new asset in the form of a property. They used it as to 75% as a guest house, and the remaining 25% as their residence.

A trust deed recorded that the property would be held by them upon trust as to 75% for Mr Mudd and as to 25% for his wife. Mr Mudd claimed that 75% of the cost of acquisition of the premises qualified for roll-over relief in relation to his earlier disposal of his accountancy practice.

It was held that he was entitled to relief only in respect of 56.25% of the premises, being 75% x 75% of his undivided share of the premises. The same principle would extend to registered civil partners who are also partners in business.

Limited liability partnerships

14.16 A limited liability partnership (LLP) is treated for CGT purposes in the same way as any other partnership while it is trading, despite being a body corporate (see **6.23**). The LLP itself is regarded as transparent for CGT purposes, with each member being charged to tax on his share of any gains accruing to the LLP (*TCGA 1992, s 59A*).

However, when an LLP ceases to trade, it loses its tax 'transparency' and reverts to its corporate status. This applies unless there is merely a temporary break in trading where, for example, the LLP has ceased to carry on one trade and disposed of its assets in order to raise funds to start another trade (*TCGA 1992, s 59A(2), (3)*).

Any gains rolled over or postponed by a member of the LLP might escape as a result of the reversion to corporate status but for a special rule that deems the member to have realised a chargeable gain immediately before the LLP ceased to be transparent. This rule operates as set out below:

- Where, immediately before 'the time of cessation of trade' (see below), an LLP member holds an asset (or an interest in an asset) that he acquired for a consideration treated as reduced by virtue of a roll-over relief claim under *s 152* or *s 153*, he is treated as if a chargeable gain equal to the amount of the reduction accrued to him immediately before that time.
- Where a gain postponed by virtue of a *s 154(2)* claim (see **14.34**) made by an LLP member has not accrued before the time of cessation of trade, he is treated as if that gain accrued immediately before that time.
- 'The time of cessation of trade', is the time when *s 59A(1)* ceases to apply to the LLP, ie when it loses its tax transparency (*TCGA 1992, s 156A*).

Groups of companies

14.17 The trades carried on by members of a group of companies (as defined) are treated as a single trade for roll-over relief purposes. The rules specific to companies are examined in **9.26** and **9.36.**

ASSETS

14.18 Both the old assets and the new assets must fall within one of the nine classes listed in *TCGA 1992, s 155*, but they do not have to fall within the same class as each other. These classes are summarised in **Table 14.1**, and explained further in the following paragraphs.

Table 14.1

Class	
Class 1, Head A (see **14.19**)	1. Any building or part of a building, and any permanent or semi-permanent structure in the nature of a building, occupied (as well as used) only for the purposes of the trade. 2. Any land occupied (as well as used) only for the purposes of the trade.
Class 1, Head B	Fixed plant or machinery that does not form part of a building or of a permanent or semi-permanent structure in the nature of a building.
Class 2	Ships, aircraft and hovercraft
Class 3	Satellites, space stations and spacecraft (including launch vehicles)
Class 4	Goodwill
Class 5	Milk quotas and potato quotas
Class 6	Ewe and suckler cow premium quotas
Class 7	Fish quotas
Class 7A	Payment entitlements under the single payment scheme for farmers
Class 8	Certain rights and assets of Lloyd's underwriters

Land and buildings

14.19 Head A of Class 1 is excluded where the trade is a trade of dealing in or developing land. However, Head A can apply where a profit on the sale of any land held for the purposes of the trade would not form part of the trading profits.

Head A does not apply where the trade is a trade of providing services for the occupier of land in which the trader has an estate or interest. A lessor of tied premises is treated as both occupying and using the premises for the purposes of the trade (*TCGA 1992, s 156*).

Fixed plant or machinery

14.20 It was established in *Williams v Evans* (1982) 59 TC 509, Ch D that in Head B of Class 1, the word 'fixed' applies to both plant and machinery. Motor vehicles, for example, would normally be excluded. HMRC apply four tests in determining whether an item of plant or plant or machinery is fixed:

(a) In the context of the particular trade, is the object plant or machinery as opposed to, for example, trading stock or part of a building?

(b) Does the taxpayer intend to hold the object in a particular location indefinitely for use in his trade?

(c) Is the location of the object in a particular site essential to its function in the trade?

(d) What means of permanent fixing are available, or necessary, without rendering the object part of the land or buildings, and without damaging or destroying the object? (CG60970).

HMRC will not include in this category items of plant and machinery that have become part of a building, such as lifts or escalators. Those items may well qualify for roll-over relief, but under class 1, Head A rather than Head B (CG61001).

Ships, aircraft and hovercraft

14.21 For the purposes of class 3 in **Table 14.1** hovercraft are as defined in *Hovercraft Act 1968, s 4*. The definition of 'ships' is taken from *Merchant Shipping Act 1995, s 742* as 'every description of vessel used in navigation not propelled by oars'. HMRC accept that 'ships' for this purpose includes fishing boats, motorised cruisers and yachts, and that 'aircraft' includes aeroplanes, helicopters, airships and hot air balloons (CG61060).

Goodwill

14.22 Goodwill is not defined in *TCGA 1992*, possibly because it means different things for different businesses. HMRC's current guidance, included in their CGT manual at paras CG68000–CG68330, acknowledges that goodwill comprises a variety of elements within a business (CG68010). However, the key roll-over relief case involving goodwill: *Balloon Promotions Ltd v HMRC* [2006] SpC 524 is mentioned only briefly, and the bulk of the HMRC guidance appears to ignore entirely the view of the Special Commissioner in that case.

In *Balloon Promotions Ltd* a franchisee operating a restaurant business sold the business to the franchisor and allocated part of the consideration to goodwill not inherent in the property. HMRC contended that there was no saleable goodwill and that the consideration represented compensation for early termination of the franchise agreements. The Special Commissioner held that goodwill was attached to the franchisee's business, and that the consideration obtained for it qualified for roll-over relief.

In relation to the disposal and acquisition of business assets the point of contention is whether the goodwill is inseparable from the business, or is inseparable from a particular asset used by the business, such as a building (see **15.9**). It is fair to say that the issue of goodwill as it attaches to a business property, or not as the case may be, is a controversial one.

HMRC's view is that only goodwill which is not personal goodwill or inherent goodwill can be freely transferred, although inherent goodwill may be sold where the associated building is also transferred to the purchaser.

Although goodwill is classified as a type of intangible asset for the corporate intangible asset regime (see **14.23**), other intangible assets such as copyrights, are not classified as goodwill for the purposes of roll-over relief.

Companies: intangible assets

14.23 Classes 4 to 7A in **Table 14.1** do not apply to companies, except where transitional rules apply for acquisitions before 1 April 2002, because those assets listed are now included in the corporation tax regime for intangible assets (*CTA 2009, pt 8*). *Corporation Tax 2010/11* (Bloomsbury Professional) contains detailed coverage of the intangible assets regime at Chapter 10.

Acquisition of 'other assets'

14.24 The legislation refers to investment in 'other assets' but by concession, where a person disposes of a trade (or a trade asset) and repurchases the same asset later for purely commercial reasons, HMRC will regard that asset as a 'new asset' unless the disposal and reacquisition 'appears to have been carried out for avoidance purposes'. This concession may be applied to partnership changes resulting in reacquisition of fractional shares in partnership assets (ESC D16).

However, it was held in *Watton v Tippett* (1997) 69 TC 491, CA that a gain arising on a part disposal of land and buildings cannot be rolled over against the acquisition of the part retained after the part disposal.

By concession, capital expenditure to enhance the value of other assets is treated as incurred in acquiring other assets provided that:

- the other assets are used only for the purposes of the trade; or
- on completion of the work, the assets are immediately taken into use and used only for the purposes of the trade (ESC D22).

Another concession applies where a person carrying on a trade uses the proceeds from the disposal of an old asset to acquire a further interest in another asset that is already in use for the purposes of the trade. That further interest is treated as a new asset taken into use for the purposes of the trade (ESC D25).

A right to unascertainable future consideration may be received as part of the consideration for disposal of the old asset. Roll-over relief is not available on a later disposal of that right because the right is not among the classes of asset listed in *TCGA 1992, s 155* (CG14970).

NEW ASSETS TO BE USED 'ON ACQUISITION'

14.25 A new asset must be taken into use for the purpose of the business 'on the acquisition' of the asset if it is to form part of a roll-over relief claim (*TCGA 1992, s 152(1)*).

HMRC interpret this as meaning that the asset must be taken into use at the time any contracts are completed – by conveyance or delivery – and possession has been obtained. See also **14.27** regarding the period of ownership, in relation to the restriction of relief where there is non-business use.

However, allowance is made for necessary alterations, adaptations or other steps required before the asset can be taken into use. HMRC guidance indicates that relief should not be denied solely on the grounds that the asset was not brought into use as soon as it was acquired, provided that it was brought into use as soon as practicable after the acquisition and without unnecessary delay. HMRC would expect the interval to be short in most cases (CG60830).

In *Milton v Chivers* (HMIT) SpC 57 [1995] the Special Commissioner held that the phrase 'on the acquisition' did not mean 'immediately on the acquisition' but it did mean that the taking into use and the acquisition must be 'reasonably proximate' to one another.

By concession (ESC D24), HMRC will allow relief where a new asset is not taken into use for the purposes of a trade immediately on acquisition but:

- the owner proposes to incur capital expenditure on enhancing its value;
- any work arising from such expenditure begins as soon as possible after acquisition and is completed within a reasonable time;
- the asset is taken into use – and in the case of land and buildings, occupied – for the purpose of the trade (and for no other purpose) on completion of the work; and

- the asset is neither let nor used for any non-trading purpose in the period between acquisition and the time it is taken into use for the purpose of the trade.

HMRC regard this approach as an interpretation of *TCGA 1992, s 152(1)* that gained judicial approval in *Steibelt (Inspector of Taxes) v Paling* (1999) 71 TC 376, Ch D, rather than as a concession, but have indicated that they will continue to draw on that interpretation where appropriate (CG60850).

ASSETS USED ONLY PARTLY FOR BUSINESS PURPOSES

14.26 In the following situations the taxpayer needs to calculate the acquisition or disposal consideration relating to a deemed 'separate asset' qualifying for roll-over relief:

- Where, during the period of ownership (or any substantial part of it), part of a building or structure is used for the purposes of a trade and part is not so used, then the part used for trade purposes – together with any land occupied for purposes ancillary to it – is treated as a separate asset. HMRC regard this rule, together with the reference in Head A of Class 1 of the list of qualifying assets to 'any building or part of a building', as applying to the new assets as well as the old assets. The rule applies only to buildings, and can apply to both the old and the new assets. Assets in other classes must be used for the purpose of the business and for no other purpose (*TCGA 1992, s 152(6)*; CG60520).
- If the old asset was not used for the purposes of the trade throughout the period of ownership (see **14.27**), then a part of the asset representing its use for the purposes of the trade is treated as a separate asset used wholly for the purposes of the trade. This part is to be calculated having regard to the time and extent to which it was, and was not, used for the purposes of the trade (*TCGA 1992, s 152(7)*). This rule can apply to assets other than buildings (CG60528).

Any period of ownership before 31 March 1982 is ignored for these purposes. Any apportionment of consideration for the above purposes is to be made in a just and reasonable manner and where appropriate HMRC will seek to ensure that all parties to a transaction are bound by the same apportionment of the total consideration (*TCGA 1992, s 152(11)*; CG60300).

Example 14.3

Khaled bought a freehold property on 1 September 2001 and let it to a tenant for three years before occupying and using it for the purpose of his trade on 1

September 2004. He used the whole of the property for the purpose of the trade until he sold it on 1 September 2010 for £150,000.

A chargeable gain of £90,000 accrued. Two-thirds of the gain arising, ie £60,000, may be rolled-over if Khaled reinvests the proceeds of £150,000 in qualifying assets.

The period of ownership

14.27 HMRC consider that the period of ownership of an asset for roll-over relief purposes is the period of beneficial ownership and possession. This period may not be the same as the period from the time of the acquisition and the time of disposal, as defined for the general purposes of CGT. For example, *TCGA 1992, s 28* provides that where an asset is acquired under an unconditional contract, the date on which the acquisition is made is the date the contract is made (and not, if different, the date on which the asset is conveyed or transferred). However, beneficial ownership may not be obtained until completion and the period of ownership for roll-over relief begins when beneficial ownership is obtained, but HMRC have indicated that they will not pursue 'trivial adjustments' (CG60528).

OPERATION OF THE RELIEF

Full relief

14.28 Roll-over relief is given without restriction if an amount equal to the net consideration for the disposal (after deducting allowable costs of disposal) of the old asset is reinvested in a new, qualifying asset. For this purpose the net consideration for the old asset is compared with the cost of acquisition, including allowable incidental costs, of the replacement asset (CG60770).

First, the actual consideration for the disposal is reduced and treated as if it were of such an amount as would give rise to neither a gain nor a loss. Where indexation allowance is available on the disposal (see **9.11**) this means that the disposal proceeds are deemed to be equal to the sum of the original cost plus the indexation allowance. Then the amount of this reduction is deducted from the amount (or value used for CGT purposes) of the consideration for the acquisition of the new asset.

Where the taxpayer is a company the application of indexation allowance can result in a greater gain accruing on the disposal of the second asset, than would accrue in total on the disposal of both assets without roll-over relief. This is because the roll-over relief claim reduces the base cost of the second asset and thus reduces the effect of indexation allowance. The advantage is that the tax due on the disposal of the first asset is postponed for some years.

For the interaction of roll-over relief with other CGT reliefs see **14.44–14.46**.

Example 14.4

On 11 September 2003 Art Ltd sold a warehouse for £300,000, which cost £100,000 on 1 December 1994. The incidental costs of disposal were £6,000. Art Ltd acquired a freehold property on 1 November 2003 also for £300,000 and incurred incidental costs of acquisition amounting to £5,000. The total cost of acquisition is £305,000 and full roll-over relief is due because this exceeds the net proceeds of £294,000. The freehold building was sold on 21 May 2010 for £500,000.

The taxable gain on the disposal of the freehold property is calculated as follows:

Warehouse	£	£
Disposal proceeds June 2003		300,000
Less incidental costs of disposal		(6,000)
Less: cost in 1994	100,000	
Indexation allowance: 0.250 × £100,000	25,000	(125,000)
Chargeable gain rolled over:		169,000
Freehold		
Disposal proceeds in May 2010		500,000
Costs of acquisition in Nov 2003	305,000	
Less rolled-over gain	(169,000)	
	136,000	
Indexation allowance 0.224 × 136,000	30,464	(166,464)
Chargeable gain:		333,536

Partial relief

14.29 Some relief may be available if only a part of the consideration for the disposal of the old assets is reinvested in new assets. The part not reinvested must be less than the amount of the gain if any relief is to be obtained. In this situation:

(a) the chargeable gain is reduced to the amount not reinvested; and

(b) the amount of this reduction is deducted from the consideration for the acquisition of the new asset.

The reduction in (a) and (b) does not affect the tax treatment of the other parties to the transactions (*TCGA 1992, s 153(1)*).

Example 14.5

Bernard sold a qualifying asset in October 2007 for £150,000, realising a chargeable gain of £50,000. He acquired a new qualifying asset in June 2010 for £120,000. Bernard is treated in effect as having reinvested the cost of the old asset, ie £100,000, first.

The remaining £20,000 invested is treated as derived from the gain, so that £30,000 of the gain was not reinvested. The chargeable gain accruing on disposal of the old asset is reduced by £20,000 to £30,000, and the acquisition cost of the new asset is also reduced by £20,000.

Assets held on 31 March 1982

14.30 Assets held by non-corporate taxpayers on 6 April 2008, which were also held by the same taxpayer in the same capacity on 31 March 1982, are automatically rebased to their market value at 31 March 1982. Before 6 April 2008 all taxpayers could elect for all their assets held on 31 March 1982 to be rebased to that date, this rebasing election still applies for companies (see **9.6**). Rebasing excludes from tax any gains arising before 31 March 1982.

Halving relief applies to the 'deferred charge' arising where roll-over relief was obtained on a disposal before 6 April 1988 of an asset held on 31 March 1982. If no adjustment were made on the occasion of a post-1988 disposal of the new asset, the pre-1982 element of the deferred gain would be taxed. In broad terms and subject to certain exceptions, where the deferred gain accrues after 5 April 1988, it is halved (see **9.10**) (*TCGA 1992, Sch 4*). Halving relief only applies to taxpayers subject to corporation tax from 6 April 2008.

DEEMED CONSIDERATION AND DEEMED DISPOSALS

14.31 Any provision of *TCGA 1992* fixing the amount of consideration deemed to be given for the acquisition or disposal of an asset – for example, where a transaction between connected persons is treated as having a consideration equal to the market value of the asset – is applied before roll-over relief. This means that in some cases the amount that the taxpayer needs to 'reinvest' to secure full relief will be greater than the proceeds actually received (*TCGA 1992, s 152(10)*).

HMRC do not consider that roll-over relief is available where there is a deemed disposal and reacquisition of the same asset, because the deemed consideration for the deemed disposal is not available to be applied in acquiring 'other assets'. However, relief may be available where a qualifying asset is deemed to be disposed of or deemed to be acquired. For example, gains arising when a capital sum is derived from an asset (see **2.12**), or when an asset is appropriated to trading stock (see **4.35**), may be the subject of a claim. A deemed acquisition of a qualifying asset, for example, acquisition of an asset as legatee, may also give rise to roll-over relief.

Expenditure reimbursed from public funds

14.32 *Wardhaugh v Penrith Rugby Union Football Club* (2002) 74 TC 499, Ch D established that for roll-over relief purposes the amount or value of the consideration taken to be applied in the acquisition of the new asset is the amount before any reduction under *TCGA 1992, s 50*. That section provides that a CGT computation excludes any expenditure met directly or indirectly by the Crown or by any government, public or local authority. HMRC argued that *TCGA 1992, s 152(10)* (see **14.31**) applied, but the court disagreed on the basis that *TCGA 1992, s 50* related to the non-deductibility of acquisition expenditure. It was not a provision that fixed the amount of the consideration deemed to be given for the acquisition of an asset.

DEPRECIATING ASSETS

14.33 Special rules apply where the new assets are 'depreciating assets'. The provisions of *TCGA 1992, ss 152* and *153* (roll-over relief for business assets) and *TCGA 1992, s 229* (roll-over relief on disposals to employee share ownership trusts) are modified and the following definitions are applied for the purpose of the special rules described below:

- the 'held-over gain' is the amount by which, under the normal rules, the chargeable gain on the first asset ('asset No 1') is reduced, with a corresponding reduction of the allowable expenditure on another asset ('asset No 2'); and
- where a gain of any amount is described as being 'carried forward to any asset', this refers to a reduction of that amount in a chargeable gain, coupled with a reduction of the same amount in expenditure allowable in respect of the asset (*TCGA 1992, s 154(1)*).

An asset is a 'depreciating asset' at a particular time if it is a wasting asset (as defined in *TCGA 1992, s 44*), or will become a wasting asset within ten years. *TCGA 1992, s 44* provides that, subject to certain exceptions, an asset is a wasting asset if it has a predictable life not exceeding 50 years. An asset is a depreciating asset, therefore, if it has a predictable life of no more than 60 years (*TCGA 1992, s 154(7)*).

Postponing the held-over gain

14.34 Where asset No 2 is a depreciating asset, the gain accruing on asset No 1 is not carried forward as described above. Instead, the taxpayer is treated as if the held-over gain did not accrue until the first of the following events occurs:

- he disposes of asset No 2;
- he ceases to use asset No 2 for the purposes of a trade carried on by him; or
- the expiration of a period of ten years beginning with the acquisition of asset No 2 (*TCGA 1992, s 154(2)*).

By concession, no gain is deemed to accrue under this rule where the asset ceases to be used for the purpose of the trade because of the taxpayer's death (ESC D45).

Acquisition of a third asset

14.35 The taxpayer might acquire asset No 3, a non-depreciating asset, before the postponed gain is deemed to accrue as set out in **14.34**. In such a case he could make a claim to roll over the gain on the disposal of asset No 1 against the acquisition cost of asset No 3. The time limits for reinvestment (see **14.7**) would be regarded as met and the initial claim, relating to the acquisition of asset No 2, would be treated as withdrawn. The claim to roll-over relief against the cost of asset No 3 would be limited to the amount of the gain that was held over on the acquisition of asset No 2 (*TCGA 1992, s 154(4), (5)*).

The amount invested in asset No 3 may be less than the net proceeds of asset No 1. In that event the above rule might give rise to a CGT liability because only partial relief would be available. However, the taxpayer may ask for the postponed gain to be treated as derived from two separate assets. The effect would be to split the gain on disposal of asset No 1 into two parts:

- the first part being rolled over against the acquisition of asset No 3 (as in **14.28**); and
- the second part being postponed (as in **14.34**) (*TCGA 1992, s 154(4), (6)*).

Example 14.6

On 25 May 2008, Farmer Gooney sold a barn making a gain of £84,000. On 28 September 2010 he acquired a leasehold interest in a vineyard at a cost of £105,000, which had 35 years to run at that time. Gooney immediately started to cultivate the vineyard as part of his farm, and submitted a roll-over relief claim.

If the new asset had not been a depreciating asset, the gain of £84,000 would be reduced to nil and the cost of acquiring the leasehold reduced to £21,000 (£105,000 less £84,000). However, the cost of acquiring the leasehold vineyard is not reduced. The held-over gain of £84,000 is treated as accruing on the earlier of:

(a) the date of disposal of the leasehold interest;

(b) Gooney ceasing to use the leasehold for the purposes of a trade; and

(c) 28 September 2020, being ten years following the date of acquisition of the leasehold.

On 31 March 2012 Gooney purchased additional agricultural land at a cost of £100,000, and immediately used it in his farming business. Gooney made a claim for roll-over relief in respect of this new land, but continued to use the leasehold vineyard for the purposes of his business. None of the events (a) to (c) above had yet occurred.

The result of this latest roll-over claim is as follows.

Asset No 1 – barn

	£
Disposal proceeds	84,000
Less roll-over relief to Asset No 3 – agricultural land	84,000
Revised gain	NIL

Asset No 2 – Leasehold vineyard

Previous claim withdrawn – no liability on postponed charge

Asset No 3 – agricultural land

	£
Cost of acquisition	100,000
Less roll-over relief	84,000
Revised cost	16,000

Transfer to a European Company or Societas Europaea ('SE')

14.36 The treatment of the postponed gain is modified where the taxpayer transfers asset No 2, or shares in a company that holds asset No 2, to an 'SE' in circumstances in which *TCGA 1992, s 140E* (merger leaving assets within UK tax charge) applies. The postponed gain is not brought into charge. Instead, the SE is treated as though it claimed the roll-over relief *TCGA 1992, s 154(2A)*).

CLAIMS

Time limits

14.37 The time limits set out in **14.38** and **14.39** begin with the end of the tax year or accounting period in which the disposal takes place, or the one in which the new assets are acquired, whichever is the later. See **14.41** regarding provisional relief. The time limits may be extended in the event of an assessment being made to recover tax lost through fraud or neglect. A claim may be made after a CGT assessment has become final.

Individuals, trustees and personal representatives

14.38 A taxpayer within self-assessment has to submit the claim within four years after the end of the tax year to which the claim relates (*TMA 1970, s 43*). There is a temporary extension to the claims period for taxpayers who are not within self-assessment for the year of the claim (see **1.46**), but a taxpayer who is eligible to claim roll-over relief would normally be required to be within self-assessment.

Companies

14.39 A company must claim within four years from the end of the accounting period to which the claim relates (*FA 1998, Sch 18, para 55).*

How to claim

14.40 A claim must be in writing and must specify:

- the claimant;
- the assets disposed of;
- the date of disposal of each of those assets;
- the consideration received for the disposal of each of those assets;
- the assets acquired;
- the dates of acquisition of each of those assets (or the dates on which unconditional contracts for acquisition were entered into);
- the consideration given for each of those assets; and
- the amount of the consideration received for the disposal of each of the specified assets that has been applied in the acquisition of each replacement asset (CG60605).

HMRC provide a claim form for individuals, PRs and trustees to use in their self-assessment helpsheet HS290.

Provisional relief

14.41 In some cases the CGT payable on the gain arising on the disposal may become due before a claim to roll-over relief can be established. Provisional relief is available to ensure that the funds available for reinvestment are not depleted by a payment of tax that would be recovered later. The taxpayer is required to make a declaration, in his tax return for the tax year (or accounting period) in which the disposal took place, that:

(a) the whole (or a specified part) of the consideration will be applied in the acquisition of, or of an interest in, other assets ('the new assets') which on the acquisition will be taken into use, and used only, for the purposes of the trade;

(b) the acquisition will take place as mentioned within the time limits for reinvestment set out in *TCGA 1992, s 152(3)* (see **14.7**); and

(c) the new assets will be within the classes listed in *TCGA 1992, s 155* (see **14.18**).

The declaration may be made on the form provided in HMRC's helpsheet HS290. Until the declaration ceases to have effect (see **14.42**), relief will be available as if the taxpayer had acquired the new assets and made a claim for relief. The rules set out in *s 152* regarding partial business use, successive trades, deemed consideration and apportionments are applied accordingly (*TCGA 1992, s 153A*).

Declaration ceasing to have effect

14.42 The declaration ceases to have effect:

- if it is withdrawn before the 'relevant day', on the day on which it is withdrawn;
- if it is superseded by a valid claim to roll-over relief, on the day on which it is superseded;
- in other cases, on the 'relevant day' (*TCGA 1992, s 153A(3)*).

The 'relevant day' for CGT is the third anniversary of 31 January following the tax year in which the disposal of the old assets took place. For corporation tax, it is the fourth anniversary of the last day of the accounting period in which the disposal took place (*TCGA 1992, s 153A(5)*).

Once a declaration has ceased to have effect all necessary adjustments are to be made, including the making or amending of assessments, irrespective of any time limits that would otherwise apply. If the taxpayer who has obtained provisional relief dies before the relevant day and before having made a valid claim to roll-over relief, HMRC will ask his personal representatives to withdraw the declaration (*TCGA 1992, s 153A(4)*; CG60705).

Interest and penalties

14.43 Interest may be charged on any tax ultimately found to be payable in the event that the taxpayer does not proceed with reinvestment, or partial relief only is obtained. HMRC guidance says: 'The deterrent of frivolous declarations lies in the taxpayer's liability to pay interest from the time the tax should have been paid if the declared intention does not lead to an acquisition. Only if, exceptionally, the declaration is clearly found to have been made fraudulently or negligently should you consider the possibility of penalties' (CG60704).

INTERACTION WITH OTHER RELIEFS

Taper relief

14.44 Taper relief was abolished on 6 April 2008 and is discussed at **17.22–17.41**. The gain to be rolled over on a disposal made before 6 April 2008 was computed before taper relief was given. This is because taper relief applied only to 'chargeable' gains, and the effect of roll-over relief is to reduce the total amount of a chargeable gain. The new asset acquired does not pick up the qualifying holding period for taper relief accrued on the old asset, thus a roll-over relief claim could result in a significant loss of taper relief.

On disposals of business assets that attracted the 75% taper relief, the assessable gain could be reduced to such a level where the net gain would be covered by the annual exemption. In such a case, the taxpayer would opt to have the gain automatically reduced by taper relief rather than claim roll-over relief. Entrepreneurs' relief can apply on the disposal of certain assets, but not in all of the situations where taper relief previously applied (see **Chapter 11**).

Incorporation

14.45 Roll-over relief under *TCGA 1992, s 152* takes precedence over relief on the transfer of a business to a company under *TCGA 1992, s 162* (see **15.17**).

Roll-over relief on the transfer of a business to a company in exchange for shares is given automatically under *TCGA 1992 s 162*, although the taxpayer may elect to disapply the relief on such a transfer after 5 April 2002. If a *TCGA 1992, s 152* roll-over relief claim is made later, the computation of any *TCGA 1992, s 162* relief given may be reopened and revised.

However, HMRC consider that this is not possible once there has been a disposal of any of the shares and an assessment of a chargeable gain on that disposal has become final and conclusive (CG61560).

Entrepreneurs' relief

14.46 The HMRC view is that roll-over relief under *TCGA 1992, s 152* takes priority over entrepreneurs' relief (CG64136). Any part of the gain not rolled-over may be eligible for entrepreneurs' relief.

Chapter 15

Incorporation of a business

INTRODUCTION

15.1 Where a sole trader or partners in a partnership transfer a business to a company, this will normally involve the transfer of all the assets of the business into the ownership of the company. In some cases the business owners may wish to retain certain assets such as property in their own hands, but this can restrict the CGT relief available on incorporation (see **15.8**).

The transfer of the assets to the new company is a disposal for CGT purposes. Normally the new company and the individuals who become the shareholders in that company are then connected persons, as those shareholders will control the company (*TCGA 1992, s 286(6)*). In this case the value of consideration must be taken as the open market value of the assets that are transferred.

The assets of the business may include; stock, plant and machinery (see **4.27**), land, buildings, investments and goodwill. The goodwill may not have been included on the balance sheet of the original business, but it will have a value. However, some forms of goodwill are not separable from the proprietors, so cannot be transferred to the company (see **15.9**).

Taxable capital gains are likely to arise on the land, buildings, investments and goodwill, but these gains can be deferred with a form of roll-over relief known as incorporation relief (*TCGA 1992, s 162*). Guidance on this form of roll-over relief is found in the HMRC Capital Gains Manual at paras CG65700–CG65864.

Incorporation relief is automatic if the conditions apply but it may be disapplied by election. Where incorporation relief does not apply hold-over relief for gifts of business assets may be available, as discussed in **15.20** and **Chapter 13** (*TCGA 1992, s 165*). Entrepreneurs' relief (see **Chapter 11**) can also be used independently or in conjunction with holdover relief to reduce any residue of gains not covered by hold-over relief (see **Chapter 13**).

EFFECT OF THE RELIEF

15.2 The effect of incorporation relief is that the total of the chargeable gains less allowable losses accruing on the transfer of assets (the 'old assets') to the company is deducted from the acquisition cost of the shares received in exchange for those assets.

The gains are therefore deferred until a subsequent disposal of the shares. Where the shares are not all of the same class, the relief is apportioned by reference to the market value of the shares (*TCGA 1992, s 162(2), (3)*).

Full relief is available only where the business assets are exchanged wholly for shares in the company. However, full CGT relief may not always be desirable, as other exemptions or reliefs may be preferred.

Partial relief

15.3 If the transfer is made partly for cash, the gains are apportioned by reference to the value of the shares and the other proceeds received. The amount of relief available is found by applying the fraction A/B to the gain on the old assets, where:

- A is the 'cost of the new assets', ie the shares; and
- B is the value of the whole of the consideration received in exchange for the business.

The cost of the shares (A) is found by adding together the items of expenditure that would be allowable as a deduction (under *TCGA 1992, s 38(1)(a)*) in the event of a chargeable gain arising on a disposal of the shares. This will normally be the market value of the assets transferred to the company (see **15.13**). The relief cannot exceed the cost of the shares. The gains attributed to the shares are rolled over, while the remaining gains are immediately chargeable to CGT (*TCGA 1992, s 162(4), (5)*).

See **15.13** regarding the consideration received for the transfer and how relief is restricted where part of the consideration is not in the form of shares.

Partnerships

15.4 Where the business transferred to the company was carried on in partnership, incorporation relief is computed separately for each individual partner based on the consideration he receives. Relief is not denied to the individuals where one of the partners is a company, so long as the whole of the business is transferred to a company, but as indicated in **15.5** the corporate partner is not eligible for relief.

This means that it is possible to obtain incorporation relief for a partner who transfers his interest in the business in exchange for shares, while his fellow partner who receives only cash for his interest is unable to roll over any capital gain arising. This provides considerable flexibility when arranging the transfer of a business previously carried on by a partnership.

THE CONDITIONS

15.5 The gains arising on the transfer of assets to the company are automatically deferred if the conditions are met. No claim is required, but the relief can be disapplied by election (see **15.11**). The key conditions are set out below:

(a) the transfer must be made by a person other than a company (see below);

(b) the business must be transferred as a going concern (see **15.7**);

(c) the transfer must include the whole assets of the business, or the whole of those assets other than cash (see **15.8**); and

(d) the transfer must be made wholly or partly in exchange for shares issued by the company to the transferor – these shares are known as the 'new assets' (*TCGA 1992, s 162(1)*).

Incorporation relief is available, therefore, for transfers of a business (see **15.6**) by an individual, trustee or personal representative. 'Company' includes any unincorporated association (but not a partnership), so that condition (a) means that relief is not available where an unincorporated association transfers a business to a company (*TCGA 1992, s 288(1)*). The company need not be specially formed for the purpose, it can be an existing company. The company does not to have to be resident in the UK, or liable to UK tax.

Incorporation relief is not available where a business conducted by a sole trader or ordinary partnership is transferred to an LLP. This is because for CGT purposes the LLP is treated exactly like an ordinary partnership (see **6.23**). Where the business of an LLP is transferred entirely to a company, incorporation relief may apply. However, where the new company is invited to join the LLP as a member and the LLP continues trading as a going concern, the business remains owned by the LLP and incorporation relief cannot apply.

Business

15.6 The relief applies to the transfer of a 'business', which is not defined in the legislation (*TCGA 1992, s 162(1)*). HMRC regard 'business' as taking its normal meaning, which is 'wider than trade' (and would probably include a profession or vocation). HMRC guidance recognises that it is not always easy to draw the line between a business and other activities, but a claim that the passive holding of investments or an investment property amounted to a business is likely to be resisted (CG65712). Having said that, the commercial letting of furnished holiday accommodation may well be accepted by HMRC as a 'business', as it is treated as being a trade for various CGT reliefs (*TCGA 1992, s 241(3), (3A)*).

HMRC regard the Malaysian tax case *American Leaf Blending Co Sdn Bhd v Director-General of Inland Revenue* [1978] STC 561, heard by the Privy Council, as useful authority and an indication that property letting activities may constitute a business if carried on by a company but not where those activities are carried on by a private individual. Lord Diplock said:

> 'In the case of a private individual it may well be that the mere receipt of rents from property that he owns raises no presumption that he is carrying on a business. In contrast … in the case of a company incorporated for the purpose of making profits for its shareholders any gainful use to which it puts any of its assets prima facie amounts to the carrying on of a business.'

While the carrying on of a business usually called for some activity, that activity may be 'intermittent with long intervals of quiescence in between', Lord Diplock added. HMRC stress the importance of looking at the context in which the courts have considered the meaning of 'business', and add that the word may be interpreted differently when contrasting individuals and companies.

HMRC will provide businesses with written confirmation of the application of tax law to specific transactions, where there is material uncertainty, or the issue is commercially significant, under the non-statutory business clearance service, see the HMRC manual: Non-Statutory Business Clearance guidance. This service applies to all tax law as it affects UK businesses. Where the question to be addressed is whether the activities of the taxpayer are considered to be a 'business' or a 'trade' for a particular provision it is unclear whether this non-statutory clearance procedure can be used by the taxpayer.

Going concern

15.7 The business must be transferred as a 'going concern' together with all of the assets of the business (*TCGA 1992, s 162(1)*). HMRC take this to mean that the transfer must comprise 'something more than a collection of assets'.

HMRC guidance refers to an Australian case, *Reference under the Electricity Commission (Balmain Electric Light Co Purchase) Act 1950* [1957] 57 SR (NSW) 100, cited in *CIR v Gordon* (see below), where Sugerman J said:

> 'To describe an undertaking as a "going concern" imports no more than that, at the point of time to which the description applies, its doors are open for business; that it is then active and operating, and perhaps also that it has all the plant etc which is necessary to keep it in operation, as distinct from its being only an inert aggregation of plant.'

In *Gordon v CIR* (1991) 64 TC 173 CS Lord Hope said the Special Commissioner had considered the ability of the business to continue as a going concern for some time in the future after the transfer to the company, but the question whether the activities could be carried on without interruption should be directed to the date of the transfer, and not to some later date (CG65716). Lord Hope referred to *Kenmir Ltd v Frizzell* [1968] 1 WLR 329 in which Widgery J said that the vital consideration was 'whether the effect of the transaction was to put the transferee in possession of a going concern, the activities of which he could carry on without interruption'.

Whole of the assets of the business

15.8 The transfer must include the whole assets of the business, or the whole of those assets other than cash. HMRC regard cash as including sums held in a bank deposit or current account (*TCGA 1992, s 162(1)*; CG65719).

If an asset is a business asset it must be transferred to the company. Whether an asset is on the balance sheet is not conclusive, and an asset may remain a business asset after it has been taken off the balance sheet. See **15.9** regarding goodwill.

The requirement that all assets (except cash) must be transferred to the company may be unattractive to the business proprietor. For example, transfers of land and buildings may result in substantial stamp duty land tax liabilities.

As an alternative to securing incorporation relief under *TCGA 1992, s 162* the proprietor may consider retaining assets outside the company and transferring the remaining chargeable assets to the company for a consideration less than market value. In those circumstances hold-over relief for gifts, under *TCGA 1992, s 165* (see **15.20**), may be available.

Goodwill

15.9 The goodwill of the business may not appear on the balance sheet, but goodwill can be the most valuable asset to be transferred to the company. It is important, however, to achieve a realistic valuation of the transferable goodwill as HMRC frequently challenge valuations that appear over optimistic.

The latest HMRC approach to defining and valuing goodwill is set out in their CGT manual at paras CG68000–CG68330. The definition of goodwill is now based on the reputation of the business which is built up over its lifetime, so a young business has very little goodwill and a more established business should expect to carry a significant value of goodwill. The HMRC view is that goodwill generated within a business cannot be separated from that business when the business is transferred as a going concern (CG68010–CG68050). However, this overarching definition is qualified by the following conditions which will restrict the value of goodwill that can be transferred to the company:

- Personal goodwill. This derives from the technical skills, and personal attributes of the business proprietor, such as the personal skills of an author or chef. This goodwill cannot be separated from the individual to be transferred into the company.
- Inherent goodwill. This is connected to the location where the business is carried out. The HMRC view is that this type of goodwill can be transferred, but generally only when the premises in which the business is run is also transferred to the company. The attachment of this type of goodwill to the property value has implications for stamp duty land tax, as at present HMRC are insisting that SDLT be paid on the goodwill attached to a property when the property is transferred as part of the sale or incorporation of a business.

Once the personal and inherent aspects of the goodwill are isolated the balance should be free goodwill that can be transferred to the company, without the need to also transfer the business property. It should be noted that the allocation of goodwill in the sale or transfer agreement does not dictate the tax treatment of the goodwill. Although any apportionment of the total transfer value by HMRC should be done on a just and reasonable basis.

Where a significant value is placed on the goodwill to be transferred to the company it is advisable to use the post-transaction valuation procedure (form CG34), to attempt to agree the value with HMRC (see **1.35**). This procedure may not always achieve an agreed valuation in time for the tax return filing date, as all valuations of free goodwill must be dealt with by HMRC Shares and Assets Valuation office. This office has a library of information covering various trades and types of businesses, which sets out how goodwill and other intangible assets are commonly valued in those trades.

Example 15.1

In November 2010, Herman transferred his music business including all the assets and liabilities to Musiqware Limited in consideration for 1,000 shares in Musiqware Limited. Herman started the business in June 2002 and ran it from that date in his own name. He did not elect under *TCGA 1992, s 162A* to disapply incorporation relief. The only chargeable asset of the business is goodwill, which is judged to be free goodwill based on the future value of the music sales. The value of the business transferred is agreed as follows:

	Value £
Free goodwill (based on the value of the music sales)	250,000
Non-chargeable assets	100,000
Cash	25,000
	375,000
Creditors	(255,000)
Net value of the business	120,000

The gain arising on the transfer is £250,000. The consideration for the business is wholly in the form of shares, so the shares are worth £120,000. The amount of the gain to be rolled over cannot exceed the cost of the shares, which is £120,000.

Thus, £120,000 of the gain is rolled over and the balance of £130,000 is chargeable to CGT in 2010/11. Musiqware Limited can claim a corporation tax deduction for the cost of the goodwill it has purchased from Herman under the intangibles regime. Although Herman is connected with Musiqware Limited as he controls all the shares, the intangibles regime applies as the goodwill was wholly created after 31 March 2002 (*CTA 2009, s 882*).

Liabilities

15.10 The company may well assume some or all of the liabilities of the business, although there is no requirement for liabilities as well as assets to be transferred to the company. The company's assumption of liabilities represents additional consideration for the business, but by concession (ESC D32), HMRC do not take this point because they recognise that the transferor does not receive cash to meet the tax liability that would arise by reference to that consideration (CA65745).

HMRC also recognise that the transfer of liabilities reduces the value of the shares issued to the transferor, see **Example 15.3**. ESC D32 reads:

> 'Where liabilities are taken over by a company on the transfer of a business to the company, HMRC are prepared for the purposes of the "rollover" provision in *TCGA 1992, s 162* not to treat such liabilities as consideration. If therefore the other conditions of *s 162* are satisfied, no capital gain arises

on the transfer. Relief under *s 162* is not precluded by the fact that some or all of the liabilities of the business are not taken over by the company.'

Any personal liabilities of the transferor assumed by the company, including his capital account and any tax liability relating to the transfer of the business, are outside the terms of this concession and are treated as part of the consideration. The concession does not affect the calculation of the net cost of the shares (CG65745).

Where incorporation relief is obtained by concession, the taxpayer is required by statute to account for the deferred gain becoming chargeable (*TCGA 1992, ss 284A, 284B*).

Example 15.2

Walter carries on an antiquarian bookselling business. He decides to form a company, Bookend Limited, to carry on the business. In August 2010 he transfers the whole of the business undertaking, assets and liabilities to Bookend Limited in exchange for shares. The business assets and liabilities transferred are valued as follows:

		Value	Chargeable gain
Assets	£	£	£
Freehold shop premises		180,000	100,000
Goodwill		36,000	36,000
Fixtures and fittings		4,000	0
Trading stock		52,000	0
Debtors		28,000	0
		300,000	
Liabilities			
Mortgage on shop	50,000		
Trade creditors	20,000	(70,000)	
		230,000	136,000

Bookend Ltd issues 230,000 £1 ordinary shares, valued at par, to Walter. The amount of chargeable gain rolled over on transfer of the business to Bookend Ltd is:

£136,000 × (£230,000/£230,000) = £136,000

See **15.12** regarding the formula to calculate the relief due.

ELECTION TO FOREGO INCORPORATION RELIEF

15.11 Incorporation relief under *TCGA 1992, s 162* does not have to be claimed. For transfers prior to 6 April 2002 the relief was mandatory if all the conditions were met. For transfers made after that date the taxpayer may elect to disapply the relief (*TCGA 1992, s 162A*).

For transfers occurring before 6 April 2008 the dis-application of incorporation relief would crystallise a gain for taper relief. This would be desirable when the shares of the new company were sold within two years of incorporation, which would not allow enough time for full business asset taper relief to build up, or indeed because taper relief was about to be abolished. The available business asset taper relief and the CGT annual exemption could reduce or eliminate the tax liability. For disposals made on and after 6 April 2008 it may be more desirable to claim entrepreneurs' relief on the full gain leaving the residue to be covered by the annual exemption (see **15.19**). The uncertainty surrounding future rates of CGT may also encourage the taxpayer to pay tax on the gain in the current period at a known rate, rather than defer the gain to date where the rate of CGT may well be higher.

Once an election under *TCGA 1992, s 162A* is made, all necessary adjustments – eg by means of discharge or repayment of tax – are made to give effect to it (*TCGA 1992, s 162A(1), (6)*).

If two or more individuals owned the business transferred to the company – including ownership by a partnership of which they are partners – then each of them is entitled to elect to disclaim incorporation relief as he sees fit in relation to his own share of the gain accruing on the old assets and his share of the new assets (*TCGA 1992, s 162A(7), (8)*).

The election must be made by a notice given to HMRC no later than:

- the first anniversary of 31 January following the tax year in which the transfer took place, where the transferor has disposed of all the new assets by the end of the tax year following the one in which the transfer took place; or
- the second anniversary of 31 January following the tax year in which the transfer took place in any other case.

HMRC advise taxpayers to write to them if they do not want *s 162* to apply to their gains (Helpsheet HS276). The election could also be made by an amendment to the tax return.

For the purpose of this time limit a disposal of new assets by the transferor is ignored if it is a disposal to a spouse or civil partner falling within the no gain, no loss provisions of *TCGA 1992, s 58* (see **3.62**). A later disposal by the transferee spouse or civil partner is treated as a disposal by the transferor unless it is a disposal to the transferor (*TCGA 1992, s 162A(2)–(5)*).

Example 15.3

James and Jill ran a computer software business in partnership sharing all profits equally until they transferred the business to JJ Limited in June 2009 in exchange for shares in the company. The asset of goodwill was not shown in the partnership balance sheet. In May 2010 they sold their shares for £2 million more than the net asset value of the partnership business prior to incorporation, producing a gain of £1 million each. This excess represented the goodwill that was owned by the partnership but had no acquisition cost for CGT.

In the absence of an election to forego incorporation relief, the gain of £2 million would be rolled over against the cost of the shares and a gain of the same amount would arise on the sale of the shares. James and Jill cannot claim entrepreneurs' relief on the disposal of the shares because they had not owned the ordinary shares in JJ Limited for the minimum 12 months to qualify for that relief.

If an election under *TCGA 1992, s 162A* is made, incorporation relief does not apply and the gain of £2 million on the goodwill is eligible for the entrepreneurs' relief as it accrues in June 2009. Entrepreneurs' relief applies at this time to reduce the amount chargeable to 5/9th of the gain, or £555,555 each, to be taxed at 18%. The gains accruing on other assets would also have to be considered. The election under *TCGA 1992, 162A* must be made by 31 January 2012 (the first anniversary of 31 January following the tax year in which the transfer took place) because the shares were sold by the end of the 2010/11 tax year following the tax year (2009/10) in which the incorporation took place. The claim for entrepreneurs' relief must also be made by 31 January 2012.

COMPUTING THE RELIEF

15.12 The chargeable gains and allowable losses accruing on the transfer of chargeable assets to the company are computed and the net gains are aggregated. Calculating the incorporation relief can be confusing as there are two figures arising from the disposal of the old assets:

(A) the net gain realised on those assets; and

(B) the net value of the assets transferred to the company.

In addition the consideration given by the company may involve two amounts:

(C) the cost of the new shares issued by the company; and

(D) the value of any other consideration.

See **15.13** regarding the task of identifying and quantifying the consideration for the transfer. Some of the consideration for the assets must be shares issued by the company, but there may be other consideration such as cash or a loan account (see **15.16**). Where no other consideration is given for the old assets the value of (D) will be nil, and the value of (B) will equal (C).

The amount of incorporation relief is found using this formula using the values for the list above:

$$(C/(C + D)) \times A$$

Where there is consideration other than shares the amount of the gain that can be relieved using incorporation relief is restricted, leaving the balance of the gain immediately chargeable to CGT (see **15.16**). This is best explained by a number of examples. In each case John transfers his trading business to JDMS Ltd, and the figures of gain and consideration are labelled as per the above list.

Example 15.4

(A): net gain on the assets transferred to JDMS Ltd was £100,000.

(B): the net value of the assets transferred was £210,000.

The only consideration given by JDMS Ltd was an issue of 210,000 ordinary shares of £1 each.

(C): The cost of the shares is £210,000. The amount of incorporation relief is calculated as:

$$\frac{C}{(C + D)} \times £100{,}000$$

ie $$\frac{210{,}000}{210{,}000} \times £100{,}000 = £100{,}000$$

The gain arising on the transfer to the company will be:

	£
Amount of the gain on the old assets	100,000
Less incorporation relief	100,000
Gain or loss remaining	NIL

	£
Base cost of the new shares:	
Actual cost	210,000
Less incorporation relief	100,000
Revised base cost of new shares	110,000

Example 15.5

(A): net gain on the assets transferred to JDMS Ltd was £100,000.

(B): the net value of the assets transferred was £75,000.

The only consideration is 75,000 shares issued at £1 per share.

(C): The cost of the shares is £75,000.

The total gain is £100,000, but the incorporation relief is restricted to the cost of the shares: £75,000.

The taxable gain arising on the transfer to the company is:

	£
Amount of the gain on the old assets	100,000
Less incorporation relief	75,000
Net gain subject to CGT immediately	25,000

The base cost of the new shares becomes:

	£
Actual cost	75,000
Less incorporation relief	75,000
Revised base cost	NIL

Example 15.6

(A): net gain on the assets transferred to JDMS Ltd was £100,000.

(B): the net value of the assets transferred was £180,000,

In exchange JDMS Ltd supplied the following consideration.

	£
110,000 shares of £1 each with no premium	110,000
Balance left outstanding on loan account	70,000
Total consideration	180,000

(C): The cost of the new shares is £110,000.

(D): The value of other consideration is £70,000

The amount of incorporation relief becomes:

$$\frac{C}{(C + D)} \times £100{,}000$$

ie $$\frac{110{,}000}{180{,}000} \times £100{,}000 = £61{,}111$$

The gain arising on the transfer to JDMS Ltd is:

	£
Amount of the gain on the old assets	100,000
Less incorporation relief	61,111
Net gain chargeable to CGT	38,889

CGT will be payable on the gain of £38,889, but this could be subject to a claim for entrepreneurs' relief (see **Chapter 11**)

The base cost of the new shares in JDMS Ltd is:

	£
Actual cost	110,000
Less incorporation relief	61,111
Revised cost	48,889

Consideration for the transfer

15.13 The transfer must be made wholly or partly in exchange for shares actually issued by the company to the transferor – these shares are known as the 'new assets' (*TCGA 1992, s 162(1)*). It is important that the necessary documentation is prepared to demonstrate what has been transferred to the company and precisely what the company has given in return.

HMRC accept that there may sometimes be a delay in issuing the shares, where, for example, the authorised capital of the company has to be increased. Relief is not denied so long as the issue of shares takes place 'fairly promptly' after the reason for the delay has gone. The task should not be left until the company's first accounts are prepared (CG65720).

Relief is not available if the shares are issued:

- in consideration for something other than the transfer of the business; or
- to settle a loan account representing cash consideration.

Consideration in the form of shares

15.14 The transferor does not have to acquire any specific level of shareholding in the company. The number of shares may be decided in advance of the transfer, leaving the share premium to be calculated later by reference to the value of the business assets transferred to the company. The transferor is not required to work for the company.

As indicated in **15.2**, where the shares are not all of the same class, the relief is apportioned by reference to their relative market values.

The shares issued do not have to be ordinary shares, but if, for example, redeemable preference shares are issued the relief may be denied by virtue of the anti-avoidance provisions in *ITA 2007, s 684*. In such a case the taxpayer should consider requesting an advance clearance under *ITA 2007, s 701*.

The cost of the shares

15.15 As indicated in **15.12**, the effect of the relief is that the net gains accruing on the transfer of assets (the 'old assets') to the company is reduced. That reduction is then apportioned among the shares and goes to reduce the allowable expenditure otherwise deductible on a future disposal of each new share (*TCGA 1992, s 162(2)*), as shown in **Examples 15.4–15.6** above.

The cost of the new shares is found by adding together the items of expenditure that would be allowable as a deduction in computing the chargeable gain arising on a disposal of the new assets. The reduction is apportioned between shares of different classes on the basis of their relative market values.

The date of disposal of the old business is taken to be the date of acquisition of the shares.

The transferor and transferee company will normally be connected persons (see **3.20**), so that the chargeable assets will pass to the company at market value. The transferor's cost of acquiring the shares is, therefore, normally the market value of what he gives for those shares, ie the value of the business.

HMRC regard the value of the business as, broadly, the difference between its assets and liabilities – concession ESC D32 relating to liabilities (see **15.10**) is not in point. This may mean that incorporation relief is restricted because the amount of the relief set against the cost of the shares cannot exceed that cost (see **Example 15.1**). That cost may be very small in the case where the business has significant liabilities.

Consideration other than shares

15.16 Where part of the consideration for the transfer is in a form other than shares, a proportion of the gains accruing on the transfer will become chargeable to CGT. Such consideration would include a credit balance on the transferor's loan or current account with the company (except where the balance represents consideration which is to be satisfied in the form of shares and there is a delay in issuing the shares) (see **15.13**). HMRC do not accept that cash consideration or other consideration can be regarded as being given for one or more specified assets (CG65742).

It may well be beneficial to arrange for part of the consideration to be in the form of a loan account balance, given that:

- any gain accruing on that part of the consideration may well be covered by the CGT annual exemption; and
- the transferor may not wish to 'lock in' all of the consideration in the form of shares in the company.

INTERACTION WITH OTHER RELIEFS

15.17 The interaction of the reliefs available on the disposal of business assets is summarised below.

(a) Incorporation relief under *TCGA 1992, s 162* is applied before taper relief (see **15.18**).

(b) Roll-over relief for replacement of business assets (*TCGA 1992, s 152*) takes precedence over the other CGT reliefs, because it reduces the consideration to be taken into account in computing the gain on disposal.

(c) Incorporation relief on the transfer of a business to a company (*TCGA 1992, s 162*) follows, because it reduces the net chargeable gains accruing on the assets transferred to the company.

(d) Hold-over relief for gifts of business assets (*TCGA 1992, s 165*) also reduces the chargeable gains, but since incorporation relief under *TCGA 1992, s 162* is automatic (unless an election is made to forego it), it must take precedence over *TCGA 1992, s 165* relief.

(e) Entrepreneurs' relief (*TCGA 1992, ss 169H–169S*) can apply to gains not relieved by incorporation relief or hold-over relief (see **15.19**).

Taper relief

15.18 Taper relief was abolished for disposals made from 6 April 2008, but it will remain relevant while claims for incorporation relief are finalised for 2007/08. It is clear that incorporation relief (under *TCGA 1992, s 162*) is applied before taper relief.

For taper relief purposes, the period of ownership of the old assets transferred to the business is ignored in calculating the qualifying holding period of the new shares. This means that where incorporation relief is obtained without restriction, taper relief that would otherwise be due in respect of the assets transferred is lost. However, as indicated in **15.11**, the taxpayer may elect under *TCGA 1992, s 162A* for the relief not to apply where the transfer takes place after 5 April 2002 (*TCGA 1992, s 162A*; CG65860).

Example 15.7

On 1 November 2007 Jeremy transferred his business as a going concern to Fisher Ltd in return for shares in the company, and the conditions for relief under *TCGA 1992, s 162* were met. The business had commenced on 1 October 2003. A chargeable gain would accrue in 2007/08 on the transfer of goodwill to Fisher Ltd in the absence of incorporation relief, but the effect of *s 162* is that the gain is deducted instead from the acquisition value of Jeremy's Fisher Ltd shares.

Jeremy disposes of his shares in Fisher Ltd on 1 December 2008, after taper relief was abolished. By that date Jeremy had held the Fisher Ltd shares for over 12 months, and the other qualifying conditions for entrepreneurs' relief applied (see **Chapter 11**). That relief reduces the chargeable gain by 4/9ths, subject to the taxpayer's lifetime cap.

An election to forego the incorporation relief (made within the time limits set out in *TCGA 1992, s 162A* see **15.11**) would give rise to a chargeable gain, accruing on 1 November 2007, on the disposal of goodwill to the company. However, the qualifying holding period in respect of that goodwill would cover four complete years (1 October 2003 to 1 November 2007) so that only 25% of the 2007/08 gain would be chargeable after deduction of taper relief.

The entrepreneurs' relief claim to reduce the gain arising in 2008/09 can be submitted by 31 January 2011, whether or not the claim to disapply incorporation relief had been made. Jeremy would also need to consider the different rates of CGT that apply in 2007/08 and 2008/09.

Entrepreneurs' relief

15.19 The HMRC view is that roll-over relief under *TCGA 1992, s 152* takes precedence over entrepreneurs' relief, and where part of the gain is not rolled-over entrepreneurs' relief can apply to that part (CG64136). As incorporation relief is a form of roll-over relief it must be presumed that HMRC believe incorporation relief takes precedence over entrepreneurs' relief.

However, this view is not clearly stated in the HMRC Capital Gains Manual at the time of writing. An alternative view is that entrepreneurs' relief takes priority over incorporation relief for the following reasons:

- Incorporation relief operates by deducting a sum from the gain that would be taxed, but for the incorporation relief given, so the gain must be calculated first. The sum deducted from the gain is also used to reduce the base cost of the shares acquired.
- The taxpayer needs to claim entrepreneurs' relief whereas incorporation relief under *TCGA 1992, s 162* is applied automatically if the conditions are met, subject to the election to disapply the relief (*TCGA 1992, s 162A*).

The cautious approach would be to disapply incorporation relief using the election (see **15.11**) and claim entrepreneurs' relief. The alternative is to structure the incorporation so incorporation relief does not apply (see **15.20** and **Chapter 13**).

Incorporation: using hold-over relief

15.20 A hold-over relief claim may be made on the transfer of a business to a company where *s 162* relief is either not available or is restricted. Hold-over relief may be useful if the sole trader or partners wish to retain assets outside the company, but the relief is restricted where there is actual consideration, either in the form of shares or a credit balance on a director's loan account with the company.

In order to qualify for hold-over relief the transfer to the company must be a disposal otherwise than by way of a bargain at arm's length, including a transaction deemed to be such because it is between connected persons.

Table 15.1 sets out some of the key features, of incorporation relief (*TCGA 1992, s 162*) and hold-over relief (*TCGA 1992, s 165*), to be considered by a taxpayer contemplating the incorporation of a business.

Table 15.1

Incorporation relief	*Hold-over relief for gifts of business assets*
Relief is automatic unless an election is made to disapply it	Relief must be claimed
Relief need not apply to all partners	Relief need not be claimed by all partners
Relief is given in full or in part on all chargeable assets transferred, depending on the extent of consideration other than shares	Relief may be claimed either on all assets or on certain assets only
Relief is available only if all the assets (or all the assets except cash) are transferred	Relief may be claimed even if some non-cash assets are not transferred
Gain is rolled over against the cost of the shares issued to the transferor(s) as consideration	Gain is held over against the cost of the chargeable asset(s) acquired by the company
Business must be transferred as a going concern	The transfer of one or more assets used for the purpose of the trade, etc will suffice
Loss of taper relief up to the date of incorporation	Loss of taper relief up to the date of the transfer

Further reading

15.21 This chapter covers only the capital gains considerations for the incorporation of a business, for a full discussion of all the tax and practical issues involved with incorporation see Roger Jones, *Incorporating a Business* (3rd edition) (Bloomsbury Professional).

Chapter 16

Enterprise Investment Scheme

INTRODUCTION

16.1 The Enterprise Investment Scheme (EIS) is designed to encourage individuals to invest in small unquoted trading companies. The conditions the company which issues the EIS shares has to comply with (the EIS company), have been amended frequently in past years. The focus of EIS relief is now on smaller companies. The EIS company must have no more than 50 full-time equivalent employees, and gross assets of no more than £7 million before the EIS share issue and £8 million afterwards (*ITA 2007, ss 186, 186A*).

Income tax relief at the rate of 20% of the amount subscribed for EIS shares is available, although this tax relief is restricted by the taxpayer's income tax liability for the year. Various other conditions apply as discussed in Chapter 3 of *Income Tax 2010/11* (Bloomsbury Professional). The CGT reliefs examined in this chapter provide for:

- gains to be free of CGT after the EIS shares have been held for three years – see **16.3**; and
- deferral of a capital gain reinvested in EIS shares within, broadly, one year before and three years after the disposal giving rise to the gain – see **16.10**.

HMRC guidance on the EIS is available at www.hmrc.gov.uk/eis/index.htm, and in the Venture Capital Schemes manual at paras VCM20000–VCM43660. The CGT reliefs for investments in venture capital trusts (VCTs) are examined in **17.2**.

CGT DISPOSAL RELIEF

16.2 A gain accruing on an individual's disposal of EIS shares is not a chargeable gain providing certain conditions are met. EIS shares are shares that have attracted income tax relief under the EIS scheme as set out in *ITA 2007, Pt 5*. There are detailed conditions in relation to the individual, the company and its activities.

Disposal relief is not available to trustees. For HMRC guidance regarding this exemption, see HMRC's Venture Capital Manual at VCM30000–VCM32350 and the HMRC tax return helpsheet HS297.

Conditions

16.3 A gain arising on a disposal of EIS shares is not a chargeable gain if:

(a) the disposal is made after the end of the 'relevant period' (see below) defined by reference to *ITA 2007, s 159* – this is normally three years;

(b) the shares have qualified for EIS income tax relief;

(c) that income tax relief has not been withdrawn; and

(d) there would be a chargeable gain but for this relief (*TCGA 1992, s 150A*).

The income tax relief condition in (b) means that disposal relief is limited by reference to the maximum annual subscription for which income tax relief is available, and the actual tax relief given (see **16.5**). From 6 April 2008 income tax relief can be given on up to £500,000 of shares issued in a tax year. The limit was previously £400,000 (*ITA 2007, s 158*).

A gain accruing on a disposal within the relevant period is a chargeable gain, and any loss accruing is an allowable loss. However, a loss accruing on disposal of the shares after the end of the relevant period is also allowable (see **16.4**).

A gain that does not qualify for disposal relief is a chargeable gain. For gains realised before 6 April 2008, business asset taper relief should be available (see **17.22**). However, later gains will only qualify for entrepreneurs' relief if the shareholder held at least 5% of the ordinary shares of the EIS company and was either an employee or officer of the company, or of a company in the same group for 12 months to the date of disposal (see **11.9**).

The term 'relevant period' is defined in *TCGA 1992, Sch 5B, para 19(1)* and *ITA 2007, s 159*, where the relevant period is further split into periods A, B and C. These periods all end immediately before the 'termination date' relating to those shares. The termination date is the later of:

- the third anniversary of the issue date of the shares; and
- the third anniversary of the commencement of the trade (*ITA 2007, s 256*).

For shares issued before 6 April 2000, the relevant period is normally the period of five years from the date of issue of the shares.

Losses

16.4 Disposal relief is excluded where a loss accrues on the disposal, with the result that a loss is an allowable capital loss. If disposal relief was not excluded, a loss would not be an allowable loss because *TCGA 1992, s 16(2)* provides that a loss is not an allowable loss if a gain accruing on the same disposal would not be a chargeable gain.

The loss is an allowable loss whether or not EIS income tax relief is withdrawn. However, in calculating the loss the taxpayer's allowable expenditure is reduced by the amount of the income tax relief obtained and not withdrawn. Relief for the loss may be claimed against income rather than set off against future capital gains, see **17.16** (*TCGA 1992, s 150A(1), (2), (2A)*; *ITA 2007, s 131*). This restriction of loss relief also applies for the disposal of BES shares acquired before 1 January 1994 where the income tax relief has not been withdrawn (*TCGA 1992, s 150*).

Example 16.1

On 6 April 2006 Christina subscribed £100,000 for new ordinary shares in an EIS company and obtains income tax relief of £20,000. She sold the shares on 20 May 2010, after the termination date, for £90,000 and none of the income tax relief had been withdrawn. The restriction of allowable expenditure turns her loss into a gain, but that gain is not a chargeable gain.

2010/11	£	£
Sale proceeds		90,000
Allowable expenditure	100,000	
less income tax relief not withdrawn	(20,000)	
		(80,000)
Gain not chargeable to tax:		10,000

Example 16.2

Ralph subscribes £200,000 for EIS shares and obtains income tax relief of £40,000. He disposes of the shares before the termination date for £150,000, and £30,000 of the income tax relief is withdrawn. His allowable loss is:

	£	£
Consideration		150,000
Allowable expenditure	200,000	
less income tax relief not withdrawn	(10,000)	
		(190,000)
Allowable loss		40,000

Restriction of disposal relief

16.5 Disposal relief is restricted where the taxpayer did not obtain income tax relief on the whole of the amount subscribed for the shares, unless that restriction was due solely to the fact that income tax relief is limited to the amount of the taxpayer's income tax liability.

This restriction applies to gains but not losses. It is normally a consequence of the subscription limit (see **16.3**) for income tax relief purposes. The fraction of the gain that is exempt in such a case is found by applying the fraction A/B to the gain, where:

- A is the amount of the income tax relief obtained; and
- B is an amount equal to tax at the basic rate (currently 20%) for that year on the amount subscribed for the shares (*TCGA 1992, s 150A(3)*; *ITA 2007, ss 6, 989*).

Example 16.3

Richard subscribes £250,000 for shares in an EIS company in the tax year 2002/03, when the maximum amount on which income tax relief can be obtained is £150,000. He obtains income tax relief of £30,000 (20% × £150,000) for that year although the basic rate relief on the full subscription would be £50,000. He sells the shares in 2010/11 for £400,000. His chargeable gain is:

2010/11	£
Consideration	400,000
Allowable expenditure	(250,000)
Gain	150,000
Exemption:	
£150,000 × (30,000/50,000)	(90,000)
Chargeable gain	60,000

Identification rules

16.6 Where it is necessary to identify shares disposed of with acquisitions made at different times, or to establish whether the shares disposed of were shares that attracted income tax relief, the EIS identification rules in *ITA 2007, s 246* are applied instead of the rules in *TCGA 1992*.

Broadly speaking, identification is made on a first in, first out basis. There are detailed rules for identification of shares acquired on the same day (*ITA 2007, s 246(3)*).

Reorganisations and rights

16.7 For disposal relief the rules in *TCGA 1992, s 127* (where the new shares step into the shoes of the old shares) are to be applied, on a reorganisation of share capital within *TCGA 1992, s 126*, separately to each of the following kinds of shares:

- shares that have attracted income tax relief, where the investment has formed the basis of a deferral relief claim (see **16.10**) and there has been no chargeable event affecting the deferral relief;
- other shares that have attracted income tax relief; and
- shares that have not attracted income tax relief (*TCGA 1992, s 150A(6), (6A)*).

The effect of this rule is that shares of each kind are treated as a separate holding of original shares and identified with a separate new holding following the reorganisation. See **16.24** for rules regarding share reorganisations and deferral relief.

Where there is a rights issue in respect of an existing holding of ordinary shares, and either the existing shares or the new shares attract income tax relief and the other shares did not. In this case the provisions of *TCGA 1992, ss 127–130* (which broadly treat the old and new shares as a single holding) are disapplied and the taxpayer is treated as acquiring new shares at the date of the rights issue for the amount paid for those new shares (*TCGA 1992, s 150A(7)*).

Exchange of shares

16.8 Where the rules in *TCGA 1992, ss 135* and *136* apply to exchanges of shares and securities in a company (A) for those in another company (B), the effect for the capital gains position of shareholders is normally that there is no disposal of the original holding in company A. Companies A and B are treated as if they were the same company and the exchange is treated as a reorganisation of its share capital.

These rules are disapplied for EIS shares held in company A, unless:

- company B has issued shares eligible for EIS income tax relief and has issued certificates to investors in respect of those shares (as required by *ITA 2007, ss 204–205*);
- the shares in company B are new ordinary shares carrying no present or future preferential rights to dividends, or to assets in a winding-up, and no present or future right to be redeemed; and
- the shares in company B are issued on or after 29 November 1994, and after the termination date for company A's issue of EIS shares.

The rules in *TCGA 1992, ss 135* and *136* may also apply where a new company (C) meeting the conditions in *ITA 2007, s 247,* acquires EIS shares in exchange for new shares in company C (*TCGA 1992, s 150A(8), (8A–8D)*).

The allowable expenditure deducted in computing the gain or loss on a disposal of EIS shares is adjusted in any case where the income tax relief was reduced following a reorganisation of share capital before 29 November 1994 (as provided by *TCGA 1992, s 150A(9)*).

Reduction of income tax relief

16.9 Disposal relief is restricted if the EIS income tax relief was reduced because either or both of (a) or (b) below applied before the disposal (but after 28 November 1994):

(a) value is received from the company in circumstances where income tax relief is reduced under *ITA 2007, s 213*;

(b) there is a repayment, redemption, repurchase or payment in circumstances where income tax relief is reduced under *ITA 2007, s 224*.

In these circumstances the gain is computed in the normal way (applying any restriction required by *TCGA 1992, s 150A(3)* as mentioned in **16.5** above) and the exemption is then reduced by an amount found by applying the fraction A/B to the gain, where:

- A is the amount of the reduction in income tax relief; and
- B is the amount of income tax relief before the deduction.

Where the *TCGA 1992, s 150A(3)* restriction applies, the above fraction is applied to the exempt part of the gain and the deduction is made from that part (*TCGA 1992, s 150B*; VCM30100–VCM30200).

Example 16.4

In May 2006, Sidney subscribes £80,000 for shares in an EIS company. This would normally provide him with income tax relief of £16,000 (20% × £80,000) but his income tax liability for the 2006/07 tax year is only £15,000, so his income tax relief is restricted to £15,000. This restriction of income tax relief does not reduce the exempt gain. However, Sidney receives £5,000 of value from the EIS company in 2008. He sells the shares in 2010/11 for £200,000. His chargeable gain is:

2010/11		£	Gain £
Consideration		200,000	
Allowable expenditure		80,000	
Gain, potentially exempt		120,000	120,000
Exemption reduced by value received:	120,000 × (5,000/15,000)	(40,000)	
Exempt gain			(80,000)
Chargeable gain subject to CGT:			40,000

CGT DEFERRAL RELIEF

16.10 Deferral of CGT is available where a chargeable gain accrues to an individual ('the investor') at any time after 28 November 1994 on the disposal of an asset and the investor makes a 'qualifying investment' (see **16.14**). Deferral relief is discussed in detail in *Capital Gains Tax Roll-over, Hold-Over and Deferral Reliefs 2010/11* (Bloomsbury Professional).

The relief is also available where the gain accrues on a deemed disposal under the rules for EIS deferral relief, VCT deferral relief (abolished for shares issued after 5 April 2004), or reinvestment relief under *TCGA 1992, s 164A* (abolished for investments made after 5 April 1998). The time of the actual or deemed disposal giving rise to the gain is the 'accrual time'.

The asset disposed of – or deemed to be disposed of – may be any chargeable asset. The investment must be made, generally, within a period beginning one year before and ending three years after the accrual time (*TCGA 1992, Sch 5B, para 1(3)*).

There is no limit to the amount of the gain that can be deferred, but an individual cannot claim income tax relief for any amount subscribed for eligible EIS shares that exceeds £500,000 (see **16.3**) in a tax year (*ITA 2007, s 158*).

For HMRC guidance regarding CGT deferral relief, also referred to as reinvestment relief, see their Venture Capital Schemes Manual at paras VCM38000–VCM41650.

Residence condition

16.11 The investor must be an individual, or trustee of a qualifying settlement (see **16.12**), who is resident or ordinarily resident in the UK:

- at the time when the gain accrues; and
- at the time the EIS shares are issued.

There are two further conditions to be satisfied in relation to residence status:

- the investor must not be regarded as resident in a territory outside the UK by virtue of any double taxation relief arrangements; and
- relief is not available if the effect of those arrangements is that he would not be liable to CGT in the UK on a disposal of the EIS shares (disregarding for this purpose the exemption for a disposal of EIS shares in *TCGA 1992, s 150A*, see **16.2**) (*TCGA 1992, Sch 5B, para 1(1), (4)*).

Trustees

16.12 Trustees cannot claim EIS income tax relief or disposal relief. However, deferral relief is available to the trustees of a settlement where the asset on the disposal of which the chargeable gain accrued is settled property (a 'trust asset') (*TCGA 1992, Sch 5B, para 17(1)*).

Deferral relief applies to:

(a) settled property in which there is no interest in possession (an interest in possession is, broadly, an immediate right to income of the settlement) so long as *all* the beneficiaries are individuals;

(b) settled property in which the interests of the beneficiaries are interests in possession, if *any* of the beneficiaries are individuals (*TCGA 1992, Sch 5B, para 17(2)*).

Discretionary trusts and accumulation and maintenance trusts will fall within (a).

Where (b) applies but at the time of the disposal of the trust asset not all the beneficiaries are individuals, only a proportion of the gain that would accrue to the trustees on the disposal qualifies for deferral relief (*TCGA 1992, Sch 5B, para 17(3)*).

Deferral relief may be denied if the interests of the beneficiaries change between the time of the disposal and the time of the acquisition of the qualifying investment. Where either (a) or (b) above applies, relief is available only if it applies both at the time of the disposal of the trust asset, and at the time of acquisition of the qualifying investment (*TCGA 1992, Sch 5B, para 17(4), (5)*).

There is a further condition where (b) applies. If not all the beneficiaries are individuals, the 'relevant proportion' (see below) at the time of acquisition of the qualifying investment must not be less than the relevant proportion at the time of the disposal of the trust asset (*TCGA 1992, Sch 5B, para 17(5)*).

If both individuals and others have interests in possession, 'the relevant proportion' is the proportion that A bears to B, where:

- A is the total amount of the income of the settled property representing interests held by beneficiaries who are individuals; and
- B is the total amount of all the income of the settled property (*TCGA 1992, Sch 5B, para 17(6)*).

There are complex anti-avoidance provisions relating to settled property (*TCGA 1992, Sch 5B, para 18*; see also VCM41500–VCM41650).

Postponing the gain

16.13 Deferral relief must be claimed (see **16.17**). The investor specifies the amount of the qualifying expenditure on the 'relevant shares' (ie the amount he has subscribed for the EIS shares) that is to be set against a corresponding amount of the gain.

The investor may well wish to limit the amount of his claim in order to utilise:

- any unused part of his CGT annual exemption;
- taper relief (for disposals before 6 April 2008 – see **16.25**);
- entrepreneurs' relief (for disposals made on or after 6 April 2008 – see **16.26**); or
- capital losses carried forward from earlier tax years.

Any part of the gain that has been matched with qualifying expenditure is treated as not having accrued at the accrual time (see **16.10**), but it is treated as accruing if there is a 'chargeable event' (see **16.19**) in relation to any of the shares (*TCGA 1992, Sch 5B, para 2(2)*).

Any amount of the original gain that has not had expenditure set against it in this way is 'unmatched', and qualifying expenditure is 'unused' to the extent that it has not already been set against a chargeable gain (*TCGA 1992, Sch 5B, para 2(1), (3), (4)*).

The 'relevant shares' are the EIS shares acquired by the investor, and where the investment is made before the gain accrues, which are still held by the investor at that time. This rule is modified to allow for bonus issues and reorganisations (*TCGA 1992, Sch 5B, para 19(1A–1D)*).

The actual proceeds of the disposal on which the gain accrued do not have to be applied directly in subscribing for the new shares (VCM38100).

Example 16.5

Kylie sold a commercial property in June 2010 and made a chargeable gain of £350,000. She subscribed for eligible shares in an EIS company of £140,000 in November 2010, and a further £200,000 for EIS shares in May 2011. Kylie's CGT position for 2010/11 is:

2010/11	£
Gain	350,000
Less deferred under EIS provisions:	(339,900)
Gain	10,100
Less annual exemption	(10,100)
Taxable gain for 2010/11	Nil

Kylie could claim deferral relief on up to £340,000 of chargeable gains, but she has chosen to limit the claim to avoid wasting her 2010/11 annual exemption, which cannot be carried forward (see **16.25**).

Qualifying investment

16.14 The investor makes a qualifying investment if:

(a) he subscribes for 'eligible shares' in a company and the shares are issued to him at a 'qualifying time'. If the accrual time (see **16.10**) is later than the qualifying time, the investor must still hold the shares at the accrual time;

(b) he subscribes for the shares (other than any bonus shares) wholly in cash;

(c) the company is a 'qualifying company' in relation to the shares. For instance, it must be an unquoted trading company and comply with the detailed conditions in *ITA 2007, ss 181–199*;

(d) the shares (other than any bonus shares) are fully paid up when they are issued. Shares are not fully paid up for this purpose if there is any undertaking to pay cash to any person in the future in relation to the acquisition;

(e) the investor subscribes for the shares, and they are issued, for bona fide commercial purposes and not as part of arrangements the main purpose (or one of the main purposes) of which is the avoidance of tax (see below);

(f) the issuing company or a qualifying 90% subsidiary must carry on the qualifying activities, so where the relevant trade is carried on in partnership the conditions in *ITA 2007, s 183* are not met, see Revenue & Customs Brief 77/09;

(g) the shares (other than any bonus shares) are issued in order to raise money for the purpose of a qualifying business activity;

(h) all of the money raised by the issue of the shares (other than bonus shares), is employed wholly for the purpose of that qualifying business activity no later than the end of the period of two years beginning with either the issue of the eligible shares or, if later, the commencement of the qualifying trade; and

(i) the total amount of relevant investments made by the company in the 12-month period ending with the issue of the EIS shares does not exceed £2 million.

The condition in (h) above is still satisfied if an amount of money is employed for another purpose, so long as that amount is not significant (*TCGA 1992, Sch 5B, para 1(2), (5)*). For shares issued before 22 April 2009, 80% of the money had to be so employed within a year of the share issue or commencement of trade, see *Skye Inns and Mr Richards* [2009] TC00304.

The condition in (i) only applies for EIS shares issued on or after 19 July 2007.

HMRC consider that the condition in (e) above excludes a subscription that is motivated by benevolence. HMRC also consider that deathbed investments are 'unlikely to be made for genuine commercial reasons' (VCM12140).

Eligible shares

16.15 Shares are eligible shares for deferral relief purposes if they are new ordinary shares which, throughout the following period, carry no present or future preferential right to dividends or to a company's assets on its winding-up, and no present or future right to be redeemed. That period:

(a) begins with the issue of the shares; and

(b) ends immediately before the 'termination date' relating to those shares (*TCGA 1992, Sch 5B, para 19(1)*; *ITA 2007, s 173(2)*).

The termination date is the later of:

- the third anniversary of the issue of the shares; and
- the third anniversary of the commencement of the trade (*TCGA 1992, Sch 5B, para 19(1)*; *ITA 2007, s 256*).

Example 16.6

Play-time Ltd issued eligible shares on 1 January 2006 and used the funds for the purposes of a trade that commenced on 30 November 2005. The termination date is 1 January 2009. If Play-time's trade had commenced on 1 April 2006 the termination date would be 1 April 2009.

Time limits for reinvestment

16.16 The qualifying time in **16.14**(a) is any time in the period beginning one year before and ending three years after the accrual time, or any other such time as HMRC may allow (*TCGA 1992, Sch 5B, para 1(3)*).

HMRC guidance indicates that they will extend the standard time limits where the claimant can show that he:

- had a firm intention to comply with them, but
- was prevented from complying by some fact or circumstance beyond his control, and
- acted as soon as he reasonably could after ceasing to be so prevented.

Each case is considered on its own merits but examples of circumstances outside the claimant's control might include death or serious illness of a vital party at a crucial time, unsettled disputes or litigation, or unexpected delay in receipt of disposal consideration.

HMRC say that a mere change of intention at a late stage, or a lack of funds due to the claimant having spent or invested the disposal consideration elsewhere, will not normally be regarded as circumstances beyond his control. If the claimant chooses to defer applying for the EIS shares until late in the standard reinvestment period, a subsequent issue of shares outside that period will not normally be regarded as a circumstance beyond his control. (See VCM38030 and VCM68060, which refers to venture capital trust shares – VCT deferral relief was abolished in 2004 – but should be read for this purpose as referring to eligible shares in a qualifying EIS company.)

Claims

16.17 The procedures and time limits for claims to deferral relief are set out by reference to the provisions for claims to income tax relief for an investment in EIS shares. *ITA 2007, s 202* is applied with some modifications, so that:

(a) a claim may not be made earlier than the time when the requirement in *ITA 2007, s 176* is first satisfied – broadly, this requirement is that the trade (or research and development) concerned has been carried on for four months;

(b) a claim may not be made later than five years after 31 January following the tax year in which the shares were issued; and

(c) no claim may be made unless the claimant has received a compliance certificate (form EIS3) from the company, certifying that the conditions for EIS relief (other than those relating to the investor) are satisfied in relation to the shares.

The company is required, before issuing the EIS3 certificate, to declare to HMRC that certain conditions have been, and remain, satisfied. Further details of the company's obligations in this regard, and penalties for non-compliance, are set out in *ITA 2007, s 205* (*TCGA 1992, Sch 5B, para 6*).

The time limit in (b) for submitting a claim has not been amended by *FA 2008, Sch 39* so remains at the fifth anniversary of the normal filing date for the self-assessment tax return. Note, the advice on HMRC helpsheet HS297 is incorrect on this point.

There is no provisional relief. A claim may not be made before the shares are issued. The investor is required to submit to HMRC part 2 of form EIS3 completed by the company, which includes a claim form. The claim may be made either in the tax return or separately. The form EIS3 should show:

- the amount paid on subscription for the shares;
- the company in which the investment has been made;

- the date the shares were issued;
- the office that deals with the company and the company's tax reference; and
- the chargeable gains against which deferral relief is claimed (VCM38500).

Although there is no statutory clearance procedure, HMRC officers may give a provisional opinion on the basis of the information available to them, subject to review following receipt of a claim. Investors asking about the qualifying status of a company are referred to an officer of the EIS company. HMRC's Small Company Enterprise Centre will assist the company with regard to its qualifying status (VCM38550).

Failure of conditions

16.18 The shares forming the investment are treated as never having been eligible for relief if the condition in **16.14**(g), relating to the purpose of the share issue, is not met (*TCGA 1992, Sch 5B, para 1A(3)*).

The shares cease to be eligible shares on the date of an event occurring after they have been issued, if as a result of that event any of the following conditions is not satisfied:

- the qualifying company condition in **16.14**(c); or
- the condition in **16.14**(f) relating to who carries on the qualifying activities (*TCGA 1992, Sch 5B, para 1A(1), (2)*); or
- the investment condition in **16.14**(i).

If the condition in **16.14**(h) above relating to the company's use of the money subscribed is not met, the shares are treated as:

- never having been eligible shares if the claim is made after the time limit mentioned in **16.14**(h) has expired; or
- ceasing to be eligible shares on the expiration of that time limit in any other case (*TCGA 1992, Sch 5B, para 1A(4), (4A)*).

A notice, given by either the company or HMRC as appropriate, is required before any of these provisions can take effect (*TCGA 1992, Sch 5B, para 1A(5), (6), (7)*).

Chargeable events

16.19 The effect of a chargeable event is explained at **16.21**. There is a chargeable event in relation to the shares if, after the qualifying investment has been made:

(a) the investor disposes of the shares otherwise than as a no gain, no loss transfer between spouses or civil partners;

(b) the shares are disposed of (but not to the investor) by a person who acquired them on a disposal that the investor made within marriage or civil partnership;

(c) the investor becomes not resident or ordinarily resident in the UK, while holding the shares and before the termination date – but see below regarding a temporary change of residence status;

(d) a person who acquired the shares on a disposal within marriage or civil partnership becomes a non-resident while holding them and before the termination date; or

(e) the shares cease (or are treated as ceasing) to be eligible shares, for example, where the company carries on non-qualifying activities (*TCGA 1992, Sch 5B, para 3(1)*).

A temporary change of residence status does not give rise to a chargeable event as described in (c) or (d) above where the investor or the transferee, leaves the UK to take up an employment or office where all of the duties are performed outside the UK and he returns to take up residence in the UK within three years. The individual must not have disposed on the shares in the meantime (*TCGA 1992, Sch 5B, para 3(3), (4)*).

The investor or the company is required to notify HMRC of the chargeable event within 60 days or, in specified cases, within 60 days of coming to know of the event. *TCGA 1992, Sch 5B, para 16* sets out the detailed notification requirements and HMRC information powers (VCM40900).

Death of investor or transferee

16.20 An event within **16.19**(a)–(e) above is not a chargeable event, in relation to shares held by the deceased immediately before his death, if the event occurs at or after the time of the death of either the investor, or a person who acquired any of the relevant shares on a disposal within marriage or civil partnership (*TCGA 1992, Sch 5B, para 3(5)*).

Effect of chargeable event

16.21 Broadly, the 'deferred gain' (see below) becomes chargeable if a chargeable event (see **16.19**) occurs. A chargeable gain accrues on the occasion of a chargeable event in relation to any of the shares. The amount of the chargeable gain is equal to the part of the deferred gain that is attributable (see below) to the shares involved in the chargeable event (*TCGA 1992, Sch 5B, para 4(1)*).

The 'deferred gain' is the amount of the original gain that has been matched against qualifying expenditure, less the amount of any gain treated as accruing as a result of an earlier chargeable event (*TCGA 1992, Sch 5B, para 4(7)*).

The deferred gain attributable to any shares is found by attributing a proportionate part of the gain to each of the relevant shares held immediately before the chargeable event occurs (*TCGA 1992, Sch 5B, para 4(6)*; VCM38250).

Example 16.7

Monique subscribes £40,000 for eligible EIS shares on 4 July 2008 and makes a claim to defer a chargeable gain of £20,000 accruing on the disposal of an investment property on 15 July 2005. She sells the shares on 26 April 2010, before the termination date. The whole of the deferred gain of £20,000 becomes chargeable on 26 April 2010 and will be subject to CGT at 18% subject to deduction of her annual exemption and any available losses.

Example 16.8

Finbar subscribes £70,000 for eligible EIS shares on 17 August 2007 and makes a claim to defer a chargeable gain of £30,000 accruing on the disposal of land on 3 April 2005. He sells 50% of the shares on 13 July 2010 before the termination date. The same proportion of the deferred gain, ie £15,000, becomes chargeable on 13 July 2010, and will be subject to CGT at 18% or 28% depending on the level of Finbar's taxable income for 2010/11 and other gains made after 22 June 2010.

See **16.26** for the interaction with entrepreneurs' relief.

Identification rules

16.22 It may be necessary for this purpose to determine whether deferral relief is attributable to the shares disposed of (including disposal by means of a no gain, no loss disposal within marriage or civil partnership).

Identification is generally made on a first in, first out basis and the normal identification rules in *TCGA 1992, Pt IV, Ch I* are modified accordingly. There are detailed rules for identification of shares acquired on the same day and to cater for reorganisations (*TCGA 1992, Sch 5B, para 4(2)–(5)*; VCM38280).

Chargeable person

16.23 The chargeable gain accruing on the occurrence of a chargeable event is treated as accruing, as the case may be, to:

(a) the person who makes the disposal;

(b) the person who becomes a non-resident;

(c) the person who holds the shares when they cease (or are treated as ceasing) to be eligible shares.

With regard to (c), if the investor has transferred some of his shares on a no gain, no loss disposal within marriage or civil partnership and the transferee retains those shares at the time of the chargeable event, then the gains accruing to the investor and the transferee are computed separately (*TCGA 1992, Sch 5B, para 5*).

Reorganisations and rights

16.24 The rules in *TCGA 1992, s 127* (where the old shares stand in the shoes of the new shares) are to be applied, on a reorganisation of share capital within *TCGA 1992, s 126*, separately to each of the following kinds of shares. The effect of this rule is that shares of each kind are treated as a separate holding of original shares and identified with a separate new holding following the reorganisation:

(a) shares which attract neither income tax relief or deferral relief;

(b) shares to which only CGT deferral relief is attributable;

(c) shares to which deferral relief is not attributable, but income tax relief does apply; and

(d) shares to which both CGT deferral relief and income tax relief (and thus disposal relief) are attributable (*TCGA 1992, Sch 5B, para 7(1)*).

Where there is a rights issue in respect of an existing holding of ordinary shares, and either the existing shares or the new shares fall into the categories (b), (c) or (d) above, then the provisions of *TCGA 1992, ss 127–130* (treating the old and new shares as a single holding) do not apply to the existing holding (*TCGA 1992, Sch 5B, para 7(2)*). The taxpayer is treated as having acquired the new shares at the date of the rights issue and for the amount paid for the new shares. Any shares acquired on a rights issue may qualify for deferral relief, but a separate claim will need to be made.

If a company (B) that has only subscriber shares acquires all the shares in an EIS company (A) in exchange for shares of a 'corresponding description' (see below) in company B, and the conditions in *TCGA 1992, s 135* are met so that *TCGA 1992, s 127* applies, the share exchange is not treated as involving a disposal of the shares in company A. The shares in company B attract deferral relief in place of the shares in company A and there are detailed rules setting out the effect of this treatment.

Shares in company B are of a 'corresponding description' where, if they were shares in company A, they would be of the same class and carry the same rights as the original shares. Shares are of the same class where they would be so treated if dealt with on the Stock Exchange (*TCGA 1992, Sch 5B, para 8*).

From 22 April 2009 deferral relief may be lost where the EIS company is taken over and the acquiring company issues its own shares in exchange for the original EIS shares. If the original EIS shares attracted both income tax relief and deferral relief, neither of which has been withdrawn at the time of the share exchange, then *TCGA 1992, ss 135–137* is disapplied, and the EIS shares are treated as being disposed of for the purposes of *TCGA 1992, Sch 5B, paras 3, 4*. The result is the deferred gain comes into charge, but for other provisions of *TCGA 1992* the EIS shares are *not* treated as being disposed of, thus no other gain or loss attached to the EIS shares comes into charge at the time of the share exchange (*TCGA 1992, Sch 5B, para 9*).

Interaction with taper relief

16.25 Taper relief was withdrawn for disposals made on and after 6 April 2008. For disposals before that date the taxpayer may restrict the amount of his deferral relief claim to preserve an amount of gain which will be reduced by taper relief, and covered by any unused part of the annual exemption (*TCGA 1992, Sch A1, para 16(1)*).

Where a gain becomes chargeable after it has been postponed or deferred, using EIS deferral relief, taper relief can apply if the date the gain becomes chargeable falls before 6 April 2008. In that case taper relief on the deferred gain is calculated by reference to the date of the original disposal. No further taper relief is available for the period from that date to the date of the chargeable event.

Normally, the qualifying holding period for taper relief purposes (see **17.23**) ceases when the asset is disposed of. However, where a taxpayer is a serial investor in EIS shares the holding periods of EIS shares issued by different companies may be combined, in certain circumstances (*TCGA 1992, s 150D, Sch 5BA*). This extension of the qualifying holding period is less important for disposals made after 5 April 2002 as the maximum business asset taper relief of 75% is achieved after the asset has been held for just two complete years.

This special treatment applies where:

(a) a chargeable gain ('the original gain') accrues on the disposal of shares ('the original shares') to which EIS deferral relief and/or income tax relief was attributable;

(b) all or part of the original gain is deferred by being matched with an investment in qualifying EIS shares;

(c) a chargeable gain ('the revived gain') is deemed to accrue on a later disposal ('the relevant disposal') of the second EIS shares; and

(d) the original shares were issued after 5 April 1998 and disposed of after 5 April 1999 (*TCGA 1992, Sch 5BA, para 1(1), (2)*).

The qualifying holding period of the original shares in these circumstances is the period beginning with the date of issue of the original shares and ending with the date of the relevant disposal. Therefore, the holding periods of the two investments are taken together. However, a period when neither the original shares nor the reinvestment shares were held does not count for the purposes of taper relief (*TCGA 1992, Sch 5BA, para 1(3), (4)*).

The extent to which the business asset rate of taper relief is available is determined, broadly, on the assumption that the original shares and the reinvestment shares are the same asset (*TCGA 1992, Sch 5BA, para 1(3), (4)*; VCM43010).

Interaction with entrepreneurs' relief

16.26 The HMRC view is that entrepreneurs' relief takes precedence over EIS deferral relief under *TCGA 1992, Sch 5B*, as that relief merely defers a gain and does not reduce it (CG64135). Thus, any chargeable gain remaining after the application of entrepreneurs' relief may be deferred by investing in EIS shares, and electing for the defined amount of the gain to be deferred.

However, for gains arising on or after 23 June 2010, the taxpayer will have to choose between EIS deferral relief and entrepreneurs' relief. If the gain is subject to entrepreneurs' relief, the full gain, within the taxpayer's lifetime cap (see **11.5**) is subject to CGT at 10%. Only any excess gain above the lifetime cap can be deferred using EIS.

There are special transitional arrangements where a gain that arose before 6 April 2008 has been deferred by way of a claim under EIS deferral relief. Where the deferred gain becomes chargeable after 5 April 2008 due to a relevant chargeable event (see **16.21**), such as the disposal of those EIS shares, entrepreneurs' relief would not normally apply. However, where the deferred gain originally accrued before 6 April 2008, it can be reduced by entrepreneurs' relief under *FA 2008, Sch 3, para 8*, if the conditions for that relief apply (see **11.44**). When the reduced gain comes back into charge on or after 23 June 2010 it is chargeable to CGT at 10%, if this was the first chargeable event in respect of those EIS shares to occur since 6 April 2008 (see **Example 16.9**).

The gain that accrues on the disposal of the EIS shares themselves may be eligible for entrepreneurs' relief if the EIS company is the shareholders' personal company at the time of the disposal, and the employment condition applies (see **11.10–11.11**).

Example 16.9

John sold his software company in June 2000 making a gain of £900,000. This gain would have qualified for entrepreneurs' relief if it had been in force at that time. On 10 April 2003 John invested the gain in EIS shares issued by MRC Ltd, and successfully claimed EIS deferral relief. This claim removed any possibility to reduce the gain by taper relief as the full gain was covered by EIS deferral relief. John could restrict his claim to EIS relief to leave an amount in charge subject to taper relief and the annual exemption, but that claim must be submitted to HMRC by 31 January 2010.

John sold his entire holding of the EIS shares issued by MRC Ltd in July 2010. If John makes a claim for entrepreneurs' relief to apply to the disposal of the software company shares, the full gain of £900,000 is subject to CGT at 10%. John must make his claim for entrepreneurs' relief by 31 January 2012.

Anti-avoidance rules

Reinvesting in the same company or a group company

16.27 The taxpayer is not entitled to deferral relief if the gain he wishes to defer arose on the disposal of holding shares in a company (A) and:

- the qualifying EIS company that issues the EIS shares (see **16.14**) is company A itself; or
- the qualifying EIS company is either a member of the same group of companies (see below) as company A at the time of the disposal of the company A shares, or a member of such a group when the EIS shares are issued (*TCGA 1992, Sch 5B, para 10(1)*).

EIS shares in a 'relevant company' (see below) are not regarded as a qualifying investment where the shares are issued after the taxpayer has already made a qualifying investment in a company (B) (the 'acquired holding') and obtained deferral relief on the disposal of either an asset (A) or shares in a company (A). A company is a 'relevant company' for this purpose if:

- where the taxpayer has disposed of any of the acquired holding in company B, it is either company B itself or a company that was a member of the same group of companies as company B at any time since the acquisition of the 'acquired holding' of shares in company B;
- it is company A, ie it is the company the disposal of whose shares gave rise to the deferral relief claim by virtue of the acquisition of the holding in company B; or
- it is a company which was a member of the same group of companies as company A at the time of the disposal of shares in company A or the time of the acquisition of the holding in company B (*TCGA 1992, Sch 5B, para 10(2), (3)*).

A group of companies for this purpose comprises a company that has one or more 51% subsidiaries, together with those subsidiaries (*TCGA 1992, Sch 5B, para 10(4)*).

Pre-arranged exits

16.28 Where an individual subscribes for EIS shares in a company no deferral relief is available if there are 'relevant arrangements' in place (see below) that include any of the following:

(a) arrangements with a view to the repurchase, exchange or other disposal of the EIS shares (or of other shares in or securities of the same company) – subject to an exception for certain exchanges of shares, etc;

(b) arrangements for the cessation of a trade carried on, or to be carried on, by the company or a person connected with it, except where the arrangements apply only on a winding-up for bona fide commercial reasons that does not feature in the relevant arrangements;

(c) arrangements for the disposal of the company's assets (or of the assets of a person connected with the company), or of a substantial amount of those assets, subject to the exception mentioned in (b) for a winding-up; and

(d) arrangements the main purpose of which (or one of the main purposes of which) is to provide protection for people investing in shares in the company against the risks attached to the investment, however that protection is provided, but excluding protection that a company would reasonably be expected to provide for itself (or, in the case of the parent company of a trading group, for its subsidiaries).

'Relevant arrangements' are the arrangements under which the shares are issued and any other arrangements, made before that share issue, in relation to it or in connection with it. 'Arrangements' include any scheme, agreement or understanding, whether or not legally enforceable (*TCGA 1992, Sch 5B, paras 11, 19(1)*).

Put and call options

16.29 Special rules apply to put and call options granted during period A (see **16.32**). These do not affect the above rules relating to pre-arranged exits (*TCGA 1992, Sch 5B, para 12(4)*).

Options granted after shares are issued

16.30 Shares issued to the investor cease to be eligible shares on the date of the grant, during the 'relevant period' (see **16.32**), of:

(a) a put option granted to the investor, where the exercise of the option would bind the grantor to buy the shares from the investor; or

(b) a call option granted by the investor, where the exercise of the option would bind the investor to sell the shares to the grantee.

The shares affected by this rule are those to which the option relates, ie the shares that would be treated as disposed of in pursuance of the option if the option were exercised immediately after the grant, and there was an immediate disposal of the shares acquired on exercise of the option (*TCGA 1992, Sch 5B, para 12*).

Options granted before shares are issued

16.31 If an option within (a) or (b) in **16.30** is granted before the date on which the shares are issued, the shares are treated as never having been eligible shares (*TCGA 1992, Sch 5B, para 12(2)(a)*).

Period A

16.32 Period A for shares issued after 5 April 2000 is the period beginning with the incorporation of the company, or if the company was incorporated more than two years before the date on which the shares were issued, two years before that date. It ends immediately before the termination date (see **16.15**) (*TCGA 1992, Sch 5B, para 19(1)*; *ITA 2007, s 159*).

Value received by the investor

16.33 A chargeable event may arise if the investor receives value other than 'insignificant' value from the company at any time in the 'period of restriction'. The whole of the deferred gain becomes chargeable – there is no apportionment even if the value received represents only a part of the investment (*TCGA 1992, Sch 5B, para 13A*).

The 'period of restriction' is the period beginning one year before the shares are issued and ending immediately before the termination date (see **16.15**) relating to the shares (*TCGA 1992, Sch 5B, para 19(1)*).

An amount is of 'insignificant value' if it is no more than £1,000, or it is greater than £1,000 but is insignificant in relation to the investment set against gains in a deferral relief claim.

HMRC guidance says that 'insignificant' should be given its dictionary meaning of 'trifling or completely unimportant'. HMRC also consider that if a receipt of value falls within periods of restriction relating to more than one share issue, there is no apportionment and the receipt must be taken into account in regard to each issue (VCM40300, VCM40350).

However, no amount of value received is treated as a receipt of insignificant value if arrangements existed, in the period of 12 months prior to the share issue, which provided for the investor (or an 'associate' of his) to receive value from the issuing company (or a person connected with it) in the period of restriction. 'Associate' takes its meaning from *ITA 2007, s 253* except that brothers and sisters are excluded (*TCGA 1992, Sch 5B, paras 13A(2)–(5), 19(1)*).

The shares are treated as never having been eligible shares if the investor receives value before the date of issue of the shares. If he receives value after that date, the shares cease to be eligible shares on the date when the value is received. There is no receipt of value by virtue of a disposal of shares that gives rise to a chargeable event (see **16.19**) (*TCGA 1992, Sch 5B, para 13(1), (6)*).

Receipts of insignificant value during the period of restriction are aggregated for this purpose, and a chargeable event arises if the total value of the receipts is not an amount of insignificant value (*TCGA 1992, Sch 5B, para 13(1B)*).

The investor receives value from the company if the company does anything that is mentioned in the first column of **Table 16.1** below, and the value received by the investor in each case is as set out in the second column (*TCGA 1992, Sch 5B, paras 13(2), (8), 13A(1)*).

Table 16.1

The company	**The value received is**
repays, redeems or repurchases any of its share capital or securities belonging to the investor or pays him to give up his right to any of the share capital or any security on its cancellation or extinguishment;	the amount received by the investor or, if greater, the market value of the share capital, securities or debt
repays, under arrangements connected with the acquisition of the shares, any debt owed to him other than a debt incurred by the company (i) on or after the date of issue of the shares, and (ii) otherwise than in consideration of extinguishment of a debt incurred before that date; or	
pays him to give up his right to any debt on its extinguishment;	
releases or waives his liability to the company or discharges, or undertakes to discharge, his liability to someone else (a liability that is not discharged within 12 months of the time when it ought to have been discharged is treated as released or waived for this purpose);	the amount of the liability
makes a loan or advance to him that is not repaid in full before the shares are issued (see below);	the amount of the loan or advance less the amount of any repayment made before the issue of the shares
provides a benefit or facility for him;	the cost to the company of providing the benefit or facility less any consideration given for it by the investor
disposes of an asset to him for no consideration, or for a consideration less than (or worth less than) the asset's market value; or	the difference between the market value of the asset and the consideration (if any) given for it
acquires an asset from him for a consideration more than (or worth more than) the asset's market value;	
makes any payment to him other than a 'qualifying payment' (see below)	the amount of the payment

The investor also receives value from the company if a person connected with the company (as defined in *ITA 2007, s 166*) either buys any of its share capital or securities belonging to the individual, or pays him for giving up a right in relation to any share capital or securities of the company. In this case the value received is the amount received by the investor or, if greater, the market value of the share capital or securities (*TCGA 1992, Sch 5B, paras 13(5), 13A(1)*).

A loan is regarded as being made by the company to the investor where he incurs a debt to the company (other than an 'ordinary trade debt'), or a debt due from the investor to a third party is assigned to the company. An 'ordinary trade debt' is a debt for goods or services supplied in the ordinary course of a trade or business, so long as the credit period is no longer than six months and no longer than that normally given to customers of the business (*TCGA 1992, Sch 5B, para 13(3), (11)*).

A debt or a liability is disregarded if a qualifying payment (see below) would discharge it, and a benefit or facility is disregarded if payment of equal value would be a qualifying payment (*TCGA 1992, Sch 5B, para 13(9)*).

A 'qualifying payment' includes:

- a payment (by any company) of reasonable remuneration for service as an officer or employee, having regard to the duties of that position;
- a payment or reimbursement (by any company) of travelling or other expenses wholly, exclusively and necessarily incurred by the payee in the performance of duties as an officer or employee of that company;
- the payment (by any company) of any interest representing no more than a reasonable commercial return on money lent to that company;
- the payment (by any company) of a dividend or other distribution not exceeding a normal return on any investment in that company's shares or securities;
- a payment for the supply of goods that does not exceed their market value;
- a payment for the acquisition of an asset that does not exceed its market value;
- the payment (by any company), of a reasonable and commercial rent for property occupied by the company;
- reasonable and necessary remuneration paid (by any company) for services rendered to that company in the course of a UK trade or profession where the payment is included in the profits of that trade or profession for tax purposes; and

- a payment in discharge of an ordinary trade debt (*TCGA 1992, Sch 5B, para 13(7)*).

The scope of these provisions is widened so that:

- a payment or disposal to the investor includes a payment or disposal made to him indirectly, or to his order, or for his benefit;
- anything received by an associate of the investor is treated as received by the investor; and
- a reference to a company includes a reference to a person who is connected with the company at any time in the 'relevant period' (see below) (*TCGA 1992, Sch 5B, para 13(10)*).

The 'relevant period' for shares issued after 5 April 2000 is the period beginning with the incorporation of the company, or if the company was incorporated more than two years before the date on which the shares were issued, two years before that date. It ends immediately before the termination date (*TCGA 1992, Sch 5B, para 19(1)*; *ITA 2007, s 159*).

Value received by another person

16.34 Value received by persons other than the investor may give rise to a chargeable event, see **16.19**. Detailed rules are set out in *TCGA 1992, Sch 5B, paras 14, 14AA* and *14A*.

Example 16.10

In November 2005, Reggie realised a gain of £1,500,000 when he disposed of his personal company, Scream Ltd, of which he owned all the ordinary shares and was a director. On 7 October 2008 he reinvested all of this gain by subscribing for eligible EIS shares in Perrin Ltd. In May 2010 Reggie's wife received £5,000 from CJ Ltd, which amounts to a return of value as CJ Ltd is an associated company of Perrin Ltd, and this creates a chargeable event for the Perrin Ltd shares. Reggie claims entrepreneurs' relief in respect of the gain arising on the disposal of Scream Ltd, but his capital gains tax position for 2010/11 becomes:

2010/11	£	£
Deferred gain now chargeable	1,500,000	
Gain subject to entrepreneurs' relief within the lifetime cap applicable at the date of the gain	(1,000,000)	1,000,000
Chargeable gain	500,000	1,000,000
Less annual exemption for 2010/11	(10,100)	
Taxable gain	489,900	1,000,000
CGT due at 28%/10%	137,172	100,000

Reggie's total CGT liability for 2010/11 will be £237,172, which is payable by 31 January 2012, although most of his money is still invested in Perrin Ltd.

Replacement value

16.35 Value received by the investor (the 'original value') may be disregarded where, broadly:

- the shares were issued after 6 March 2001 or the original value was received after that date;
- the original value was received in any of the circumstances set out in **Table 16.1** (see **16.33**), except for value received in connection with the repayment of a debt;
- the person from whom the original value was received (the 'original supplier') receives replacement value in the form of a 'qualifying receipt', from the person who received the original value (the 'original recipient');
- the replacement value is not less than the original value; and
- the receipt of replacement value is not disregarded.

In broad terms, a 'qualifying receipt' may arise by means of a payment by the original recipient or the transfer of an asset between him and the original supplier for a consideration greater or less than market value. The detailed rules are set out in *TCGA 1992, Sch 5B, paras 13B, 13C.*

Investment-linked loans

16.36 If an 'investment-linked loan' (see below) is made by any person, at any time in the relevant period, to an individual who subscribes for eligible shares (or to his associate), the shares are treated as:

- never having been eligible shares, if the loan is made on or before the date of the issue of the shares; and
- ceasing to be eligible shares when the loan is made, if it is made after that date.

A loan is 'investment-linked' if it would not have been made – or would not have been made on the same terms – if the individual had not subscribed for, or had not been proposing to subscribe for, the shares.

A loan is regarded as made by a person to an individual if the person gives him any credit, or a debt due from the individual to someone else is assigned to that person (*TCGA 1992, Sch 5B, para 16*).

HMRC have said that their primary concern is why the lender made the loan rather than why the borrower applied for it and relief is not necessarily denied just because a loan is used to finance the investment. HMRC said in Statement of Practice 6/98:

> 'The test is whether the lender makes the loan on terms which are influenced by the fact that the borrower, or an associate of the borrower, has acquired, or is proposing to acquire, the shares.
>
> The rules would not have effect to deny or withdraw relief where a person proposing to acquire shares receives a loan from a bank, if the bank would have made a loan on the same terms to a similar borrower who was intending to use it for a different purpose. But if, for example, a loan is made on a specified security which consists of, or includes, the shares in question, it would be one which would not otherwise have been made on the same terms.
>
> In such a case, the loan would be linked with the shares, and the investor would not qualify for relief in respect of them. This would apply only where the shares, or any rights associated with them, are specified as all or part of the security. It would not apply, for example, in any case where the lender had recourse against the borrower's assets generally.
>
> In considering the terms of any particular loan, HMRC will have regard to such features as the qualifying conditions which must be satisfied by the borrower, the existence of incentives or benefits offered to the borrower, the time allowed for repayment, the amount of repayment'.

Chapter 17

Other reliefs

INTRODUCTION

17.1 Various exemptions for certain persons, assets or gains are examined in **Chapter 1**. Double taxation relief is examined at **3.64–3.69**. The following provisions which reduce or defer liability to CGT or corporation tax on chargeable gains are discussed in **Chapter 2**:

- small part disposals – **2.5**;
- no gain, no loss disposals – **2.7**;
- assets lost, destroyed or becoming of negligible value – **2.10**;
- capital sums applied in restoring the asset – **2.17**.

The CGT reliefs that are most likely to be met in practice are discussed in the following chapters:

- entrepreneurs' relief – **Chapter 11**;
- main residence relief – **Chapter 12**;
- hold-over relief for gifts – **Chapter 13**;
- roll-over relief for replacement of business assets – **Chapter 14**;
- incorporation relief – **Chapter 15**; and
- enterprise investment scheme reliefs – **Chapter 16**.

This chapter examines the following reliefs:

- disposal relief and deferral relief for investments in venture capital trusts – **17.2**;
- relief for losses on loans to traders – **17.11**;
- share loss relief for unquoted shares – **17.16**;
- taper relief (for disposals before 6 April 2008) – **17.22–17.41.**

VENTURE CAPITAL TRUSTS

17.2 Venture capital trusts (VCTs) are quoted companies, similar to investment trusts, which specialise in investing in small unquoted trading companies. An approved VCT is exempt from corporation tax on chargeable gains.

The main conditions for approval include the requirement that at least 70% of the company's investments are in qualifying unquoted trading companies (including companies listed on the alternative investment market or AIM), with at least 30% of the investments being in eligible shares and no single holding representing more than 15% of the investments. The definition of eligible shares is to be changed to include preference shares as well as ordinary shares, and the proportion of the investment the VCT must hold in eligible shares will increase to 70%. These changes are to apply for shares issued from a date to be announced, likely to be late in 2010.

There are also limits on the value of the company's (or group's) gross assets, and on the size of company the VCT can invest in. The investee company must employ no more than 50 full-time equivalent employees at the time the shares are issued to the VCT (*ITA 2007, s 297A*). The investee company also cannot raise more than £2 million using any of the venture capital schemes (CVS, EIS and VCT), within a 12-month period (*ITA 2007, s 292A*).

The reliefs available for VCT investors are similar to those available for investments in enterprise investment scheme shares (see **Chapter 16**):

- income tax relief (including an exemption for dividends – see Chapter 3 of *Income Tax 2010/11* (Bloomsbury Professional);
- capital gains tax disposal relief; and
- capital gains tax deferral relief (only for VCT shares issued before 6 April 2004).

Disposal relief

17.3 A gain is not a chargeable gain if it accrues to an individual on a 'qualifying disposal' (see below) of ordinary shares in a company which:

- was a VCT when he acquired the shares; and
- is still a VCT at the time of the disposal.

Any loss accruing where these conditions are met is not an allowable loss. Shares are ordinary shares if they form part of the company's ordinary share capital (*TCGA 1992, s 151A (7)*; *ITA 2007, s 989*).

A 'qualifying disposal' is a disposal of shares, made by an individual, which meets the following conditions:

(a) the individual has attained the age of 18 at the time of the disposal;

(b) the shares were not acquired in excess of the 'permitted maximum' (see below) for any tax year ; and

(c) the taxpayer acquired the shares for bona fide commercial purposes and not as part of a scheme or arrangement the main purpose of which, or one of the main purposes of which, is the avoidance of tax (*TCGA 1992, s 151A(2)*).

Disposal relief is available regardless of whether the taxpayer subscribed for the shares or acquired them from someone else. The 'permitted maximum' in (b) above requires, broadly speaking, that in any tax year the market value of all VCT shares acquired by an individual (or his nominees) must not exceed £200,000 at the time of acquisition. This limit was £100,000 per tax year for VCT shares acquired before 6 April 2004 (*TCGA 1992, s 151A(6)*; *ITA 2007, s 263*).

HMRC guidance indicates that the restriction in (c) above is likely to apply only in 'exceptional' circumstances, where, for example, artificial arrangements are made to convert shares that do not qualify for disposal relief into qualifying shares (VCM66050).

Identification rules

17.4 It may be necessary to identify shares disposed of with particular acquisitions of shares in order to establish whether a disposal relates to shares acquired in excess of the permitted maximum for a particular tax year. For this purpose, the following rules replace the normal rules for identification of share and securities (see **4.3**):

- disposals of shares acquired by the same person on the same day are identified first with any shares acquired in excess of the permitted maximum, and then with other shares;

- a first-in, first-out basis applies to disposals of shares acquired on different days – disposals are identified first with the earliest acquisitions, and then with later acquisitions (*TCGA 1992, ss 151A(4), 151B(1)*); and

- a person who disposed of VCT shares acquired at a time when the company was not a VCT is treated as having disposed of those shares before he disposed of any other shares acquired in the same company when it did qualify as a VCT (*TCGA 1992, s 151A(5)*).

Reorganisations and rights

17.5 On a reorganisation of share capital of a VCT within *TCGA 1992, s 126,* the rules in *TCGA 1992, s 127* (equation of original shares and new holding) are to be applied separately to each of the following kinds of shares:

(a) VCT shares that are eligible for both CGT disposal relief and income tax relief;

(b) VCT shares that are eligible for CGT disposal relief but not income tax relief;

(c) VCT shares that are eligible for income tax relief but not CGT disposal relief; and

(d) other VCT shares (*TCGA 1992, s 151B(2), (3)*).

The effect of this rule is that shares of each kind are treated as a separate holding of original shares and identified with a separate new holding following the reorganisation.

Where there is a rights issue in respect of an existing holding of ordinary shares, and either but not both the existing shares or the new shares fall within (a)–(c) above, then the provisions of *TCGA 1992, ss 127–130* (which broadly treat the old and new shares as a single holding) do not apply to the existing holding (*TCGA 1992, s 151B(4)*).

Exchange of shares

17.6 Where the rules in *TCGA 1992, ss 135* and *136* apply to exchanges of shares and securities in a company (A) for those in another company (B), their broad effect is that there is no disposal of the original holding in company A. Companies A and B are treated as if they were the same company and the exchange is treated as a reorganisation of its share capital.

Those rules do not apply to an exchange of shares where:

- the shares in company A are shares falling within **17.5**(a) or (b) above; and
- the shares in company B are not ordinary shares in a VCT (*TCGA 1992, s 151B(5)*).

Withdrawal of company's approval as a VCT

17.7 A person holding shares eligible for disposal relief is deemed to dispose of and reacquire those shares at their market value if the company's approval as a VCT is withdrawn. He is deemed to dispose of the shares at the time the withdrawal takes effect (ie the date on which the notice of withdrawal is issued) and to reacquire them immediately for a consideration equal to their market value at that time. The effect of this rule is to preserve the benefit of disposal relief for the period for which approval applied.

There are detailed rules relating to identification of shares in these circumstances, and the effect of any reduction in income tax relief, any chargeable event under the deferral relief rules, and the death of the shareholder (*TCGA 1992, s 151B(6), (7), (8)*).

If a provisional VCT approval is withdrawn and the company does not meet the conditions for approval subsequently, disposal relief is not available at all.

If full approval is withdrawn – so that the investor's shares are deemed to be disposed of and reacquired as mentioned above – and the company subsequently regains its VCT status, HMRC consider that the shares do not become eligible again for disposal relief because the company will not have been a VCT at the time of the deemed reacquisition (VCM66950).

Deferral relief

17.8 An individual could defer a chargeable gain on the disposal of any asset by subscribing for ordinary shares in a VCT before 6 April 2004. Relief was available for subscriptions of up to £100,000 per tax year. No deferral relief was available unless the taxpayer received income tax relief on the subscription. The relief was withdrawn with effect for VCT shares issued after 5 April 2004 (*TCGA 1992, s 151A(3)* and *Sch 5C*, repealed by *FA 2004*).

Although new investments in VCTs do not qualify for deferral relief, gains already deferred may be brought back into charge by reason of a chargeable event (see **17.10**), so a brief summary of this relief remains relevant.

The relief was available to individuals who were resident or ordinarily resident in the UK both at the time when the gain accrued and at the time the qualifying investment was made. An individual was excluded from relief if he was regarded for the purposes of double taxation relief arrangements as resident in a territory outside the UK and the effect of those arrangements was that he would not be liable to UK tax on a gain arising on a disposal (ignoring for this purpose the disposal relief in **17.3**).

The shares had to be subscribed for within a period beginning one year before, and ending one year after, the disposal on which the gain accrued. It is possible, therefore, to use VCT deferral relief to defer gains accruing up to 5 April 2005. HMRC have statutory powers to extend these time limits, but no extension can result in deferral relief being available for VCT shares issued after 5 April 2004 (*TCGA 1992, Sch 5C, para 1* repealed by *FA 2004*).

Deferral relief for investment in VCT shares operated in a broadly similar manner to deferral relief for investment in enterprise investment scheme shares (see **Chapter 16**).

Claims

17.9 Deferral relief using VCT shares must be claimed within five years after 31 January following the later of:

- the tax year in which the gain accrued; or
- the tax year in which the VCT shares were issued.

The last possible accrual date for a gain that could be deferred using VCT shares was 5 April 2005. A claim for deferral relief for 2004/05 had to be submitted to HMRC by 31 March 2010. This date is the deadline for the five-year claim periods which became four years on 1 April 2010 (see **1.46**).

Chargeable events

17.10 The deferred gain becomes chargeable if, broadly speaking:

- there is a disposal of the VCT shares (other than a no gain, no loss disposal to a spouse or civil partner);
- the investor's spouse or civil partner disposes (to someone other than the investor) of VCT shares originally acquired from the investor under a no gain, no loss disposal;
- VCT shares are exchanged for non-VCT shares;
- the investor, or a spouse or civil partner who has received the shares on a no gain, no loss transfer, becomes non-resident within a three-year qualifying period (five years for shares issued before 6 April 2000);
- HMRC withdraw the company's approval as a VCT; or
- income tax relief for the VCT investment is withdrawn or reduced in circumstances other than those outlined above.

The deferred gain is not clawed back on the death of the investor or on the death of a spouse or civil partner who acquired the shares on a no gain, no loss disposal (*TCGA 1992, Sch 5C, paras 3–6*, repealed by *FA 2004* with effect for shares issued after 5 April 2004).

When the deferred gain becomes chargeable it is taxed at the rate of CGT that applies at the time of that chargeable event, which may be 18% or 28% in 2010/11. It is possible for the taxpayer to retrospectively claim entrepreneurs' relief in respect of the deferred gain (see **11.44**), in which case the deferred gain may be subject to CGT at 10% when it comes into charge.

LOANS TO TRADERS

17.11 Where a person (A) incurs a debt to another person (B), no chargeable gain accrues to the original creditor (B) on his disposal of the debt, except in the case of a debt on a security, and money held in a foreign currency bank account that does not represent currency acquired for personal expenditure outside the UK (*TCGA 1992, ss 251, 252*).

For individuals, trustees and personal representatives, a debt is, therefore, not normally subject to CGT unless it is a 'debt on a security' (meaning, broadly, marketable loan stock).

Most loan stock is a type of 'qualifying corporate bond', which is an exempt asset (*TCGA 1992, s 115*). Therefore, as a general rule, gains on simple debts are exempt from CGT and no relief is available for losses.

However, *TCGA 1992, s 253* provides for allowable losses incurred on loans made after 11 April 1978 to UK traders. Relief is not available for amounts taken into account in computing income for tax purposes.

For companies, profits (and losses) on loans are generally treated as income (and deductions in computing income) under the 'loan relationship' rules. Such profits and losses are outside the scope of corporation tax on chargeable gains, regardless of whether the company is a borrower or a lender. Where part of a loan becomes irrecoverable on or after 1 April 1996, relief under *TCGA 1992, s 253* is available only to a company if the loan relationship rules do not apply to the loss. For further discussion of the loan relationship rules see Chapter 14 of *Corporation Tax 2010/11* (Bloomsbury Professional).

Conditions

17.12 Relief is available for a 'qualifying loan', ie a loan in relation to which:

(a) the borrower uses the money wholly for the purposes of a trade, profession or vocation, other than a trade, etc involving the lending of money, which he carries on;

(b) the borrower is UK resident;

(c) the borrower's debt is not a 'debt on a security' as defined in *TCGA 1992, s 132*, (*TCGA 1992, s 253(1), (2)*).

In *Taylor Clark International Ltd v Lewis* [1998] STC 1259, the judge identified three characteristics of a 'debt on a security' in relation to a business debt. It should be assignable, interest-bearing, and have a structure of permanence. A debt is not a debt on a security just because it is supported by a propriety security. If the debt is not marketable or assignable it is not a 'debt on a security'.

Where the money is lent to company A and that company lends it on to company B, and company B is a trading company in the same group, relief is available for the loan to company A as if company A had used the money for the purpose for which company B used it while a member of the group (*TCGA 1992, s 253(2)*).

HMRC accept that bank overdrafts and credit balances on directors' loan accounts, but not ordinary trade debts, are capable of being qualifying loans. HMRC consider that a loan used for 'mixed purposes' would not qualify. However, a proportion of a loan used partly for trade purposes and partly for non-trade purposes would qualify – for example, a loan for the construction of premises part of which are used for trade purposes (CG65932, CG65933).

Relief for irrecoverable loans

17.13 A taxpayer who has made a qualifying loan may make a claim for an allowable capital loss in respect of that loan if at the time he makes the claim (or at an earlier time, see below) all the following apply:

- any amount of the outstanding principal has become irrecoverable;
- the claimant has not assigned his right to recover the amount; and
- the claimant and the borrower were not each other's spouses, civil partners, or companies in the same group, either at the time the loan was made or at any later time.

The amount of the allowable loss is the amount of the outstanding principal that has become irrecoverable. It is specifically provided that no relief is due if that amount is treated as a debit on a loan relationship (as discussed in **17.11**) (*TCGA 1992, s 253(3)*).

The taxpayer may specify an earlier time than the date of the claim (and possibly obtain the benefit of the allowable loss in an earlier tax year) if the outstanding amount was irrecoverable at that earlier time. However, the earlier time must be:

- for CGT purposes, not more than two years before the beginning of the tax year in which the claim is made; or
- for corporation tax purposes, not before the first day of the earliest accounting period ending not more than two years before the time of the claim (*TCGA 1992, s 253(3A)*).

HMRC accept that a loan has become irrecoverable where they come to the view that there was in fact 'no reasonable prospect' of recovery of the loan at the date of the claim (or at the earlier time mentioned above). They take account of funds potentially available as well as those currently available, and take the view that the initial presumption should be that the loan remains recoverable if the borrower continues to trade, even at a loss (CG65950).

If there is a short period between the loan being granted and the date on which it is claimed to have become irrecoverable, HMRC may wish to establish what happened to the business in that period, and may examine in particular:

- what happened to make the loan irrecoverable so soon after it was made; and
- whether there was a reasonable prospect of recovery at the time the loan was made (CG65951).

A loan is not treated as becoming irrecoverable if it has become so in consequence of the terms of the loan, any arrangements surrounding the loan, or any act or omission by the lender. HMRC guidance regards these conditions as anti-avoidance measures to exclude arrangements ranging from a gift presented as a loan to sophisticated schemes 'such as the siphoning of resources out of a company which then becomes unable to repay its loan' (*TCGA 1992, s 253(12)*; CG65958).

Relief for payments made by a guarantor

17.14 Relief may be available to a taxpayer who has guaranteed the repayment of a qualifying loan (or a loan that would be a qualifying loan but for the condition in **17.12**(c)). An allowable loss is treated as accruing to such a taxpayer who has made a claim to relief, if at the time he made the claim:

- any amount of the outstanding principal or interest has become irrecoverable from the borrower;
- the taxpayer has made a payment under the guarantee, either to the lender or to a co-guarantor, relating to that amount;

- the taxpayer has not assigned any right, accruing to him in return for making the payment, to recover that amount;
- the lender and the borrower were not each other's spouses or civil partners, or companies in the same group, either at the time the loan was made or at any later time; and
- the taxpayer and the lender were not each other's spouses or civil partners, or companies in the same group, either at the time the guarantee was given or at any later time.

The amount of the allowable loss is:

- the amount of the payment made by the taxpayer in respect of the outstanding principal or interest that has become irrecoverable from the borrower, *less*
- any contribution payable to him by any co-guarantor (*TCGA 1992, s 253(4)*).

A loan is not treated as becoming irrecoverable if it has become so in consequence of the terms of the loan, any arrangements surrounding the loan, or any act or omission by the lender or guarantor (*TCGA 1992, s 253(12)*).

A claim in respect of a payment made under a guarantee must be made:

- for CGT purposes; by the fourth anniversary of the end of the tax year in which the payment was made.
- for corporation tax purposes; by the fourth anniversary of the end of the accounting period in which the payment was made (*TCGA 1992, s 253(4A)*).

Recovery of loan or payment made under guarantee

17.15 If the taxpayer recovers any part of a loan or guarantee payment that has given rise to an allowable loss, the amount recovered is treated as a chargeable gain accruing at the time of recovery. The amount of the gain is so much of the loss as corresponds to the amount recovered. There are corresponding provisions for companies (*TCGA 1992, s 253(5)–(8)*).

The taxpayer is treated as recovering an amount if he receives – or directs someone else to receive – money or money's worth either in satisfaction of his right of recovery or in return for assigning that right. If he assigns the right under a bargain made otherwise than at arm's length (see **3.5**) he is treated as receiving money or money's worth equal to the market value of the right (*TCGA 1992, s 253(9)*).

Example 17.1

Patricia lent £10,000 to her sister Judy in June 2003 to help her continue in business. In May 2010, Judy's business collapsed and it was clear that she would not be able to repay the loan.

Patricia made a claim in her 2010/11 tax return that the loan had become irrecoverable at 6 April 2010. She may set off the resulting loss of £10,000 against any chargeable gains accruing in 2010/11, and carry any unused allowable loss forward indefinitely. Any part of the sum of £10,000 that is repaid at a later date will give rise to a chargeable gain equal to the amount repaid.

SHARE LOSS RELIEF

17.16 This relief, also known as VC loss relief, turns an allowable capital loss into a loss qualifying for income tax relief under *ITA 2007, Pt 4, Ch 6*, or corporation tax relief under *CTA 2010, Pt 4, Ch 4*. It may arise on the loss, disposal or negligible value of shares that qualify for EIS relief (see **Chapter 16**), or other unquoted shares. The EIS shares do not have to satisfy any further requirements for this loss relief, but the other shares do have to satisfy a number of requirements as discussed in **17.19**.

This relief is available only to individuals and investment companies, not trustees. HMRC guidance says it is intended 'to provide investors in unlisted trading companies with some degree of financial insurance against failure' (*ITA 2007, s 131*; VCM45010).

Relief for individuals

17.17 An individual who has subscribed for shares in a 'qualifying trading company' (see **17.19**), and incurs an allowable loss for CGT purposes on the disposal of the shares in a tax year, may claim relief from income tax on:

(a) an amount of his income for that tax year equal to the amount of the loss; or

(b) the whole of his income, where his income is less than the amount of the loss.

Alternatively, he may claim relief for the amount in (a) or (b) for the preceding tax year. No part of any loss may be relieved more than once. Once a loss has been relieved against income, it is no longer an allowable loss for CGT purposes. This relief must be claimed no later than 12 months after 31 January following the end of the tax year in which the loss was incurred (*ITA 2007, s 132*).

For this purpose an individual 'subscribes' for shares if:

- the company issues the shares to him in return for money or money's worth; or
- he acquires them from his spouse or civil partner by means of a lifetime transfer made while the individual was living with the spouse or civil partner, and the spouse or civil partner acquired the shares by subscription, although the subscription need not have been made during the marriage or civil partnership (*ITA 2007, s 135*).

Any bonus shares connected to the shares the individual subscribed for are treated as subscribed shares.

The disposal giving rise to the loss must be:

- a disposal by way of a bargain made at arm's length for full consideration;
- a disposal by way of a distribution in a dissolution or winding-up of the company;
- a disposal involving the entire loss, destruction, dissipation or extinction of the asset (see *TCGA 1992, s 24(1)*); or
- a deemed disposal arising on a claim that the value of the asset has become negligible under *TCGA 1992, s 24(2)* (see **2.10**) (*ITA 2007, s 131(3)*).

There are detailed rules concerning company reorganisations and exchanges of shares; identification of shares disposed of with acquisitions; and value shifting *(ITA 2007, ss 145–149*).

Order of reliefs

17.18 Income tax relief claimed under *ITA 2007, s 132* for the tax year in which the loss accrued takes priority over income tax relief claimed for the preceding year, for the purpose of establishing what losses remain and what income remains chargeable.

Income tax relief claimed under *ITA 2007, s 132* for either the year of the loss or the preceding year takes priority over trading losses for which a claim has been made under either *ITA 2007, s 64* (set-off against general income) or *ITA 2007, s 72* (losses in early years of a trade available for set-off against general income of preceding years) (*ITA 2007, s 133(4)*).

Qualifying trading company

17.19 A 'qualifying trading company' (see **17.17**) is a company that meets the conditions in (a)–(d) below:

(a) The company either meets the following four requirements on the date of the disposal:

- the trading requirement (*ITA 2007, s 137*);
- the control and independence requirement (*ITA 2007, s 139*);
- the qualifying subsidiaries requirement (*ITA 2007, ss 140, 191*); and
- the property management requirement (*ITA 2007, ss 141, 188, 190*); or

it ceased to meet any of those requirements at a time within three years before the disposal date and since that time it has not been:

- an excluded company,
- an investment company, or
- a trading company.

(b) The company has either:

- met all of the requirements in (a) for a continuous period of six years ending on the date of disposal; or
- has met all of the requirements in (a) for a shorter continuous period ending on that date (or at that time) and has not before the beginning of that period been an excluded company, an investment company or a trading company; and

(c) The company has met following requirements:

- gross assets of no more than £7 million before the issue of the shares and no more than £8 million after the issue of the shares (*ITA 2007, s 142*);
- was an unquoted company when the shares were issued and there were no arrangements in existence for the company to become quoted (*ITA 2007, s 143*).

(d) The company has carried on business wholly or mainly in the UK throughout the 'period from incorporation, or if later 12 months before the shares were issued, and ending on the date of disposal (*ITA 2007, s 134(5)*).

Several detailed definitions are provided, including:

- 'the trading requirement' is defined by reference to the qualifying trade rules for the purpose of the enterprise investment scheme (*ITA 2007, s 189*);
- 'excluded company' means, broadly, a company (i) whose trade consists wholly or mainly of dealing in land, commodities or futures, or in shares, securities or other financial instruments, or is not carried on a commercial basis, or (ii) which is the holding company of a group other than a trading group, or (iii) which is a building society or a registered industrial and provident society.

Various definitions and conditions are modified where the shares were issued before 6 April 1998.

Relief for companies

17.20 A similar relief to that described in **17.17** is available to an investment company that incurs an allowable loss for corporation tax purposes on the disposal of shares, for which it subscribed, in a qualifying trading company. The company disposing of the shares must meet both of the following conditions:

(a) it is an investment company on the date of disposal and (i) has been an investment company for a continuous period of six years ending on that date, or (ii) has been an investment company for a shorter continuous period ending on that date and was not a trading company or an excluded company before the beginning of that period; and

(b) it was not, at any time when it held the shares, associated with (or a member of the same group as) the qualifying trading company (*CTA 2010, s 69*).

The company may make a claim, within two years after the end of the accounting period in which the loss was incurred, for the allowable loss to be set against income for corporation tax purposes as follows:

- income of that accounting period; and
- income of preceding accounting periods ending within a specified period (see below) if the company was then an investment company.

The specified period is the period of 12 months ending immediately before the accounting period in which the loss is incurred, and an apportionment may be required if that period was longer than 12 months. The loss is relieved against income of later periods before income of earlier periods (*CTA 2010, ss 70–72*).

There are detailed rules setting out the interaction between losses, charges and management expenses; specifying the order of reliefs; and providing various definitions (*CTA 2010, s 71*).

COMPULSORY PURCHASE ROLL-OVER RELIEF

17.21 Where land is purchased by an authority that has compulsory purchase powers, and the proceeds are reinvested in acquiring new land, a form of CGT roll-over relief may be available under *TCGA 1992, s 247*. The taxpayer – who may be an individual, trustee or company – may claim to defer the gain by setting it against allowable expenditure on replacement land acquired within one year before and three years after the disposal.

This relief operates in a broadly similar manner to roll-over relief for replacement of business assets (see **Chapter 14**). However, the roll-over relief is restricted where the original proceeds are only partly reinvested. Relief will also be denied where:

- the landowner advertised the land for sale, or otherwise indicated a willingness to sell;
- the replacement property attracts main residence relief (see **Chapter 12**) within six years following its acquisition.

For further discussion of this relief see Chapter 7 of *Roll-over, Hold-over and Deferral Reliefs 2010/11* (Bloomsbury Professional).

Example 17.2

David owns freehold land with an agreed 31 March 1982 value of £98,000. Part of the land is made the subject of a compulsory purchase order and compensation of £70,000 is agreed on 10 August 2010. The market value of the remaining land is £175,000. The chargeable gain accruing on the disposal is £42,000, computed as shown below. David acquires new land for £80,000 in December 2009, and claims roll-over relief:

	£	£
Disposal consideration August 2010		70,000
Market value in March 1982:		
£98,000 × [70,000/(70,000 + 175,000)]		(28,000)
Chargeable gain		42,000
Consideration for disposal		70,000
Allowable cost of land compulsorily purchased	28,000	
Deemed consideration for disposal		(28,000)
Roll-over relief		42,000
Allowable cost of replacement land £80,000 – £42,000		38,000

TAPER RELIEF

17.22 Taper relief was abolished for disposals made after 5 April 2008. The effect of the relief was to reduce the amount of chargeable gains accruing on disposals of business and non-business assets according to the type of asset and number of whole years the asset had been held, as set out in the following table.

Table 17.1

Gains on disposal of business assets		**Gains on disposal of non-business assets**	
Number of whole years in qualifying holding period	Percentage of gain chargeable	Number of whole years in qualifying holding period	Percentage of gain chargeable
1	50	–	–
2 or more	25	–	–
		3	95
		4	90
		5	85
		6	80
		7	75
		8	70
		9	65
		10 or more	60

The relief was obtained by multiplying the amount of the gain by the percentage, given by the table in *TCGA 1992, s 2A(5)* (reproduced above), for the number of whole years in the qualifying holding period. **Table 17.1** applies to disposals made after 5 April 2002 and before 6 April 2008. For earlier disposals of business assets, the rate of taper relief for business assets was lower than shown, so that a higher percentage of the gain was chargeable.

For disposals made after 6 April 2004 business assets broadly encompass all shares in unlisted trading companies, and all assets used by a business for its trade or by an employee or office holder for that employment or office, but reference should be made to the detailed descriptions at **17.29**. Assets that do not qualify as business assets are non-business assets.

Taper relief was available to disposals by individuals when disposing of any chargeable assets, personal representatives when disposing of assets comprised within an estate, and trustees' disposals of assets held within a settlement. This contrasts with the more restricted scope of entrepreneurs' relief (see **Chapter 11**).

Qualifying holding period

17.23 The 'qualifying holding period', measured at the time of disposal, is the period after 5 April 1998 for which the asset had been held at the time of its disposal. In the case of a non-business asset held at both 17 March 1998 and 6 April 1998 a 'bonus year' is added.

The qualifying holding period may be reduced where the taxpayer had limited exposure during a period of ownership to fluctuations in the asset's value (*TCGA 1992, Sch A1, para 10*, CG17916, CG17917, CG17928).

Example 17.3

John acquired a lease of land on 1 June 2001. He acquired the freehold on 1 December 2002, extinguishing the lease, and sold the freehold on 1 November 2007. The qualifying holding period for taper relief runs from 1 June 2001 to 1 November 2007, giving six complete years.

Inactive company

17.24 The qualifying holding period does not run for periods from 17 April 2002 where the asset comprises shares in a close company which is inactive (*TCGA 1992, Sch A1, para 11A*). HMRC regard a company as unlikely to be active if it is in liquidation and there are 'no winding-up activities' and no other activities. However, a company will be treated as active where:

- the directors, or some other person, are dealing with the company's post-cessation business affairs (eg paying off creditors, closing bank accounts or selling off assets) and the company remains in being;
- the company is intended to remain in being in order to start another business later and there is a gap between winding up the first business and starting the next. The time spent winding up the affairs of the first business 'counts as active' (CG17921e).

Where a company's business ceases and there is a period in which the company is neither settling the affairs of that business nor preparing to start a new one, that period is regarded as a time when the company is 'inactive'.

A company is treated as active regardless of the above rules if:

- it is the holding company of a group of companies that contains at least one active company;

- it has a qualifying shareholding in a joint venture company; or
- it is the holding company of a group of companies any member of which has a qualifying shareholding in a joint venture company.

Example 17.4

Alan realised a gain of £10,000 on disposal of an asset that was a non-business asset throughout the period of ownership. He acquired the asset on 1 August 2000 and sold it on 31 October 2006. The qualifying holding period is six years and 80% of the gain, ie £8,000, is chargeable.

Transfers between spouses or civil partners

17.25 Where an asset is transferred between spouses or civil partners who were living together the transfer is treated under *TCGA 1992, s 58(1)* as giving rise to no gain, no loss. On a subsequent disposal the transferee spouse is treated, for taper relief purposes, as having acquired the asset when the transferor spouse acquired it. This means that the qualifying holding period is the entire period of ownership of both spouses falling after 5 April 1998.

The conditions that determined whether an asset qualified as a business asset or not, may depend on the employment and other shareholding rights of the individual who held the asset (see **17.33**). Thus, on the transfer of an asset between spouses the asset could lose its status as a business asset:

- Where shares or securities were transferred, the company in which those shares or securities were held had to be a 'qualifying company' of the transferee spouse or civil partner throughout the combined period of ownership after 5 April 1998. If it was not a qualifying company throughout the combined period, then an apportionment of business and non-business asset holding periods was required (*TCGA 1992, Sch A1, para 15*).
- Where other assets are transferred, the asset is treated as a business asset at any time before the transfer if the business asset conditions were satisfied by the transferor spouse or civil partner at that time. For the period after the transfer, business asset status depended entirely on whether the conditions were met in relation to the transferee.

The rate of taper relief

17.26 Taper relief was given at a higher rate for the disposal of business assets rather than non-business assets. However, an asset may not be a business asset throughout its 'relevant period' of ownership. This period is whichever is the shorter of the period after 5 April 1998 for which the asset had been held at the time of disposal, and the period of ten years ending with the time of disposal. As taper relief was abolished on 5 April 2008, the relevant period of ownership cannot exceed ten years.

Note the relevant period of ownership is not the same as the qualifying holding period discussed in **17.23**.The relevant period is not increased by the 'bonus year' that may be added to the qualifying holding period. Any period that is not counted for the purposes of taper relief because of an anti-avoidance rule (*TCGA 1992, Sch A1, paras 10* and *12*) is excluded from the qualifying holding period and is not included in the relevant period of ownership.

If the person making the disposal did not acquire the asset but created it, the date of acquisition for taper relief is the date on which the asset was created. HMRC consider that this date is to be determined as a question of fact on the basis of the available evidence (*TCGA 1992, Sch A1, paras 1–3*; CG17900).

Example 17.5

Martin acquired an asset on 1 June 1994 and used it for non-business purposes until he sold it on 6 April 2007. The relevant period of ownership is the shorter of (i) nine years, being the whole period of ownership after 5 April 1998, and (ii) the period of ten years ending with the time of the disposal. The relevant period of ownership is, therefore, nine years. The qualifying holding period will be ten years, including the 'bonus year'.

There are two situations that complicate the taper relief computation:

- where the asset qualified as a business asset for only part of the relevant period (see **17.27**). This may well occur due to the change in the definition of a business asset during the period of ownership (see **17.29**);
- where the asset is used partly for business purposes and partly for non-business purposes, so the asset has a mixed use (see **17.28**). Note only assets other than shares or securities can have mixed use, as a holding of shares either qualifies completely as a business asset, or not at all, at any point in time.

Business asset for only part of the relevant period

17.27 In this situation the gain is divided into parts, and those parts are treated as separate gains arising on the disposal of a separate business asset and a non-business asset. Each of these deemed separate assets is treated as being owned for the whole of the relevant period of ownership.

The apportionment of the gain between the deemed business and non-business asset is made on a just and reasonable basis, assuming the total gain arose or accrued at the same rate throughout the period of ownership (*TCGA 1992, Sch A1, paras 3, 21*).

Example 17.6

Nicola acquired shares on 1 March 1997. They did not meet the conditions for business asset status until 6 April 2000, when the rules were relaxed. She disposed of the shares on 6 April 2007, realising a gain of £90,000. Nicola held the shares for nine whole years after 5 April 1998; this is the relevant period of ownership. During that period the shareholding was a non-business asset for two years and a business asset for the remaining seven years.

Non-business asset

Gain £90,000 × 2/9ths = £20,000

Qualifying holding period is ten years (nine years plus a 'bonus year')

Percentage of gain chargeable is 60%, ie £12,000

Business asset

Gain £90,000 × 7/9ths = £70,000

Qualifying holding period is nine years

Percentage of gain chargeable is 25%, ie £17,500

Total amount chargeable is £12,000 + £17,500 = £29,500

Mixed use

17.28 Where an asset qualified as a business asset, part of that asset may at the same time be put to non-business use. This could apply where part of the property was used for business purposes (qualifying business use), but other areas were used as a residential accommodation (non-business use), for example a small hotel where the owners live in part of the property. In such a case it is necessary to find the 'relevant fraction' representing the proportion of use, during the mixed-use period that is non-qualifying. The relevant fraction of the mixed-use period is treated as a period throughout which the asset was not a business asset. The asset is taken to have been a business asset for the remainder of the period. The relevant fraction is to be recalculated where the proportion of non-qualifying use varies (*TCGA 1992, Sch A1, para 9*).

Example 17.7

Edward sold a property on 5 April 2007. Throughout the four-year period of ownership he used three-quarters of the property for the purpose of his retail trade and he let the remaining quarter to private tenants, which did not qualify for business asset taper relief. The 'relevant fraction' is one quarter. A gain of £80,000 arose on the disposal. Edward needs to split this gain into two parts, one deemed to accrue on the disposal of a non-business asset and the other deemed to accrue on disposal of a business asset.

Non-business asset

Gain £80,000 × relevant fraction 1/4 = £20,000

Qualifying holding period is four years

Percentage of gain chargeable is 90%, ie £18,000

Business asset

Gain £80,000 × 3/4 = £60,000

Qualifying holding period is four years

Percentage of gain chargeable is 25%, ie £15,000

Total amount chargeable is £18,000 + £15,000 = £33,000

Complications arose where the different parts of the property were disposed of separately, which could be the case where the property consisted of commercial premises with flats above. In this case HMRC insist that the taper relief be apportioned on the gain of each separate disposal according to the business and non-business use of the whole building (CG17959).

Further complications arose where main residence relief applied to part of the property to remove part of the gain from charge (see **Chapter 12**), in which case the operation of the relief could actually increase the tax charge if the HMRC guidance was followed. The HMRC approach was successfully challenged in *IS Jefferies & LA Jefferies* (TC00235). The taxpayers argued that the gain removed from charge by main residence relief should not be included in the taper relief computation. Thus, the taper relief should only apply to the business part of the property, giving full business asset taper on the remaining gain. HMRC will not appeal the *Jefferies* case so the decision can be used as a reference in any similar mixed-use taper case.

What is a business asset?

17.29 There are separate rules for determining whether shares and securities (see **17.30**) and other assets (see **17.35**) qualify as business assets. The rules for both categories of asset were altered with effect from 6 April 2000, and from 17 April 2002 for shares; then again from 6 April 2004 for other assets. The rules that apply to earlier periods of ownership remain relevant to disposals in later periods. It is thus essential to look at the qualifying factors for the asset under each set of the rules to determine if the asset qualified as a business asset or not for that period.

Shares and securities

17.30 Any reference in the taper relief rules to shares of a company includes any securities of the company and any debentures that are deemed by *TCGA 1992, s 251(6)* to be securities of the company, and are subject to CGT. Non-qualifying corporate bonds issued in 'paper for paper' transactions will generally qualify as securities by virtue of *FA 2002, Sch 10, para 8.* An 'interest in' shares or securities is an interest as a joint or co-owner.

Qualifying company

17.31 For shares to qualify as business assets, the company must be a 'qualifying company' by reference to the individual shareholder (*TCGA 1992, Sch A1, para 4*). This requires the company to be a trading company, and not have significant activities that are not trading. The shareholder must also qualify in relation to the size of their shareholding and their employment relationship with the company, or a group company. There are special rules for non-trading companies see **17.34**.

Trading company

17.32 From 17 April 2002, a trading company is one which carried on trading activities whose activities did not include to a substantial extent activities other than trading activities (*TCGA 1992, Sch A1, para 22A*). This is exactly the same definition that is now used for 'trading company', in the entrepreneurs' relief provisions (see **11.12**).

For periods before 17 April 2002, a trading company was one which either:

- existed wholly for the purpose of carrying on one or more trades; or
- fell within the above definition apart from any purposes capable of having no substantial effect on the extent of the company's activities.

HMRC regard 'wholly' above as meaning solely. In this context, there must be no purpose other than for the company to trade, but the generation of investment income did not automatically mean that a company's purpose is not wholly trading.

For all periods 'trade' means any trade, profession or vocation within the meaning of the Income Tax Acts which is conducted on a commercial basis with a view to the realisation of profits. An asset used for a business of commercial letting of furnished holiday accommodation that meets the conditions set out in *ITTOIA 2005, ss 323–325* is regarded as an asset used for a trade (*TCGA 1992, Sch A1, para 22*).

Shareholder qualification

17.33 From 6 April 2000 if the company was an unlisted trading company, or the unlisted holding company of a trading group, there were no additional requirements for the shareholder to meet for the shares to be business assets, and the company to be the shareholder's qualifying company. If the trading company was listed, the shareholder or the eligible beneficiary of a settlement had to be either an employee or officer of the company or of a company in the same trading group.

If the shareholder was not an employee or officer of the listed company/group company he had to hold at least 5% of the voting rights of the company, which would be very unlikely. In relation to settlements the trustees need to be able to exercise at least 5% of voting rights.

For disposals of shares in a trading company before 6 April 2000 the individual shareholder (which includes a trustee or personal representative) must be able to exercise either:

- at least 25% of the voting rights of the company; or
- at least 5% of the voting rights of the company and, also the shareholder or eligible beneficiary must be a full-time working officer or employee of the company or of a company in the same group or part of the same commercial association.

Where the company did not qualify as a trading company, the conditions in **17.34** had to apply.

Non-trading company

17.34 Large companies could not always prove that they were trading companies, and employees who held shares in those companies, particularly through employee share schemes could not tell whether the company was trading or not. For this reason the conditions were changed with effect from 6 April 2000, so shares held by employees or officers of non-trading companies, or of a company in a non-trading group, would be business assets, and the company would be the qualifying company of that employee/shareholder.

This is subject to the proviso that the individual did not have a material interest in the company or any other company having control of it. A material interest was defined as more than 10% of any of the following:

- the issued shares of any particular class;
- the voting rights;
- the right to receive dividends;
- the right to assets in a winding-up.

Present rights to acquire shares in the future, and future rights to acquire shares later, must be taken into account in applying the 10% test. It was also necessary to take into account the holdings and rights of connected persons including, for example, spouses/civil partners, brothers and sisters, lineal descendants and ancestors (*TCGA 1992, Sch A1, paras 6(4)–(7), 6A*).

These provisions also applied to trustees, if an eligible beneficiary was an officer or employee of the company in which the trustees held shares or a company having a relevant connection with it, and neither the trustees of the settlement, nor any person connected with them could have a material interest in the company or any company which controls it.

Assets other than shares

17.35 There were four basic situations that can cause an asset to qualify as a business asset and they are summarised in **17.36–17.39**. The asset must be used wholly or *partly* for one of these qualifying purposes. If, at any point in time, only part of the asset was used for one of these qualifying purposes, and part is not, the asset had mixed use for taper purposes (see **17.28**).

In all of these situations the payment of rent for the use of the asset, at a commercial level or otherwise, had no effect on the availability for taper relief (CG17940a). This position is reversed under entrepreneurs' relief, which restricts the tax relief available on an associated disposal of an asset used by a company or partnership, where any rent was received for the use of that asset for a period since 6 April 2008 (see **11.38**). This is also similar to the position that existed under retirement relief, which was abolished from 5 April 2003.

Used for own trade

17.36 Where an individual carried on a trade as a sole trader, or was a partner in a business carrying on a trade, and an asset was wholly or partly used for the purposes of that trade, it qualified as a business asset (*TCGA 1992, Sch A1, para 5(2)(a)*).

This situation also applied where the owner of the asset was a trustee or personal representative, and the trading partnership that used the asset included a trustee of the same settlement or personal representatives of the same deceased person.

Used by a qualifying company

17.37 Where the company that used the asset was the asset owner's qualifying company (see **17.31**), the asset qualified as a business asset. This also applied where the asset was used by a company that was a member of the trading group, of which the qualifying company was the holding company. From 6 April 2000 all unlisted companies qualified as the individual's qualifying company, with no restrictions on the percentage of shares held or the employment of the individual.

Used for purposes of employment

17.38 Assets used for the purpose of an office or employment qualified as business assets where:

- the individual or eligible beneficiary of a settlement who owned the asset held a full-time office or employment with any person (ie individual, partnership or company) who carried on a trade, and the asset was used for the purpose of that office or employment;
- the individual or eligible beneficiary of a settlement was an officer or employee of a trading company which was a member of the same trading group, or the same commercial association of companies, as a company which was the individual's qualifying company (see **17.31**).

Let to sole trader or trading partnership

17.39 From 6 April 2004 property let to an individual or partnership who used that property for the purposes of the (lessee's) trade, qualified as a business asset.

Interaction with losses

17.40 Allowable losses were not subject to taper relief but they were set off against 'untapered' chargeable gains. Where the taxpayer had more than one chargeable gain arising in a tax year, any allowable losses (whether realised in the current year, or carried forward or back to the current year) were set against untapered gains in the order that results in the largest reduction in those gains, ie the order that maximised the available taper relief. See **1.20** regarding the interaction between losses carried forward and the CGT annual exemption.

Example 17.8

Adam has unrelieved capital losses of £20,000 available to carry forward to 2007/08. His gains for that year are as set out in the following table:

2007/08	**Disposal A Business asset**	**Disposal B Non-business asset**	**Disposal C Non-business asset**
Gains	£20,000	£30,000	£14,000
Qualifying holding period in years	2	7	4
Percentage of gain chargeable	25%	75%	90%
Loss set-off	Nil	£6,000	£14,000
Net gains before taper relief	£20,000	£24,000	Nil
Chargeable gain	£5,000	£18,000	Nil

The losses are allocated first against the gain accruing on disposal C, which qualifies for the lowest rate of taper relief. Taper relief is most valuable in relation to disposal A, so the remaining losses are allocated against disposal B. Total chargeable gains, after losses and taper relief, are £23,000 (*TCGA 1992, s 2A(6)*).

Special rules

17.41 There are a number of special rules that affect the calculation of taper relief, such as:

- the treatment of options (see **Chapter 4**);
- interaction with roll-over relief (see **Chapter 14**);

17.41 *Other reliefs*

- interaction with incorporation relief (see **Chapter 15**);
- assets derived from other assets (*TCGA 1992, Sch A1, para 14*);
- postponed gains; and
- value shifting (*TCGA 1992, Sch A1, para 12*).

Index

[*All references are to paragraph number*]